Warrior, Dancer, Seductress, Queen

Women in Judges and
Biblical Israel

THE ANCHOR BIBLE REFERENCE LIBRARY is designed to be a third major component of the Anchor Bible group, which includes the Anchor Bible commentaries on the books of the Old Testament, the New Testament, and the Apocrypha, and the Anchor Bible Dictionary. While the Anchor Bible commentaries and the Anchor Bible Dictionary are structurally defined by their subject matter, the Anchor Bible Reference Library will serve as a supplement on the cutting edge of the most recent scholarship. The series is open-ended; its scope and reach are nothing less than the biblical world in its totality, and its methods and techniques the most up-to-date available or devisable. Separate volumes will deal with one or more of the following topics relating to the Bible: anthropology, archaeology, ecology, economy, geography, history, languages and literatures, philosophy, religion(s), theology.

As with the Anchor Bible commentaries and the Anchor Bible Dictionary, the philosophy underlying the Anchor Bible Reference Library finds expression in the following: the approach is scholarly, the perspective is balanced and fair-minded, the methods are scientific, and the goal is to inform and enlighten. Contributors are chosen on the basis of their scholarly skills and achievements, and they come from a variety of religious backgrounds and communities. The books in the Anchor Bible Reference Library are intended for the broadest possible readership, ranging from world-class scholars, whose qualifications match those of the authors, to general readers, who may not have special training or skill in studying the Bible but are as enthusiastic as any dedicated professional in expanding their knowledge of the Bible and its world.

David Noel Freedman
GENERAL EDITOR

THE ANCHOR BIBLE REFERENCE LIBRARY

Warrior, Dancer, Seductress, Queen

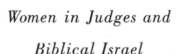

Women in Judges and Biblical Israel

SUSAN ACKERMAN

Doubleday

NEW YORK   LONDON   TORONTO   SYDNEY   AUCKLAND

THE ANCHOR BIBLE REFERENCE LIBRARY

PUBLISHED BY DOUBLEDAY
a division of Bantam Doubleday Dell Publishing Group, Inc.
1540 Broadway, New York, New York 10036

THE ANCHOR BIBLE REFERENCE LIBRARY, DOUBLEDAY,
and the portrayal of an anchor with the letters ABRL are
trademarks of Doubleday, a division of Bantam Doubleday Dell
Publishing Group, Inc.

Book Design by Dana Leigh Treglia

Library of Congress Cataloging-in-Publication Data
Ackerman, Susan.
Warrior, dancer, seductress, queen: women in Judges and
biblical Israel / Susan Ackerman.—1st ed.
p.   cm.—(The Anchor Bible reference library)
1. Bible.   O.T.   Judges—Criticism, interpretation, etc.
2. Women in the Bible.   I. Title.   II. Series.
BS1305.6.W7A29   1998
222'.32083054—dc21   97-37992
                                             CIP
ISBN 0-385-48424-0

In memory of my paternal grandmother

Eunice Hamilton Ackerman

(1898–1977)

on the occasion of the one-hundredth

anniversary of her birth

ACKNOWLEDGMENTS

In Spring 1990, the Reverend Gordon K. McBride asked me to deliver the annual Lenten Lecture Series at Saint Paul's Episcopal Church in Tucson, Arizona. The topic I chose was "Women in the Book of Judges," and the five lectures I gave on Deborah, Jael, Sisera's mother, Manoah's wife, and the Levite's concubine form the basis for the first five chapters of this volume. My initial thanks, now that this book is complete, are thus owed to Reverend McBride and to the congregation of Saint Paul's for giving me the opportunity to begin my work on Judges' women, as well as to others in Tucson who heard the lectures and encouraged me to develop them further, especially David and Rosanne Keller of the Episcopal Diocese of Arizona; William G. Dever, Pamela Gaber, Shoshana Green, Dane A. Miller, and Beth Alpert-Nakhai, my colleagues and students in the Department of Near Eastern Studies at the University of Arizona; and Herbert N. Schneidau and John Bormanis, my colleague and student, respectively, in the University of Arizona's Department of English.

In the summer of 1990, I moved from the Department of Near Eastern Studies at Arizona to the Department of Religion at Dartmouth College, and as this book developed at Dartmouth, I received immeasurable help from the institution, especially from the Dartmouth College Class of 1962 Junior Faculty Fellowship. This fellowship, coupled with sabbatical support from Dartmouth's Dean of Faculty Office, made it possible for me to write an initial draft of this manuscript during the academic year 1993–94, and I am very grateful to the class of 1962 for this opportunity. The Class of 1962 Fellowship, along with the Religion Department's Dickinson fund, in addition made it possible for me to hire students to assist in my bibliographic endeavors, and I would like to thank Kristen A. Pollard, from the Dartmouth College class of 1993, Richard N. Fried, class of 1994, and Blake T. Wentworth, class of 1995, for their help. The librarians at Dartmouth College were also unstinting in the time and help they offered me as my research developed, and I owe a particular thanks to Patricia A. Carter and the staff of Baker Library's Interlibrary Loan Office. I further would like to thank my colleagues in the Religion Department at Dartmouth, who read and critiqued drafts of several chapters of this volume. Professors Amy M. Hollywood and A. Kevin Reinhart were especially conscientious in commenting on the Introduction and Chapter 6, respectively, and Chapter 6 benefited as well from the discussions I held with members of Dartmouth's Mediterranean Studies Faculty Seminar, especially Professors Phyllis B. Katz (Classics), Gene R. Garthwaite (History), and Dale F. Eickelman (Anthropology). Finally, among my Dartmouth colleagues, I would like to thank the faculty of the Women's Studies Program, especially those who participated in the Feminist Inquiry Faculty Seminar at which I presented a version of Chapter 4, and Professors Marlene E. Heck of the Departments of Art History and History, Shalom Goldman, formerly of Dartmouth's Asian Studies Program, and William C. Scott, of the Department of Classics.

Among colleagues at other institutions, I have been helped by the late Steven H. Lonsdale of Davidson College, Susan Niditch of Amherst College, William H. Propp of the University of California at San Diego, and Neal A. Walls of Emory University, all of whom read and commented extensively on substantial portions or, in some cases, all of this manuscript. The series editor of the Anchor Bible Reference Library, David Noel Freedman, was particularly diligent in the performance of his task, and my book has been greatly improved by his extensive comments. I am also grateful for the more informal editorial help I received from Michael F. Lowenthal, formerly of the University Press of New England, and for the advice and support of Peter Anderson, Laura Smoller, and Richard Voos.

Some of the material presented in Chapter 3 of this book has previously been published in volume 112 of the *Journal of Biblical Literature* (1993) and in *Women and Goddess Traditions: In Antiquity and Today* (Studies in Antiquity and Christianity; ed. K. L. King with an Introduction by K. J. Torjeson; Minneapolis: Fortress, 1997). A version of Section I of Chapter 4 has previously appeared in print in *Bible Review* 9/3 (June 1993).

Unless otherwise noted, the translations of biblical and other ancient texts are my own.

Susan Ackerman
Hanover, New Hampshire
May 1997

CONTENTS

ABBREVIATIONS

AB	Anchor Bible
ABD	D. N. Freedman (ed.), *Anchor Bible Dictionary*
AJSL	*American Journal of Semitic Languages and Literature*
ALUOS	*Annual of Leeds University Oriental Society*
ANEP	J. B. Pritchard (ed.), *Ancient Near East in Pictures*
ANET	J. B. Pritchard (ed.), *Ancient Near Eastern Texts Relating to the Old Testament* (3d ed.)
AOAT	Alter Orient und Altes Testament
BA	*Biblical Archaeologist*
BAR	*Biblical Archaeologist Reader*
BARev	*Biblical Archaeology Review*
BASOR	*Bulletin of the American Schools of Oriental Research*
B.C.E.	Before the Common (or Christian) Era
BDB	F. Brown, S. R. Driver, and C. A. Briggs, *Hebrew and English Lexicon of the Old Testament*
BHS	*Biblia hebraica stuttgartensia*
Bib	*Biblica*
BJRL	*Bulletin of the John Rylands University Library of Manchester*
BJS	Brown Judaic Studies
BN	*Biblische Notizen*
BZ	*Biblische Zeitschrift*
BZAW	Beihefte zur *Zeitschrift für die alttestamentliche Wissenschaft*
CAH	*Cambridge Ancient History*
CBQ	*Catholic Biblical Quarterly*
CBQMS	Catholic Biblical Quarterly Monograph Series
C.E.	Common (or Christian) Era
CTM	*Concordia Theological Monthly*
EA	The El-Amarna tablets according to the numeration of J. A. Knudtzon, *Die El-Amarna-Tafeln* 1–2
ErIsr	Eretz Israel

EvQ	*Evangelical Quarterly*
ExpTim	*Expository Times*
HAR	*Hebrew Annual Review*
HS	*Hebrew Studies*
HSM	Harvard Semitic Monographs
HSS	Harvard Semitic Studies
HTR	*Harvard Theological Review*
HUCA	*Hebrew Union College Annual*
IB	*Interpreter's Bible*
ICC	International Critical Commentary
IDB	G. A. Butterick (ed.), *Interpreter's Dictionary of the Bible*
IEJ	*Israel Exploration Journal*
Int	*Interpretation*
IOSCS	International Organization for Septuagint and Cognate Studies
JAAR	*Journal of the American Academy of Religion*
JANESCU	*Journal of the Ancient Near Eastern Society of Columbia University*
JAOS	*Journal of the American Oriental Society*
JB	A. Jones (ed.), *Jerusalem Bible*
JBL	*Journal of Biblical Literature*
JEA	*Journal of Egyptian Archaeology*
JEOL	*Jaarbericht . . . ex oriente lux*
JFSR	*Journal of Feminist Studies in Religion*
JHS	*Journal of Hellenic Studies*
JJS	*Journal of Jewish Studies*
JNES	*Journal of Near Eastern Studies*
JNSL	*Journal of Northwest Semitic Languages*
JRS	*Journal of Roman Studies*
JPSV	Jewish Publication Society Version
JSOT	*Journal for the Study of the Old Testament*
JSOTSup	Journal for the Study of the Old Testament—Supplement Series
JSS	*Journal of Semitic Studies*
KAI	H. Donner and W. Röllig, *Kanaanäische und aramäische Inschriften* 1–3
KJV	King James Version
KTU	M. Dietrich, O. Loretz, and J. Sanmartín, *Die keilalphabetischen Texte aus Ugarit: Einschliesslich der keilalphabetischen Texte ausserhalb Ugarits* 1, *Transkription*
LCL	Loeb Classical Library
LXX	Septuagint

MT	Masoretic Text
NAB	New American Bible
NEB	New English Bible
NJB	H. Wansbrough (ed.), *New Jerusalem Bible*
NJPS	New Jewish Publication Society Version
NRSV	New Revised Standard Version
NTS	*New Testament Studies*
OBT	Overtures to Biblical Theology
OLP	*Orientalia lovaniensia periodica*
OLZ	*Orientalische Literaturzeitung*
Or	*Orientalia* (Rome)
OTL	Old Testament Library
OTS	*Oudtestamentische Studiën*
PRU	J. Nougayrol and Ch. Virolleaud, *Le palais royal d'Ugarit* 1–6
4QSam[a]	First copy of Samuel from Qumran Cave 4
RB	*Revue biblique*
REB	Revised English Bible
RS	Ras-Shamra
RSV	Revised Standard Version
SBLDS	Society of Biblical Literature Dissertation Series
SBLMS	Society of Biblical Literature Monograph Series
SBLRBS	Society of Biblical Literature Resources for Biblical Study
SBT	Studies in Biblical Theology
SNTSMS	Society for New Testament Studies Monograph Series
TDOT	G. J. Botterweck and H. Ringgren (eds.), *Theological Dictionary of the Old Testament* 1–5
TToday	*Theology Today*
TZ	*Theologische Zeitschrift*
UF	*Ugarit-Forschungen*
Ugaritica 5	J. Nougayrol, E. Laroche, Ch. Virolleaud, and C. F. A. Schaeffer, et al., *Ugaritica 5, Nouveaux textes accadiens, hourrites et ugaritiques des archives et bibliothèques privées d'Ugarit, Commentaires des textes historiques (première partie)*
USQR	*Union Seminary Quarterly Review*
UT	C. H. Gordon, *Ugaritic Textbook*
VT	*Vetus Testamentum*
VTSup	Vetus Testamentum, Supplements
WTJ	*Westminster Theological Journal*
ZAW	*Zeitschrift für die alttestamentliche Wissenschaft*
ZDPV	*Zeitschrift des deutschen Palästina-Vereins*

ABBREVIATIONS OF BIBLICAL BOOKS

Cant	Song of Songs	Josh	Joshua
	(Song of Solomon)	Judg	Judges
1 Chr	1 Chronicles	1 Kgs	1 Kings
2 Chr	2 Chronicles	2 Kgs	2 Kings
Dan	Daniel	Lev	Leviticus
Deut	Deuteronomy	Matt	Matthew
Esth	Esther	Mic	Micah
Exod	Exodus	Nah	Nahum
Ezek	Ezekiel	Neh	Nehemiah
Gen	Genesis	Num	Numbers
Hag	Haggai	Prov	Proverbs
Heb	Hebrews	Ps, Pss	Psalms
Hos	Hosea	1 Sam	1 Samuel
Isa	Isaiah	2 Sam	2 Samuel
Jer	Jeremiah	Tob	Tobit
Jdt	Judith	Zech	Zechariah

INTRODUCTION

—————— ⊗⊗⊗ ——————

"Now the House Was Full of Men and Women"[1]

FEMALE CHARACTERS IN THE BOOK OF JUDGES

At first glance, the narrative that opens the book of Judges looks a lot like most of the stories found in the Hebrew Bible: it is a story about men. It begins in Judg 1:1 by recording the death of one man, the Israelite war leader Joshua, and continues in 1:2–36 by recounting the exploits of other men: first, the soldiers of the two southern tribes of Judah and Simeon as they do battle against the cities of Jerusalem, Bezek, Hebron, Debir, and Hormah; then, the struggles of six tribes of the north as they seek to seize territory in the Ephraimite hills, in the Jezreel valley, and along the coastal plain. The text finally concludes in 2:6–9 by reinvoking the name of Joshua and by eulogizing his deeds; it also adds in 2:10 a notice concerning the deaths of those men who were of the same generation as Joshua, who had come into the land with him and who had engaged in Israel's battles of conquest.

Even the one episode in this recital that mentions a woman (1:11–15) initially seems as if it, too, is a story really about men. The text describes how the clan of the Judahite chieftain Caleb has gone forth to wage war against the people of Kiriath-sepher, also known as Debir, and how Caleb has prefaced this attack with a promise that he will give his daughter Achsah to whichever of his soldiers takes the city.[2] The setting of this story—the field of battle—is thus an arena traditionally reserved for the affairs of men, and within this androcentric theater, the role assigned to Achsah appears not much more than that of pawn, fighting men's fodder in a wartime game of chess.[3] One man willingly gives her up in order to gain his real objective, the capture of Debir, and another—Caleb's nephew Othniel—takes her as the trophy that signifies the occasion's larger, and its true prize, the conquering of the city and the defeat of its people.[4]

Still, not all here is quite as it seems, for while this wartime game of

men's "give and take" is concluded quickly, by Judg 1:13, the tale of
Achsah continues for another two verses, both of which work to under-
mine the story's earlier, male-centered point of view. In verse 14, for
example, Achsah speaks out, urging her bridegroom to ask her father
for a marriage gift of land, and, by so doing, begins already to counter-
mand our expectations regarding her pawn-like status.[5] In verse 15, expectations are further contravened. Although that text does intimate that
Othniel ignored his new wife's exhortations found in verse 14, it nevertheless suggests that the husband's neglect is *not* to be taken as a signal of
Achsah's lack of influence or authority. Instead, because Achsah quickly
takes over the charge of asking Caleb for land, Othniel's silence high-
lights her ability to act as an agent independent of him.[6] Achsah asks,
moreover, for very specific land, the basins of Gulloth-mayim, which
are two pools of water or, perhaps, two wells. This suggests that, in
addition to an ability to assert herself by speaking out, Achsah possesses
a pragmatic streak, recognizing the need to control a source of water if
she and her husband are to have a viable future in Israel's agriculturally-
and pastorally-based economy. It is further of note that Achsah asks for
the two pools of Gulloth *over and above* land that had already been promised to her somewhere in the Negev. A scene that begins with a supposedly pawned-off woman thus shifts by its end to present her as something very different: as assertive, as practical, and as one who, at least to
some degree, can lay claim to land ownership. This metamorphosis in
turn suggests a revised reading of the surrounding narrative, as the inclusion of the brief tale of Achsah in the midst of Judg 1:1–2:10 serves to
indicate how Judges' opening chapters, which initially appeared to be
so exclusively about men, are not just a description of a man's world
after all.

This conclusion could well describe the book of Judges as a whole.
Like 1:1–2:10, Judges at first glance seems to be a book about men.
It is about the great men who led Israel during her premonarchical
days: Othniel, Gideon, Tola, Jair, Jephthah, Ibzan, Elon, and Abdon. It
is about the mighty fighters who prevailed over Israel's foes: Shamgar
ben Anat, who slaughtered six hundred Philistines with an oxgoad; Samson, who slew one thousand men with the jawbone of an ass. It is about
men's cunning strategies that confounded their enemies: the left-handed
Ehud, who murdered King Eglon of Moab while the monarch was in
his toilet; the trickster Samson, whose enigmatic riddle about a lion and
honey baffled the Philistines who attended his marriage feast. Yet scat-

tered throughout this book of men are numerous "Achsahs," women whose stories are interspersed with the tales of men and women who, like Achsah, exert themselves in the narrative as actors in their own right.

In addition to Achsah, I count ten of these women in the book of Judges.[7] Three appear in the twinned chapters of Judges 4 and Judges 5: Deborah, who is labeled as a judge and a prophet in Judg 4:4 and who, in 4:6–16 and especially 5:1–23, is described as a hero in the military encounter between the tribes of Israel and the Canaanite forces under the leadership of Sisera; Jael, Deborah's cohort in the battle against Sisera and the woman who ultimately kills the Canaanite commander (4:17–22; 5:24–27); and Sisera's mother, who watches from the window of her great house, waiting in vain for her son to come home (5:28–30). Wartime also provides the setting for the stories of the fourth and fifth "Achsah-like" women of Judges: the woman of Thebez, who, trapped in a tower by the royal pretender Abimelech, shatters (literally) his kingly claims by dropping a stone upon his head (9:50–57); and Jephthah's daughter, who, after her father's battle against the Ammonites, learns that she will be the victim of his rash and impulsive vow to sacrifice to God the first thing he sees upon returning home (11:29–40).

Judges' next three female actors are the women in the life of the hero Samson: Manoah's wife, who gives birth to Samson after she receives from God's angel a divine promise that her barrenness will be ended and that she will bear a son (13:2–24); the Timnite woman, Samson's Philistine wife, who wheedles from her husband the answer to his lion-and-honey riddle (14:1–15:8); and Delilah, Samson's flirtatious mistress, who also tricks Samson by discovering that the secret of his godly strength lies in his uncut hair (16:4–22). In the concluding chapters of Judges, there appear two more women characters of note: Micah's mother, who erects a votive statue to God in order to protect her son from the deity's curse (17:1–5), and the Levite's concubine,[8] a woman who seeks to leave the home of her Levite master and return to her Judahite father only to find herself, first, reclaimed by the Levite against her will and, then, brutally raped and murdered by the Benjaminites of Gibeah on the way back to the Levite's house (19:1–30).

Other Benjaminite tribesmen subsequently seize wives for themselves from the daughters of Shiloh who dance in that village's vineyards (21:20–23), and, although no individuals among these daughters are identified by name, they as a group should still be considered alongside our list of Judges' women actors.[9] Two other groups of women also are worthy of mention: the wise ladies who attend Sisera's mother and who comfort her when her son fails to return home from war in a timely fashion (5:29) and the virgin companions of Jephthah's daughter who accompany the girl on the two-month retreat that precedes her sacrifice (11:37–38).[10]

I. THE SCOPE OF THE INQUIRY

This is truly a remarkable collection of women characters. Only a few other of the Bible's books can claim such a concentration: the book of Genesis, whose women characters include the matriarchs Sarah, Rebekah, Rachel, and Leah, their maids Hagar, Zilpah, and Bilhah, the two daughters of Lot, and Judah's daughter-in-law Tamar;[11] the book of Ruth, which, in addition to its depiction of its title character, presents a complex portrait of Ruth's mother-in-law, Naomi, and a briefer representation of Naomi's other daughter-in-law, Orpah;[12] and the book of Exodus, which especially in chapters 1–4 describes no fewer than seven noteworthy women.[13] These are the midwives Shiphrah and Puah, who defy the orders of the Egyptian pharaoh and let male Hebrew children live; Moses' mother, later identified as Jochebed (Exod 6:20; Num 26:59), and Moses' sister, elsewhere named as Miriam, both of whom engineer the survival of one particular Hebrew child, the baby boy Moses; the pharaoh's daughter, who, in conjunction with her maid, lifts Moses out of the Nile to be raised in the pharaoh's court; and Zipporah, Moses' wife, who averts disaster by circumcising Gershom, her son by Moses, and presumably also Moses (the text is unclear)[14] when "the Lord met him and tried to kill him" (Exod 4:24; NRSV translation).[15]

Yet, though these Exodus women are extraordinary in their actions, showing themselves willing, for example, to defy the pharaoh's decree that all male Hebrew children must die, it is crucial that we realize that the tradition depicts these women as using their attributes of boldness and defiance in the service of a single goal, the preservation of the lives of Hebrew sons in general and of Moses in particular. The women of Ruth also are presented as single-mindedly focused on one objective, the finding of a man who can assume the responsibility of sheltering each of these otherwise destitute widows. Thus the Moabite Orpah returns to the house of her birth family to seek a second husband there,

and although Ruth, also a Moabite, eschews this option in favor of going to Israel with Naomi, upon their arrival in Naomi's hometown of
Bethlehem, both of these women determinedly devote themselves to
acquiring marital security for Ruth and, through her, security for Naomi.[16] Likewise in Genesis, the women characters all assume essentially
the same role as they seek to ensure the continuation of Abraham's patriarchal line. Sometimes, this means a woman bears an Abrahamic descendant or descendants herself, often after a prolonged period of barrenness
(Sarah, Rebekah, Rachel, Leah); sometimes a maid bears an Abrahamic
child or children on behalf of her mistress (Hagar, Zilpah, Bilhah); sometimes women resort to deception to become impregnated by the patriarchal seed (Lot's daughters, Tamar). But whatever the method, the role
these women perform in the narrative is always the same.

Judges' women stand in striking contrast. Ethnically, they are a mixed
lot: most are Israelite, but Jael is a Kenite, Sisera's mother is a Canaanite,
and the Timnite woman is Philistine. In terms of social status, they also
run the gamut, from virtual chattel—the Levite's concubine of Judges
19—to nobles and aristocrats—the chieftain's daughter Achsah in Judges
1. Even more remarkable are the ways in which Judges' women can be
depicted in defiance of traditional gender expectations. While many are
identified using the typical female epithets of wife, mother, mistress,
daughter, sister, and bride, others are described in ways not usually associated with the female sphere. Deborah, Jael, and the woman of Thebez,
for example, are all noteworthy for the actions they take within the
traditionally male domain of battle, and Deborah is also described as a
religious functionary (a prophet) and as one of Israel's political leaders (a
judge). Elsewhere in biblical tradition, these offices are occupied almost
exclusively by men.[17]

Even those Judges women who do remain primarily defined by the
men in their lives need not necessarily subordinate themselves to these
men and their concerns. Micah's mother, Jephthah's daughter, and Manoah's wife, for example, while all nameless in the text, identified only
by the son, father, or husband with whom they stand in closest relation,
still take independent action.[18] The mother of Micah dedicates a votive
statue to God, and Jephthah's daughter persuades her father to delay her
sacrifice for two months so that she can join other young women in a
ritual lamentation. The divine messenger who announces Samson's impending birth initially makes his revelation known just to Manoah's wife,
not to Manoah, and it is only the wife who understands that the recep-

tion of this divine epiphany does not mean certain death.[19] Also to be
recalled here is the portrayal of Achsah, which, although it begins by
depicting her as a disempowered bride, an object of barter in the hands
of men, quickly turns to describe her as a woman who takes charge of
her own destiny: she is assertive, pragmatic, and lays claim to land ownership. The women of Genesis, Exodus, and Ruth could again be considered by way of contrast, for in those books not only do all the women
characters play a single role in the text, but the goal each assembly of
women pursues—be it motherhood (Genesis), the prevention of man-
slaughter (Exodus), or the securing of a male provider (Ruth)—is one
that ultimately serves an androcentric agenda of either male descent or
male leadership.[20]

It is further of note that even in those cases where the women of
Judges are like the women of Genesis, Exodus, and Ruth and thus of a
single "type," the Judges women are still remarkable for the diverse
characterizations they can present within the context of the same role.
While one newlywed, Achsah, can act in ways that are readily described
as thoughtful and mature, another, Samson's Timnite wife, can be accused of filling her wedding celebration with reckless cajolery and
self-interested deception. While, during a time of war, one woman, Deborah, can follow an Israelite victory in battle by singing a hymn of exultation, another, Jephthah's daughter, sees post-victory jubilation quickly
turn into mourning as she finds herself lamenting her impending death
as the victim of her father's wartime vow. Micah's mother embodies
generosity as she dedicates two hundred pieces of silver to God to expiate the guilt of her son; Delilah seeks only her own gratification and
enrichment when she reveals the secret of Samson's great strength
and receives a fortune in Philistine silver in exchange. Sisera's mother,
engaging in pitiful fantasies as she waits in vain for her son's return home,
seems at best naive but more likely slow-witted; the waiting lady who
stands with her, however, is especially identified as wise. Then there is
Jael, a woman who savagely pierces Sisera's head in what Robert Alter
has called "a phallic aggressive act,"[21] to be contrasted to the Levite's
concubine, who lies brutally raped and murdered, the prey of the Benjaminite men's sexual aggression.

It is this remarkable assembly of women and the multitude of roles they
play in the book of Judges that I wish to explore in this volume. Six

"types" of women's roles particularly attract my attention. I will begin in Chapter 1 by describing the first of these, the role Deborah and Jael play in Judges 4 and, especially, Judges 5 as military heroes; of primary interest to me will be the fact that these two women are depicted as military actors in Judges even though ancient Israelite tradition generally envisioned wartime activities as belonging exclusively to the domain of men. In Chapter 2, I will continue to focus my attention on this sort of representation whereby Judges' women play a role in an arena more characteristically associated with the world of men by discussing the portrayals of the same two women of Chapter 1, Deborah and Jael, as they perform the traditionally male function of cult specialist. Chapter 3 will again consider women who assume the sorts of power usually the prerogative of men, focusing in particular on the role of Sisera's mother in Judg 5:28–30. This woman, I will argue, is depicted as a queen mother serving in her son's royal court and so should be imagined as wielding the same kinds of political, economic, and religious authority that queen mothers commanded elsewhere in the biblical world.

Chapter 3, however, will also document the more typically "female" experience of powerlessness that Sisera's mother endures as she watches vainly from a window, hoping against hope that her son will return at the end of the Israelite-Canaanite war. This sort of occasion, where women find their activities limited to the home and centered around their domestic roles, especially their roles as men's mothers, wives, and daughters, will occupy my attention further in Chapters 4, 5, and 6. I will discuss mothers in Chapter 4, specifically the role of a mother-to-be, Manoah's wife, and the ways in which she overcomes her barrenness to give birth to a son. In Chapter 5, I will concentrate on wives and more generally on women defined in terms of their sexual relationships with men, contrasting, for example, the tale of a woman like Delilah, who is able to render her will supreme in her dealings with her lover Samson, to the experience of the Levite's concubine, who finds herself subject to the demands of her Judahite father, her Levite master, and, ultimately, her Benjaminite molesters. Then, in Chapter 6, I will move from the story of the Benjaminites' rape of the Levite's concubine to study the story of how other Benjaminite tribesmen seize the daughters of Shiloh when those young women dance in the vineyards. Here, I will reevoke some of the questions of Chapter 5 about women's sexual autonomy—why must these Shilonite daughters fall victim to the sexual aggressions of the Benjaminite men?—and will also return to some of the issues raised in Chapter 2, asking more specifically whether there is a religious character to the young women's revels.

This observation—that Chapter 6 will reevoke some of the earlier discussions of Chapters 2 and 5—brings to the fore another consideration that will guide this study, namely, that even though each chapter proposes to focus on the representation of one central female figure or figures in the book of Judges and the "type" of role played by such a figure or figures in the biblical text, it is nevertheless my contention that none of these individuals can be studied in isolation. Rather, because my interest is in Judges' rendering of its women as character "types," I believe it necessary to compare the ways in which other women of the same "type" are presented elsewhere in biblical tradition. In some cases, as in my comparison of the Shilonite daughters of Chapter 6 with the women discussed in Chapters 2 and 5, this comparative data will come from within the book of Judges itself. In Chapter 1, similarly, although its primary concern is the battlefield exploits of Deborah, I will also examine other women in Judges who participate in some sort of wartime activity: first, as noted above, Jael, the murderer of Sisera, whose story is found alongside Deborah's in Judges 4 and 5; then, the woman of Thebez described in Judges 9, who, like Jael, smashes an enemy commander's head and so brings to an end a military conflict.

But it is hardly my intent to restrict my search for comparative data to Judges alone. Instead, I aim to embrace in my discussion relevant materials from elsewhere in the biblical corpus and, often, materials from elsewhere in the biblical world. In fact, in several of my chapters, the Judges woman on whom I will focus has no counterparts within the book of Judges itself, and in these cases, my search for comparative data will immediately take me to materials that come from other books of the Hebrew Bible and from other parts of the ancient Near Eastern and eastern Mediterranean regions. Manoah's wife, for example, the primary subject of Chapter 4, is the only barren woman depicted in the book of Judges, so my discussion of other women who fill the same role will quickly turn from her story in Judges to consider stories of barren women found elsewhere in the Hebrew Bible: Sarah, Rebekah, and Rachel from the book of Genesis, and, from the books of Samuel and Kings, Hannah and the Shunammite woman. Next, I will move beyond the Hebrew Bible tradition to consider a prebiblical legend of infertility, the Canaanite Epic of Aqhat; then, casting an even wider net, I will conclude by arguing that in the ancient Israelite imagination, the state of virginity is, in some ways, analogous to that of being barren. This consideration will suggest in turn a comparison between the New Testament story of the virgin birth and the Judges story of the birth of Samson.

II. SOME QUESTIONS OF METHOD

Because of this structure I propose to follow—to use the six chapters in this book to consider six different roles played by women in the book of Judges and then to bring forward comparative data to analyze the place of these character "types" within the larger context of biblical tradition—it is possible, at least to some degree, to read the six essays in this volume as six independent studies: the "women and war" analysis in Chapter 1, the "queen mother" investigation in Chapter 3, the "abduction of dancing maidens" examination in Chapter 6, and so on. Nevertheless, it is my intent that, however discrete each of my analyses may seem, this volume should be comprehended as a conceptual whole. While it is true, that is, that each chapter *can* to some extent be read as a separate discussion, I do see all six as interrelated. In part, this interrelationship stems from the demands of the material itself, given that many of the Judges women I describe are so multidimensional in their characters that I have often found it necessary to discuss the same woman in more than one of this book's chapters: Jael, for example, is considered both in Chapter 1, as a woman involved in military action, and in Chapter 2, as a cult specialist and provider of religious sanctuary. More important, though, is the fact that the six chapters of this book are united through a common set of presuppositions. To put forward those presuppositions briefly, my work takes its inspiration from the methodologies of historians of religion and thus determines to treat both the story of the focal character with whom I begin each chapter and the various texts to which I compare that character's story according to the categories of religious literature. My goal in this effort is to sketch the place occupied by these pieces of religious literature—and, consequently, by the "types" of women characters this literature represents—within the larger arenas of Israelite theological belief and ritual practice. To state the matter more briefly still, I want to use Judges' stories about its women and those stories' kindred texts to describe the place of Judges' "types" of women characters within the ancient Israelite religious imagination and, even more generally, to discuss the place these "types" of women occupied within the actual practice of ancient Israelite religion.

I will have more to say about the specifics of this methodology below, but by way of prologue, I wish first to describe my reasons for embracing this sort of history-of-religions approach. My aim is to chart something of a middle course between the two conflicting methods of inquiry that have been employed in most previous examinations of Judges' women.[22] By so doing, I hope to avoid some of the problems that practitioners of these methods have faced.

The first of these two methods to which I refer is a purely historical means of analysis that tends to consider Judges' women characters by discussing these characters' roles in the light of the actual historical circumstances and events of the twelfth and eleventh centuries B.C.E. (the period of time Judges purports to describe).[23] This method's questions are simple and straightforward: "what did women in premonarchical Israel really do in their lives?" or "what were women's roles and relationships in the period of the judges really like?" Two closely related articles by Jo Ann Hackett, both of which consider most of the women found in Judg 3:12–16:31, can serve as examples.[24] The subtitle of the earlier piece (1985), "In the Days of Jael: Reclaiming the *History* of Women in Ancient Israel" (emphasis mine), is particularly telling, as it identifies explicitly Hackett's historiographical interests. So, too, does the fact that Hackett uses the words "history," "histories," "historians," and "historiography" no less than thirteen times in the six sentences that comprise this article's first paragraph.[25] In the pages that follow, Hackett also enthusiastically dons the historian's mantle as she outlines the specific focus of her inquiry: to take the larger questions concerning women's status and power that have arisen out of the recent women's history and social history movements and to use these questions to ask about the status of women during the period of the judges. "My goals are simple," she writes,

> . . . first, to employ recent understandings of women's lives in order to give us new insight into the status of Israelite women; second, since there are analogies between Israel and other societies, to add our knowledge of women in ancient Israel, on a historical and sociological level, to the growing body of research about women the world over.[26]

Yet, as noble as these goals may be—and as much as I, personally, am in sympathy with Hackett's objectives—I believe her sort of enterprise is fraught with difficulties, and difficulties, moreover, that are (at least to my mind) all but insurmountable. The basic problem is this: how reliably, really, can the book of Judges respond to the historian's "what really happened" sorts of inquiries? The stumbling blocks are many. An initial question concerns matters of date, as the overwhelming bulk of the text of Judges, at least in the form in which it has come down to us, is the work of a school of writers, called the Deuteronomists (because of their writings' close relationship to the book of Deuteronomy), whose work was compiled in the last quarter of the seventh century B.C.E.[27] This means that Judges postdates by some *four to five hundred years* the events the book claims to describe. Hackett responds by positing that there were oral and written traditions that antedated the Deuteronomistic text and were used by the Deuteronomists in their redacting of Judges, and she further resolves to base her reconstructions only on those parts of this older tradition that she feels are "relatively free of editorial reworking."[28] But, while I agree with this part of Hackett's methodological premise—a careful reading of Judges *can* extract minimally redacted pre-Deuteronomistic materials—I feel much less confident than she that these pre-Deuteronomistic traditions, whether oral or written, can transmit accurate historical information about the lives of women in Israel's premonarchical past.

Concerning oral traditions, for example, recent studies have repeatedly documented the failure of this sort of material to provide historically reliable data. Most significant for students of the Hebrew Bible are the conclusions of Homeric scholars concerning the historicity of the *Iliad* and the *Odyssey* since these giants of Homeric literature are—in their epic character, in their self-presentation as second-millennium B.C.E. history, in their eighth-century B.C.E. date of written composition, and in their eastern Mediterranean place of origin—closely akin to the book of Judges and, indeed, closely akin to large portions of the biblical text (especially the stories of Israel's origins and early days found in Genesis–I Samuel). Ian Morris sums up the Homeric case succinctly: "The much-vaunted oral tradition was not in any sense a 'chronicle,' a repository of antiquated institutions and world-views."[29] Instead, oral tradition is a constantly changing and evolving phenomenon, "intimately linked to the present, consisting only of what the parties to the oral performance thought proper."[30] Or, to put the matter more bluntly, "The institutions, attitudes, and conditions of action that we find in the *Iliad* and *Odyssey* must of necessity be derived in some way from those of the functioning societies that Homer himself knew."[31] The biblicist need only substitute "Judges" for "the *Iliad* and *Odyssey*" and "the Deuter-onomists" for "Homer" to appreciate the impossibility of assuming a historically accurate oral tradition underlying the current Judges text.

The search for historically reliable data in whatever written sources lie embedded in the current text of Judges (including even the demon-strably archaic poem found in Judges 5) is likewise an extremely prob-lematic enterprise.[32] An initial concern is these sources' transparently religious agenda: to catalogue the mighty acts that God did on behalf of Israel during the people's early days in the land. Within such a theologi-cally-oriented construct, any attempt to find "history" at all is difficult, at least any attempt to find "history" in the more secular and human-centered sense in which we usually think of that term. The attempt to find historically reliable data concerning ancient Israelite women's status and lives is more difficult still. The maxim "winners write history" must here stand to the fore, as Judges, like all the texts of the Hebrew Bible, reflects in large part the literary activity of only a small and privileged segment of the Israelite population.[33] In many cases, as in the bulk of the texts found in Genesis, Exodus, Leviticus, Numbers, and Deuter-onomy, the group whose literary activity is reflected is the priestly elite. In other cases, biblical texts reflect the perspective of Israel's prophetic leadership. In both these instances, moreover, and in the case of the scribal class responsible for almost all the rest of the Bible's writings, the perspective is exclusively male.[34] Within these sorts of sources, any attempt to find a history of women, and especially a history of nonaristo-cratic women, is gravely compromised. It is perhaps even impossible.

It is small wonder, then, that discussions that use the texts of Judges to describe women's actual work and lives in ancient Israel are often disparaged, dismissed, for example, by J. Cheryl Exum as "useless exer-cises in historical literalism."[35] Thus, in her several studies considering various women characters in Judges, Exum rejects any historical inquiry in favor of a formalist literary approach.[36] More specifically, Exum pur-sues a methodology that involves a close reading of single units of text, "examining in detail the interconnections of form and content."[37] For example, in her 1985 article, "'Mother in Israel': A Familiar Figure Re-considered," which considers two episodes from the book of Judges— the story of Samson's mother and the use of the epithet "mother" to describe Deborah—Exum writes, "My approach here involves primarily a literary method of close reading, which pays careful attention to the portrayal of women in selected texts."[38] Similarly, in her longer investi-gation of the story of Samson's mother, "Promise and Fulfillment: Narrative Art in Judges 13," Exum describes how her study "proposes to focus attention on the relationship between literary structure and meaning in this material on the premise that proper delineation of form contributes to proper articulation of meaning."[39] "Aspects of Symmetry and Balance in the Samson Saga," Exum's longer-still examination of the entire Samson tale (Judges 13–16) and the women within it (especially Samson's Timnite wife and Delilah), also begins by noting her interest in the narrative's "literary patterns," which, "since form is a vehicle of meaning," provide "a significant and reliable guide to the theological emphases of the saga in its present form."[40] The crucial questions asked here are diametrically opposed to those of the previously described historical approach: not "what actually happened?" or "what was really going on?" but instead "what are the means by which a story is told?" or "what techniques of style and craft has a narrator used?" This information is in turn used to consider not "what did women in ancient Israel really do in their day-to-day lives?" but "what is a story's narrative impact concerning women?" or, most basically, "regarding women, what is a story really trying to *say*?"[41]

Others who have brought this sort of literary approach to bear on a discussion of Judges' women include Phyllis Trible,[42] who has used the techniques of rhetorical criticism in studies that analyze the stories of Jephthah's daughter and of the Levite's concubine. Both these pieces are found in Trible's book *Texts of Terror,* which, notably, is subtitled *Literary-Feminist Readings of Biblical Narratives.*[43] "Literary" is a key word as well in the subtitle of Mieke Bal's 1987 book, *Lethal Love: Feminist Literary Readings of Biblical Love Stories,* in which Bal considers, along with other materials, the Judges story of Samson and Delilah using a literary strategy in general and the methodology of narratology in particular.[44] Narratology is again the guiding method for Bal in her 1988 book *Death and Dissymmetry: The Politics of Coherence in the Book of Judges,* which documents the pivotal role Bal believes women's stories play in communicating Judges' political and ideological message. An approach that analyzes narrative structure also informs three other recently published discussions of women in Judges, Danna Nolan Fewell's article "Judges" that appeared in *The Women's Bible Commentary* in 1992 and two pieces by Lillian R. Klein, "A Spectrum of Female Characters in the Book of Judges" and "The Book of Judges: Paradigm and Deviation in Images of Women," both a part of Athalaya Brenner's 1993 edited collection, *A Feminist Companion to Judges.*[45]

Yet, while the techniques of literary criticism are certainly enjoying a

surge of popularity in biblical scholarship today, they, like the previously
described methods of historicism they seek to replace, are not without
their pitfalls. Most dangerous is the literary critic's tendency to take
methodologies developed in fields such as English and comparative literature, used there to describe American and European fiction of the En-
lightenment and post-Enlightenment eras, and then to apply these tools
to a text that is decidedly not of the place, not of the time, and, most
significantly, not of the genres that this sort of analysis is meant to address.[46] That is, while Judges is manifestly not history, it is just as surely
not a modern novel or a collection of contemporary short stories. The
best of the literary critics acknowledge the Bible's dissimilarities and try
to make reasonable accommodation; Bal, for example, notes that the
presuppositions of literary analysis are peculiar to today's literary experience and warns practitioners against uncritically forcing these projec-
tions back upon biblical materials.[47] But all too often, caveats like these
fall on deaf ears, yielding literary-critical inquiries that assume, without
serious reflection and without sundry reservations, the synonymity of
ancient and recent writings.[48] Such investigations are—at best—open to
serious criticism. At worst, they are doomed to fail.

Judges, I conclude, is best analyzed neither as a chronicle of ancient
history nor as the stuff of contemporary fiction.[49] What this means for
my discussion of its women characters is that, on the one hand, I will
not assume any historical reality that underlies the narratives I will be
describing. To put the matter more bluntly, I will not suppose that any
of the stories I will consider actually happened, nor will I suppose the
women actors of these stories actually lived. In fact, in the case of certain
of Judges' women, the book's female military heroes, for example, I will
not even assume that the "type" of character the Judges woman represents ever existed within Israelite society. In essence, this is nothing
more than common sense: can we really imagine warrior women thriv-
ing within the context of Israel's highly androcentric culture?[50] On the
other hand, however, I refuse to succumb to literary nihilism. This
means that, while I will not assume a historical reality for any of the
stories or characters I will be discussing, I do believe it is crucial to
assume a historical reality for the authors who wrote these stories and
for the audience for whom these authors wrote. I further believe it is
crucial to assume that this historical reality matters, that the biblical au-

thors shaped their stories about various "types" of women in a certain way and that the biblical redactors preserved certain versions of tales about women because these narratives somehow "worked" within the context—the mind-set and the worldview—of the authors' and redactors' day. Unlike a formalist literary critic, then, I will care about the dates of Judges' texts, I will care about these texts' authorship, I will care about these texts' editing, and I will particularly care about the social world in which these texts were constructed and transmitted. I will care even more about the religious aspects of that social world, for I do take the Bible to be primarily a religious document.[51] I thus assume that its literature is most properly analyzed according to the genres of religious texts, in particular, in the case of Judges, the genres of myth, legend, epic, and, in certain cases, folktale.[52]

I also maintain that a crucial component in the analysis of any myth, legend, epic, or folktale is the comparison of the focal piece of literature to other texts of the same topic and type. I therefore assume that in the case of the materials that interest me, the depictions of women found in the book of Judges, that after my initial analysis of a Judges story, I will need to describe how the Judges representation of a woman character is related to similar representations of women found elsewhere: first, elsewhere in the book of Judges itself; second, elsewhere in the rest of biblical literature; third, elsewhere in Israelite tradition (in extrabiblical literature and in the archaeological record); and, finally, elsewhere in the biblical world (in the religious literature and in the archaeological record of other ancient Near Eastern and eastern Mediterranean peoples with whom the Israelites interacted). I will want, that is, to undertake precisely the comparative task I discussed earlier, at the end of Section I. Then, as adumbrated at the beginning of Section II, I will want to use this body of comparative data to apprehend the place of Judges' various "types" of women within the larger arena of ancient Israelite religious literature and within the even larger province of the actual practice of ancient Israelite religion. The question I will pose in this regard is easily stated: what are the theological and ideological influences and suppositions concerning women—more simply put, what are the religious beliefs—that motivated the biblical writers to craft their portraits of Judges' women in the ways that they did?

This sort of question is familiar terrain and is, in fact, practically second nature to anyone who has ever engaged in this sort of a history-of-religions type of analysis. Yet I also want to raise a second and more wide-ranging type of query within the history-of-religions domain, in-spired to do so by Jonathan Z. Smith, perhaps the foremost theoretician of a history-of-religions methodology writing today. In his work, Smith consciously departs from older history-of-religions interpretations by in-sisting that a study of a text's history, or what Smith prefers to call its trajectory, must play a role in its analysis.[53] A body of material, that is, must be discussed within the context of the history of tradition, taking into account continuities with older ideologies and beliefs but concur-rently asking what it is that has changed. What this sort of evolutionary question means for my inquiry is that, after identifying the ideological influences and beliefs that inspired Judges' authors to depict the book's women characters in the ways that they did, I will want to ask what role, if any, those same ideological influences and beliefs played in the materi-als to which I compare Judges' various texts. As we will see, ideologies on occasion are held in common throughout the various retellings of a certain "type" of woman's story; the several biblical and extrabiblical portraits of, for example, queen mothers all look very much the same (Chapter 3). A great deal of the literature I will be surveying, however, comes from texts separated in date by as much as a millennium, and often in these narratives, we will find that there are significant differences in the ways in which a "type" of character is rendered. These permuta-tions, I will argue, are inspired by a number of factors: by changes in the literary genre that was used in the telling of the tales of Deborah and of other female military heroes (Chapter 1); by shifts in Israel's political, social, and especially religious circumstances over time, which in turn generated shifting Israelite attitudes concerning a woman like Jael's ap-propriate political, social, and especially religious roles (Chapter 2); by variations in the biblical writers' assumptions about what could consti-tute "barrenness" among women, which in turn occasioned the encom-passing of something like the New Testament story of the virgin birth in the term's definition (Chapter 4), and, similarly, by variations in the biblical writers' assumptions about what could constitute proper behav-ior in a woman's exercise of sexual autonomy, which in turn generated contrasting portraits of, say, Delilah and the Levite's concubine (Chapter 5); finally, by differences in the geographical regions from which the several versions of the "abduction of dancing maidens" tale come, resulting in differences in the various tales' emphases and concerns (Chapter 6).

My endeavor is in short a dual essay. First, it is a synchronic description of a specific Judges character and story and of that character's kindred actors and that story's kindred texts. This book's main title, *Warrior, Dancer, Seductress, Queen,* by listing some of the major character "types" I will discuss, intends to address this part of my inquiry. Simultaneously, though, I want to engage in a diachronic study, based on the assumption that the ways in which a particular "type" of woman character was imagined in the biblical world could hardly have remained static throughout the approximately one-thousand-year time span that defines the era of the Israelite cult. The book's subtitle and, especially, the word "and" within it—*Women in Judges and Biblical Israel*—speaks to this sort of evolutionary concern.

My overall goal is to examine Judges' stories about its women characters and to compare kindred representations of women from elsewhere in the biblical world in order to illuminate the place that six "types" of women occupied within the ancient Israelite religious imagination and within the more general sphere of ancient Israelite religion. Smith has written, "The more I read in Jewish and Christian materials, the more I become convinced that many elements yield themselves far better to the sensitive historian of religions than to other disciplinary approaches."[54] This is a conviction that, at least in studying the roles of women in the book of Judges, I share. The point of this book is to illustrate the insights that such a history-of-religions analysis can offer.

NOTES

———— ∞∞∞ ————

[1]Judg 16:27 (NRSV translation).

[2]An almost identical version of this story is found in Josh 15:14–19.

[3]Danna N. Fewell points out that the name Achsah, meaning "bangle" or "anklet," also implies her status as "a trinket" or "an ornament" in this story. See Fewell's "Deconstructive Criticism: Achsah and the (E)razed City of Writing," *Judges and Method: New Approaches in Biblical Studies* (ed. G. A. Yee; Minneapolis: Fortress, 1995), 133.

[4]According to some versions, for example, the Alexandrinus codex of the Septuagint, Othniel is Caleb's brother. See R. G. Boling, *Judges* (AB 6a; Garden City, NY: Doubleday, 1975), 56; J. M. Myers, "Judges: Introduction and Exegesis," IB 2 (Nashville: Abingdon, 1953), 692.

[5]Retaining the MT *wattĕsîtēhû*, "and she urged him," as opposed to the Septuagint and Vulgate, which read a masculine form of the verb, "and he urged her." See further P. G. Mosca, "Who Seduced Whom? A Note on Joshua 15:18//Judges 1:14," *CBQ* 46 (1984), 18–22 (this reference brought to my attention by Fewell, "Deconstructive Criticism," 135, n. 38); also, Mieke Bal, *Death and Dissymmetry: The Politics of Coherence in the Book of Judges* (Chicago: University of Chicago Press, 1988), 152–55 (although Bal's analysis of the second problematic phrase of this verse, *wattiṣnaḥ mēʿal haḥămŏr* [preferring "she clapped her hands from on top of her ass" to the more traditional "she alighted from her ass"], seems to me misguided).

[6]The text here is enigmatic; my reading follows most closely that of J. A. Soggin, *Joshua: A Commentary* (OTL; Philadelphia: Westminster, 1972), 161, with notes on pp. 166–67. Others interpret the specifics of this episode very differently. For example, Boling, *Judges*, 64, who reads "he urged her" in verse 14 (see above, n. 5), believes that, while Othniel urged his wife to ask Caleb for a field, she ignored his request and substituted her own desire for two basins of water. Alternatively, both Fewell and Lillian R. Klein suggest that verse 14 implies that Othniel does in fact follow his wife's urging and ask Caleb for a field; then, in verse 15, after that petition has been granted, Achsah returns to Caleb with an additional request for two basins of water. See Fewell, "Judges," *The Women's Bible Commentary* (ed. C. A. Newsom and S. H. Ringe; London: SPCK; Louisville, KY: Westminster/John Knox, 1992), 68; Klein, "A Spectrum of Female Characters in the Book of Judges," 25; idem, "The Book of Judges: Paradigm and Deviation in Images of Women," 58; both in *A Feminist Companion to Judges* (ed. A. Brenner; The Feminist Companion to the Bible 4; Sheffield: Sheffield Academic Press, 1993). Cf. Fewell, "Deconstructive Criticism," 134.

[7]Klein, "A Spectrum of Female Characters," 24, similarly speaks of "eleven fully differentiated females"; cf. Athalaya Brenner, "Introduction," *A Feminist Companion to Judges,* 9, who, counting every woman even mentioned in the book of Judges, finds "19 female personae or collective personae in all." See also Gale A. Yee's comments on and catalogue of Judges' women in "Introduction: Why Judges?" *Judges and Method,* 1–5.

[8]On the meaning of concubine here, see my comments in Chapter 5 and, as there, Fewell, "Judges," 75; M. O'Connor, "The Women in the Book of Judges," *HAR* 10 (1986), 278, n. 5.

[9]Although Judg 21:20–23 does not specify that the women dance in the vineyards *per se* but only that their Benjaminite abductors conceal themselves there, we are surely meant to understand that the women, if not dancing right *in* the vineyards, were dancing nearby. See further Chapter 6, n. 80.

[10]There are also several women or groups of women in Judges who are mute and/or are acted upon rather than being actors in the narrative themselves. These women include: (1) the wives and concubine of Gideon (8:30–31); (2) the prostitute mother of Jephthah (11:1); (3) the legal wife of Gilead, Jephthah's father (11:2); (4) the thirty daughters and thirty daughters-in-law of Ibzan of Bethlehem (12:9); (5) the sister of Samson's Timnite wife (15:1–2); (6) the prostitute of Samson (16: 1–3); (7) the virgin daughter of the Ephraimite residing in Gibeah (19:24); and (8) the young virgins of Jabesh-Gilead (21:12 and 14).

[11]There are many articles discussing one or several of these Genesis women; the one book-length study that considers them all is S. P. Jeansonne, *The Women of Genesis: From Sarah to Potiphar's Wife* (Minneapolis: Fortress, 1990). Also note the materials collected in *A Feminist Companion to Genesis* (ed. A. Brenner; The Feminist Companion to the Bible 2; Sheffield: Sheffield Academic Press, 1993).

[12]On Ruth's women, see, for example, the discussions of P. Trible, "A Human Comedy," Chapter 6 in *God and the Rhetoric of Sexuality* (OBT 2; Philadelphia: Fortress, 1978), 166–99; of K. P. Darr, "'More than Seven Sons': Critical, Rabbinical, and Feminist Perspectives on Ruth," Chapter 2 in *Far More Precious than Jewels: Perspectives on Biblical Women* (Louisville, KY: Westminster/John Knox, 1991), 55–84, especially 73–76; and the articles collected in *A Feminist Companion to Ruth* (ed. A. Brenner; The Feminist Companion to the Bible 3; Sheffield: Sheffield Academic Press, 1993).

[13]On Exodus' women, see, for example, the evocative comments of P. Trible, "Depatriarchalizing in Biblical Interpretation," *JAAR* 41 (1973), 34, and the fuller discussions of J. C. Exum (who brought Trible's discussion to my attention), "'You Shall Let Every Daughter Live': A Study of Exodus 1:8–2:10," *The Bible and Feminist Hermeneutics* (*Semeia* 28; ed. M. A. Tolbert; 1983), 63–82, and of E. Schuller,

"Women of the Exodus in Biblical Retellings of the Second Temple Period," *Gender and Difference in Ancient Israel* (ed. P. L. Day; Minneapolis: Fortress, 1989), 178–81.

[14]See my discussion of this passage in Chapter 2 and the references cited there.

[15]Some might add other biblical books to my list: 2 Samuel, perhaps, with its descriptions of David's various wives, of David's daughter Tamar, and of the wise women of Tekoa and of Abel-Beth-Ma'acah (see J. A. Hackett, "1 and 2 Samuel," *The Women's Bible Commentary*, 85–95; also, the articles collected in *A Feminist Companion to Samuel and Kings* [ed. A. Brenner; The Feminist Companion to the Bible 5; Sheffield: Sheffield Academic Press, 1994]), or the book of Esther, possibly, which includes a representation of Queen Vashti in addition to its portrayal of its title character (see S. Niditch, "Short Stories: The Book of Esther and the Theme of Woman as a Civilizing Force," *Old Testament Interpretation: Past, Present, and Future. Essays in Honor of Gene M. Tucker* [ed. J. L. Mays; D. L. Petersen; K. H. Richards; Nashville: Abingdon, 1995], 195–209; S. A. White, "Esther: A Feminine Model for Jewish Diaspora," *Gender and Difference*, 161–77; idem, "Esther," *The Women's Bible Commentary*, 124–29). But in Esther, Vashti disappears after the first chapter, leaving the book with only one woman actor, and in 2 Samuel, the stories of women, though many, are generally subsumed within larger men's stories of political intrigue and palace machinations. Even the most notorious of 2 Samuel's women, Bathsheba, is basically a character acted upon rather than being an actor in the text (although this situation does change dramatically in 1 Kings 1–2). See further Chapter 5 and, as there, the discussions of G. A. Yee, "'Fraught with Background': Literary Ambiguity in II Samuel 11," *Int* 42 (1988), 240–53; idem, "Bathsheba," *ABD* 1 (ed. D. N. Freedman; New York: Doubleday, 1992), 627b; and A. Berlin, "Characterization in Biblical Narrative: David's Wives," *JSOT* 23 (1982), 70–76; idem, *Poetics and Interpretation of Biblical Narrative* (Sheffield: JSOT Press, 1983), 25–27. See also my discussion in Chapter 3 of the way in which another of David's wives, Michal, is treated in 2 Samuel.

[16]See further my discussion of the Ruth story in Chapter 5.

[17]There are no other female judges mentioned in the Bible; for the tradition's few other female prophets, see my brief comments in "Isaiah," *The Women's Bible Commentary*, 164–65, and my longer discussion of the prophet Huldah in Chapter 2.

[18]I have considered the issue of named versus nameless women in Judges below in Chapters 2 and 5; in addition, see Bal, *Death and Dissymmetry*, 43–93, 217–24; Brenner, "Introduction," 10–14; J. C. Exum, "Feminist Criticism: Whose Interests Are Being Served?" *Judges and Method*, 75–86; C. Meyers, "The Hannah Narrative in Feminist Perspective," *"Go to the Land I Will Show You": Studies in Honor of Dwight W. Young* (ed. J. Coleson and V. Matthews; Winona Lake, IN: Eisenbrauns, 1994), 120–22 (reprinted as "Hannah and her Sacrifice: Reclaiming Female Agency," *A Feminist Companion to Samuel and Kings*, 96–99).

[19]See further my discussion in Chapter 2 and, as there, the comments of R. Alter, "How Convention Helps Us Read: The Case of the Bible's Annunciation Type-Scene," *Prooftexts* 3 (1983), 123–24; Y. Amit, "'Manoah Promptly Followed His Wife' (Judges 13.11): On the Place of the Woman in Birth Narratives," *A Feminist Companion to Judges,* 149–50; Bal, *Death and Dissymmetry,* 74; J. C. Exum, "Promise and Fulfillment: Narrative Art in Judges 13," *JBL* 99 (1980), 43–59; idem, "'Mother in Israel': A Familiar Figure Reconsidered," *Feminist Interpretation of the Bible* (ed. L. M. Russell; Philadelphia: Westminster, 1985), 82–84; idem, "Samson's Women," Chapter 3 in *Fragmented Women: Feminist (Sub)versions of Biblical Narratives* (Valley Forge, PA: Trinity Press International, 1993), 61–93, especially pp. 63–68; idem, "Feminist Criticism," 79; E. Fuchs, "The Literary Characterization of Mothers and Sexual Politics in the Hebrew Bible," *Feminist Perspectives on Biblical Scholarship* (ed. A. Y. Collins; Chico, CA: Scholars Press, 1985), 123–25; also, the remarks of J. A. Hackett, "In the Days of Jael: Reclaiming the History of Women in Ancient Israel," *Immaculate and Powerful: The Female in Sacred Image and Social Reality* (ed. C. W. Atkinson; C. H. Buchanan; M. R. Miles; Boston: Beacon, 1985), 29, 32; idem, "Women's Studies and the Hebrew Bible," *The Future of Biblical Studies: The Hebrew Scriptures* (ed. R. E. Friedman and H. G. M. Williamson; Atlanta: Scholars Press, 1987), 158, 160; Klein, "A Spectrum of Female Characters," 26–27; S. Niditch, "Samson as Culture Hero, Trickster, and Bandit: The Empowerment of the Weak," *CBQ* 52 (1990), 610–12; O'Connor, "Women in the Book of Judges," 280; and A. Reinhartz, "Samson's Mother: An Unnamed Protagonist," *JSOT* 55 (1992), 32.

[20]See also in this regard the comments of Fuchs, "Mothers," 129, and of Exum, "'You Shall Let Every Daughter Live,'" 81.

[21]"From Line to Story in Biblical Verse," *Poetics Today* 4 (1983), 635; also, idem, *The Art of Biblical Poetry* (New York: Basic Books, 1985), 49.

[22]As exceptions, I think only of S. Niditch, "Eroticism and Death in the Tale of Jael," *Gender and Difference,* 43–57; P. L. Day, "From the Child Is Born the Woman: The Story of Jephthah's Daughter," *Gender and Difference,* 58–74.

[23]On the use of historical analyses more generally in the study of the book of Judges, see Yee, "Why Judges?" 5–9.

[24]"In the Days of Jael," 15–38; "Women's Studies," 141–64. In limiting her discussion to 3:12–16:31, Hackett considers only the collected stories of the book's actual "judges" (excluding, however, for reasons unclear to me, the story of the judge Othniel in 3:7–11) and so deals with neither the introductory materials concerning conquest and settlement (1:1–3:6) nor the supplemental stories of Micah's shrine and Micah's Levite (Judges 17–18), of the Levite's concubine (Judges 19), and of the civil war that followed this woman's rape and murder (Judges 20–21). In setting these parameters, Hackett follows the generally accepted source analysis of

Judges (see, for example, the chart of R. G. Boling, "Judges, Book of," *ABD* 3, 1116a). But the split between Judg 3:7–16:31 and the rest of the book may not be as clear-cut as Hackett and Boling suggest; see, for example, the comments of G. W. Ahlström, *The History of Ancient Palestine* (Minneapolis: Fortress; Sheffield: Sheffield Academic Press, 1993), 377, on the relationship between Judges 1–16 and 17–21; also, the attempts of J. C. Exum, "The Centre Cannot Hold: Thematic and Textual Instabilities in Judges," *CBQ* 52 (1990), 413, n. 8; Fewell, "Judges," 67–77; and O'Connor, "Women in the Book of Judges," 277–93, to read *all* the narratives of Judges' women, from Judges 1 through Judges 21, synthetically.

[25]"In the Days of Jael," 15.

[26]"In the Days of Jael," 16.

[27]On this date, see further Chapter 2 and, as there, F. M. Cross, *Canaanite Myth and Hebrew Epic: Essays in the History of the Religion of Israel* (Cambridge, MA: Harvard University Press, 1973), 274–89, especially 284, 287; R. E. Friedman, *The Exile and Biblical Narrative: The Formation of the Deuteronomistic and Priestly Works* (Chico, CA: Scholars Press, 1981), 1–26; R. D. Nelson, *The Double Redaction of the Deuteronomistic History* (Sheffield: JSOT Press, 1981), passim but especially 13–28, 119–28.

[28]"In the Days of Jael," 37, n. 34; see also the caveats she raises in "Women's Studies," 154.

[29]"The Use and Abuse of Homer," *Classical Antiquity* 5 (1986), 88.

[30]"Use and Abuse of Homer," 88.

[31]"Use and Abuse of Homer," 90.

[32]On the date of Judges 5, see my comments in Chapter 1 (and also Chapters 2 and 3), and, as in all these chapters, the discussions of D. N. Freedman, "Divine Names and Titles in Early Hebrew Poetry," *Pottery, Poetry, and Prophecy: Studies in Early Hebrew Poetry* (Winona Lake, IN: Eisenbrauns, 1980), 83–85; of B. Halpern, "The Resourceful Israelite Historian: The Song of Deborah and Israelite Historiography," *HTR* 76 (1983), 379, n. 2; idem, *The First Historians: The Hebrew Bible and History* (San Francisco: Harper & Row, 1988), 102–3, n. 36; and of L. E. Stager, "Archaeology, Ecology, and Social History: Background Themes to the Song of Deborah," VTSup 40 (Jerusalem Congress Volume, 1986; ed. J. A. Emerton; Leiden: Brill, 1988), 224; also idem, "The Song of Deborah—Why Some Tribes Answered the Call and Others Did Not," *BARev* 15/1 (January/February 1989), 64, n. 1.

[33]The discussion of C. Meyers, *Discovering Eve: Ancient Israelite Women in Context*

(New York and Oxford: Oxford University Press, 1988), 11–14, is particularly tren-
chant; less fully, Exum, "Feminist Criticism," 66.

[34]The occasional scholarship that posits a female author or authors at certain points in Judges and elsewhere in the Hebrew Bible (e.g., M. Bal, *Murder
and Difference: Gender, Genre, and Scholarship on Sisera's Death* [Bloomington and
Indianapolis: Indiana University Press, 1988], 2, 112–15, 124–34, and F. van Dijk-
Hemmes, "Mothers and a Mediator in the Song of Deborah," in *A Feminist Companion to Judges,* 110–14, with respect to Judges 5; Hackett, "In the Days of Jael," 32–33,
and "Women's Studies," 160, with respect to Judges 5 and Judges 11; A. J. Bledstein,
"Is Judges a Women's Satire of Men Who Play God?" in *A Feminist Companion to
Judges,* 34–54, with respect to the book of Judges as a whole; A. J. Bledstein, "Fe-
male Companionships: If the Book of Ruth Were Written by a Woman . . . ," in *A
Feminist Companion to Ruth,* 116–33, and F. van Dijk-Hemmes, "Ruth: A Product
of Women's Culture?" in *A Feminist Companion to Ruth,* 134–44, with respect to the
book of Ruth; J. W. H. Bos, "Out of the Shadows: Genesis 38; Judges 4:17–22;
Ruth 3," *Reasoning with the Foxes: Female Wit in a World of Male Power,* [*Semeia* 42;
ed. J. C. Exum and J. W. H. Bos; 1988], 49, with respect to Genesis 38; H. Bloom,
"The Author J," in H. Bloom and D. Rosenberg, *The Book of J* [New York: Vintage
Books, 1990], 9–55, with respect to the Yahwistic source in the Tetrateuch; S. D.
Goitein, "Women as Creators of Biblical Genres," *Prooftexts* 8 [1988], 1–33, and A.
Brenner and F. van Dijk-Hemmes, *On Gendering Texts: Female and Male Voices in the
Hebrew Bible* [Leiden: Brill, 1993], passim, with respect to female authorship in the
Bible in general) is so highly speculative that it has convinced few. Phyllis Bird's
comments in "Women's Religion in Ancient Israel," *Women's Earliest Records From
Ancient Egypt and Western Asia* (BJS 166; ed. B. S. Lesko; Atlanta: Scholars Press,
1989), 285–86, n. 8, are particularly salient; she observes that, while the Hebrew
Bible itself does attribute some literary pieces to women, "these few works have all
been transmitted to us in the compositions of scribal guilds, which I would view as
male associations. Hence I believe that we have no *direct* or *unmediated* access to the
words or lives of women in the Hebrew scriptures" (emphasis Bird's).

[35]"'Mother in Israel,'" 157, n. 16.

[36]The ahistorical impulses of literary criticism are most pointedly discussed by
J. Kugel, "On the Bible and Literary Criticism," *Prooftexts* 1 (1981), 231–34, and
also described more briefly by Bal, *Murder and Difference,* 74, and by A. Cooper
and B. R. Goldstein, "Biblical Literature in the Iron(ic) Age: Reflections on
Literary-Historical Method," *HS* 32 (1991), 51.

[37]This description of method is taken from P. Trible, "A Daughter's Death:
Feminism, Literary Criticism, and the Bible," *Backgrounds for the Bible* (ed. M. P.
O'Connor and D. N. Freedman; Winona Lake, IN: Eisenbrauns, 1987), 1.

[38]P. 74.

[39]P. 44.

[40]*JSOT* 19 (1981), 3.

[41]On the sorts of questions asked by a feminist literary analysis, see further Exum, "Feminist Criticism," 69–70.

[42]On the use of literary analyses more generally in the study of the book of Judges, see Yee, "Why Judges?" 9–12.

[43]OBT 13; Philadelphia: Fortress, 1984.

[44]Bloomington and Indianapolis: Indiana University Press.

[45]Fewell's article is found on pp. 67–77; Klein's articles are on pp. 24–33 and 55–71, respectively. I might also note here one other study that considers most of Judges' women: O'Connor, "Women in the Book of Judges," 277–93. This article's methodological approach is somewhat mixed. Some of O'Connor's language and concerns seem more in line with literary analysis; he speaks, for example, of the "thematic shape of Judges," of women as an "abiding metaphor of the book," and of his intent to focus on "the shape of the received text" (p. 279; on this sort of vocabulary as signaling a literary analysis, see Bal, *Murder and Difference,* 74). But O'Connor goes on to remark that the themes he identifies as central to Judges are "deeply inscribed in the source materials used in the redaction" of the book's final form (p. 279), a remark that belongs squarely within the school of historical-critical inquiry (given that literary-critical analysis takes as one of its fundamental tenets the reading of a text solely in its received form; see Bal, *Death and Dissymmetry,* 4; Trible, "A Daughter's Death," 1). O'Connor also, in discussing the metaphor of women as he finds it in Judges, describes the crucial question as being one of private versus public domain, noting that "women, here as elsewhere in pre-modern society, are set to do duty as representatives of the private, as men do duty as tokens of the public. Women are typically on the inside, the domestic sphere, while men are on the outside, the common sphere" (p. 279). Such remarks are highly reminiscent of Hackett's historical inquiries concerning the position and status of women in ancient Israelite society.

[46]On this last point, see the particularly salient comments of Kugel, "On the Bible and Literary Criticism," 218–19.

[47]*Murder and Difference,* 93.

[48]Again, Kugel's comments are especially enlightening, as he calls for "some deeper awareness of assumptions, and a greater consciousness of the historical situation of today's literary criticism of the Bible." "In this connection," he adds, "it is

the very *differentness of the Bible* [emphasis mine] that calls out for consideration" ("On the Bible and Literary Criticism," 234).

[49]Katharine Sakenfeld has similarly discussed the conflicting approaches of historical and literary scholarship, using as an example the interpretation of the story of the daughters of Zelophehad in Numbers 27 and 36; see "Feminist Biblical Interpretation," *TToday* 46 (1989), 154–68. Sakenfeld also describes a third type of interpretation, which she characterizes as being "also within the literary realm" but which "concentrates much more on reading the text as a product of its own culture" (p. 161). This approach is, in some ways, much closer to my own, although it lacks both the special focus on religious ideology and the broadly comparative perspective that I consider essential. It has, moreover, only rarely been used in studies of Judges' women (I think only of E. Fuchs, "Marginalization, Ambiguity, Silencing: The Story of Jephthah's Daughter," *JFSR* 5 [1989], 35–45, and G. A. Yee, "Ideological Criticism: Judges 17–21 and the Dismembered Body," *Judges and Method,* 146–70).

[50]But see Hackett, "In the Days of Jael," 26–28; idem, "Women's Studies," 156–57; Meyers, *Discovering Eve,* 174; G. A. Yee, "By the Hand of a Woman: The Metaphor of the Woman Warrior in Judges 4," *Women, War, and Metaphor: Language and Society in the Study of the Hebrew Bible* (*Semeia* 61; ed. C. V. Camp and C. R. Fontaine; 1993), 111–12.

[51]This *pace* R. Alter, "Convention," 116–17.

[52]These genres are those most closely kindred to the kinds of narrative materials we find in Judges. Elsewhere in the biblical text, other categories of religious literature—including hymns, sermons, oracles, canon law, and theological discourse—may provide the more appropriate *comparanda*.

[53]*Map Is Not Territory: Studies in the History of Religions* (Chicago and London: University of Chicago Press, 1993), xi.

[54]*Map Is Not Territory,* 108.

Chapter 1

"Awake! Awake! Utter a Song!"

DEBORAH, WOMEN, AND WAR

> *Wondering how a good woman can murder*
> *I enter the tent of Holofernes,*
> *holding in one hand his long oiled hair*
> *and in the other, raised above*
> *his sleeping, wine-flushed face,*
> *his falchion with its unsheathed*
> *curved blade. . . .*

FROM THE POEM "JUDITH,"
BY VICKI FEAVER[1]

The apocryphal book of Judith presents its protagonist as everything a paragon of Israelite womanhood should be: beautiful, pious, unassuming, and wise. But the book also depicts Judith as someone who defies Israel's ideals of femininity as she goes forth from her village of Bethulia to assassinate Holofernes, the Assyrian general who is oppressing the town. In her 1994 poem "Judith," Vicki Feaver addresses this unexpected dissonance, asking already in the poem's first line "how a good woman can murder." As the verse unfolds, Feaver answers through a psychological meditation on Judith's past, imagining how Judith remembers the greatest wrongs that fate has dealt her, the untimely death of her husband from heatstroke and the utter emptiness, "like the emptiness of a temple with the doors kicked in," that consumed her in the years that followed. Judith's murder of Holofernes becomes her revenge for these and others of life's arbitrary acts, so that by the poem's last lines, Judith finds her supposed dilemma is really no quandary at all. Beheading Holofernes is "easy," Feaver writes, "like slicing through fish."

In this chapter, the question that guides me is much the same as the one that opens Feaver's poem, the question of how a good woman like Judith—or Deborah, the Judges woman who is my focus in this essay—can so defy Israelite paradigms of gender-appropriate behavior that she can be presented as assuming a leadership role in Israel's military affairs. Yet though I, like Feaver, sense that there is a dissonance between the decorum Israelite society normally expected of its women and the Bible's portrayals of Judith, of Deborah, and of other Israelite women who triumph in battlefield endeavors, I do not feel that I, as a biblical scholar, can claim the same luxury allowed the poet and explain these warring women's behavioral discord by conjuring up details from their psychological pasts. The biblical scholar, I maintain, is instead compelled to consider only the "hows" and "whys" actually presented in the Bible's text, and, as I have already indicated in the Introduction, I believe that because the Bible is primarily a religious document, the essential "hows" and "whys" that must be considered are those that stem from ancient Israel's religious practices and beliefs. What I seek through my analysis of the biblical materials, therefore, is a description of those aspects of ancient Israelite religion that allowed the Bible's authors to overturn their culture's stereotypes concerning appropriate gender activities in order to present militaristic portraits of Judith, of Deborah, and of the tradition's kindred women.

This list, moreover—of Judith, Deborah, and the tradition's kindred women—is important, for as I have also described in the Introduction, it is my belief that, unlike Feaver, who can consider the story of Judith in isolation, I have an obligation to examine the stories of Judith, Deborah, and these stories' related narratives in conjunction with one another; this because of my assumption that the narrative traditions that show women acting as military heroes during times of war exist within the context of an ideological continuum. I have further intimated in the Introduction, and will argue at greater length below, my contention that the motif of warring women found in the literature of Israel's ancient Near Eastern and eastern Mediterranean neighbors should be examined alongside the biblical texts. Indeed, I will suggest in the fourth and last section of this chapter that it is the influence of Canaanite myths concerning the warrior goddess Anat that has led Israelite tradition to promulgate and sustain a corpus of narratives in which women are portrayed as heroes in battlefield affairs.

The Introduction has finally summarized my conviction that this inquiry should proceed in the order I have just indicated, meaning that even though I will eventually argue for the interrelatedness of the Canaanite and several Israelite stories, I consider it essential that I first analyze each tale individually. I will begin in Section I by discussing the story of Deborah, the most prominent of the female military heroes depicted in the book of Judges. Next, I will turn to consider her two Judges compatriots, Jael and, in Section II, the woman of Thebez. Also in Section II, I will describe the Apocrypha's story of the wartime acts of Judith. Then, after examining Canaan's woman warrior mythology in Section III, I will put forward in Section IV an explanation that accounts for the commonalities I find in all these stories yet also elucidates factors I believe are distinctive to each. By the end of this chapter, this explanation will allow me to suggest that the biblical traditions associating women with war are so pervasive and, simultaneously, so multivalent that militaristic female imagery can appear even in texts that seemingly have nothing to do with women's heroics in times of battle. I will discuss in particular passages found in the love poetry of the Song of Songs and prophecies from the second half of the book of Isaiah.

I. WOMEN AND WAR IN JUDGES 5

The story of Deborah is found in Judges 4 and 5. She is first introduced in Judg 4:4 as a prophet and a judge. Both titles indicate her role as someone who serves as an intermediary between the human world and the divine, bringing the word of God to the people of Israel. This task is certainly an important one within Israelite society, indeed, envisioned by the passage's authors as being so important that Deborah is even assigned a special location from which to carry out her work, a tree known as the palm of Deborah, located in the hill country of Ephraim between Ramah and Bethel. As Judg 4:5 tells us, Deborah used to sit under this tree while the Israelites came to her to seek her judgment and advice.

Judges 4 next turns to consider one particular piece of advice Deborah delivers, the instructions she gives to a man named Barak. It is God's mandate, Deborah declares in verses 6–7, that Barak assemble Israel's militia and go forth to wage war against the forces of the Canaanites.

They are under the command of Sisera, the leader of the army of King Jabin, who reigns in the city of Hazor (v 2). According to verse 8, Barak expresses reluctance about answering this call to arms without Deborah's help. He insists that, as the representative of the divine, she accompany him to the site of the battle. Deborah agrees (v 9), although the only role Judg 4:14a ascribes to her at the time of the war is that she provides Barak with a final exhortation to go forth and fight. In 4:14b–16, the actual description of the battle, only Barak and his victory over Sisera are mentioned.

In fact, although the narrative continues for another eight verses (through v 24), Deborah never again appears in the Judges 4 text. Even more striking is Deborah's absence from two other biblical texts in which Barak is lauded. In 1 Sam 12:11, Barak's name, but not Deborah's, is found along with the names of Jerubbaal, Jephthah, and Samson—*her* fellow judges—in a list of Israel's premonarchical deliverers.[2] The author of Heb 11:32 lists the same premonarchical deliverers found in the Samuel text—Gideon (another name for Jerubbaal),[3] Barak, Samson, and Jephthah—and then adds, from the period of the monarchy, David, Samuel, and the prophets. The judge and prophet Deborah, though, is still missing.[4]

Given the description of Deborah's prophetic and judicial functions in Judg 4:4–7 and her role as Barak's main source of spiritual support in 4:8–14a, this tendency in 4:14b–24; 1 Sam 12:11; and Heb 11:32 to ignore her contribution to the war effort is surprising. It is even more surprising if we compare the depiction of Deborah found in Judges 5. Judges 5 is another version of the Judges 4 story and thus recounts once again the tale of the battle that took place between the Israelite militia and Sisera's Canaanite army. But, despite the fact that these texts share a common subject, the two renditions of this war story are ultimately very different.

Sometimes, the differences are perfunctory. For example, while Judges 4 tells the story of the battle in prose, the Judges 5 version is in verse. Commentators also agree that, although Judges 4 appears first in the biblical text as we have it today, the poetic traditions of Judges 5 predate the Judges 4 prose by several centuries. In fact, most scholars believe that Judges 5 is among the oldest of all texts found in the Hebrew Bible, and a date in the late twelfth or eleventh century B.C.E. is frequently advanced.[5] Judges 4 stems from the Deuteronomistic period of composition in the seventh century B.C.E.

More significant, however, are the different understandings found in Judges 4 and 5 regarding the roles played by the story's major characters. In particular, while Judges 4, as described above, relegates Deborah to an advisory role in the war against Sisera, Judges 5 is unambiguous and emphatic in its depiction of Deborah as Israel's chief military commander. Conversely, Barak, lauded in Judges 4; 1 Sam 12:11; and Heb 11:32 as *the* military hero of the Israelite-Canaanite battle, appears in Judges 5 only as Deborah's second-in-command.

Judges 5 signals Deborah's primacy over Barak in several ways. First, she is mentioned in the poem four times to Barak's three. More important, in the three times that Barak is mentioned, he never appears independent of Deborah but is always cited in association with her; on each of these three occasions, moreover, he somehow appears as secondary. For example, in 5:1, although both Deborah and Barak are described as singing the Israelites' postwar victory song, she seems to have been the major performer, as her name comes first in the verse and the verb *šwr,* "to sing," is rendered in the third-person *feminine* singular (*wattāšar*). Also in 5:12 and 5:15, Deborah's name occurs first and Barak's name is found only in the second lines of the couplets that make up these verses. Furthermore in 5:12, it is only Deborah who receives the command to sing out, which is the command to stand forth and sound the cry of reveille that will summon the Israelite troops into battle. Barak, I will argue below, is merely a recipient of this call. Even more telling is 5:7. Although, like much of Judges 5, this text is difficult to understand, what seems to be indicated is that the Canaanite oppression of the Israelites ceased when *Deborah* arose to lead the people. Barak is not even mentioned.[6]

It is, moreover, at least possible that the reference in Judg 5:7 to Deborah's "arising" to lead her people means to describe Deborah as actually rising up to lead Israel's troops into military combat. To be sure, the poem makes no explicit mention of Deborah carrying weapons of war or fighting. But the poem also makes no explicit mention of Barak doing these things, although both ancient Israelite tradition (Judges 4) and modern commentators assume that he did.[7] Could not this same assumption hold for Deborah? Note that the sole piece of Judges 5 evidence suggesting Barak's involvement in the battle—the notice in verse 15 that the tribe of Issachar rushed forth at his heels—is immediately preceded by a description of how the chiefs of Issachar were "with" Deborah.[8] Should we not envision Issachar's leaders as being "with" Deborah on the battlefield in the same way that we see the tribe as a whole rushing to fight behind Barak? The paired lines in the poem could indicate as much. In fact, they might even be said to insist on this point since, according to the norms of biblical poetry, paralleled lines should have paralleled meanings.

Nevertheless, whatever the role Judg 5:7 and 15 mean to assign Deborah in the actual combat against the Canaanites, and whatever the claims of Judges 4, 1 Samuel 12, and Hebrews 11 concerning Barak's status as the battle's real military hero, the overall conclusion regarding Judges 5 is clear: in the poetic version of Israel's fight against the Canaanites, it is Deborah's contribution to the war effort that is primary. She musters the troops and sends them forth into battle (v 12), earns the poem's acclaim as the people's deliverer (v 7), and leads in the performance of the postwar victory song (v 1). Titles such as general, commander, war leader, and even warrior come readily to mind.[9]

After introducing Deborah as its hero in verse 1, verse 2 of Judges 5 begins by describing the preparations of the Israelite army as it readies itself for battle against its Canaanite foes. Unfortunately, however, the obscure language that can characterize all poetry is particularly oblique in this verse. While hardly explicit, the second line is the most direct: it speaks of how the people "offered themselves willingly" (NRSV translation) or "volunteered" (*hitnaddēb*). Although the activity for which these Israelites volunteered is not specified, the implication is that it was for military service since the voluntary nature of Israel's tribal army and its basic character as a call-up militia are well attested in biblical literature. This interpretation is strengthened by comparing verse 9 of the poem, where a description of those who volunteered (*hitnaddēb*) appears again, this time referring to Israel's military commanders.[10]

The war for which this volunteer army assembles is sacred or holy in nature, as is indicated by the first line of verse 2, Hebrew *biprōaʿ pĕrāʿôt bĕyiśrāʾēl*. Scholars have recently suggested several possible translations, including: "the leaders took the lead in Israel";[11] "when they cast off restraint in Israel";[12] "when men wholly dedicated themselves in Israel";[13] "in the very beginning in Israel."[14] Yet the translation intimated in one ancient Greek version, adopted by many older English texts, and resurrected in 1991 in the NRSV still seems to me the best: "when locks were [or "are"] long in Israel."[15] The general allusion here concerns—

as did the description of "volunteering" in verse 2b—the Israelite army's preparations for battle. The specific reference is to certain ritual observances required of Israel's soldiers before they engage in holy war.[16]

Traditions detailing these ritual observances come particularly to the fore in Deut 20:1–20 and 23:9–14. These texts describe the essence of Israel's holy war ideology: that God fights alongside the Israelite human army in battle and that Israelite soldiers must therefore avoid certain behaviors that might compromise a sanctified state. Deuteronomy 23:12–14 dictates, for example, that the Israelites must urinate and defecate outside their military encampments. While we might expect that this is for reasons of sanitation, the biblical text in fact does not raise this issue at all; it stresses instead the need to preserve the camp's holiness. Sexual activity is also considered religiously unclean. In 2 Sam 11:6–13, this is why Uriah the Hittite, summoned home by King David from the front, refuses to sleep with his wife Bathsheba even though David gets Uriah drunk in an effort to encourage him to do so. Deuteronomy 23:10–11 further describes how rules about sexual purity were so strict in times of holy war that a man who had an involuntary ejaculation in the night had to be exiled from a military encampment until he could be ritually cleansed.

Another behavior that could apparently compromise an Israelite's state of wartime sanctity was for him to cut his hair. Particularly illustrative here are traditions concerning the Nazirites. These Nazirites were individuals specially consecrated to the deity, and to mark themselves as such they had to fulfill three main conditions. They were forbidden to come into contact with a corpse, even one belonging to a close relative. They were prohibited from drinking wine and other intoxicating beverages. Finally, they were required to keep their hair uncut (Num 6:1–7). The story of the most famous of the biblical Nazirites, Samson, climaxes with Samson's unwitting failure to keep this vow concerning uncut hair (Judges 13–16). The result of his failure was catastrophic: it meant the loss of his special and sanctified relationship with God and his subsequent defeat at the hands of the Philistines. The army described in Judg 5:2 seeks to avoid a similar fate at the hands of the Canaanites. They therefore allow their hair to grow long in order to facilitate a state of special sanctity.

Only when Israel's soldiers have entered into this state of special sanctity required in times of holy war can the name of Yahweh, the God of

Israel, be invoked. The invocation is found in the third and last line of verse 2. The verse reads in its entirety:

> *When locks were long in Israel,*
> *When the people volunteered,*
> *Bless Yahweh!*

In verse 3, the invocation of Yahweh continues, as Deborah speaks in the first person:

> *Hear, O kings! Give ear, O rulers!*
> *I to Yahweh, I will sing,*
> *I will sing out to Yahweh, the God of Israel.*

Commentators generally assume that the song Deborah proposes to sing here is some version of the poem as we have it in Judges 5, meaning that the reference is to the hymn that was sung "after the fact," so to speak, recounting the victory the Israelites had secured against the Canaanites and describing the means by which that battle had been won. Such an interpretation is certainly possible, especially since it is consistent with other Israelite traditions that describe women as the singers of Israel's victory songs.[17] But it is not without its problems. In particular, one would not typically expect an announcement concerning the singing of a victory hymn to be found in verse 3, in what appears to be the midst of the Judges 5 narrative flow.[18] Rather, the announcement should more properly come at the beginning of the poem's description of the battle, and as I have already noted, such an announcement is in fact found in the poem's first verse. To interpret verse 3 as referring also to a postwar victory song is thus to brand the text as redundant and impugn it as disruptive.

   An alternative explanation of the "song" of verse 3 seems therefore to be required. One possibility is to build upon a discussion of Judg 5:12 put forward by Baruch Halpern, who has suggested that the command to Barak to "Arise" in 5:12b should be understood as the song Deborah is ordered to sing in 5:12a.[19] Or, to put the matter another way: in verse 12a Deborah is told to sing a song of reveille that in verse 12b calls forth Barak and summons him to participate in the Israelite–Canaanite battle. I propose to understand the description of Deborah's song to Yahweh in verse 3 similarly, interpreting her words in that verse also as a reveille.

This one summons Yahweh, the divine warrior, to go forth into battle against Sisera.

If this interpretation holds, then the second stanza of the poem, verses 4–5, represents Yahweh's response to this call to arms. The text, which depicts Yahweh as a mighty warrior roused for battle, reads:

> *Yahweh, when you went forth from Seir,*
> *When you marched out from the steppe of Edom,*
> *The earth trembled, yea the heavens shook.*[20]
> *The clouds shook water,*
> *The mountains quaked,*[21]
> *Before Yahweh, the one of Sinai,*
> *Before Yahweh, the God of Israel.*

Regardless, though, of whether verses 4–5 describe Yahweh's response to reveille, it is beyond question that what is presented in this stanza is a vivid depiction of the way in which Israel's holy war ideology envisioned Yahweh as the divine warrior. Israel's warrior god comes from the southern desert, from the territory of Edom, also known as Seir. Edom/Seir is south and east of the Dead Sea and lies on the main highway leading from Israel to the Sinai Peninsula. According to biblical tradition, this is the very place of the mountain of God. Judges 5:4–5 thus describe the march of Yahweh as Yahweh leaves God's mountain abode to go north and enter into the Israelite battle against the Canaanites. This march to battle is truly a cosmic event: the ground trembles as Yahweh sets out; the clouds unleash a mighty storm; an earthquake shakes the mountains. Such is the might of Yahweh, the divine warrior, as this God prepares for battle.

In the face of such awe-inspiring imagery, the third stanza of the poem, verses 6–7, might seem incongruously mundane. There are several problems here concerning the specifics of translation,[22] but commentators generally agree that what is described in these verses is the effect that the tumult associated with times of war can have on day-to-day activities like commerce and travel:

> *In the days of Shamgar ben Anat,*
> *In the days of Jael, caravans*[23] *ceased,*
> *Travelers*[24] *took to the twisted by-ways.*
> *Settlements in unwalled hamlets*[25] *ceased,*

> In Israel they ceased,[26]
> Until you arose,[27] O Deborah,
> Till you arose,[28] a mother in Israel.

Yet, although these verses lack the grandeur of the preceding lines, I believe that they are anything but incongruous when compared to Stanza 2. I propose instead to read Stanza 2 and Stanza 3 as purposely paired, as two sides of what one might call a poetic diptych. These two parts of the poem, that is, while thematically distinct, are meant to be read as a single unit, with each piece of the diptych balancing and serving to complement the image suggested by the other. As Stanza 2 sets the scene for Israel's holy war as a cosmic activity, Stanza 3 is meant to show the counterpart of the cosmic, the earthly context of the battle.

Judges 5 masterfully uses syntax to convey this complementarity, juxtaposing in Stanzas 2 and 3 grammatically paired descriptions of the diptych's cosmic and earthly parts. Stanza 2, for example, begins its description of the cosmic aspect of the holy war with two temporal cola (v 4a):

> Yahweh, <u>when you went forth</u> (běṣēʾtěkā) *from Seir,*
> <u>When you marched out</u> (běṣaʿděkā) *from the steppe of Edom.*

Stanza 3 likewise begins its description of the more earthly aspects of the holy war with two temporal cola (v 6a):

> <u>In the days</u> (bîmê) *of Shamgar ben Anat,*
> <u>In the days</u> (bîmê) *of Jael, caravans ceased.*

At first glance, this double construction might seem redundant: why should the poem need two separate verses to describe the setting of the holy war in time? And why does the poem use the same particle, *bě,* "when, in," to introduce the temporal setting in both stanzas (*běṣēʾtěkā* and *běṣaʿděkā* in Stanza 2; *bîmê* [twice] in Stanza 3)? Such a pedestrian repetition could seem evidence of a stylistic gaffe. But if one appreciates the poetic strategy of diptych at work, then the purpose of the juxtaposed constructions and the duplicated *bě* becomes obvious. The point is to communicate through paralleled temporal cola and through repetition the notion that there are two levels—the cosmic and the earthly—on which the war against Sisera is to be fought. As verse 4a establishes a setting for the war in cosmic time, verse 6a describes the earthly equivalent.

Interpreting Stanza 2 and Stanza 3 as a poetic diptych also explains why Stanza 2 uses much the same language to celebrate the march forth of the divine warrior Yahweh in verses 4b–5 that Stanza 3 uses to celebrate the emergence of Yahweh's human counterpart in the holy war, the earthly war leader Deborah, in verse 7. Indeed, the point of verses 4b–5 and 7 is to suggest that, in addition to there being two spatial spheres in which the war against Sisera is to be fought, there are also two kinds of actors who will be involved: the divine commander Yahweh and the human commander Deborah. The poem's structure again points to the intentionality of this parallelism. Stanza 2 concludes (vv 4b–5):

> *The clouds shook water,*
> *The mountains quaked,*
> *Before Yahweh, the one of Sinai,*
> *Before Yahweh, the God of Israel.*

Compare the last lines of Stanza 3 (v 7):

> *Settlements in unwalled hamlets ceased,*
> *In Israel they ceased,*
> *Until you arose, O Deborah,*
> *Till you arose, a mother in Israel.*

Several points of comparison suggest themselves here. The repetition of the phrase "(un)til you arose" (*šaqqamtî*) in lines 3 and 4 of verse 7 is reminiscent of the repetition of "before Yahweh" (*mippěnê yhwh*) in lines 3 and 4 of verses 4b–5. Both passages evoke a personal name in their third lines: Yahweh in verse 5; Deborah in verse 7. Both passages end with the same word, Israel, in line 4. And particularly significant is the way in which this word "Israel" is used in the paralleled titles of Yahweh and Deborah: Yahweh is "the God of Israel" in verse 5, and Deborah is "a mother in Israel" in verse 7. This phrasing, along with the entire poetic structure of verses 4b–5 and 7, is designed to make us read these two figures as paired. Yet the dichotomy of cosmos/earth is still maintained, for although Yahweh is the God *of* Israel and so transcends the earthly sphere, Deborah is a mother *in* Israel, someone firmly rooted within the human world.[29] Yahweh is thus the divine warrior who will metaphorically lead the Israelite army into battle, while Deborah is God's human representative who will actually take the lead in conducting the war on earth.[30]

In addition to locating dichotomies of cosmic/earthly and divine/human in Stanzas 2 and 3, I also posit there a dichotomy of male and female. The male member of the dichotomy is Yahweh; this despite the fact that many theologians today prefer to use nongendered language and nongendered imagery in referring to the Bible's deity. In ancient Israel, however, Yahweh was typically understood as male. This is certainly the case in Judges 5, where, for example, all the verb forms used in the divine warrior hymn of verses 4–5 are masculine. However, Yahweh's human counterpart in the war against Sisera is a woman, Deborah. Deborah is even lauded in verse 7 with a very female-specific epithet: she is called "a mother in Israel."

At first glance, the phrase "a mother in Israel" is a curious title to apply to Deborah. There is no mention in Judges 5 of Deborah having any children, nor is she even described as being married (although some commentators have mistakenly paired her with Barak).[31] Also in Judges 4, Deborah's marital status is ambiguous. She is described in 4:4 as *'ēšet lappîdôt,* usually translated as "the wife of Lappidoth," but also plausibly rendered "a fiery woman." And even if "the wife of Lappidoth" is the correct translation, meaning that Judges 4 does understand Deborah as being married, it is striking that the Judges 4 text makes no mention of Deborah as having any children. This silence is telling, for as Halpern has conclusively shown, Judges 4, in addition to being written later than Judges 5, is literarily dependent on the poem.[32] This means that the prose tradition must have been aware of the poem's "mother in Israel" epithet. Yet, despite this and despite the even more significant fact that everywhere else, the prose redactor requires an absolutely literal rendition of the poetry's metaphorical language,[33] Judges 4 does not insist on interpreting "a mother in Israel" according to its "plain meaning" or its biological sense. Why here—and only here—does the prose suspend literalism's standards? The most plausible explanation is that the prose redactor knows of some other, less literalistic definition of "a mother in Israel" that it is his intention—and also, by implication, the intention of Judges 5—to evoke.

As to what this less literalistic meaning might be, evidence is scant,

for the phrase "a mother in Israel" is used in only one other place in the
Hebrew Bible, in 2 Sam 20:19. Like that of Judges 5, the context of this
passage is military. Earlier in 2 Samuel 15–18, King David had faced an
attempt by his son Absalom to usurp the throne. Now in 2 Samuel 20,
David faces a second rebellion, this one led by Sheba, son of Bichri,
a member of the tribe of Benjamin. In the case of Absalom's revolt,
David had delayed in responding, but the king realizes in retrospect that
this had been a mistake. He thus reacts to Sheba's treachery with alacrity,
dispatching first the commander Amasa and then his chief general Joab
to pursue Sheba. Sheba takes refuge in the city of Abel-Beth-Ma'acah
in the far north of Israel. Joab's forces begin to besiege the city, but the
siege is halted when a wise woman appears and challenges Joab's inten-
tions. She asks how he can seek to destroy her city, which she describes
as part of the heritage of Yahweh and as "a mother in Israel" (v 19). She
arranges instead for Sheba to be executed and his head thrown out over
the city wall to Joab. The destruction of Abel-Beth-Ma'acah is thus
averted.

In discussing this incident, and especially the phrase "a city that is a
mother in Israel," the standard commentaries tend to define the idiom only in terms of its geopolitical significance: "*a city that is a mother
in Israel* means one that has dependent villages called 'daughters' (compare *villages,* literally 'daughters,' in Num 21.25, 32; Josh 15.45; Judg
11.26)."[34] But Claudia V. Camp, while not denying the validity of this
traditional interpretation, has argued that a geopolitical meaning is not
all that the phrase "a mother in Israel" implies. Rather, Camp urges that
"a mother in Israel" in 2 Samuel 20 be examined within the context of
the wise woman's entire speech. She suggests that once this is done, it
becomes clear that "a mother in Israel" has important connotations that
extend beyond a simple reference to a mother city and daughter towns.[35]

Camp's argument begins by noting what she sees as a distinctive
structure in verse 19, where the woman says to Joab, "You are seeking
to destroy a city that is a mother in Israel (*'ēm bĕyiśrā'ēl*)," and then asks,
"Why would you swallow up the heritage of Yahweh (*naḥălat yhwh*)?"
Camp interprets these two statements almost as if they were a poetic
couplet, arguing that *'ēm bĕyiśrā'ēl,* "a mother in Israel," and *naḥălat yhwh,*
"the heritage of Yahweh," are parallel terms.[36] For support, she compares
2 Samuel 14, the story of the wise woman of Tekoa. In verse 16 of that
text, the woman, a mother (*'ēm*) pleading with King David for the life
of her son, also evokes the image of God's "heritage" (*naḥălat 'ĕlōhîm*).[37]

Camp comments, "Both of the women are particularly concerned with the possible destruction of the 'heritage of Yahweh (or God)' . . . an entity somewhat differently conceived in each case but, in both cases, associated by a parable or metaphor (i.e., symbolically) with a 'mother.'"[38] Hence this conclusion:

> When the "heritage of Yahweh" is placed in parallelism with "a mother in Israel," we might expect the latter term to carry a metaphorical surplus of meaning beyond the obvious "biological" association of city and surrounding towns.[39]

Next, to determine what is comprised by this metaphorical surplus of meaning, Camp looks to the opening lines of the wise woman's speech (20:18). There, the woman tells us the one other thing we know about Abel-Beth-Ma'acah: that, according to proverbial wisdom, the city had a reputation of being skilled in the mediation of disputes. "They used to say of old," according to the woman, "'let them inquire in Abel,' and thus they would bring about resolution."[40] To label Abel as "a mother in Israel," Camp infers, is to claim it as a city that protects "the heritage of Yahweh" through what Camp describes as "good and effective counsel."[41]

Camp concludes her discussion of "a mother in Israel" at this point, but it seems to me that implicit in her analysis is one further step. If the city Abel-Beth-Ma'acah embodies what it means to be "a mother in Israel" by using skills in persuasive counseling to protect "the heritage of Yahweh," then could one not argue—as was in fact assumed by the ancient midrashic tradition—that the wise woman who speaks for the city also deserves the "mother in Israel" designation?[42] Does not she, too, use effective counsel to protect her city, which she describes as part of "the heritage of Yahweh," from destruction?

Certainly there can be no doubt about the wise woman's counseling skills, as 2 Samuel 20 emphatically portrays her as being as gifted a counselor as the city for which she speaks. Twice in the text the woman is called wise: first, when she appears to speak to Joab (*iššâ ḥăkāmâ;* v 16); second, when she approaches the people "in her wisdom" (*běhokmātāh*) to inform them of her plan to decapitate Sheba and throw his head over the city's walls (v 22). Presumably, she has to persuade the people of Abel to agree with this proposed course of action, but a description of this is lacking in the text, which jumps quickly from the woman's presentation of her plan to the execution of it. The narrative thereby suggests that the woman's counsel was so convincing that the people of Abel voiced no dissent. Her counsel was also effective enough earlier in the story immediately to deter potential opposition, as her short (two-verse) speech to Joab about Abel-Beth-Ma'acah's heritage and its mother role (vv 18–19) caused him to reconsider his siege of the city and require only that Sheba be given to him as captive (vv 20–21). The conclusion that follows is clear: if Camp is right in arguing that what makes the city Abel-Beth-Ma'acah "a mother in Israel" is its ability to use "good and effective counsel" to protect "the heritage of Yahweh," then the wise woman of Abel should likewise be "a mother in Israel," one who uses her skills in persuasive counseling to protect her city from destruction at the hands of Joab.

This understanding in turn suggests a further step of analysis, namely, that we look at additional aspects of the wise woman's character to see if she embodies other attributes integral to her "mother in Israel" role. Here, another part of Camp's work is crucial, for by comparing Abel's wise woman to others in the Bible who speak with their attackers during a military engagement, Camp has shown that the woman of 2 Samuel 20 is not only depicted as a skilled counselor but also as a military commander. To demonstrate, Camp notes three texts: first, 2 Sam 2:18–23, in which Saul's general Abner speaks to Asahel, Joab's brother, as Asahel pursues him; second, 2 Sam 2:24–28, where Abner speaks again to an opponent, this time to Joab after Asahel has been killed; and, finally, 2 Kgs 18:17–36, in which the Rabshakeh, head of Sennacherib's Assyrian army, speaks to King Hezekiah's representatives in Jerusalem. As Camp points out, the speech-maker in each of these episodes is the head of his military faction. Thus, too, should the wise woman of Abel who speaks to Abel's attackers be considered the head of her military faction, the people of Abel-Beth-Ma'acah. The woman's status as military leader is, in addition, indicated by the fact that her counterpart in the conversation at Abel is Joab. One might indeed ask why David's chief general agrees to speak with an otherwise unknown woman. The answer is that the two are equals: they speak as one military commander to another.[43]

Yet, in addition to emerging in 2 Samuel 20 as a military leader, the woman of Abel-Beth-Ma'acah simultaneously characterizes herself as "one of those who are peaceable and faithful (*šĕlūmê 'ĕmûnê*) in Israel" (v 19).[44] While these two portraits—military commander and paragon of peaceableness—initially may appear contradictory, an examination of the Hebrew terms used in 20:19, passive participles derived from the roots *šlm* and *'mn,* suggests that they are not. Particularly significant is *šlm,* for although the noun *šālôm* (English shalom) and its related verbal forms are commonly translated as "peace" and "to be at peace," respectively, the Hebrew in fact conveys a far richer meaning. The word *šālôm* describes a state of cosmic harmony, reflecting the wholeness and complete unity that exists when all of Israel lives in a perfect covenant relationship with its God.[45] While the connotations conveyed by the English word "peace" can certainly correspond to this Israelite vision of harmony, perfect *šālôm* may also require that Yahweh's people fight against the kinds of disorder and chaos that threaten cosmic concord. Similarly, what the Bible means by *'ĕmûnâ,* "faithfulness," and its related verbal forms is perfect dedication to the Israelite covenant ideal.[46] In Israelite thinking, such dedication again can require that the covenant community fight to uphold what the tradition regards as Israel's covenantal standards. To the modern sensibility, the decisions of the wise woman of Abel—to stand forth in a military confrontation with Joab and to execute Sheba in order to protect her city—may seem antithetical to the concepts of peaceableness and faithfulness. Her actions, however, are in perfect keeping with the Bible's understanding of *šlm* and *'mn.*

In the end, then, 2 Samuel 20 reveals three basic characteristics embodied by the wise woman of Abel-Beth-Ma'acah and, by implication, by anyone who is "a mother in Israel." First, as argued by Camp, "a mother in Israel" must be a good and effective counselor and must use her skills in counseling to protect the heritage of Yahweh. Extending such protection on occasion can involve the use of military force, and hence "a mother in Israel" must be willing to step forth as a commander who leads those under her protection in military encounters. Such military endeavors, however, must always be informed by a commitment to Israel's covenantal unity and wholeness (what 2 Samuel 20 describes as peaceableness and faithfulness).

This richness of meaning seems to me precisely what Judges 5 has in mind when it describes Deborah as "a mother in Israel." Certainly the poem's depiction of Deborah's mustering of an Israelite tribal army to fight the Canaanite forces of Sisera indicates both a passionate commitment to the heritage of Yahweh and a willingness to use military leadership to protect that inheritance.[47] Deborah's attributes of "good and effective counsel" are less obviously indicated in the text, but verses 14–18, which detail the musings of each tribe about whether to respond to the call to battle, suggest the need for a leader like Deborah to possess skills in persuasive counseling that can be brought to bear when influencing recalcitrant tribes.[48] Even more significant in this regard is the fact that later Israelite tradition remembers Deborah *foremost* as having gifts in counseling and mediation, as her prosaic biographer in Judges 4 describes her *primarily* as the one who rendered judgments for the Israelites who sought her under her palm in Ephraim (4:4–5); this observation attains even greater importance if we recall Halpern's thesis that the prose redaction in Judges 4 was literarily dependent on Judges 5 and thus should have derived its sense of Deborah's counseling role from the poem.[49] As for Deborah's traits of peaceableness and faithfulness, or as I have preferred to interpret, her commitment to a covenantal unity and wholeness in Israel, I can do no better than Camp, who writes:

> Abel is characterized . . . as a city with a long reputation for wisdom and faithfulness to the tradition of Israel. It is, therefore, a mother in the same way Deborah was . . . a symbol of the unity that bound Israel together under one God Yahweh.[50]

This enhanced appreciation of what it means to call Deborah "a mother in Israel" also agrees well with the overall interpretation of diptych that I have posited in verses 4–5 and 6–7 of Judges 5. Recall there that paired with the epithet lauding Deborah as "a mother in Israel" was the phrase describing Yahweh as "the God of Israel." My discussion of the term "mother in Israel" shows how appropriate this pairing is. Deborah as "a mother in Israel" stands forth as a woman passionately committed to Israel's well-being. As such, she is the perfect human counterpart of Yahweh, who as "the God of Israel" likewise displays a passionate commitment to the Israelite community. Moreover, Yahweh was primarily worshiped in Israel—especially during the premonarchical period from which Judges 5 dates—as the God who delivered the Israelites from the oppressions of Egypt and redeemed the people from the experience of slavery. Deborah's intent in Judges 5 is much the same: she endeavors to liberate her people from Canaanite domination. She and Yahweh are thus the worthiest of partners. In fact, the poem's descriptions of Yahweh as "the God of Israel" and of Deborah as "a mother in Israel," although brief, are so evocative that they reveal in shorthand all the dichotomies I have located in Stanzas 2 and 3. Yahweh represents the cosmic, the divine, and the male in the role of war leader who extends protection to the community of Israel; Deborah represents the earthly, the human, and the female as she steps forth as military commander to ensure the security of Yahweh's people.

These dichotomies of cosmic/earthly, divine/human, and male/female continue to be emphasized in the stanzas of Judges 5 in which the actual Israelite-Canaanite battle is described. As I have already mentioned, the preparations for war outlined in the early verses of the poem climax with the final call to arms in verse 12:[51]

> *Awake! Awake, O Deborah!*
> *Awake! Awake! Utter a song!*
> *Arise Barak!*
> *Capture your captives, O son of Abinoam!*

Particularly significant here is the fourfold cry to Deborah to "awake" (Hebrew *'ûrî*). Elsewhere in the Bible, the cry to "awake" frequently goes out from the Israelite people to Yahweh, and in each of these cases, the cry is found in a military context, as the Israelites beseech Yahweh to march forth and do battle against some enemy force.[52] For example, Ps 7:7 (in the Bible's English versions, 7:6) reads:

> *Arise, O Yahweh, in your anger;*
> *Lift yourself up against the fury of my enemies!*
> *Awake ('ûrâ), O my God;*[53]
> *Assign a judgment!*

Military imagery is even more pronounced in Isa 51:9–10. These verses address themselves to the "arm of Yahweh," asking it to gird itself and go out to war:

> *Awake ('ûrî)! Awake! Gird on strength, O arm of Yahweh!*
> *Awake as in the days of old, the generations of long ago!*

Similar pleas to Yahweh to "awake" are addressed to the divine warrior in Pss 44:24 (English 44:23) and 59:5–6 (English 59:4–5). But in Judges 5, it is Deborah who is called on to "awake." In the light of the Psalms and Isaiah comparisons, this might be considered an anomaly. I prefer instead to interpret Judg 5:12 as further evidence of the poetic strategy of diptych at work. The call to "awake" can come to Deborah rather than to Yahweh because Yahweh and Deborah are paired as divine and human equivalents.

In the next verse of Judges 5, verse 13, the battle begins. The Israelite troops are described first:

> Then the remnant[54] came down against[55] the nobles,
> The people of Yahweh came down for him[56] against the warriors.

In verses 14–18, this description of the march of the Israelite troops continues, as each tribe and its contribution to the war effort are listed. There are certain problems in the translation of these verses, as it is not necessarily clear that all of the ten tribes mentioned actually went forth to engage Sisera in battle.[57] However, a comparison with other biblical poems that catalogue the tribes of Israel (Genesis 49; Deuteronomy 33), as well as a sensitivity to the kinds of archaic language used in Judges 5,[58] suggests that the poem's intent is to celebrate the participation of each tribe in the amassing of the Israelite militia.[59]

In verse 19, the poem turns to describe the Canaanite force that stood in opposition to this Israelite army:

> The kings came, they fought,
> Then fought the kings of Canaan.

Yet for obvious reasons, the constitution of the Canaanite force is of much less interest to the Israelite poetic tradition than was the makeup of Israel's militia, and so Judges 5 quickly moves in verse 19b to describe the battle itself and the Israelite victory:

> At Taʿanach by the waters of Megiddo,
> They [i.e., the kings of Canaan] took no spoils of silver.

The Israelite triumph is further depicted in verses 20–21:

> From heaven fought the stars,
> From their courses they fought against Sisera.
> The Wadi Kishon swept them away,
> The wadi attacked them,[60] the Wadi Kishon.

Commentators have puzzled over these verses and especially over the reference to the torrential flood of the Wadi Kishon. The problem here is that the Kishon does not in fact flood like typical Near Eastern wadis, whose normally dry streambeds can be transformed into rampaging torrents when filled with the runoff from a heavy rain. Rather, when the Kishon is in flood, its waters just overflow its banks to spread out across the Megiddo plain and turn it into a muddy swamp. For this reason, some have envisioned a scenario in verses 20–21 whereby the wheels of the Canaanite chariotry become clogged in a morass of silt, allowing the Israelite troops, who are on foot, to descend from their positions in the foothills and defeat their entrapped foes.[61] But this explanation, while consistent with the region's topographical reality, hardly conforms to the plain meaning of the text, which insists that the Wadi Kishon attacked (qdm) the Canaanite troops and swept (grp) them away. How to explain this discrepancy? Surely the poetic tradition was not just ignorant of the Kishon's normal behavior. Rather, it is crucial to realize here the Israelite belief that it is Yahweh, and only Yahweh, who has the ability to redirect natural phenomena, causing the Jordan to part (Josh 3:14–17), the sun to stand still (Josh 10:12–14), and the desert to bloom (Isa 35:1). This suggests that however improbable, the geographical imagery of verses 20–21 is intentionally unsound for it is meant to demonstrate a profound theological point: that in Judges 5, the very forces of nature are commanded by Yahweh to deviate from their usual behavior in order to wage war on Yahweh's and Israel's behalf.[62] The waters that sweep through the bed of the Wadi Kishon, along with the stars that fight from their courses in the heavens, thus become part of the cosmic army Yahweh leads into battle against Sisera. The dichotomies introduced in verses 4–5 and 6–7 again manifest themselves, as Yahweh's divine soldiers from the heavens (vv 20–21) fight together with Deborah's human recruits on earth (vv 14–18) to ensure the defeat of Sisera's Canaanite army (v 19).

Still, the defeat of Sisera's army is not the end of the battle, for Sisera himself escapes. He flees to the tent of a woman named Jael to seek refuge. Jael initially seems to respond with magnanimity (vv 24–25):

Most blessed of women be Jael,
A woman of the Kenite community,[63]
Of tent-dwelling women most blessed.
He asked for water, she gave him milk,
She brought him ghee in a lordly bowl.

But then (vv 26–27):

> *She reached out*[64] *her hand to the tent peg,*
> *Her right hand to the laborers' hammer.*
> *She hammered Sisera, she smashed his head,*
> *She struck and pierced his temple through.*[65]
> *Between her feet, he sunk, he fell, he lay,*
> *Between her feet he sunk, he fell,*
> *Where he sunk,*
> *He fell there, dead.*

Thus the battle that one woman, Deborah, has begun, another woman, Jael, has finished. Here, then, is one final resonance of the structuring diptych of Judges 5, as the female and human assassin Jael brings to a close the holy war initiated by the male divine warrior Yahweh.[66]

II. THE WOMAN OF THEBEZ AND JUDITH

Because Israel is generally portrayed in the book of Judges as a highly androcentric culture, it seems surprising to find these two remarkable portraits of Deborah and Jael as military heroes in Judges 5. Still more surprising is the fact that these portraits are not isolated occurrences in Judges. Rather, in Judges' prose narratives, there is another story of a woman who, like Jael, smashes an enemy's head and thus brings to an end a period of war. This is the woman of Thebez, who acts against a man named Abimelech, the final scion of the house of Gideon.

The Gideon story is found in Judges 6–8 and begins by describing how the judge Gideon arose to lead the Israelites in a battle against the Midianites. Then, after an Israelite victory had been secured and as this tale comes to its end, the people approach Gideon with a request: "Rule over us, you and your son and your grandson also; for you have delivered us out of the hand of Midian" (8:22). What the people are asking is that Gideon serve them as king and that he establish his family as a royal dynasty. Gideon responds by invoking the traditional belief of Israel's premonarchical period, which maintains that Yahweh is Israel's only true king. "I will not rule over you," he says, "and my son will not rule over you. Yahweh will rule over you" (8:23).

Abimelech, however, does not share his father's theological point of view. In Judges 9, after Gideon dies, Abimelech goes to his mother's kin in Shechem and persuades them to anoint him as king.[67] Once they agree, Abimelech proceeds, in good royal fashion, to eliminate all potential rivals by killing off his seventy half-brothers. The precise manner of their death is not specified in the text, but Judg 9:5 does tell us that they were all killed (beheaded?) "upon a single stone" ('al 'eben 'eḥāt). The biblical authors rightly perceive this fratricide as contrary to the laws of God, and they therefore describe Yahweh as sending an evil spirit that comes between Abimelech and his followers, the lords of Shechem. The result is deceit, treachery, and, ultimately, civil war.

The final episode in this civil war takes place at Thebez, a small town to the north and east of Abimelech's main power base at Shechem.[68] Abimelech's initial assault on Thebez is reported to be successful, as, according to Judg 9:50, "he encamped against Thebez and he captured it." But as the narrative continues, all the people of Thebez—"all the men and the women and all the lords of the city"—fled to a tower in the midst of the town, shut themselves in, and climbed to the tower's roof (v 51). Abimelech begins to attack this tower. His plan is to use a strategy he had previously used in destroying a similar tower in Shechem: to stack piles of brushwood around the tower and then to set fire to it, immolating the people who have taken refuge inside. As he prepares to lay the fire at Thebez, however, a lone woman ('iššâ 'aḥat) throws down a millstone on top of Abimelech's head and crushes his skull.

Like the head-smasher Jael, this head-smashing woman should surely be remembered as "most blessed of women," a female who secures a victory in battle against one of Israel's most odious foes. Moreover, as pointed out by T. A. Boogaart, the way in which the woman of Thebez attacks Abimelech avenges perfectly Abimelech's original crime.[69] Abimelech had murdered his seventy half-brothers by killing them upon a stone; the woman ambushes Abimelech by dropping a stone upon his head. J. Gerald Janzen has augmented Boogaart's analysis by drawing attention to the way the Hebrew root 'ḥd, "one," is used in Judges 9 to emphasize the tale's ironies of retribution. At the beginning of the story, the seventy brothers are murdered upon a single ('eḥāt) stone; at its end, the agent who smashes Abimelech's head with a stone is a lone ('aḥat) woman. Janzen further notes that in 9:37, Abimelech is assigned the title "Headman" (rō'š 'eḥād) by the biblical tradition, yet he is defeated in 9:53 by having his head (rō'š) smashed with a stone.[70]

According to Judg 9:54, however, the victory that should have been assigned to the woman of Thebez is apparently to be denied to her. Once his skull was crushed, Abimelech

> . . . quickly called to the boy who bore his armor and said to him, "Draw your sword and kill me lest they say of me that a woman slew him." And his boy pierced him through, and he died.

But the biblical authors have one final irony to recount concerning this story. In 2 Sam 11:14–17, Joab, King David's general, leads the Israelite army in an attack on the Ammonite city of Rabbah. In doing so, Joab sends Israel's forces too near the wall of Rabbah, where many are killed by Ammonite archers. As it turns out, Joab has purposely sacrificed this wall-attacking contingent because it included Uriah the Hittite, whose wife, Bathsheba, was the object of David's amorous desires. Still, in 2 Sam 11:18–21, Joab imagines that before David learns that the attack has brought about Uriah's death, the king will be angry at his general for making a poor command decision. Joab even supposes that David might evoke the story of Abimelech at Thebez. "Who killed Abimelech son of Jerubbaal?"[71] Joab envisions the king as asking, "Did not a woman throw down upon him an upper millstone from the wall so that he died at Thebez? Why did you draw so near the wall?" (v 21). Joab's ruminations here demonstrate that, ironically, whatever Abimelech might have wished when he had his armor-bearer pierce him through, tradition *does* remember that Abimelech's death came at the hands of a woman. Still, Abimelech's female attacker remains nameless and, beyond Judges 9 and 2 Samuel 11, forgotten.[72]

In striking contrast to the nameless and forgotten woman of Thebez stands the woman whom I discussed briefly at the beginning of this chapter, Judith, who has an entire book of the Apocrypha named after her. This book purports to describe an attack mounted by Holofernes, the general of the Assyrian king Nebuchadnezzar, against the Israelite town of Bethulia in the late sixth century B.C.E. Nebuchadnezzar, however, was king of *Babylon* in the *early* sixth century B.C.E., and the town of Bethulia, although mentioned some twenty times in the text of Judith, is described nowhere else in the Hebrew Bible or in the Apocrypha. Such a collocation of misinformation suggests that the book of Judith belongs to the genre of folktale as opposed to that of historical narrative. Most scholars prefer a date of composition in the second century B.C.E.

The first half of this folktale (Judith 1–7) describes the military aggressions of the Assyrian army. The goal of the army's attack is ultimately Jerusalem and its temple, but in order to reach that city, Holofernes' troops have to march through a small pass guarded by the towns of Bethulia and Bethomesthaim (another location that is otherwise unknown). Holofernes besieges Bethulia by cutting off the town's water supply. After thirty-four days of this, the people are ready to surrender. As Judith 7 comes to an end, Uzziah, the chief of the town elders, persuades them to wait for five more days to see if God will miraculously intervene and deliver the town.

At this point in the story Judith appears. Judith 8 begins by describing attributes of this woman I have already noted: her beauty and above all her piety, which is particularly evidenced by the fact that she has worn sackcloth and fasted each day for the three years since her husband's untimely death. She is also presented as a compelling speaker, delivering to Uzziah and to all the elders of Bethulia an impassioned plea urging them not to capitulate to Holofernes. Uzziah responds by praising her wisdom (8:29) but claims that he is required by his promise to surrender the town. Judith then hints at—but does not describe—a plan she has to save Bethulia. She withdraws, with the elders' blessings, to put this plan into action.

Judith 9 describes how the widow prays to Yahweh, urging God to allow her to defeat the Assyrians. "By the deceit of my lips strike down the slave with the prince and the prince with his servant; crush their arrogance by the hand of a woman" (v 10; NRSV translation). Judith next retires into her living quarters to bathe, to anoint herself with precious oils, to comb out her hair and put on a tiara, and to dress herself in festive attire. She and her maid then leave Bethulia's gates and make their way to the Assyrian camp. There, her beauty astonishes the Assyrian guards on patrol and, after she is finally brought to him, Holofernes. Additionally, albeit ironically, Holofernes praises her for her wisdom because of the fiction she presents to him: that Yahweh is angry with the people of Bethulia and of Jerusalem because they have transgressed and that Yahweh intends to favor Holofernes and his army in battle in order to punish these sinners. Totally beguiled, Holofernes urges her to eat with him and clearly hopes that she will stay the night.

For the first three nights of her sojourn in the Assyrian camp, Judith refuses this offer and instead establishes a pattern of withdrawing to a spring outside the camp to bathe and to pray. On the fourth night, Judith accepts Holofernes' invitation to an intimate supper in his tent, but she turns Holofernes' intended seduction toward her own purposes by getting her host drunk. As soon as he lies passed out on his bed, she takes his sword from his bedpost and beheads him. She then leaves the camp as she had been wont to do each night, this time, though, going back to Bethulia to inform the people of her triumph. Judith 16 describes Judith's victory in this way (16:7–9; NRSV translation):[73]

> *For she put away her widow's clothing,*
> *To exalt the oppressed in Israel.*
> *She anointed her face with perfume,*
> *She fastened her hair with a tiara,*
> *And put on a linen gown to beguile him.*
> *Her sandal ravished his eyes,*
> *Her beauty captivated his mind,*
> *And the sword severed his neck!*

The book of Judith also describes how Judith plays a crucial role in planning the military actions undertaken by her people after they have been informed that Holofernes is dead. She instructs the Bethulian army to amass at dawn at the town's gates as if it were preparing to attack the Assyrian camp. The Assyrians, she predicts, will rush into Holofernes' tent to summon him, only to discover what the Bethulians know already: that he has been beheaded. In the ensuing panic, the Assyrians will flee, and the Israelites will be able to overtake and slaughter them. This scenario is presented in Jdt 14:1–10. In 14:11–15:7, Judith's proposal is followed, and everything she has forecast comes to pass. Judith is thus portrayed as the mastermind whose strategies lead to the defeats of both Holofernes and his Assyrian army. The titles of general, commander, war leader, and warrior earlier assigned to Deborah come once more to mind.

III. THE CANAANITE WARRIOR GODDESS ANAT

There is at least one other woman warrior mentioned—albeit quite obliquely—in the Hebrew Bible. This is the Canaanite warrior goddess Anat, whose name appears embedded in certain Israelite place names

(Anathoth, Beth-Anoth, and Beth-Anath) and also is found as a part of some of the Bible's personal names (Shamgar ben Anat, Anathoth, and Anthothiyah). The Bible, however, is otherwise silent about the goddess Anat. It is instead Canaanite mythological texts, especially those found by archaeologists at the Late Bronze Age site of Ugarit (c. 1550–1200 B.C.E.), that provide a picture of the goddess' main attributes. Anat is also well known from texts and iconographic representations from Egypt, where—especially during the period of the militaristic New Kingdom (c. 1575–1087 B.C.E.)—she seems to have been adopted by the Egyptians as their own and to have become a very popular goddess.

In Egypt, depictions of Anat show her holding a shield and spear.[74] She is also described as a shield to Pharaoh Ramses III in a text dating from the Twentieth Dynasty (twelfth century B.C.E.),[75] and a Nineteenth Dynasty poem (thirteenth century B.C.E.) likens her to a part of the king's war chariot.[76] An Egyptian mythological passage characterizes her as "a woman acting (as) a warrior, clad as a male and girt as a female."[77]

At Ugarit, Anat's warlike nature is similarly indicated. In one text, she is said to be an eater of flesh and a drinker of blood (*KTU* 1.96.3–5).[78] Elsewhere, she is described as wearing a necklace made of her enemies' skulls and a girdle made of their hands (*KTU* 1.3.2.11–13). As that particular passage continues, the delight Anat takes in her militaristic adventures is so great that after she returns home victorious from an actual fight, the goddess magically transforms her furniture into soldiers so as to prolong the thrill of the battle (*KTU* 1.3.2.20–22):

> *She arranged chairs as the warriors;*
> *She arranged tables as the troops;*
> *Footstools as the heroes.*

Anat then goes to war against these household furnishings (*KTU* 1.3.2.23–28):

> *She fought hard and looked,*
> *Anat battled and saw.*
> *Her liver swelled with laughter,*
> *Her heart was filled with joy,*
> *The liver of Anat was exultant.*
> *As she plunged knee-deep in the blood of the mighty,*
> *Up to her hips in the gore of the warriors.*

This description of Anat at war against her furniture is a part of what is usually called the Baal-Anat cycle, a complex series of myths that recount the various military endeavors that Anat undertakes in conjunction with her brother-consort Baal. The first major episode of this cycle describes a conflict that pits Anat and Baal against a dragon-like deity of the sea, alternately called Yamm, which means "Sea"; Nahar, meaning "River"; or Lôtan, a name etymologically related to Hebrew Leviathan, the chaos dragon referred to in several biblical texts.[79] A second episode depicts the struggles of Anat and Baal against the Canaanite god of sterility and death, Mot. The significant point for us in each of these battle scenes concerns the way in which tradition ascribes to both Baal and Anat the victory over these foes.

The story of the fight against Mot, for example, begins by describing how Baal, who has been declared king of the gods, sends an embassy to Mot's underworld abode, demanding that Mot pay homage in Baal's court. Mot is scornful. He says to Baal (*KTU* 1.5.1.6–8):

> *No, but you will come down into the throat of Mot, the son of El,*[80]
> *Into the maw of the hero, beloved of El.*

As the myth progresses, it turns out that Mot has been right to scorn. Baal finds himself not only denied Mot's obeisance, but also descending as Mot's slave into the underworld (*KTU* 1.5.2.2–4):

> *[One lip to ea]rth, one lip to heaven,*
> *[He (i.e., Mot) stretched out his] tongue to the stars.*[81]
> *Baal entered his gorge,*
> *He descended into his mouth.*

This descent into the underworld means, at least metaphorically, that Baal has died. When word reaches Anat, she reacts first by engaging in rituals of lamentation typical of the Semitic world, cutting her flesh and pulling out her hair.[82] The text reads (*KTU* 1.6.1.2–7):

> *She cut her skin with a stone,*
> *She cut herself [with a razor].*
> *She shaved her cheeks and her beard,*
> *[She harrowed] the shoulders of her arms.*

> *She plowed her chest like a garden,*
> *She harrowed her back like a valley.*
> *"Baal is dead! What will become of the people?*
> *The son of Dagan, what will happen to the masses?"*

Anat, however, is hardly one simply to sit and mourn (*KTU* 1.6.2.26–35):

> *A day, two days passed,*
> *The days became months,*
> *As the maiden Anat sought him.*
> *Like the heart of a cow for her calf,*
> *Like the heart of a ewe for her lamb,*
> *So was the heart of Anat after Baal.*
> *She seized El's son Mot.*
> *With a sword, she cleaved him,*
> *With a sieve, she winnowed him,*
> *With fire, she burned him,*
> *With millstones, she ground him,*
> *In the field she sowed him.*

Shortly thereafter, Baal is freed from the underworld.

Baal's release from the underworld, however, does not bring to an end his confrontations with Mot, for the god of death reappears after seven years to challenge Baal again. This challenge is ultimately unsuccessful, but what is important to note is that in lodging his complaint, Mot harks back to the humiliation he had suffered seven years earlier. He says (*KTU* 1.6.5.11–19):

> *On account of you, O Baal, I suffered shame,*
> *On account of you, I suffered splitting with the sword,*
> *On account of you, I suffered burning with fire,*
> *On account of you, [I suffered grinding] with millstones,*
> *On account of you, [I suffered winnowing] with a sieve.*
> *On account of you, I suffered [ ] in the fields,*
> *On account of you, I suffered sowing in the sea.*

Technically, Mot's speech is correct: it is "on account of Baal" that Mot had previously suffered the indignities of splitting, burning, grinding, winnowing, and sowing. But curiously unmentioned here is Anat, even though she was the actual agent who effected Mot's defeat. To put the matter another way: while it was Anat who cleaved, winnowed, burned, ground, and scattered Mot, it seems to be Baal whom Mot singles out for blame. Why this transposition? I believe it is because Mot—and, by extension, Canaanite mythography—regards the military exploits of the god Baal and the goddess Anat as inextricably intertwined. Baal *can* in a sense lay claim to the victory over Mot because Anat's triumphs in battle are also Baal's.

Even more telling in this regard is the story of the battle Baal and Anat wage against Yamm/Nahar/Lôtan. As in the conflict with Mot, this narrative begins with a description of how Baal becomes the prisoner of the god of the sea. Eventually, Baal is able to fight his way free of Yamm's dominion by using a magical club (*KTU* 1.2.4.23–27):

> *The club danced in Baal's hands,*
> *Like an eagle in his fingers.*
> *He struck the head of Prince Yamm,*
> *Between the eyes of Judge Nahar.*
> *Yamm collapsed, he fell to the ground,*
> *His joints trembled, and his face fell.*
> *Baal destroyed and drank Yamm,*
> *He finished off Judge Nahar.*

Yet the mythological tradition also preserves this speech by Anat (*KTU* 1.3.3.38–40):

> *Did I not smite Yamm, the beloved of El?*
> *Did I not finish off Nahar, the great god?*
> *Did I not muzzle the dragon and destroy it?*[83]

The answer to these rhetorical questions of Anat's is clearly meant to be "yes," as the next two lines of Anat's delivery make plain (*KTU* 1.3.3.41–42):[84]

> *I smote the crooked servant,*
> *The tyrant with the seven heads.*

But does not Anat's claim here logically contradict the description quoted above of Baal's triumph over Yamm? Not, I propose, if we follow the line of interpretation I advanced concerning the story of Mot and suggest again that, according to Canaanite mythological tradition, the battles of Baal and Anat are inextricably intertwined. Thus, as her victory over Mot was credited to him, so, too, can his victory over Yamm be ascribed to her. It is almost as if Baal and Anat are reckoned as two sides of the same coin.

IV. ANAT AND ISRAELITE TRADITIONS
OF WOMEN AND WAR

These descriptions of Baal and Anat as two characters who serve to balance and complement the actions of one another bring to mind once more Judges 5 and the way that text uses a structuring principle of poetic diptych in order to convey points of theological complementarity. In fact, the portrayal found in the Baal-Anat cycle of a male and female warrior who fight in concert parallels precisely one of the three dichotomies I have identified in the Judges 5 diptych: the male/female dichotomy whereby Yahweh's battle against Sisera is conducted in conjunction first with Deborah and then with Jael. I find it impossible to evaluate this shared Canaanite and Israelite motif as coincidental. Instead, I intend to borrow from a line of interpretation first suggested by Stephen G. Dempster and argue that those in Israelite culture responsible for the text of Judges 5 adopted older Canaanite mythological traditions concerning Baal and Anat and adapted them in describing the holy war Israel waged against Sisera.[85] I also intend to develop this thesis further by proposing that Canaanite traditions regarding Anat influence Israel's depictions of Judith and the woman of Thebez. In addition, I believe Anat traditions affect some militaristic portrayals of women whom I have not as yet had occasion to mention. I will even argue by the end of this chapter that there are holy war texts in the Hebrew Bible in which no woman character is present but in which the kind of female warrior imagery Israel inherited from Canaan's Anat lore still resonates.

To begin with Judges 5: several pieces of evidence suggest the dependency of this text on the Canaanite myths of Baal and Anat. First, we should consider chronological and geographical data. After spending several decades advancing theories of an Israelite invasion of Canaan— either through conquest or through gradual infiltration—a number of biblical scholars now agree that the people who came to be known as the Israelites emerged from within the context of Canaanite culture in

C. 1250–1200 B.C.E.[86] Thus, although Ezekiel's intent is to speak sarcastically when he says to the people of Jerusalem, "Your origin and your birth were in the land of the Canaanites" (16:3), in truth the prophet is right, and right not just about Jerusalem: the people of Israel were Canaanites. Undoubtedly then, these Israelites, especially during their early history, would have been intimately familiar with Canaanite mythological traditions. Recall, moreover, that most scholars date Judges 5 to the period of Israel's earliest history, to the late twelfth or eleventh century B.C.E. Those responsible for this poem thus must have been conversant with Canaanite mythic motifs. The reference in Judg 5:6 to one "Shamgar ben Anat" indeed demonstrates that Israelite authors knew at least the name of the goddess Anat. We can easily extrapolate that they also would have been familiar with Anat's character and with the names and characters of the other actors of Canaanite myth.

In fact, Dempster, along with several other commentators, has pointed out that the portrait of Yahweh drawn in Judges 5 depends extensively on older Canaanite images of the god Baal.[87] According to Canaanite myth, Baal is the storm god *extraordinaire*. He rides in a chariot of a storm cloud. He travels with an entourage of wind, thunder, and rain. Artistic representations show him holding aloft a bolt of lightning as a spear. Descriptions of Baal also depict him brandishing lightning as his weapon. When he speaks in his manifestation as the storm god, his voice is the roar of thunder. His female attendants are Misty One, daughter of Light; Dewy One, daughter of Showers; and Muddy One, daughter of Floods.[88]

Yahweh is similarly described in Judges 5 through the use of storm imagery. In verses 4–5, the clouds shake with the waters of a mighty tempest when Yahweh marches forth as the divine warrior from Sinai. The trembling of the earth described in verse 4 also can be interpreted as a reaction to Yahweh's roars of thunder. Even more telling is verse 21, where the Canaanite army is attacked and swept away by the waters of the Wadi Kishon. As discussed above, this raging wadi fights as a part of Yahweh's cosmic army, meaning that the rampaging flood must have come from rains that the storm god Yahweh has brought. And if there is yet any doubt that Judges 5 means to depict Yahweh as a storm god, we can compare Ps 68:8–10 (English 68:7–9), where verses 4–5 of Judges 5 are paraphrased and expanded upon:[89]

O God, when you went forth before your people,
When you marched in the wilderness,

> *The earth trembled, yea the heavens shook,*[90]
> *Before God, the one of Sinai,*
> *Before God, the God of Israel.*
> *Rain in abundance you did pour out, O God.*

The last line is particularly significant. It is further of note that elsewhere in Psalm 68 (v 5; English v 4), Yahweh is called "rider on the clouds" (**rkb 'rpwt*), the same epithet ascribed to Baal in Ugaritic myth (*rkb 'rpt*).[91]

Dempster has further sought to demonstrate that if Yahweh in Judges 5 is modeled after the storm god Baal, then so, too, should at least the first woman with whom Yahweh fights in concert in the poem, Deborah, be modeled after Baal's female ally in Canaanite myth, the warrior goddess Anat. Peter C. Craigie has augmented this analysis by suggesting some quite specific parallels between Deborah and Anat. Craigie points out, for example, that in the Ugaritic Epic of Aqhat, which tells the story of a battle Anat wages against a human hero Aqhat, Anat is aided by a henchman, Yatpan, whom Craigie compares to Deborah's second-in-command in Judges 5, Barak. Craigie then goes on to suggest four more points of comparison.[92] In the end, both he and Dempster agree that in Canaan and in Israel, Anat and Deborah are similarly described as females who undertake military exploits in conjunction with or on behalf of a male storm god. I would add only the results of my own analysis: that both cultures structure their literary representations of these male-female fighting teams in such a way to suggest that the victories won by one member of the pair can simultaneously be celebrated as a triumph by the other. The Israelite authors responsible for Judges 5, I conclude, derived their portrayal of Deborah as a female military hero in the battle against Sisera from older Canaanite paradigms of Anat, the warrior goddess.

Yet this is not to claim, I hasten to add, that Deborah is just Canaanite Anat with an Israelite name. Deborah lacks Anat's out-and-out bellicosity: she wears no necklace of skulls or girdle of hands; she does not eat flesh; she does not drink blood. Also, as I discussed in Section I, although there may be hints in Judges 5 that Deborah should be seen as participating in the actual combat against Sisera's troops, the biblical text certainly does not assign to Deborah the same sorts of explicit associations with weaponry and with the waging of war that are ascribed to Anat in Canaanite tradition. Nevertheless, while Deborah may want for Anat's unrestrained belligerence, she does appear Anat-like in her role as a female military champion, a woman who, through her endeavors on behalf of Israel in its battle against Sisera, takes decisive and powerful action within the battlefield arena. It is this association of a woman with the general exploits of war, I suggest, that the Judges 5 tradition derives from Canaan's Anat mythology. Thus, while Deborah is surely not just Canaanite Anat in an Israelite guise, it is still the case that Deborah's characterization in Judges 5 seems to have been powerfully influenced by the sorts of militaristic attributes associated with Anat in Canaanite myth. Dempster's language catches the nuances of this position perfectly, identifying Deborah not as Anat *per se* but as a character conceived "in the vein of Anat."[93]

Likewise, I believe, should Jael be seen as a character conceived "in the vein of Anat," a woman whose attributes of military heroism are powerfully influenced by Canaanite mythology and its descriptions of Canaan's warrior goddess.[94] Especially significant here are the ways in which both the Judges 5 characterization of Jael and the Canaanite characterizations of Anat combine militaristic imagery with imagery of sexuality and seduction. Susan Niditch has most thoroughly discussed this motif of violence paired with eroticism in the Judges 5 depiction of Jael.[95] She focuses in particular on the description found in 5:27 of Sisera dead at Jael's feet. Niditch translates:[96]

Between her legs he knelt, he fell, he lay
Between her legs he knelt, he fell
Where he knelt, there he fell, despoiled.

In analyzing the language used here, Niditch points out that *raglayim*, "legs, feet," is a Hebraic euphemism for both male and female genitalia; that the verbs *kāra'*, "to kneel," and *nāpal*, "to fall," especially when used in conjunction, can suggest the sexual posture expected of a would-be lover; that the verb *šākab*, "to lie," is frequently used in illicit sexual contexts; and that *šādûd*, "despoiled," can be used—as in Jer 4:30—to describe the fate that those who play the harlot will suffer. Erotic imagery is thus present—and multiply present—in every line of this verse. Yet Niditch hardly denies the text's more obvious connotations of violence. She writes:

Double meanings of violent death and sexuality emerge in every line. He is at her feet in a pose of defeat and humiliation; he kneels between her legs in a sexual pose. He falls and lies, a dead warrior assassinated by a warrior better than he; he is a supplicant and a would-be lover. . . . He is despoiled/destroyed. The woman Jael becomes not the object of sexual advances, with the improper nuances of *škb,* and not the complacent responder to requests for mercy, but is herself the aggressor, the despoiler.[97]

So, too, can Anat be described as a fighter who serves up bellicosity laced with passion.[98] The clearest example comes from the aforementioned Aqhat Epic, in which Anat schemes to acquire the hero Aqhat's magnificent bow and arrows. Eventually, this requires that Anat engage in battle against Aqhat, but the goddess begins her quest more peaceably, attempting to bargain with Aqhat for the bow. Delbert R. Hillers has persuasively argued that this bargaining scene is charged with sexual overtones.[99] Hillers particularly demonstrates that Aqhat's bow is a sexual symbol, a mythic representation of the phallus. Thus, when Anat requests of Aqhat his bow, she should be understood both as a warrior who seeks to acquire a mighty weapon and as a seductress who approaches Aqhat with a sexual proposition. Likewise, when Aqhat refuses the goddess, the pique Anat displays should be interpreted both as the frustration of a thwarted warrior and as the anger of a rejected lover.

Although not certain, it is likely that Anat's dual characterization as both militaristic and sensual manifests itself again further on in the Aqhat Epic. After Aqhat refuses Anat, the goddess storms off to see El, the divine patriarch, in order to obtain his permission to exact revenge. Well aware of Anat's rather rash and impulsive tendencies, El tells the goddess that she can do as she will. She then approaches Aqhat a second time, saying to him, "You are my brother, and I am [your sister]" (*KTU* 1.18.1.24). Commentators generally, and I believe correctly, interpret this line as having the same sexual connotations that were found in Anat's earlier conversation with Aqhat, given that frequently in ancient Near Eastern literature, the words "brother" and "sister" mean "lover." [100] Unfortunately, the Ugaritic clay tablet on which this episode is inscribed is so fragmentary that no definitive analysis can be secured. What is definite, however, is Aqhat's subsequent fate, described in the next complete scene in the epic. There, as Aqhat sits alone in a tent, eating, Anat's henchman Yatpan, disguised as a vulture, swoops down from above and strikes Aqhat on the head. Aqhat is killed instantly.

Crucial to note here are the several motifs that this death scene has in common with the story of Jael and Sisera. A male military hero, unaccompanied by any of his warrior companions, sits eating and drinking inside a tent. The image initially seems a peaceful one, but the scene quickly turns to violence as the hero is murdered through the agency of a woman. In both cases, moreover, the murder is effected by a blow to the head. The possibility that images of seduction are coupled with each of these acts of violence further indicates the analogous nature of the Anat/Aqhat and Jael/Sisera death scenes. I conclude that, in the same way that the Judges 5 description associating Deborah with the waging of war is derived from Canaanite imagery of the warrior goddess Anat, so, too, is the poem's depiction of Jael as an erotic assassin influenced by Canaan's Anat traditions.

These descriptions, moreover, of Anat and Jael as erotic assassins who initially seem to befriend military commanders only to turn against them while the heroes sit peacefully in a tent, eating and drinking, are highly reminiscent of the book of Judith's description of Judith's seduction-*cum*-murder of Holofernes. The Jael and Judith stories in particular are similar.[101] Patrick W. Skehan, for example, has pointed out that in the description of Judith's assassination of Holofernes in Judith 8–16, there are nine different verses in which Judith's killing deed is said to be done by the work of her "hand" or, once (13:4), her "hands."[102] Why the pervasiveness of this particular vocabulary item? One possibility, according to Skehan, is that "it could be an echo of Jael in Jgs 5, 26," who put her "hand" to the tent peg as she prepared to strike the head of Sisera.[103] Note also Jdt 16:9, which recounts how Judith's sandal ravished Holofernes' eyes and her beauty captivated his mind before the sword severed his neck. The obvious meanings of "ravish" and "captivate" in this text are sexual, but in Greek, which is the original language of Judith, both verbs have militaristic connotations as well: *harpazō*, translated as "to ravish," means also "to overpower"; *aichmalōtizō*, "to captivate," means also "to make captive by the spear."[104] Compare the description of Sisera's murder in Judg 5:27 and the *double entendres* of sex and violence that Niditch located in the verbs of that verse. Finally, and of greatest significance, see the lauding of Judith in Jdt 13:18 as "blessed above all other women" (NRSV translation), an epithet surely meant to evoke the description of Jael as "most blessed of women" in Judg 5:24.

The book of Judith's depiction of its hero, however, is also striking in its similarities to the Judges 5 portrait of Deborah. Judith 16, for example, celebrates Judith's triumph over Holofernes with a victory song that is quite similar to the "Song of Deborah" found in Judges 5. Particularly significant is the fact that Jdt 16:1 identifies Judith as the singer of the hymn (NRSV translation):

> *And Judith said:*
> *Begin a song to my God with tambourines,*
> *Sing to my Lord with cymbals.*
> *Raise to him a new psalm,*
> *Exalt him, and call upon his name.*

Compare Judg 5:1 and its identification of Deborah as the primary singer of the Judges 5 victory song. Recall also Judith's role in Jdt 14:1–15:7 as the strategist who masterminds the Bethulian attack on the Assyrian army, to which compare Deborah's role in Judges 5 as the one who arises to deliver Israel from Sisera's Canaanite troops.

Another point of similarity between Judith and Deborah has been suggested by Toni Craven, one of the most sensitive interpreters of the book of Judith.[105] In describing Judith's hero, Craven writes, "Faith makes this childless woman a mother to Israel and a model of true freedom."[106] In support of this assertion, Craven cites the maternal imagery found in Jdt 16:4, where Judith sings of Holofernes (NRSV translation):

> *He boasted that he would burn up my territory,*
> *And kill my young men with the sword,*
> *And dash my infants to the ground,*
> *And seize my children as booty,*
> *And take my virgins as spoil.*

All of these things Judith refers to here as hers—territory, young men, infants, children, and virgins—are elements that I have earlier followed Camp in describing as a part of the *naḥălat yhwh*, "the heritage of Yahweh." I have also earlier followed Camp in arguing that a primary charge of "a mother in Israel"—be it Deborah, the woman of Abel-Beth-Maʿacah, or the city of Abel itself—is to protect Yahweh's precious inheritance. And how is the "mother in Israel" to effect this protection? Through her wisdom and through her skills in persuasive counseling; through her faithfulness to the covenant of Israel; and through a willingness to go to war on behalf of Yahweh if it is necessary to defend the covenant ideal. Judith possesses all these attributes. Wisdom is a charac-

teristic ascribed to Judith both by the elders of Bethulia (8:29) and by
Holofernes (11:21). Persuasive counseling is a skill Judith manifests both
in her speech to the town elders convincing them to let her go forth on
her own to try to defeat Holofernes (8:11–34) and in her speech outlin-
ing the plan of attack that should be followed after Holofernes' death
(14:1–10). Faithfulness to Yahweh's covenant is something Judith exhib-
its through her constant ritual devotions (prayer, fasting, the wearing of
sackcloth). Her willingness to fight on behalf of Yahweh in defense
of that covenant, while demonstrated throughout chapters 8–16, is perhaps most evident in her prayer to Yahweh in Judith 9, where she asks
for Yahweh's help and blessing as she goes forth to stage her one-woman
attack. Thus, although the title "mother" is never used of Judith, Craven
is certainly correct to understand her as being—like her counterpart
Deborah—"a mother in Israel."

Given, moreover, that Judith is so like Deborah in her "maternal"
role and in other respects; given, in addition, that Judith is equally, indeed, even more like Jael in her characterization as an erotic assassin;
and given, finally, the thesis with which I began this section—that Anat
traditions influenced the representations of both Deborah and Jael in
Judges 5—we cannot help but conclude that the book of Judith's depiction of its hero must also have been influenced by paradigms of the
Canaanite warrior goddess. Judith, that is, represents a third Israelite
manifestation of the Anat tradition that assigns a role of military heroism
to females during times of war.

Still, despite the common use of Anat traditions in the depictions of
Deborah, Jael, and Judith, there are important differences between the
ways Anat imagery is used in Judges 5 to depict Deborah and Jael and
the way it is used by the authors of Judith to portray their protagonist.
Note, for example, that in the book of Judith, after Holofernes' death,
although it is Judith who concocts the plot that leads to the slaughter of
the Assyrian army, her role as a military leader does not involve an actual
position of battlefield command; she does not, that is, participate in the
mustering of the troops, in the sounding of the reveille, or in the actual
combat. Yet at least two and possibly all three of these more militaristic
endeavors are ascribed to Deborah in Judges 5. Even more significant
are the differences between the book of Judith's depiction of its hero
and the portrayal of Jael in Judges 5. Although in both texts, Judith and

Jael are depicted as Anat-like erotic assassins, Jael is much more like Anat in that militaristic language stands firmly to the fore in her representation. Erotic imagery, conversely, remains highly veiled in the description of Jael, so veiled, in fact, that in much the same way that Hillers had to tease forth the imagery of Anat's eroticism from the Aqhat Epic and its symbolic use of the bow, so, too, were the skills and sensitivities of an interpreter like Niditch required in order to locate sexual language in the verbs of the Judges 5 text. But this primary focus on bellicosity is completely downplayed in the story of Judith's murder of Holofernes. There, Judith is foremost the seductress and not the belligerent fighter. It was thus the *militaristic* meanings of the verbs "to ravish" and "to captivate" that had to be teased forth from the Judith 16 text and not their erotic connotations; note also in this regard that even though Judith leaves Bethulia with the intention of murdering Holofernes, she only provisions herself with a weapon—the sword that hangs over Holofernes' bed—when fate puts it into her hand.

Why should this be, that even though the portrayals of Deborah and Jael, on the one hand, and Judith, on the other, are both heavily influenced by the imagery of Canaanite Anat, these three Israelite women stand in certain ways so counter to one another, the portrayal of Judith deriving itself only minimally from Anat's predominant role as a warrior and depending almost exclusively on Anat's secondary attributes of sensuality, while the representations of Deborah and Jael have as their primary inspiration Anat's militaristic qualities and allude only obliquely, and only in the case of Jael, to the goddess' erotic characteristics? Perhaps the most obvious answer is to posit historical devolution, arguing that, as Israelite tradition became more and more distanced in time from its Canaanite heritage, it lost more and more of the specific motifs it had borrowed from its mother culture. Thus the Canaanite image of Anat as a female predominantly characterized by bellicosity, so pronounced when borrowed into a twelfth- or eleventh-century B.C.E. text like Judges 5, all but disappears by the time it is appropriated by the second-century B.C.E. book of Judith.

This explanation, however, fails to satisfy me completely, and my reasons are two. First, I believe that a close reading of the Bible's stories of its female military heroes makes it difficult to sustain a theory of historical devolution, especially a simply described one that posits an unwavering trajectory from an original position of the primarily fierce woman to a later stance of the woman as primarily seductress. The book of Judith, chronologically the latest of the Israelite texts I have described, proves to be the most serious stumbling block here, for arguably the woman Judith, although depicted as heavily reliant on attributes of sexuality and seductiveness, is still—after Deborah and Jael in Judges 5—the biblical woman most immediately involved in the actual waging of war. However, in portrayals that come from the millennium that separates Judges 5 and Judith—for example, the Judges 4 portrayal of Deborah as adviser to Barak—while an association of women with the business of war is still present, the notion that women could undertake actual military endeavors is lost.

Thus a chronological explanation that posits a move from originally "fierce" to secondarily "erotic" just will not do. In addition, the underlying assumption of such a theory, that Israel moves during its history from a position of "more Canaanite influence" to "less Canaanite influence," disregards a consensus that increasingly is emerging among historians of Israelite religion: that originally Canaanite religious beliefs and behaviors remained present and vital throughout the entire lifetime of the Israelite cult, from the last centuries of the second millennium B.C.E. well into the postexilic and Hellenistic periods (the sixth century B.C.E. and beyond). Evidence in support of this thesis is manifold and includes both archaeological materials, of which an ever-increasing corpus attests to widespread Israelite participation in allegedly "Canaanite" rituals,[107] and biblical data: Israel's heavy reliance on Canaanite mythological motifs in prophetic passages from the sixth century B.C.E., for example,[108] and texts such as 2 Kings 23, which indicates that supposedly "Canaanite" cult practices and cult objects existed and even prevailed in the Jerusalem temple of the late seventh century B.C.E.[109] Even more significant for our purposes is the abundance of Canaanite mythological imagery found in the apocalyptic chapters of the book of Daniel (Daniel 7–12), since these chapters date from the second quarter of the second century B.C.E., roughly contemporary with the book of Judith.[110] This material demonstrates that it is a mistake to speak of Canaanite influence as lessening in Israel by the time of Judith's composition. Instead, Daniel makes clear that Canaanite traditions were fully available in the second century B.C.E., as they in fact were throughout the Israelite period. The only question concerns when and to what degree Israel's various religious thinkers and actors chose to make use of them.

Which brings us once more to the differences between the Judges 5 depictions of Deborah and Jael and the book of Judith's portrayal of

Judith: assuming, now, that the authors of the twelfth- or eleventh-century B.C.E. Judges 5 and the authors of the second-century B.C.E. book of Judith had equal access to a Canaanite portrait of Anat in which the goddess exhibited primarily militaristic attributes and only second-arily sexual ones, why did the authors of Judges 5 follow the lead of their prototype in assigning Anat's bellicose attributes predominant em-phasis while the authors of Judith chose to accentuate Anat's erotic char-acteristics and mute bellicosity? Let us consider first the case of Judges 5 and recall the theory I have put forward to explain the roles of Deborah and Jael in that text and, more generally, the male/female dichotomy I identified in Section I as integral to the entire poem: that the Judges 5 pairing of the male storm god Yahweh with the women Deborah and Jael is derived from the similar pairing of the storm god Baal with his female ally Anat found in Canaanite myth. Yet this theory, I must in the same breath admit, offers no explanation of the two other dichotomies of cosmic/earthly and divine/human that I previously have argued characterize Judges 5, for these particular juxtapositions are not well par-alleled in the Baal-Anat corpus of myths. Indeed, in the myths of the Baal-Anat cycle, dichotomies such as cosmic/earthly and divine/human are not even a possibility, given that the Baal-Anat stories take place in exclusively cosmic space (heaven) and include only divine actors (gods).

Still, I do not find this failure to find parallels between the Baal-Anat mythology of Canaan and the cosmic/earthly and divine/human dichotomies of Judges 5 an insurmountable difficulty for my thesis. I suggested at the beginning of this section that Israel both *adopts* and *adapts* older Canaanite mythological forms for use in its sacred literature. A necessary adaptation of these older Canaanite mythological forms— at least within the kind of Israelite monolatry represented in the Hebrew Bible—is that Israel remove any references to a deity other than Yah-weh. This means that Israelite tradition must "demythologize" its Ca-naanite prototype by making all but one of its actors human. The divine Anat who is the ally of Baal in Canaanite myth is thus humanized in Judges 5 and becomes a woman—either Deborah or Jael—rather than a goddess. If Barak is a Yatpan figure, as Craigie has suggested, we can see the same demythologizing principle at work.

In addition to this humanizing of divine figures, there also must come in Israelite tradition a change in locus, for these new human characters belong on earth, not in heaven. Hence the scene of the battle in Judges 5 becomes "Ta'anach by the waters of Megiddo" (v 19). An earthly location also requires that time be defined in terms of a historical context: "in the days of Shamgar ben Anat, in the days of Jael" (v 6). Yet this historicizing process does not mean that all the elements of the mythological tradition are lost. One divine actor remains (Yahweh), as do those references that locate that divine actor in cosmic time ("Yahweh, when you went forth from Seir, when you marched out from the steppe of Edom"; v 4) and in cosmic space ("from heaven fought the stars, from their courses they fought against Sisera"; v 20). Yahweh also retains cosmic powers (the whole earth trembles when this God steps forth; vv 4–5) and commands a cosmic entourage (the stars and the rains; vv 20–21). There is thus only a partial demythologization of the older Canaanite tradition.[111] What results is a tension, whereby some mythic motifs remain embedded in the text while, simultaneously, a historical presentation is overlaid. It is within this tension that I find the source for the dichotomies of cosmic/earthly and divine/human that I have identified in Judges 5.[112]

It is also within this tension that I find the key for understanding the poem's depictions of its female heroes as primarily manifesting Anat's attributes of bellicosity and only secondarily, and only in the case of Jael, exhibiting the goddess' characterization as a seductress. Because Judges 5, even though ostensibly presented as a historical account, is demythologized only partially and retains several supernatural elements in its overall recitation, concerns of historical realism need not be absolutely observed in the depicting of the poem's women characters. Verisimilitude, that is, need not exclusively direct the poem's authors in their depictions of women or in their descriptions of what women can and cannot do. The poem thus can evoke a military role for Deborah and Jael despite the fact that such a role would not be normally found in Israel's male-dominated world.[113] Or, to state the matter in a more general fashion: Judges 5, like other myths, legends, and myth- and legend-like texts, can put forward certain types of representation and characterization that more historically situated narratives cannot. Within our own culture, for example, Paul Bunyan can have an enormous blue ox in legend, but in a more historicized recounting about American lumberjacks, the oxen must be about the same size as any other bovine and some shade of light brown or grey. Likewise, to take a case more germane to the representations under discussion, recall that even though it is allegedly depicting the earthly sphere, Judg 5:21 can ignore the regular laws of the Megiddo flood plain in order to portray the Wadi Kishon as a rampaging torrent.

Again, myth and myth-like texts make possible depictions that historical reality does not. Because of its myth-like qualities, therefore, Judges 5 can transcend the cultural stereotypes of Israelite society regarding women and portray its female characters in ways that are not bound by the usual Israelite definitions of gender-appropriate behavior. Deborah can be presented as a commander and warrior at the time of Israel's battle against Sisera, and Jael can be celebrated as the ferocious assassin who delivers the war's final blow.

In a book like Judith, however, myth-like qualities are almost completely absent. To be sure, there is still present the notion that the power of God stands behind Judith (see especially Judith's prayer in chapter 9), but, unlike the portrayal found in Judges 5, Yahweh is not directly involved in the book of Judith's military actions. The focus instead is almost exclusively on human actors and this-worldly events. This is not to say, I hasten to add, that the book of Judith is to be taken as historically accurate; as I have already noted, the story of a sixth-century B.C.E. battle between Israelite forces and Nebuchadnezzar's Assyrian army is patently false. But this does not matter. The point is that the authors of Judith *want* to make their story seem as if it could have happened, as if it does conform—and conform wholly—to the norms that govern the everyday world.

The book's female protagonist must therefore be portrayed in ways that adhere to Israel's general societal constructs. And, in Israelite society, cultural norms typically restricted women to the work of the domestic sphere. Undoubtedly, some women were occasionally able to exert themselves beyond the narrow confines of the home, and Judith's ability to participate in the deliberations of the town elders may reflect this.[114] But such opportunities for women were scarce: note that even Judith, in her discussions with Bethulia's leaders, summons them to her home rather than going forth to engage with them in public (8:10–11). Certainly there were no opportunities for women to go forth further and share with men the role of an accomplished soldier. Thus, if a character like Judith is to be believably portrayed, Israel's understanding of its world requires that she *must* rely on sexuality as her primary—indeed, almost as her exclusive—weapon. Note once more in this regard that even though Judith leaves Bethulia with the goal of murdering Holofernes, she does not gird on a sword as she goes forth. Instead, she only gains access to her implement of murder when chance puts Holofernes' own blade into her hand.

In the end, then, while the authors of Judith derive their portrait of the book's hero from the imagery associated with Canaanite Anat that is a part of their cultural background, their desire to minimize supernatural elements in their story in favor of that which is historically believable leads them to downplay the Canaanite conception of the warrior goddess as a bellicose fighter. What Judith's depicters stress instead is Judith's role as an Anat-like seductress, for her attributes of beauty and sensuality are perfectly acceptable characteristics for a woman to possess within the bounds Israelite society defined for women's lives in the everyday world.

This thesis—that a text that is more this-worldly in its orientation will minimize the notion that a fighting woman could be described primarily in terms of Anat-like militaristic imagery and that it will instead maximize the more historically believable idea of the woman as an Anat-like seductress—can be further demonstrated by turning once more to the other "women and war" texts we have examined in the book of Judges. Consider first the woman of Thebez story in Judges 9. I have already noted how the role played by this head-smashing deliverer of Israel recalls Jael's role as the smasher of Sisera's skull in Judges 5. Given, in addition, the arguments I have advanced above concerning the ways Jael's character is derived from Canaan's Anat lore, I now suggest that the Jael-like woman of Thebez carries within her character resonances of the Canaanite warrior goddess. Of special note in this regard is the way in which the woman of Thebez defeats her enemy Abimelech by smashing his head with an "upper millstone." The Hebrew phrase used for this upper millstone, *pelaḥ rekeb,* is found only here in Judg 9:53 and in the reference to the woman of Thebez story found in 2 Sam 11:21. However, the second word of the phrase, *rekeb,* is found at one other point in the Hebrew Bible with the meaning "millstone": this is in Deut 24:6, which also contains another fairly rare Hebrew word for "millstones," *rēḥayim.* The Ugaritic cognate of this second term, *rḥm,* is relatively rare as well and is used in Canaanite mythological tradition only twice with the meaning "millstones." Notably, in both instances, it describes the millstones with which Anat ground up Mot (*KTU* 1.6.2.34; 1.6.5.15–16). And, while Anat's grinding up of her enemy is not the same as the Thebez woman's smashing of her foe's head, it is still significant that Anat and the woman of Thebez use synonymous weapons to defeat their opponents. Motifs derived from the myths of the Canaanite

warrior goddess, it seems, have once more influenced a biblical rendering of a female military hero.

Note also that, while it is not exactly what one would call a mythological or otherworldly element, the notion that a millstone is even present at the *top* of a tower is at least a highly unrealistic detail in the woman
of Thebez narrative, given that the mechanics of milling dictate that a
millstone be at a tower's *base*.[115] Because, moreover, there is this unrealistic datum in the story's construction, my thesis proposes that Judges 9
need not be constrained by the normal strictures of Israelite society,
which required that women—even women who fight against Israel's
enemies in times of war—manifest primarily the attributes of sensuality
and domesticity perceived to be appropriate to their gender. Thus, in
contrast to the more determinedly "realistic" book of Judith, Judges 9
need make no mention of any characteristic of its woman hero that
concerns her sexual being. Is she young or old? Attractive or ugly? Married, single, or widowed? The text does not concern itself. Its willingness
to suspend realism's norms in the matter of the millstone frees it also
from the requirement to focus on the sexual attributes of its female military hero.

Still, Judges 9 is not Judges 5, meaning that, despite its use of certain
unrealistic motifs, Judges 9 remains primarily rooted in the everyday
world. Like the portrait of Judith, then, the portrayal of the woman of
Thebez must ultimately be rendered in a form that is acceptable within
the context of Israelite gender expectations. Thus, like Judith, this
woman has to rely on chance in securing her weapon; she cannot be
rendered as already armed. Note also in this regard that even though it
is archers to whom Joab compares the woman of Thebez in 2 Sam
11:14–21, the literary tradition in Judges 9 does not follow suit by depicting her as, say, a skilled archer who pierces Abimelech's skull with
an arrow. The reason is that the archers of 2 Sam 11:14–21 are men and
so are acting within the confines of culturally acceptable gender roles.
In Israelite thought, however, women should not exhibit such military
skill. So, in the end, if the Judges 9 portrayal of the woman of Thebez
is to conform to the dictates of historical realism, then her depicters can
show her only as dropping a handy rock and hoping that it lands on the
head of her target. While the influence of Canaan's Anat mythology
remains, the Canaanite language depicting Anat as a female fighter as
able as any male must give way to the text's interest in believability.

The portrait of Deborah found in Judges 4 versus Judges 5 demonstrates even more dramatically the effect that an interest in depicting the historically "real" has on the Bible's representations of its female military heroes. As discussed at the beginning of this chapter, Judges 4 tells in prose the same story Judges 5 recounts poetically concerning Israel's holy war against Sisera, but Deborah's role in leading this war is minimized in Judges 4 in favor of that of Barak. Notably, Judges 4 simultaneously glosses over the cosmic imagery found in its poetic antecedent: in Judges 4, there is no march forth of Yahweh from Sinai, no quaking earth, no fighting stars, no divinely-sent rains. Yahweh is present, but despite the claims of the story's postscript—"so on that day God subdued King Jabin of Canaan before the Israelites" (4:23)—the deity's only actual act during the battle is to send Sisera and his army into a panic as Barak begins his attack (4:15). Otherwise, the description of the confrontation is firmly grounded in historical language. In order for Deborah to be a believable character within such a context, her status as war leader in Judges 5 must be downplayed and in essence eliminated. Therefore in Judges 4, she serves only as Barak's adviser. The dictates of historical realism require that a man be depicted as Israel's commanding general and hero.

Jael's role in Judges 5 is also radically reinterpreted in Judges 4. In Judges 5, as we have seen, Jael—in lulling Sisera into complacency and then shattering his head as he eats and drinks—behaves in a manner highly reminiscent of Anat's ruthless attack that kills Aqhat. In Judges 4, though, the redactor seems unable to present Jael as a woman who can murder a foe in cold blood, especially a male foe who should be stronger and a more seasoned fighter than she. The redactor of Judges 4 thus suggests that Sisera must have been so weary after the battle with Barak that he fell asleep in Jael's tent. This allows Jael to come stealthily up from behind him and drive her tent peg through his head (4:21). Robert Alter has further argued that the Judges 4 description of Jael is redolent with the language of sex. Jael is said, for example, to "come" to Sisera, and this verb *bw'* can often be used in sexual contexts.[116] Similarly, as Niditch points out, the adverb "stealthily" (*l'ṭ, lṭ*), which describes the way in which Jael sneaks up on Sisera, is otherwise used in Ruth 3:7 to describe how Ruth comes secretly to Boaz in the night for sexual intercourse.[117] Jael's tent-peg weapon, moreover, is "unmistakably phallic."[118] Yet note that in the way the Judges 4 story is recounted, all this sexual language comes *before* or *during* Jael's murder of Sisera. Conversely, in the prototype of Judges 4, Judges 5, the sexual language Niditch identifies in verse 27 *follows* Jael's act of violence. Judges 4:21, that is, seems almost to portray in microcosm the very phenomenon I have been describing: in texts where mythological imagery becomes obscured in favor of historical representations, the Canaanite depictions that assign *primacy* to Anat's role as a ruthless and mighty warrior over her role as a seductress give way to portrayals more in keeping with the norms of Israelite culture. In such portrayals, the society's convictions about a woman's appropriate gender roles come to the fore so that the *initial* and *primary* focus of Judg 4:21 becomes Jael's role as a seductress.

This primary stress on a woman's sensuality, even within a context that otherwise seems militaristic, manifests itself in several other passages in the Hebrew Bible, for example, in passages from the Song of Songs. In Cant 4:4, the woman on whom that poem focuses is extolled by comparing her neck to the tower of David on which thousands of warriors' shields hang. Elsewhere, the woman's looks are compared to the spectacle of an army and its banners (6:4, 10) and her entire body is likened to the kind of defensive wall that surrounded Israelite cities and towns (8:9–10). Her breasts are further described as that wall's towers.[119] All these evocations are reminiscent of the Egyptian New Kingdom descriptions that likened Anat to a shield and to a part of the pharaoh's war chariot. Yet the purposes of these seemingly analogous descriptions are completely different. The comparisons between Anat and the pharaoh's weapons of war were meant to evoke the militaristic power and might of the goddess so as to ascribe similar attributes to the weapons. The woman in the Song of Songs, however, is compared with a wall and towers, not to commend the might of these fortifications, but in order to celebrate *her* extraordinary physique: her neck is tall and regal; her breasts are large and firm. The point is to praise qualities such as beauty and sensuality that are traditionally associated with women in Israelite culture. Again, we see here a radical reinterpretation of older Anat traditions.

A text from the prophetic corpus—Isa 42:13–14—illustrates one final way in which Israelite tradition could reinterpret the notion that women could be depicted as actual military heroes during times of conflict and war.[120] In Isa 42:13, we find yet another example of the Bible's many descriptions of Yahweh's march forth as the divine warrior. This text reads:

Yahweh goes forth like a warrior,
Like a seasoned combatant he stirs up zeal.

He shouts, yea, he raises a war cry;
He shows himself mightily against his foes.

What is this cry that Yahweh, the divine warrior, raises in marching forth to war? Katheryn P. Darr has demonstrated—contrary to previous commentators—that the answer to this question is found in the following verse.[121] Yahweh says:

I have long kept silent;
I have been mute; I have restrained myself.
Now, like a travailing woman I will cry out;[122]
I will gasp and pant.

These images seem incongruous. Yahweh as the divine warrior, I have argued above, is always imagined by Israel as male. Yet the battle cry sounded by this *male* God is that of a *woman* gasping and panting as she struggles to give birth. How can this be? The answer is that we have here one final resonance of Canaan's Baal-Anat mythology and its assumption that male and female warrior are linked inextricably. Hence the combination in Isa 42:13–14 of male war god and female battle cry. But because this text has shied so far away from associating the male divine warrior with an actual female counterpart, it assimilates Anat imagery completely into its description of Yahweh. Women's associations with war here all but disappear as the male God Yahweh fights both as Baal and Anat in the battles against Israel's enemies.

NOTES

[1]The poem can be found in Feaver's collection *The Handless Maiden* (London: Jonathan Cape, 1994), 41.

[2]Reading *brq* for the MT's otherwise unknown judge Bedan (*bdn*). This reading is supported by the Septuagint, but note the reservations expressed by P. K. McCarter, *I Samuel* (AB 8; Garden City, NY: Doubleday, 1980), 211. Also note that, although I follow here the Lucianic recension of the Septuagint, as well as the Syriac, in reading Samson for MT *šmwʾl*, Samuel, McCarter again has reservations (*I Samuel*, 211).

[3]See Judg 6:32; 7:1; 8:35.

[4]See, similarly, J. A. Hackett, "In the Days of Jael: Reclaiming the History of Women in Ancient Israel," *Immaculate and Powerful: The Female in Sacred Image and Social Reality* (ed. C. W. Atkinson; C. H. Buchanan; M. R. Miles; Boston: Beacon, 1985), 27; J. C. Exum, "'Mother in Israel': A Familiar Figure Reconsidered," *Feminist Interpretation of the Bible* (ed. L. M. Russell; Philadelphia: Westminster, 1985), 157, n. 13; G. A. Yee, "Introduction: Why Judges?" *Judges and Method: New Approaches in Biblical Studies* (ed. G. A. Yee; Minneapolis: Fortress, 1995), 2.

[5]For standard discussions concerning the date, see the references collected by D. N. Freedman, "Divine Names and Titles in Early Hebrew Poetry," *Pottery, Poetry, and Prophecy: Studies in Early Hebrew Poetry* (Winona Lake, IN: Eisenbrauns, 1980), 83–85; B. Halpern, "The Resourceful Israelite Historian: The Song of Deborah and Israelite Historiography," *HTR* 76 (1983), 379, n. 2; idem, *The First Historians: The Hebrew Bible and History* (San Francisco: Harper & Row, 1988), 102–3, n. 36; and L. E. Stager, "Archaeology, Ecology, and Social History: Background Themes to the Song of Deborah," *VTSup* 40 (Jerusalem Congress Volume, 1986; ed. J. A. Emerton; Leiden: Brill, 1988), 224; also idem, "The Song of Deborah— Why Some Tribes Answered the Call and Others Did Not," *BARev* 15/1 (January/ February 1989), 64, n. 1.

[6]The translation of Judges 5 presents numerous difficulties throughout, in part because of the general difficulties one confronts when translating poetry rather than prose and in part because of the special difficulties encountered in the translation of archaic poetry, which tends to be full of unfamiliar words, idioms, and grammatical forms. Verse 7 presents an excellent illustration of the sorts of difficulties that can arise due to the last problem mentioned, the presence of unfamiliar grammatical forms. Ostensibly, the text seems to contain a first-person utterance by Deborah, "until I arose, O Deborah, till I arose as a mother in Israel." Most commentators,

however, prefer to understand Hebrew *šaqqamtî* as an archaic second-person feminine form, thus translating, "until you arose, O Deborah, till you arose . . ." See,
among others, M. D. Coogan, "A Structural and Literary Analysis of the Song of
Deborah," *CBQ* 40 (1978), 147, n. 21.

[7]On this point, see, similarly, Hackett, "In the Days of Jael," 27; idem, "Wom-
en's Studies and the Hebrew Bible," *The Future of Biblical Studies: The Hebrew Scriptures* (ed. R. E. Friedman and H. G. M. Williamson; Atlanta: Scholars Press, 1987),
156.

[8]Reading *šārê*, "chiefs of," for MT *šāray* with almost all commentators.

[9]"Warrior," that is, in the sense of one who is engaged in warfare; this is not to
claim Deborah as a trained or professional soldier (but then, can we speak of anyone
as a professional soldier in the agriculturally- and pastorally-based economy of pre-
monarchic Israel?). See further G. A. Yee, "By the Hand of a Woman: The Metaphor of the Woman Warrior in Judges 4," *Women, War, and Metaphor: Language and
Society in the Study of the Hebrew Bible* (*Semeia* 61; ed. C. V. Camp and C. R. Fontaine; 1993), 99–132.

[10]Peter C. Craigie, "Some Further Notes on the Song of Deborah," *VT* 22
(1972), 351, n. 7, goes so far as to suggest that in verses 2 and 9, the Hithpael form
of the root *ndb* "may have the specific sense of volunteering for *war*" (emphasis
Craigie's).

[11]The RSV, assuming the existence of a root *prʿ*, "to lead," based on certain
Arabic cognates (see BDB [Oxford: Clarendon, 1980], 828b, s. v. *prʿ* I). The NEB
translates similarly, "For the leaders, the leaders in Israel."

[12]R. G. Boling, *Judges* (AB 6a; Garden City, NY: Doubleday, 1975), 107,
following a proposal made by T. H. Gaster, *Myth, Legend, and Custom in the Old
Testament: A Comparative Study with Chapters from Sir James G. Frazer's Folklore in the
Old Testament* (New York and Evanston: Harper & Row, 1969), 529.

[13]P. C. Craigie, "A Note on Judges V 2," *VT* 18 (1968), 399.

[14]Coogan, "Song of Deborah," 145, n. 11, based on "the apparent ordinal usage
of the root [*prʿ*] in Ugaritic (UT 1086.1); see further UT 471, No. 2113."

[15]The ancient Greek version in question is that of Symmachus, *en tō anakalýpsa-
thai kephalas*. Among English translations, see the JPSV (1917), "When men let grow
their hair in Israel"; the NJPS (1985), "When locks go untrimmed in Israel"; the JB
(1966) and the NJB (1985), "That warriors in Israel unbound their hair."

[16]In addition to my discussion below, see also P. D. Miller, *The Divine Warrior in*

Early Israel (Cambridge, MA: Harvard University Press, 1973), 88–90; B. A. Levine, *Numbers 1–20* (AB 4a; New York: Doubleday, 1993), 230–31.

[17]E. B. Poethig, *The Victory Song Tradition of the Women of Israel* (unpublished Ph.D. dissertation; Union Theological Seminary, 1985); see also Rita J. Burns, "Miriam's Celebration," Chapter 2 in *Has the Lord Indeed Spoken Only Through Moses? A Study of the Biblical Portrait of Miriam* (Atlanta: Scholars Press, 1987), 11–40, although I would note my disagreement with many of the specifics of Burns' interpretation, especially her differentiation of "cultic" versus "secular" victory songs.

[18]*Contra* Joseph Blenkinsopp, "Ballad Style and Psalm Style in the Song of Deborah: A Discussion," *Bib* 42 (1961), 66, who follows Hugo Gressmann, *Die Anfänge Israels* (Göttingen: Vandenhoeck & Ruprecht, 1914), 189, in seeing verse 3 as "the regular opening invocation addressed rhetorically to different categories to pay heed to the hymn of praise or oracle which is to follow."

[19]"The Resourceful Israelite Historian," 384, 396, and 401; *The First Historians,* 87.

[20]See Coogan, "Song of Deborah," 146, n. 13, on translating *ntp,* which ordinarily means "to drip," as "to shake." Alternatively, repoint and read the Niphal of *tpp,* "to shake" (so W. F. Albright, "A Catalogue of Early Hebrew Lyric Poems (Psalm LXVIII)," *HUCA* 33 [1950–51], 20, followed by F. M. Cross, *Canaanite Myth and Hebrew Epic: Essays in the History of the Religion of Israel* [Cambridge, MA, and London: Harvard University Press, 1973], 101, n. 35). BHS proposes two other possibilities, *nāmôgû,* the Niphal of *mwg,* "to melt," or *nāmôṭû,* the Niphal of *mwṭ,* "to shake." Both these readings, however, require undue emendation of the consonantal text.

[21]Reading *nāzollû,* from the root *zll,* "to shake," versus MT *nāzĕlû,* from the root *nzl,* "to drip, flow." See, among others, Boling, *Judges,* 108; Coogan, "Song of Deborah," 146, n. 14; Cross, *Canaanite Myth,* 101, n. 35; M. O'Connor, *Hebrew Verse Structure* (Winona Lake, IN: Eisenbrauns, 1980), 220.

[22]Michael O'Connor, "The Women in the Book of Judges," *HAR* 10 (1986), 282, n. 22, writes, "the vocabulary in these lines is particularly difficult; lines 7ab are virtually conjecture."

[23]Reading *'ōrĕḥôt,* "caravans" (Gen 37:25; Isa 21:13), for MT *'ŏrāḥôt,* "highways," with the versions and with the vast majority of commentators.

[24]Literally "goers on paths."

[25]The term *pĕrāzôn* occurs only here and in verse 11 of Judges 5, and thus any attempt at translation is perilous. Traditionally, scholars (e.g., G. R. Driver, "Prob-

lems in Judges Newly Discussed," *ALUOS* 4 [1962–63], 8–9) have associated the word with Hebrew *pĕrāzâ,* "hamlet, village, open region" (Ezek 38:11; Zech 2:8 [English 2:4]; Esth 9:19), and hence my admittedly paraphrastic rendition, "settlements [or "settlers"] in unwalled hamlets" (see, similarly, in translating verse 11, the analysis of Stager, "Archaeology, Ecology, and Social History," 224–26). Some, however, follow W. F. Albright, *Yahweh and the Gods of Canaan: A Historical Analysis of Two Contrasting Faiths* (Winona Lake, IN: Eisenbrauns, 1968), 49, n. 101, in translating "warriors," based on Papyrus Anastasi 1, 23, line 4. See, for example, Boling, *Judges,* 109; Coogan, "Song of Deborah," 147, n. 20; Craigie, "Further Notes," 350–51. A third alternative is offered by G. Garbini, "**Parzon* 'Iron' in the Song of Deborah?" *JSS* 23 (1978), 23–24, and a fourth by C. Rabin, "Judges V, 2 and the 'Ideology' of Deborah's War," *JJS* 6 (1953), 127.

[26]On retaining the more traditional translation of *ḥdl,* "to cease," rather than adopting the increasingly popular *ḥdl* II, "to grow plump," see, in addition to the standard lexica, Craigie, "Further Notes," 349–50; T. J. Lewis, "The Songs of Hannah and Deborah: *ḤDL*-II ('Growing Plump')," *JBL* 104 (1985), 105–8.

[27]On the form *šaqqamtî* as second-person feminine singular, see above, n. 6.

[28]The phrase '*ad š* in the third line of verse 7 is shortened to the relative *š* alone in line four, and the use of English "until" and its shorter form "till" in my translation is an attempt to reflect this.

[29]I am grateful to Robert G. Henricks, my colleague in the Religion Department at Dartmouth College, for this observation.

[30]For a similar conclusion, although a somewhat different analysis of the prosody, see Coogan, "Song of Deborah," 153–54, 156, 162, 165–66, especially 154, where Coogan writes of his Stanza IA (vv 2–5) and IB (vv 6–8), "there is an equation between the activity of Yahweh and that of Deborah." See also S. G. Dempster, "Mythology and History in the Song of Deborah," *WTJ* 41 (1978), 46–48.

[31]This is an old (nineteenth-century) suggestion, with references (although not approval) to be found in C. F. Burney, *The Book of Judges* (London: Rivingtons, 1920), 85, and in G. F. Moore, *A Critical and Exegetical Commentary on Judges* (ICC; Edinburgh: T. & T. Clark, 1903), 113. Among moderns, see only (to my knowledge) Boling, *Judges,* 95.

[32]"The Resourceful Israelite Historian," 379–401; *The First Historians,* 76–103.

[33]See again Halpern, "The Resourceful Israelite Historian," 379–401; *The First Historians,* 76–103.

[34]W. F. Stinespring and B. O. Long, "Annotations on 2 Samuel," *The New Ox-*

ford Annotated Bible (ed. B. M. Metzger and R. E. Murphy; New York: Oxford University Press, 1991), 414 OT (note on 2 Sam 20:19).

[35]"The Wise Women of 2 Samuel: A Role Model for Women in Early Israel?" *CBQ* 43 (1981), 14–29; see, similarly, P. A. H. de Boer, "The Counsellor," *Wisdom in Israel and in the Ancient Near East* (VTSup 3; *Festschrift H. H. Rowley;* ed. M. Noth and D. W. Thomas; Leiden: Brill, 1955), 60.

[36]Note also in this regard the similar semantic range of *hāmît*, "to destroy," in the first statement and *billaʿ*, "to swallow up," in the second.

[37]Several ancient versions, including the Lucianic and Theodotian recensions and the Targums, reflect an original reading in 2 Sam 14:16 of *naḥălat yhwh rather than *naḥălat ʾĕlōhîm*, making the parallel with 2 Sam 20:19 exact.

[38]"The Wise Women of 2 Samuel," 26–27.

[39]"The Wise Women of 2 Samuel," 27.

[40]The MT here, as all commentators have recognized, is problematic, deviating significantly from the Septuagint and treating the Hiphil *hētammû* as if it were intransitive. The following verse also shows signs of corruption, beginning as it does with the first-person singular *ʾānōkî*, followed by two plural passive participles in construct. P. Kyle McCarter, *II Samuel* (AB 9; Garden City, NY: Doubleday, 1984), 428–30, resolves by emending MT *wkn htmw ʾnky šlmy ʾmwny yśrʾl* to *wbdn htmw ʾšr śmw ʾmwny yśrʾl* and repointing *hētammû* as an interrogative, *hătammû*. These emendations, all based on the Septuagint, yield a translation, "Let them inquire in Abel and in Dan whether that which the trusted ones of Israel ordained has been carried out." McCarter further repoints *ʾĕmûnê*, "trusted ones," to *ʾămônê*, "architects" (see Prov 8:30), ultimately reading, "Let them inquire in Abel and in Dan whether that which the architects of Israel ordained has been carried out." This is an ingenious solution to a problematic text, but perhaps overly ingenious. I have preferred to follow Dominique Barthélemy, "La qualité du Texte Massorétique de Samuel," *The Hebrew and Greek Texts of Samuel* (1980 Proceedings IOSCS, Vienna; ed. E. Tov; Jerusalem: Academon, 1980), 31–33, in eschewing such radical emendations and instead sticking as closely as possible to the MT.

[41]"The Wise Women of 2 Samuel," 28.

[42]Bereshit Rabbah 94, 9, as pointed out by de Boer, "The Counsellor," 60. The midrashic text quotes the wise woman as saying: "Do you seek to destroy a city and myself, who am a mother in Israel?"

[43]In addition to Camp, "The Wise Women of 2 Samuel," 18, see A. Brenner,

The Israelite Woman: Social Role and Literary Type in Biblical Narrative (Sheffield: JSOT Press, 1985), 36.

[44]See above, n. 40, for the translation of 20:19.

[45]See further P. C. Craigie, *The Problem of War in the Old Testament* (Grand Rapids, MI: Eerdmans, 1978), 85–88; P. D. Hanson, "War and Peace in the Hebrew Bible," *Int* 38 (1984), 341–62, especially 347–49; idem, *The People Called: The Growth of Community in the Bible* (San Francisco: Harper & Row, 1986), 3, n. 2, 5.

[46]A. Jepson, "*'emunah*," *TDOT* 1 (ed. G. J. Bolterweck and H. Ringgren; Grand Rapids, MI: Eerdmans, 1974), 316–20.

[47]Note here Halpern's comment that Judges 5 is concerned with an "entity, 'Israel' (5:2, 3, 5, 7 *bis*, 8, 9, 11), which is 'the people of Yhwh' (5:11d, 13b, 3, 5, 23)" ("The Resourceful Israelite Historian," 381; similarly, M. C. Lind, *Yahweh Is a Warrior: The Theology of Warfare in Ancient Israel* [Scottsdale, PA, and Kitchener, Ontario: Herald, 1980], 70). The poem, that is, describes Deborah's actions on behalf of a geographical territory that is conceived of as equivalent to the people who inhabit that territory. Such an understanding corresponds exactly to the biblical sense of the *naḥălat yhwh,* in which the *naḥălâ* is both a plot of ground and the people whose inheritance that ground is. Although, then, neither the phrase *naḥălat yhwh* nor its cognates is used in Judges 5, I am confident that the poem's intent is to depict Deborah as passionately committed to the protection of Yahweh's heritage.

[48]See further de Boer, "The Counsellor," 59, who writes, speaking of Deborah, "'Mother in Israel' means counsellor of the people." Note, moreover, that if we take seriously the tradition's attribution of Judges 5 to Deborah, we see that at least some in Israelite history remembered this woman as a poet, exhibiting skills in wordsmithing not dissimilar to those displayed by her counterpart in Abel.

[49]"The Resourceful Israelite Historian," 379–401; *The First Historians,* 76–103.

[50]"The Wise Women of 2 Samuel," 28. See, similarly, Exum, who writes of Deborah, "A mother in Israel is one who brings liberation from oppression, provides protection, and assures the well-being and security of her people" ("'Mother in Israel,'" 85). Rachel Adler, "'A Mother in Israel': Aspects of the Mother Role in Jewish Myth," *Beyond Androcentrism: New Essays on Women and Religion* (ed. R. M. Gross; Missoula, MT: Scholars Press, 1977), 247, also argues that the phrase *'ēm běyiśrā'ēl,* "a mother in Israel," "connotes powerful protection." Finally, see Dempster: "'Mother' . . . should mean a 'fierce protector and guardian of her people'" ("Song of Deborah," 47).

[51]With Coogan, "Song of Deborah," 143–66, especially 154; P. C. Craigie, "The Song of Deborah and the Epic of Tukulti-Ninurta," *JBL* 88 (1969), 254;

G. Gerleman, "The Song of Deborah in the Light of Stylistics," *VT* 1 (1951), 168–80, especially 171; A. Globe, "The Literary Structure and Unity of the Song of Deborah," *JBL* 93 (1974), 493–512; and Halpern, "The Resourceful Israelite Historian," 379, I presume here the unity of the Judges 5 poem. See, however, Blenkinsopp, "Ballad Style and Psalm Style," 61–76, who argues that, "the unity of the poem is not literary but theological" (p. 62; see also p. 65).

[52]As pointed out by Dempster, "Song of Deborah," 48; Hackett, "In the Days of Jael," 27; idem, "Women's Studies," 156; Miller, *Divine Warrior,* 94–95.

[53]Reading *'ēlî,* "my God," for *'ēlay,* "for me."

[54]Although I have some reservations, I have retained the traditional translation "remnant" for *śārîd.* See, though, Halpern, "The Resourceful Israelite Historian," 385, n. 26; *The First Historians,* 100, n. 6.

[55]On translating the prepositions *l* and *b* as "against" in these two lines, see Stager, "Archaeology, Ecology, and Social History," 226.

[56]Reading *lô* for MT *lî.*

[57]The more traditional interpretation of verses 14–18 sees only six tribes—Ephraim, Benjamin, Machir, Zebulun, Issachar, and Naphtali—as participating in the Israelite-Canaanite battle, while four—Reuben, Gilead, Dan, and Asher—are said to abstain. Stager has provided the best analysis of this supposed split in tribal unity, suggesting that the four tribes who did not go to war refrained because their economic situations (dependence on maritime trade in the case of Asher and Dan, or on specialized pastoralism in the case of Reuben and Gilead) required them to interact closely with their Canaanite neighbors. These tribes could thus not afford—literally—to antagonize Canaan's non-Israelite population. Conversely, Stager argues, the six participating tribes were economically independent (supporting themselves through small-scale village agriculture) and therefore did not fear whatever ramifications might ensue if they engaged in confrontations with the Canaanites. See Stager, "Archaeology, Ecology, and Social History," 221–34; idem, "The Song of Deborah," 62–64.

However, as Halpern particularly points out ("The Resourceful Israelite Historian," 382), there remains a problem here. Unlike Meroz, the tribe or clan cursed in verse 23 for its failure to participate in the Israelite-Canaanite battle, Reuben, Gilead, Asher, and Dan incur no rebuke for their abstinence. Moreover, in verse 13, which describes how "the people of Yahweh came down," the poem sets up the expectation that *all* Israel presents itself for war. In Halpern's understanding, therefore, all ten tribes mentioned in verses 14–18 should be seen as volunteering to fight against Sisera. See further below, n. 58.

[58]Halpern, for example, suggests that Hebrew *lmh* in 5:16 should not be read in

its classical sense of "why" but instead as an older form comprised of the negative particle *l* plus the enclitic particle *mēm* (which has no translation value). This means that rather than describing Reuben's nonparticipation in the battle—"why (*lmh*) did you sit still among the hearths?"—the poem actually indicates Reuben's active involvement: "you did not (*lmh*) sit still among the hearths" ("The Resourceful Israelite Historian," 384).

[59]Missing here are three tribes known from elsewhere in biblical tradition, Judah, Simeon, and Levi. The absence of Levi, an anomalous tribe because of its landless and sacerdotal status, is not necessarily unexpected. Scholars generally assume, however, that the omission of Judah and Simeon is evidence of the great antiquity of Judges 5, demonstrating that the poem dates either from a point prior to these two tribes' incorporation into the tribal unity "Israel" or, at least, from a point before the standard membership of Israel's twelve-tribe league was finalized. The tribal names Machir (presumably for Manasseh) and Gilead (for Gad) also seem to indicate an early date, when tribal identities were more fluid.

[60]Reading *qiddĕmām* for MT *qĕdûmîm,* following the vast majority of commentators (but see Coogan, "Song of Deborah," 150, n. 48).

[61]See, for example, Boling, *Judges,* 116–17; P. C. Craigie, "Three Ugaritic Notes on the Song of Deborah," *JSOT* 2 (1977), 33.

[62]I am grateful to Ehud Ben-Or, my colleague in the Religion Department at Dartmouth College, for this observation. See also G. W. Ahlström, "Judges 5:20 f. and History," *JNES* 36 (1977), 287.

[63]For the translation of this line, see my discussion in Chapter 2 below.

[64]Repointing to read MT *tišlaḥnâ* as *tišlaḥannâ,* a third-person feminine singular form with energic *nûn,* as first proposed by Burney, *Judges,* 153, and followed in turn by F. M. Cross and D. N. Freedman, *Studies in Ancient Yahwistic Poetry* (SBLDS 21; Missoula, MT: Scholars Press, 1975), 19, n. r, and by Coogan, "Song of Deborah," 150–51, n. 52.

[65]The precise location on the head meant by the rare word *raqqâ* is uncertain. See Boling, *Judges,* 98; J. W. H. Bos, "Out of the Shadows: Genesis 38; Judges 4:17–22; Ruth 3," *Reasoning with the Foxes: Female Wit in a World of Male Power* (Semeia 42; ed. J. C. Exum and J. W. H. Bos; 1988), 51.

[66]Hackett, "In the Days of Jael," 23 and 28, finds further evidence of Jael's military characteristics in Judg 5:6. There, the phrase "in the days of Jael" is paralleled by the phrase "in the days of Shamgar ben Anat." This Shamgar, according to Judg 3:31, killed six hundred Philistines with an oxgoad. Because Jael is paired with him, Hackett argues, she should similarly be seen as a powerful fighter. See also

Hackett, "Women's Studies," 157; Yee, "By the Hand of a Woman," 110; and, on Shamgar ben Anat as a military hero, P. C. Craigie, "A Reconsideration of Shamgar ben Anath (Judg 3:31 and 5:6)," *JBL* 91 (1972), 239–40.

[67]On the compositional relationship between Judges 6–8 and Judges 9, see B. Halpern, "The Rise of Abimelek Ben-Jerubbaal," *HAR* 2 (1978), 79–100.

[68]Assuming an identification with modern Tubas. See E. H. Dyck, "Thebez," *ABD* 6 (ed. D. N. Freedman; New York: Doubleday, 1992), 443b. Alternatively, see Halpern's tentative identification of Thebez with Tirzah ("Rise of Abimelek," 80, n. 1).

[69]"Stone for Stone: Retribution in the Story of Abimelech and Shechem," *JSOT* 32 (1985), 45–56.

[70]"A Certain Woman in the Rhetoric of Judges 9," *JSOT* 38 (1987), 33–37.

[71]Reading *Ierobaal* with the Greek instead of the polemical reformulation *yĕrū-bošet* found in the MT. On Jerubbaal as an alternate name for Gideon, see above, n. 3.

[72]The issue of named versus nameless women in Judges is an interesting one and has been particularly well considered by M. Bal, *Death and Dissymmetry: The Politics of Coherence in the Book of Judges* (Chicago: University of Chicago Press, 1988), 43–93, on the namelessness of women in the book of Judges in general, and 217–24, on the namelessness of the woman of Thebez in particular; by A. Brenner, "Introduction," *A Feminist Companion to Judges* (ed. A. Brenner; The Feminist Companion to the Bible 4; Sheffield: Sheffield Academic Press, 1993), 10–14; by J. C. Exum, "Feminist Criticism: Whose Interests Are Being Served?" *Judges and Method,* 75–86; and by C. Meyers, "The Hannah Narrative in Feminist Perspective," *"Go to the Land I Will Show You": Studies in Honor of Dwight W. Young* (ed. J. Coleson and V. Matthews; Winona Lake, IN: Eisenbrauns, 1994), 120–22 (reprinted as "Hannah and her Sacrifice: Reclaiming Female Agency," *A Feminist Companion to Samuel and Kings* [ed. A. Brenner; The Feminist Companion to the Bible 5; Sheffield: Sheffield Academic Press, 1994], 96–99). See also my discussion in Chapters 2 and 5 below.

[73]On the relationship between the prose narrative of Judith 1–15 and the poem of 16:1–17, see C. A. Moore, *Judith* (AB 40; Garden City, NY: Doubleday, 1985), 252–57.

[74]See BM Stele 191, pictured in H. Gressmann, *Alterorientalische Texte und Bilder* 2 (Berlin und Leipzig: Walter de Gruyter, 1929), No. 270, and note the comments of W. F. Albright, "The Evolution of the West Semitic Deity 'An-'Anat-'Attâ," *AJSL* 41 (1925), 82 and n. 5; also see the vase of Prince Psammetichus, pictured in

B. Grdseloff, *Les débuts du culte Rechef en Egypte* (Cairo: L'Institut français d'archéologie orientale, 1942), Pl. 5 (opposite p. 28) and Pl. 6 (opposite p. 32).

[75]W. F. Edgerton and J. A. Wilson, *Historical Records of Ramses III* (Studies in Ancient Oriental Civilization 12; Chicago: The University of Chicago Press, 1936), 75; see also *ANET* (3d ed; ed. J. B. Pritchard; Princeton: Princeton University Press, 1969), 250a and n. 18.

[76]W. R. Dawson and T. E. Peet, "The So-Called Poem on the King's Chariot," *JEA* 19 (1933), 169 (verso, lines 12–14); see also *ANET,* 250a and n. 17.

[77]Papyrus Chester Beatty VII, verso i, 8–9. For text and translation, see *Hieratic Papyri in the British Museum. Third Series. Chester Beatty Gift* 1 (ed. A. H. Gardiner; London: British Museum, 1935), 62–63; see also *ANET,* 250a, n. 18; Albright, *Yahweh and the Gods of Canaan,* 129.

[78]The text here actually reads 'nh instead of 'nt, "Anat," but most scholars are certain it is Anat who is meant.

[79]Job 3:8; 41:1; Pss 74:14; 104:26; Isa 27:1.

[80]El is the patriarch of the Ugaritic pantheon and thus, at least metaphorically, is the father of all the gods.

[81]For the reconstruction of the lacunae of the first two lines, see Cross, *Canaanite Myth,* 117, n. 18.

[82]See Lev 21:5; Isa 15:2; Jer 16:6; 41:5; 47:5; 48:37; Mic 1:16.

[83]On the translation of this line, see M. Dietrich and O. Loretz, "šb, šbm, und udn im Kontext von *KTU* 1.3 III 35B–IV 4 und *KTU* 1.83:8," *UF* 14 (1982), 77–81; D. Pardee, "Will the Dragon Never Be Muzzled?" *UF* 16 (1984), 251–55.

[84]Note also in this regard *KTU* 1.83.8–10, which, although broken, most probably refers to Anat (see N. H. Walls, *The Goddess Anat in Ugaritic Myth* [SBLDS 135; Atlanta: Scholars Press, 1992], 176):

> She placed the dragon on high,
> She bound it to the heights of Lebanon.

[85]"Song of Deborah," 33–53; see also R. C. Rasmussen, "Deborah the Woman Warrior," *Anti-Covenant: Counter-Reading Women's Lives in the Hebrew Bible* (ed. M. Bal; JSOTSup 81; Bible and Literature Series 22; Sheffield: Almond, 1989), 79–93.

[86]This thesis, originally associated with the work of George E. Mendenhall

("The Hebrew Conquest of Palestine," *BA* 25 [1962], 66–87) and Norman K. Gott-wald (*The Tribes of Yahweh: A Sociology of the Religion of Liberated Israel, 1250–1050 B.C.E.* [Maryknoll, NY: Orbis, 1979]), now has several spokespersons, perhaps the most ardent among them being William G. Dever, who has written on the topic repeatedly. See, for example, W. G. Dever, "The Israelite Settlement in Canaan: New Archaeological Models," Chapter 2 in *Recent Archaeological Discoveries and Biblical Research* (Seattle and London: The University of Washington Press, 1990), 37–84; idem, "Archaeological Data on the Israelite Settlement: A Review of Two Recent Works," *BASOR* 284 (1991), 77–90; idem, "Unresolved Issues in the Early History of Israel: Toward a Synthesis of Archaeological and Textual Reconstructions," *The Bible and the Politics of Exegesis: Essays in Honor of Norman K. Gottwald on His Sixty-Fifth Birthday* (ed. D. Jobling; P. L. Day; G. T. Sheppard; Cleveland, OH: Pilgrim, 1991), 195–208; idem, "Israel, History of (Archaeology and the 'Conquest')," *ABD* 3, 545b–58b; idem, "Cultural Continuity, Ethnicity in the Archaeological Record, and the Question of Israelite Origins," ErIsr 24 (Abraham Malamat volume; 1993), 22*–33*.

[87]Dempster, "Song of Deborah," 46.

[88]The pertinent texts are *KTU* 1.4.1.16–18; 1.4.5.6–9; 1.4.7.29–35; 1.5.5.6–8; 1.19.1.42–44; *Ugaritica* 5, 3.3–4; see also EA 147.13–15.

[89]See E. Lipiński, "Juges 5, 4–5 et Psaume 68, 8–11," *Bib* 48 (1967), 185–206.

[90]On translating the root *ntp* as "to shake," see above, n. 20.

[91]The epithet is widely attested at Ugarit. See, for example, in the major texts of the Baal-Anat cycle, *KTU* 1.2.4.8, 29; 1.3.2.40; 1.3.3.38; 1.3.4.4,6; 1.4.3.11, 18; 1.4.5.60; 1.5.2.7. On the interchange of *b* and *p* in Hebrew *'rbwt* (for original **'rpwt*), see M. Dahood, *Psalms* II (AB 17; Garden City, NY: Doubleday, 1968), 136 (as pointed out by Dempster, "Song of Deborah," 46, n. 76).

[92]See "Deborah and Anat: A Study of Poetic Imagery," *ZAW* 90 (1978), 374–81. The four additional points are: (1) one of Anat's standard epithets at Ugarit, *ybmt limm*, which Craigie believes refers to the goddess as a leader or patron of warriors, is reminiscent of Deborah's role as "a mother in Israel"; (2) a second Anat epithet from Ugarit, "Mistress of Dominion" (*b'lt drkt*), is echoed in the battle cry found in Judg 5:21, which Craigie ascribes to Deborah and translates as, "You shall dominate (*tidrĕkî*), O my soul, mightily"; (3) Anat, according to a third Ugaritic epithet, is called a maiden (*rḥm*), a description that Craigie—based on Judg 5:30—believes fits the characterization of Deborah in Judges 5 (see further below, Chapter 3, n. 8); (4) Anat may be associated with a retinue of fighting stars in Ugaritic mythology, and, according to Judg 5:20, the stars are a part of Yahweh's army that fights along-side Deborah's troops. On this last point, see also Craigie, "Three Ugaritic Notes," 35–36; similarly, Dempster, "Song of Deborah," 50.

Yet, despite my overall sympathies with Craigie's thesis, I find that each of these four points presents difficulties. The translation of Anat's title *ybmt limm,* understood by Craigie as describing Anat as a patron of warriors, is, for example, a matter of dispute. Indeed, Craigie himself refuses to offer an etymology or translation of *ybmt,* arguing "it is safest simply to use the transliteration *ybmt,* understanding that it functions in some way to point to Anat's status as an independent female" ("Deborah and Anat," 377). As for *limm,* Walls has shown that Craigie's translation, "warriors," depends solely on an interpretation of an obscure mythological scene in which Craigie believes human warriors (*limm*) invade Anat's house (*KTU* 1.3 2.7–8). Most other commentators, however, translate *limm* in this passage as "humans" and see it as a reference to the people of a particular town against which Anat wages war. See Walls, *The Goddess Anat,* 97. And, even if Craigie is correct in interpreting *ybmt limm* as a term describing Anat as military leader, it is still difficult to agree with him that this term is parallel to Deborah's title "a mother in Israel," given the multivalent meanings I have determined are implicit in the latter phrase. The parallel Craigie adduces between Anat's epithet "Mistress of Dominion" (*b'lt drkt*) and the battle cry *tidrĕkî* is also suspect since most scholars prefer to derive the verb *tidrĕkî* in Judg 5:21 from the root *drk,* "to march, trample," rather than from Craigie's *drk,* "to dominate." Boling, for example, translates 5:21 as addressing Deborah and saying: "You shall trample the throat of the mighty" (*Judges,* 113). As for the third Anat epithet Craigie discusses, Anat as *rḥm,* "maiden," it is problematic that this term is nowhere used *directly* to describe Deborah (although it may well allude to her; see again, as above, Chapter 3, n. 8). Finally, it is very difficult to regard Anat as associated with an army of stars since there is only one clear context where Anat and the word *kbkbm,* "stars," appear together (*KTU* 1.3.2.41), and that passage has to do with the stars showering rain on Anat as she undertakes ablutions, not with the stars fighting alongside Anat as she wages war.

[93] "Song of Deborah," 49.

[94] See also the brief but suggestive comments of R. Alter, "From Line to Story in Biblical Verse," *Poetics Today* 4 (1983), 633; also, idem, *The Art of Biblical Poetry* (New York: Basic Books, 1985), 46; cf. J. Glen Taylor, "The Song of Deborah and Two Canaanite Goddesses," *JSOT* 23 (1982), 99–108, who identifies Jael as an Astarte figure.

[95] "Eroticism and Death in the Tale of Jael," *Gender and Difference in Ancient Israel* (ed. P. L. Day; Minneapolis: Fortress, 1989), 43–57; *War in the Hebrew Bible: A Study in the Ethics of Violence* (New York and Oxford: Oxford University Press, 1993), 113–17; see also the brief comments of D. N. Fewell and D. M. Gunn, "Controlling Perspectives: Women, Men, and the Authority of Violence in Judges 4 & 5," *JAAR* 58 (1990), 404, and the more lengthy analysis of Y. Zakovitch, "Sisseras Tod," *ZAW* 93 (1981), 364–74.

[96] "Eroticism and Death," 47; *War in the Hebrew Bible,* 114.

[97]"Eroticism and Death," 50.

[98]See Walls, *The Goddess Anat,* especially Chapter 4, "Violence and Passion," 161–215.

[99]"The Bow of Aqhat: The Meaning of a Mythological Theme," *Orient and Occident: Essays Presented to Cyrus H. Gordon on the Occasion of His Sixty-Fifth Birthday* (AOAT 22; ed. H. A. Hoffner; Neukirchen-Vluyn: Neukirchener Verlag; Kevelaer: Butzon & Bercker, 1973), 71–80.

[100]See, for example, in the Hebrew Bible, Prov 7:4; Cant 4:9, 10, 12; 5:1, 2. Of even greater note is the apocryphal book of Tobit, where the marriage of Tobias and Sarah is blessed by her father Raguel with a formula strikingly similar to Anat's words to Aqhat: "You are her brother and she is your sister" (Tob 7:11). Subsequently, Tobias refers to Sarah as "sister" (8:4); his father Tobit also calls his wife Anna "my sister" (5:21), and Raguel calls his wife Edna "sister" (7:15); for discussion, see J. Boswell, *Same-Sex Unions in Premodern Europe* (New York: Villard Books, 1994), 125–28. Finally, for the usage of "sister" and "brother" elsewhere in the ancient Near East, especially in Egyptian love poetry, see M. V. Fox, *The Song of Songs and the Ancient Egyptian Love Songs* (Madison, WI: The University of Wisconsin Press, 1985), xii–xiii, 8, 12–13, 136; J. B. White, *A Study of the Language of Love in the Song of Songs and Ancient Egyptian Poetry* (SBLDS 38; Missoula, MT: Scholars Press, 1978), 95–96, 130. Cf. H. H. P. Dressler, "The Metamorphosis of a Lacuna: Is *at.aḥ.wan . . .* a Proposal of Marriage?" *UF* 11 (1979), 211–17.

[101]In addition to my comments below, see B. Lindars, "Deborah's Song: Women in the Old Testament," *BJRL* 65 (1983), 174.

[102]"The Hand of Judith," *CBQ* 25 (1963), 94–110; the nine verses are Jdt 8:33; 9:9, 10; 12:4; 13:4, 14, 15; 15:10; and 16:5.

[103]"The Hand of Judith," 95.

[104]L. Alonso-Schökel, "Narrative Structures in the Book of Judith," *Protocol Series of the Eleventh Colloquy of the Center for Hermeneutical Studies in Hellenistic and Modern Culture* (ed. W. Wuellner; Berkeley, CA: Center for Hermeneutical Studies in Hellenistic and Modern Culture, 1975), 12.

[105]See, for example, her *Artistry and Faith in the Book of Judith* (SBLDS 70; Chico, CA: Scholars Press, 1983).

[106]"Tradition and Convention in the Book of Judith," *Semeia* 28 (1983), 60; see also Alonso-Schökel, "Judith," 15.

[107]The bibliography on archaeological materials is extensive, but of particular

note are the survey articles of W. G. Dever, "The Contribution of Archaeology to the Study of Canaanite and Early Israelite Religion," and J. S. Holladay, "Religion in Israel and Judah Under the Monarchy: An Explicitly Archaeological Approach," both in *Ancient Israelite Religion: Essays in Honor of Frank Moore Cross* (ed. P. D. Miller; P. D. Hanson; S. D. McBride; Philadelphia: Fortress, 1987), 209–47 and 249–99 respectively; also see W. G. Dever, "Material Remains and the Cult in Ancient Israel: An Essay in Archaeological Systematics," *The Word of the Lord Shall Go Forth: Essays in Honor of David Noel Freedman in Celebration of His Sixtieth Birthday* (ed. C. L. Meyers and M. O'Connor; Winona Lake, IN: Eisenbrauns, 1983), 571–87.

[108]Cross, *Canaanite Myth,* 343–46.

[109]W. G. Dever, "The Silence of the Text: An Archaeological Commentary on 2 Kings 23," *Scripture and Other Artifacts: Essays on the Bible and Archaeology in Honor of Philip J. King* (ed. M. D. Coogan; J. C. Exum; L. E. Stager; Louisville, KY: Westminster/John Knox, 1994), 143–68; S. Ackerman, *Under Every Green Tree: Popular Religion in Sixth-Century Judah* (HSM 46; Atlanta: Scholars Press, 1992), 212–17.

[110]See especially Dan 7:9–14 and the various studies of that passage by J. J. Collins: *The Apocalyptic Vision of the Book of Daniel* (HSM 16; Missoula, MT: Scholars Press, 1977), 96–104; "Apocalyptic Genre and Mythic Allusions in Daniel," *JSOT* 21 (1981), 83–100; *Daniel, with an Introduction to Apocalyptic Literature* (Forms of the Old Testament Literature 20; Grand Rapids, MI: Eerdmans, 1984), 77–78; *The Apocalyptic Imagination: An Introduction to the Jewish Matrix of Christianity* (New York: Crossroad, 1987), 79–83; *Daniel: A Commentary on the Book of Daniel* (Hermeneia; ed. F. M. Cross; Minneapolis: Fortress, 1993), 286–94.

[111]Here, I note I break with the analysis of Dempster, whose work I have heretofore embraced. He regards the mythological elements he identifies in Judges 5 as "denuded" ("Song of Deborah," 52), meaning that for him the historical is completely in the ascendent. In fact, Dempster goes so far as to suggest that the attitude of Judges 5 toward its Canaanite mythic antecedents is "satirical" ("Song of Deborah," 53), in that the mythological characters Baal and Anat are missing from Sisera's Canaanite retinue, and thus they, at least literarily, are rendered dead. Conversely, because Yahweh, Deborah, and Jael are present in the historical moment, they are alive or, to use Dempster's word, "real" ("Song of Deborah," 53). As my comments in the text should indicate, I disagree; see also the criticisms of Dempster voiced by Rasmussen, "Deborah the Woman Warrior," 87.

[112]This argument concerning the demythologization of Canaanite narrative in an Israelite context is heavily dependent on the work of Cross, who has analyzed the "Song of the Sea" in Exod 15:1–18 in a similar manner; see "The Song of the Sea and Canaanite Myth," Chapter 6 in *Canaanite Myth,* 112–44.

[113]Contrast, however, the views of Hackett, "In the Days of Jael," 26–28; idem,

"Women's Studies," 156–57; C. Meyers, *Discovering Eve: Ancient Israelite Women in Context* (New York and Oxford: Oxford University Press, 1988), 174; Yee, "By the Hand of a Woman," 111–12.

[114]For further discussion of Judith's status as widow and what this means for her ability to speak out publicly, see Chapter 5.

[115]Again, as in n. 62 above, I am grateful to Ehud Ben-Or, my colleague in the Religion Department at Dartmouth College, for this observation.

[116]"From Line to Story," 635; *Biblical Poetry,* 49; for a catalogue of such usages of *bwʾ,* see O. Margalith, "More Samson Legends," *VT* 36 (1986), 400; also, A. Reinhartz, "Samson's Mother: An Unnamed Protagonist," *JSOT* 55 (1992), 34 and n. 37 on that page.

[117]"Eroticism and Death," 45–46; *War in the Hebrew Bible,* 114. See also, on *pātaḥ,* "to open," as having sexual connotations in 4:19 and 20, Fewell and Gunn, "Controlling Perspectives," 393.

[118]Fewell and Gunn, "Controlling Perspectives," 394.

[119]Further on this imagery and its militaristic evocations, see C. Meyers, "Gender Imagery in the Song of Songs," *HAR* 10 (1987), 213–15, 217–21; idem, *Discovering Eve,* 178–79.

[120]See also K. Baltzer, "Women and War in Qohelet 7:23–8:1a," *HTR* 80 (1987), 127–32.

[121]"Like Warrior, like Woman: Destruction and Deliverance in Isaiah 42:10–17," *CBQ* 49 (1987), 567.

[122]For this translation, see Darr, "Like Warrior, like Woman," 568–70.

Chapter 2

⁓⁓⁓⁓

"Most Blessed of Women"

JAEL, WOMEN, AND THE CULT

If to avenge the shame of Israel
We are not able, as was Jael of old,
To pierce the impious heads of God's foes,
We can at least lay down our lives for him. . . .

FROM THE PLAY *ATHALIE,*
BY JEAN RACINE[1]

In Jean Racine's 1691 play *Athalie,* an anonymous Levite woman, protesting the reign of Judah's renegade Queen Athaliah, considers what actions she might take in her fight against the illicit monarch. Her answer, as quoted above, is to volunteer herself as martyr, offering to lay down her life for her God. She laments, though, that it is not enough that she only has her life to offer, that, unlike "Jael of old," she is not able to do that which is truly heroic and "to avenge the shame of Israel" by piercing "the impious heads of God's foes."

When I first came across them, I was surprised by these lines, finding it curious that among all of the women of ancient Israelite lore, Racine had chosen Jael to invoke as the Levite woman's paradigm of a hero.[2] Jael, after all, is mentioned only three times in the entire Hebrew Bible, in Judg 4:17–22; 5:6; and 5:24–27, and in all three of these texts, and in the Judges 5 passages in particular, she is arguably overshadowed by Deborah, her cohort in the Israelite battle against Sisera. Yet even though Deborah can be said to dominate, for example, in the first twenty-three verses of Judges 5, I hope that my discussion in the last chapter indicated that it is hardly the poem's intent to slight Jael. Rather, in verse 24, the text follows its lengthy celebration of Deborah's delivering of her people by lauding not Deborah but Jael with the accolade "most blessed of women." Racine's instincts, it turns out, ring true in the end, as it is surely this epithet describing "most blessed" Jael that stands behind the homage to which the Levite woman gives voice in *Athalie*.

As Judges 5 continues, it elaborates on its description of "most blessed" Jael, first, in verse 25, by depicting her as a woman perfect in her embodiment of attributes such as nurture and generosity. The text devotes only a few lines to this part of its portrayal, but the economy of the poem's language in no way detracts from its point. Indeed, quite the opposite is the case, as the verse's stark phrasing makes Jael's magnanimity stand out all the more vividly. The depiction is initially a matter of one simple act: Sisera, fleeing from the scene of his army's defeat, comes to Jael's tent and asks for water. I envision here a tired and demoralized soldier who leans gasping against the frame of Jael's tent and pants out his request for the humblest of beverages. Jael's response is to bring milk, a far richer drink, and also ghee, a yogurt-like dairy product, in order to give Sisera sustenance.[3] The ghee, moreover, is brought to Sisera in a "lordly" (*'addîrîm*) bowl. Although the poem offers no further description of this vessel, the single word *'addîrîm* seems meant to convey much. I picture a dish that is not a part of everyday use but is in some way precious, either because it is made of some rare material or because it is decorated in such a way that marks it as reserved for special occasions.[4] This implies that Jael, through her magnanimous response to Sisera's most basic of requests, makes a special occasion of the war leader's visit, providing him with the only hints of support and compassion that he has seen in his long day of battle. We can almost understand Jael acting here as a mother to Sisera's overwhelmed child,[5] and, in fact, there is a later Jewish midrash that imagines that the milk Jael gives to Sisera was suckled by him from her breasts.[6] While there is, to be sure, no basis for such a reading in the poem, the midrash is still accurate to the degree that it has sensed in the text the same attributes of Jael as have I: her extraordinary willingness to nurture and sustain the Canaanite warrior Sisera as he arrives desperate and defeated at her tent.

What the poem ultimately wishes to celebrate, though, when it calls Jael "most blessed of women" is the deed the Levite woman of *Athalie* so admires: Jael's brutal murder of Sisera in verses 26–27. Yet, as I demonstrated in the last chapter, Israelite tradition believed that this portrait of Jael as a "most blessed" assassin need not stand in conflict with a portrayal of "most blessed" Jael as a nurturer and sustainer. In fact, by immediately juxtaposing its description of Jael's magnanimous hospitality with its depiction of Jael's murderous act, Judges 5 indicates in shorthand the basis of my argument in Chapter 1: that in Israelite thinking, especially in texts closely informed by Canaan's Anat mythology, attributes such as compassion more typically associated with the female sphere could go hand-in-hand with the sorts of bellicose violence more usually ascribed to men. The question Vicki Feaver raises in her 1994 poem "Judith"— "how a good woman can murder?"—would have been rendered by her Judges 5 counterpart quite differently, with the biblical poet asking, "can we not expect that a good woman might kill?" Certainly in the portrait of Jael found in verses 24–27, the answer that is given is "yes."

This affirmative answer, however, raises in turn new questions, particularly questions about the poem's understanding of Sisera's motivations. If ancient Israelite tradition expected that a "most blessed" woman like Jael could manifest her blessedness through both compassion and murder, and if I was correct in Chapter 1 in arguing that Israelite tradition inherited this expectation from the Anat lore of its Canaanite ancestors, then one might reasonably have supposed that Judges 5 would portray Sisera—who is a Canaanite, after all—as cognizant of this possibility. But there is not even a hint or suggestion that when Sisera comes to Jael's tent, he has any suspicions about the ways in which this apparently good-hearted woman might turn against him. Instead, the poem shows Sisera as readily accepting Jael's hospitality.

How to explain this willing acquiescence? Judges 5 seems to provide no clue, as at this point the stark language of verses 24–27 appears to impede rather than enhance interpretation, threatening to leave questions about Sisera's apparent lapse in judgment unanswered and concerns about the logic of his actions unresolved. Yet, while it is within the license of poetry to tolerate such ambiguity, this sort of obfuscation is hardly the stuff of Judges 4, which, as I noted in the last chapter, is not only literarily dependent on Judges 5 but also aims for a prose rendition of the poem that is as pedantic and precise as possible.[7] Such an exacting interpretation can hardly allow the question of Sisera's ready assent to dangle, and, indeed, the prose redactor was so concerned to resolve the issue that he provided *two* explanations for Sisera's failure to perceive the danger inherent in Jael's hospitality. The prose's first and more explicit theory is found in 4:17, where the redactor suggests that there was a peace treaty that existed between the Kenite clan of Heber, who is identified as Jael's husband, and Jabin, the Canaanite king of Hazor, under whose auspices the prose narrator describes Sisera as fighting. Thus, when Sisera comes to Jael's tent in 4:18, he arrives without fear for he believes he enters into a space that is held by a political ally.

This explanation, however, will hardly suffice. For example, if we follow 4:17 in identifying the Kenites and Canaanites as political allies, then how do we explain 4:22, which shows Barak entering into Jael's tent just as willingly and incautiously as Sisera did? Would not the logic of the peace treaty suggest that this *Israelite* general should be wary of a *Canaanite* sympathizer? Similarly, how explain 4:21, where the narrator describes Jael as murdering Sisera and thus utterly violating the terms of the Kenite-Canaanite peace accord without offering *any* comment on the traitorous nature of her act? Should not narrative consistency require—at a minimum—that the text admit Jael's contradictory displays of allegiance? The peace treaty, it would appear, is no more than a clumsy fiction, intruding into the Judges 4 story imperfectly and only temporarily. When it conveniently resolves a crux, in verses 17–18, it is introduced, but by verses 21–22, when its presence becomes problematic, it is forgotten or ignored.

Our attention thus shifts to the second of the two explanations put forward by Judges 4 to account for Sisera's seemingly ill-conceived acts. This explanation has been most cogently analyzed by Benjamin Mazar.[8] What Mazar understands is that Jael is regarded by the authors of Judges 4 as a religious functionary; her tent is likewise imagined as a sacred space. According, then, to this argument in the prose, the reason Sisera flees unfearingly to Jael's tent in 4:18 is that he considers it to be a place of religious sanctuary.[9]

As I will discuss more thoroughly below, I concur with Mazar's conclusions in regard to Judges 4 and in fact believe there is even more evidence than he himself puts forward in support of his thesis. Still, Mazar's discussion provides no answer to the question that I originally raised: why does the *poetic* tradition in Judges 5 portray Sisera as acting so rashly in his coming to Jael's tent? In Section I of this chapter, it is my intention to respond to this apparent conundrum by suggesting that, despite its admittedly oblique phrasing, Judges 5 *shares* with Judges 4 the notion that Jael serves as a religious functionary and that her tent marks a sacred spot. Indeed, in line with Baruch Halpern's description of the literary dependency of the prose upon the poem, I will propose that Judges 4 *derives* its understanding of the sanctified status of Jael and of her tent from its Judges 5 antecedent.[10] Ironically, moreover, I will locate the clue that generates these conclusions precisely within the sparse and sparing language of Judges 5 that initially seemed so determined to obscure. I will contend that it is with the use of only one word, "Kenite," in verse 24, that Judges 5 signals its convictions regarding the cultic role of Jael and the sanctity of her tent.

But even though I will maintain that the poem's convictions regarding Jael's religious status and the sanctified character of her tent are the source for these motifs as they are found in Judges 4, I will ultimately argue that the two texts differ significantly in their presentations of the nature and scope of Jael's cultic authority. Describing and explaining these differences—and also the differences I find between the presentations of Deborah as a religious functionary in Judges 4 and Judges 5— will occupy my attention in this chapter's Section II. Section III will then expand on this discussion of differences by looking at the ways Judges presents the actions of three other women who play a religious role within its pages and by considering as well the ways in which women religious agents are presented elsewhere in the biblical record, especially in texts from the prophetic books. These various texts will show that, despite their occasional nods to the notion of female religious leadership, the Bible's authors generally prefer to minimize women's roles in the Yahwistic cult and, consequently, may drive women to seek opportunities for religious expression elsewhere, beyond the purview of biblical tradition.

I. JAEL AS A CULTIC FUNCTIONARY

Mazar's conclusions regarding the Judges 4 understanding of Jael as a religious functionary and of her tent as a sanctified space derive from two major pieces of evidence. The first, which concerns Jael's role as a cultic official, considers the lineage of Heber, the man who is named in 4:17 and 21 as Jael's husband and who is identified in verses 11 and 17 as a member of a small ethnic group known as the Kenites. Earlier in the book of Judges, these same Kenites are described in 1:16, where it is recounted that some among the Kenite community had joined with Israelites who were members of the tribe of Judah in moving from the "city of palms"—Jericho, just north of the Dead Sea—south into the Negev wilderness and into the vicinity of Arad. Judges 4:11 continues this tale by relating how Heber's clan had separated from this Arad-based Kenite group and had migrated to the far north of Israel, encamping in the tribal territory of Naphtali, near Elon-Bezaanannim in the vicinity of Kedesh. In both texts, the forefather of these migratory Kenites is identified as Hobab, who is further described as the father-in-law of Moses.[11]

The name of Moses' father-in-law, however, is a matter of some confusion in the biblical text. The dominant tradition, in Exod 3:1; 4:18; and 18:1–27, identifies the father-in-law as Jethro. But in Exod 2:16–22, the father-in-law is assigned the name Reuel, and, although the Hebrew is ambiguous, Num 10:29–32 seems to take the father-in-law's name to be Reuel as well. Hobab, in that text, is identified as Reuel's son.[12] In the Numbers text, moreover, as well as in the various Exodus passages, Moses' in-laws are identified as Midianites rather than Kenites.

Yet, despite these ambiguities regarding name and ethnicity, the traditions regarding Moses' in-laws are practically unanimous concerning one item: that Moses' father-in-law was a priest. It is this datum that Mazar takes as the narratives' salient point. Indeed, while it is typical of tales that have their basis in oral tradition for details regarding names, ethnicity, and setting to change over time, as stories are handed down through multiple recitations, those elements considered to be the most crucial characteristics of a narrative do tend to remain fixed throughout the process of transmission.[13] The priestly status of Moses' father-in-law, because it seems to be just such a crucial element, is thus not to be ignored. In fact, I would tend to stress the father-in-law's priestly status even more than does Mazar, for while he confines his discussion to the priestly portrait of Reuel found in Exod 2:16–22, I would consider as equally telling the priestly attributes of Jethro detailed in Exod 3:1; 4:18; and, especially, 18:1–27.[14] Two points in the Exodus 18 story strike me as particularly significant. First, in verse 12, Jethro offers sacrifices to Israel's deity and then comes with Moses and Aaron, Israel's two priestly forefathers, along with Israel's elders, to eat bread "in the presence of God" (*lipnê hā'ĕlōhîm*).[15] This episode is redolent with the imagery of cult and intimations of Jethro's priestly status (although we should note that in describing Israel's earliest history, the biblical authors do not necessarily regard the offering of sacrifice and the eating "in the presence of God" as prerogatives of priests alone).[16] Jethro also appears as a priest

or religious specialist in the next section of Exodus 18, where he coun-
sels Moses, who has been acting as Israel's sole priestly functionary since
the Israelites' escape from Egypt, regarding the establishment of a larger
cadre of cultic officials.

When coupled with Judges' genealogical information tracing Heber's
ancestry back to Hobab, the tales of the priestly status of Moses' father-
in-law suggest to Mazar, as they do to me, the conviction of Judges 4
that Heber, too, has the status of a priest. Indeed, because of the ancient
Israelite understanding that the priestly office was hereditary, we have
no choice but to assume that by associating Heber with Hobab, the
redactor of Judges 4 meant to portray Heber the Kenite as some kind of
religious official.

Mazar further proposes that by virtue of her marriage into this
priestly family, Jael, Heber's wife, is also meant to be understood as a
member of the clan's religious aristocracy. I agree, although again I
would assign much more weight than does Mazar to a text he discusses
only briefly and in a footnote,[17] Exod 4:24–26.[18] This is the narrative
that describes how Yahweh, who had previously designated Moses as
the deliverer who was to lead the Israelites out of their Egyptian bondage, now confronts Moses in a lodging place on Moses' way back to
Egypt and seeks to kill him.[19] Although Yahweh's reasons for this murderous attempt remain unclear, what is certain, and important for our
purposes, is that the deity's intent is foiled by Moses' wife, Zipporah,
the daughter of Reuel/Jethro/Hobab. Zipporah thwarts Yahweh's plan
by circumcising Gershom, her son by Moses, and by then touching a
flint to either Gershom's or Moses' genitals (euphemistically called in
Hebrew "his feet" [*raglâw*]).[20] Most commentators presume that since
Zipporah was earlier described as circumcising Gershom, the second set
of genitals she is said to touch with her knife must belong to Moses,
meaning that she either symbolically or perhaps actually circumcises her
husband. Commentators also tend to assume that the words Zipporah
utters after performing this act—"You are surely a bridegroom of blood
[or a "bloody bridegroom"] to me" (4:25)—are addressed to Moses.[21]
Regardless, though, of how one interprets the specifics of this passage,
it is beyond doubt that all sorts of ritual imagery are generally present:
the act of circumcision itself; the idea that Yahweh requires from Gershom and from Moses (at least metaphorically) a blood offering; the
highly formal and even formulaic statement that is uttered once the circumcision has been performed. Zipporah, as the agent who performs

the circumcision(s), who makes the blood offering, and who intones the liturgical pronouncement, should thus be understood as some sort of religious specialist.[22] This suggests that other women among the clan of Reuel/Jethro/Hobab might also serve as cultic functionaries, and hence we can conclude, following Mazar, that by virtue of her marriage to Heber, Jael plays such a role at the time of Israel's battle with Sisera.

In the second part of his thesis, Mazar turns his attention to Jael's tent and especially to its location at Elon-Bezaanannim ('ēlôn bĕṣaʿănannîm), "the oak in Zaanannim," which is near Kedesh (4:11). Mazar contends that this site is a sanctified space. He especially notes that the Hebrew term for oak ('ēlôn), when appended with a surname, "always refers to a holy tree."[23] In Gen 12:6, for example, legend describes how Abram (later Abraham) and his wife Sarai (later Sarah) encamp at "the oak of Moreh" ('ēlôn môreh) that is at or near Shechem. There, according to 12:7, Yahweh appears, which demonstrates that the oak of Moreh marks a sacred spot. Moreover, the name of the oak, môreh, is derived from the verb hôrâ, which means "to teach" or "to direct," indicating that what sanctifies this oak is that it stands at a site where divine teachings or directions are revealed.[24]

Other sacred oaks in Genesis include the oak of Mamre, which is near Hebron (Gen 13:18; 14:13; 18:1, 4, 8), and the oak of mourning, which is below Bethel (Gen 35:8).[25] There are also a number of sacred oaks mentioned in the book of Judges. Judges 9:37, for example, makes mention of "the diviners' oak" ('ēlôn mĕʿônĕnîm), whose very name tells us that, like the oak of Moreh, it stands at a place where the will of God is revealed. Another sacred oak is described in Judg 9:6. This text recounts how Abimelech begins his ill-fated monarchy by being made king at "the oak of the pillar" ('ēlôn muṣṣāb) that was in Shechem. The designating of a king was a religious ritual according to Israelite tradition (see especially 1 Sam 9:27–10:8 and 15:35–16:13), meaning that the oak under which Abimelech was enthroned was surely a sacred tree.

Commentators have further suggested that Abimelech's Shechemite oak is also referred to in Gen 35:4, which describes how Jacob buries all the images of foreign gods that belonged to members of his household under "the terebinth that is in Shechem" (hā'ēlâ 'ăšer ʿim šĕkem). To be sure, the tree named in this text is identified as a terebinth and not an oak, but this is not a problem, for the two words used in Hebrew for oak, 'ēlôn and 'allôn, are easily confused with the two words used for terebinth, 'ēlâ and 'allâ.[26] In fact, all four terms are derived from the same biliteral root, '*l*.[27] It is also important to note that the word "god," '*ēl,* is derived from this root. Indeed, this datum serves as final proof of the sacral nature of oaks as well as terebinths and further indicates the correctness of the second part of Mazar's thesis: that in locating Jael's tent under the oak in Zaanannim, the redactor of Judges 4 means to suggest that she is encamped at a sanctified spot.

Mazar rests his case at this point, but I believe there is another piece of evidence that is equally significant in suggesting the religious imagery associated with Jael and with her tent in the Judges 4 text. This is the fact that Judg 4:11 locates Jael's sacred oak in the vicinity of the city of Kedesh. According to Judg 4:6, this particular city of Kedesh is in the tribal territory of Naphtali, and scholars generally agree that it is to be identified with Tell Qades, a site approximately ten kilometers north of Hazor. Commentators, however, also have pointed out that there are problems raised by this equation since, according to 4:17, Sisera is said to have fled *on foot* from the site of the battle with the Israelites to take refuge at the tent of Jael. Yet Tell Qades lies almost eighty kilometers from "Ta'anach by the waters of Megiddo," the location in Issachar where, according to the Judges 5 poem, the battle takes place (5:19).[28] The internal logic of the prose version is somewhat more credible since the prose relocates the battle site from Ta'anach to the region of Mount Tabor (4:14), a more northerly point in Issachar that is only fifty kilometers from Tell Qades/Kedesh. Fifty kilometers, however, is still a formidable distance to have a defeated soldier cover without his horse-drawn chariot.

Why, then, should the prose redactor of Judges 4 so defy topographic logic in order to designate Kedesh as the site of Jael's tent? In his article comparing Judges 4 and Judges 5, Halpern demonstrates that it was mandatory that the prose version of Judges 4 choose some location in Naphtali.[29] This is due again to the phenomenon I have now mentioned several times: the prose's characteristically literal reinterpretation of the poetry, which in this case leads the prose redactor to reject the notion that the reference to the "coming down" of Issachar found in Judg 5:15 indicates that Issachar actually fought in the Israelite-Canaanite battle. Thus Barak, who is most closely identified with the tribe of Issachar in the poem, must be reinterpreted in Judges 4 as being associated with either Naphtali or Zebulun, the two tribes the redactor does believe to have participated in the battle against Sisera. Once Naphtali is chosen, the major events associated with both the preparations for and the aftermath of the battle must be located in Naphtali: Deborah must come from Ephraim to Naphtali and be present as a symbol of divine inspiration (4:9); Barak must muster his army in Naphtali (4:10); Sisera must flee into Naphtali and die (4:17–22).

Still, why does Judges 4 specify that all these events took place in Kedesh, one of the most northerly points in Naphtali's tribal territory? Why did the redactor not locate Barak's power base and Jael's tent in some more southern Naphtali city, one within easy striking distance of the region in Issachar where the battle is said to have taken place? Halpern can only suggest that it is because Kedesh is both *en route* to and associated with Hazor (see Josh 19:36–37 and 2 Kgs 15:29)[30] and that it is Jabin, king of Hazor, for whom the prose redactor interprets Sisera as fighting.[31] But I believe a more probable explanation is available. In Josh 20:7, Kedesh is designated as one of Israel's six cities of refuge, cities where one accused of murder is allowed to take asylum until his case can be brought to trial. Often, these cities of refuge are also cultic centers.[32] This is certainly true in the case of Kedesh, which, according to Josh 21:32, is listed as a city where the priestly tribe of the Levites, who otherwise had no territorial rights, were given residential and grazing privileges. Kedesh is thus a city associated with both sanctuary and cult. It is, moreover, the *only* city in Naphtali that can lay claim to this dual status. I propose that this is why Judges 4—despite the geographical difficulties—locates Jael's tent there. While Kedesh may be an illogical choice in terms of the war story's topography, the redactor insists upon it because it is the only logical choice if Jael's tent is to be interpreted as a sanctified haven.

In the end, then, three major data—Heber's priestly ancestry, the location of Jael's tent under an oak tree, and the proximity of her camping spot to the city of Kedesh—combine to suggest the validity of Mazar's thesis: that the reason the redactor of Judges 4 believes that Sisera flees to Jael's tent is because he perceives her to be some sort of religious functionary and regards her tent as demarcating sanctified space. Still unproven, though, is my contention that the source from which the author of Judges 4 derives this notion is the poetic predecessor of the prose found in Judges 5.

At first glance, indeed, my thesis would seem to be unprovable, given that two of the major elements that indicate sacrality in the prose—the oak in Zaanannim and the campsite in the vicinity of Kedesh—are not even mentioned in the poem. It is also unclear whether there is any basis in the poem for the prose's third datum, Heber's priestly ancestry. The crucial text here is 5:24. The NRSV translation of this verse reads:

> *Most blessed of women be Jael,*
> *The wife of Heber the Kenite,*
> *Of tent-dwelling women most blessed.*

Many commentators, though, prefer an alternate rendition:[33]

> *Most blessed of women be Jael,*
> *A woman of the Kenite community,*
> *Of tent-dwelling women most blessed.*

Abraham Malamat explains the reasoning behind this translation, pointing out that in texts from the Bronze Age city of Mari on the Upper Euphrates, the term *ḫibrum* describes some sort of a community unit, a clan, a band, or a tribe.[34] To Malamat, this suggests that *ḥeber,* which is the Hebrew cognate of *ḫibrum,* should be similarly translated, not as a proper name but as a common noun referring to some sort of bonded-together group. Elsewhere in the Hebrew Bible, in fact, *ḥeber* does occur with such a meaning. In Hos 6:9, for example, a "band" or a "company" of priests is referred to as a *ḥeber* (*ḥeber kōhănîm*). The Israelite place name Hebron (*ḥebrôn*), which is derived from the root *ḥbr,* also seems to draw on this idea of "band" or "company," as can especially be seen in texts that give the name Kiriath-Arba, the "City of Four," as an alternative appellation for Hebron.[35] This designation implies that Hebron is a community made up of, at least, four smaller villages that are "banded" or "bonded" together. In 2 Sam 2:3, which speaks of the "cities (*ʿārê*) of Hebron," we find a further indication that Hebron was comprised of several small communities that were banded together as one. Together, these data intimate that *ḥeber* in Judg 5:24 should likewise be taken as a reference to some sort of bonded-together group, and hence the translation of the verse's second line describing Jael as "a woman of the Kenite community." The husband Heber, who in Judges 4 provided Jael's link to a priestly clan, has been lost.

Yet in this revised translation of Judg 5:24, one piece of identifying information regarding Jael remains, her ethnic identity as a Kenite. In fact, this appears to be the *only* piece of information the poem provides about Jael's background. This suggests that Judges 5 considers Jael's Kenite identity to be a point of extreme significance. But what exactly does Judges 5 mean to imply when it describes Jael as Kenite? In particular, are there specific traits associated with the Kenites that the poem intends for us to attribute to Jael? And, especially, are there traits of the Kenites that coordinate with my thesis in this section: the possibility that Jael is portrayed not only in Judges 4 but also in Judg 5:24–27 as some sort of religious functionary?

The Kenites are but one of the many non-Israelite groups whose origins are described in legendary form in the book of Genesis. In fact, according to the Genesis legends, the Kenites are the most ancient of all the Near East's various ethnic communities, as they are depicted in Gen 4:1–16 as being descended from Cain, the first son of Adam and Eve. Genesis 4:17–24 continues by describing the first six generations of the Kenite community after Cain, culminating with the four children of Lamech and his wives Adah and Zillah. Several points in this Kenite origin legend appear significant.[36] First, the story seems to associate the Kenites with the profession of metallurgy, both through genealogy and etymology. Genealogically, Tubal-Cain, the son of Lamech by his wife Zillah, is identified in Gen 4:22 as "a worker of all tools of bronze and of iron." Etymologically, the root *qyn* that forms the basis for both the ancestral name Cain (*qayin*) and the clan appellation Kenites (*qênî*) means "to forge" or "to work metal" according to cognates found in several Semitic languages.[37] The root *qyn,* however, can also be associated with musicianship (hence Hebrew *qînâ,* "dirge" or "lament"), and, indeed, another of Lamech's sons (this one mothered by Adah) is Jubal, who is described in 4:21 as the ancestor of all who play the lyre. This suggests that, in addition to their associations with metallurgy, the Kenites can be characterized as musicians.[38] Because, moreover, Jabal, the brother of the lyre-playing Jubal, is said in 4:20 to be the ancestor of those who raise cattle, we deduce that a third attribute that defines the Kenite community is an association with herding. A herding economy typically implies a nonsedentary settlement pattern, as shepherds move from place to place to seek prime grazing land for their flocks. The dwelling of choice for such itinerants is a tent, and not surprisingly, Jabal is described in 4:20 not just as the progenitor of those who keep cattle but as the ancestor of those who live in tents. Note also that the Kenites' eponymous ancestor Cain, although originally an agriculturalist rather than a herder (4:2), becomes an itinerant after he murders his brother Abel and is forced by Yahweh to roam as "a fugitive and a wanderer on the earth" (4:12).

The Kenite origin story in Gen 4:1–24 finally contains indications that the Kenites were believed to be some sort of religious functionaries. Genesis 4:8–15, after describing Cain's fratricide and the punishment of wandering that Yahweh exacts as a result, describes how Yahweh places a special mark upon Cain, protecting him from anyone who sought to kill him. This mark, by designating Cain as one who is under divine protection, suggests—albeit paradoxically, given Cain's crime—that Cain has a special relationship with the deity. A special relationship with the deity is precisely the attribute that biblical tradition elsewhere posits for its religious functionaries. Halpern, among others, has in fact suggested that there are important correspondences between Cain and the biblical prophets, arguing that the "'mark of Cain' has a parallel in what seems to be a prophetic hairstyle or tonsure . . . probably a mark . . . of Yhwh's proprietorship."[39] Halpern has particularly in mind the story in 1 Kgs 20:35–43 that describes how an unnamed prophet disguises himself by bandaging his eyes and thus presumably covering the distinctive mark that he wore upon his forehead. Also of significance are the jeering taunts in 2 Kgs 2:23 that identify the prophet Elisha as bald and the command to Ezekiel in Ezek 9:4 to place a mark on the foreheads of all those who, like the prophet, empathize with Yahweh concerning the abominations being committed in Jerusalem. Citing 1 Kgs 20:35–36, 22:26–28, and Jer 26:16, Halpern further notes that the prophets, like Cain, can be said to enjoy Yahweh's personal protection.

Many of these characteristics attributed to the Kenites in Genesis 4 are manifest by the Kenite Jael in Judg 5:24–27. The associations with tent-dwelling are made the most explicit, as the last line of Judg 5:24 specifically identifies Jael as a tent-dwelling woman rather than as one who lives in a house. Jael also seems to have associations with herding since, according to verse 25 of Judges 5, she has at hand dairy products— milk and ghee—with which to feed Sisera.[40] She is also described as having at hand, according to verse 26, a *halmût,* a "hammer," and I suggest that this particular tool is pictured as being present in Jael's tent because the poetic tradition knew it was the sort of implement that might be used in the metallurgical work with which the Kenites are elsewhere associated. In at least one other passage in the Hebrew Bible, Isa 41:7, the root *hlm,* "to hammer," is used to describe the kind of hammering a blacksmith does on an anvil.

There are, unfortunately, no similar indications in Judg 5:24–27 that

Jael manifests the other two distinctive Kenite attributes of musicianship and cultic function. But because the poetic tradition ascribes to Jael the typical Kenite associations with tenting, herding, and smithing, I believe the poem also intends for us to envision Jael as sharing the characteristic Kenite association with music (is it only coincidence, in this regard, that the most lyrical part of Judges 5 is found in verses 24–27?)[41] as well as the Kenite association with the religious arts. If the latter is so, then, as proposed above, Sisera's reason for coming to Jael's tent in Judges 5 is the same as the explanation offered in Judges 4: the Canaanite war leader perceives Jael to be some sort of cultic functionary. He therefore seeks with her divine sanctuary from the enemies who pursue him.

Still, this conclusion raises one final question: why does Jael violate her mandate of divine protection in order to murder in a manner most brutal and cold-blooded the soldier who seeks refuge with her? Such a violent act seems clearly to stand at odds with her status as religious officiant and might even seem to intimate—contradictory to my thesis—that Jael is dedicated to anything but divine service. But, in fact, Jael's transgressing of the traditions of sanctuary provides the final clue proving that she *is* to be understood as a religious functionary. Crucial to recall here is the nature of the war that Judges 5 believes is being waged against Sisera: it is a holy war declared by Yahweh. It is thus Yahweh's will that Sisera be killed, even if committing this murder means violating a space that otherwise would be considered a divinely-sanctioned haven. But, although Yahweh requires that in this particular instance religious convention be suspended, how is it that Jael knows that this is the case? She knows because she is somehow privy to the intent of the divine, because she is, after all, a religious functionary. Jael's sanction to assassinate Sisera thus demonstrates, albeit ironically, that Judges 5 regards her as a religious specialist. It is her privileged relationship with God that reveals to her the necessity of overturning the traditions associated with religious sanctuary and murdering Sisera in her tent-*cum*-shrine.

II. WOMEN AND THE CULT IN JUDGES 4 AND 5

At the beginning of Section II of Chapter 1, I remarked that, given the highly androcentric nature of Israelite society, it was surprising to find two remarkable portraits of female military heroes in Judges 5 and even more surprising to find that these portraits were not isolated occurrences in the book of Judges. In Section II of this chapter, as we focus on women who serve as religious specialists, it is equally important to realize that, although positions of religious leadership in ancient Israel were generally assigned only to men, Jael's role as a cult functionary is no anomaly in Judges. In fact, even within the context of Judges 5, Jael is no anomaly, for as the poem's depiction of Jael as a female military hero is meant to complement its portrait of the female military hero Deborah, so, too, is the portrayal of Jael as a cult specialist in verses 24–27 complemented by the presentation of Deborah as a religious functionary in verses 1–23. In fact, in *both* Judges 4 and Judges 5, Deborah is described as a religious functionary, specifically as a prophetic intermediary who brings the word of Yahweh to the people of Israel.

In Judges 4, Deborah is explicitly named as a prophet in verse 4. In Judges 5, although the term prophet is never applied to Deborah, intimations of her prophetic status are found throughout.[42] The root of the Hebrew word for prophet, *nb'*, means "to call," and the words *nābî',* "prophet" (masculine), and *nĕbî'â,* "prophet" (feminine), are passive participles of this verb. A prophet is thus "one who is called," and this accurately describes Deborah's role in Judges 5: she is the one who is called by Yahweh to declare God's holy war and to assemble the troops for battle against Sisera.[43] It is also important to note that these responsibilities assumed by Deborah in Judges 5 are assumed by prophets elsewhere in the Hebrew Bible. In 1 Kgs 20:1–22, for example, King Ben-Hadad of Aram (modern Syria) lays siege to Samaria, the capital city of the northern kingdom of Israel. As the attack begins, an unnamed prophet appears and delivers this oracle to Israel's King Ahab: "Thus says Yahweh. Do you see all this great multitude? Behold, I am giving it into your hand today, and you shall know that I am Yahweh" (v 13). What the prophet declares here is that Yahweh intends to engage in holy war against Israel's Aramaean foes. Deborah in Judges 5 is similarly the prophetic intermediary through whom Yahweh makes clear that it is a holy war that is to be waged against Sisera's Canaanite army. Moreover, as the 1 Kings 20 story continues, the prophetic adviser of Ahab instructs the king regarding the mustering of an army to fight in Yahweh's holy war and even goes so far as to dictate who should serve in this fighting force: "the young men who are in the service of the district governors" (v 14). This parallels Deborah's role in mustering Israel's tribes for battle in Judg 5:14–18.

Yet, although the prophet of 1 Kings 20 is unnamed, this individual is portrayed by the text as decidedly male, and in this respect the parallel with Deborah in Judges 5 falters. In this respect also Deborah, as well as Jael, stands in distinction to most of the Bible's other prophets and, in addition, to its larger community of cultic functionaries, for whom maleness is likewise the norm. So how, in the light of this male-dominated cult, should we explain the two remarkable portraits of Jael and Deborah as cult specialists we have found in Judges 4 and 5?

When faced with the similar problem in Chapter 1, the need to explain the Bible's depictions of the same two women of Judges 5, Deborah and Jael, as military heroes, I looked to older Canaanite mythological traditions and their descriptions of the warrior goddess Anat. But here, in a discussion of Deborah and Jael as religious functionaries, mythological prototypes really do not offer much help. This is because in considering Jael's and Deborah's roles in the religious sphere, we are not dealing with a character type—the warring female—that was rendered as divine in Canaanite tradition and then, in Israelite literature, was reinterpreted as human. Instead, in considering religious specialists, we are dealing with a role that, by its very nature, must be understood to involve exclusively human actors. Because religious leaders, that is, exist *only* within the context of this-worldly space, it is to the earthly realm that we must look to explain Jael and Deborah as religious functionaries in Judges 4 and 5.

Ultimately, then, the crucial analytical category for discussing Jael's and Deborah's roles in the religious sphere is not mythological but sociological. More specifically, we need to undertake a sociological investigation of the ancient Israelite understanding of religious status and try to determine the ways in which that understanding of religious status was related to gender. Even more specifically, we need to undertake a sociological investigation of the ancient Israelite understandings (plural) concerning religious status as they might be related to gender, for my intent here is to build on a thesis first proposed by Jo Ann Hackett and suggest that there are varying attitudes evidenced in the biblical text regarding the status of women as religious functionaries.[44] These varying attitudes, Hackett argues, are the products of shifts in the degree of cultic centralization and bureaucratization during different periods of Israelite history. The gist of her theory is that during historical periods when the Yahwistic cult was stable and highly centralized, the Israelite social conventions that assigned only men positions of religious leadership were in full effect, and, consequently, the biblical authors tended not to portray women as exercising public and independent religious power. Instead, women religious figures were either denigrated or ignored. Conversely, during periods of cultic instability and decentralization, the gender roles that typically governed Israelite religion eroded to some degree. At these times, women were more likely to be depicted as wielding power in the religious sphere.

Judges 5 proves an admirable test case for Hackett's thesis. I have previously described how this text dates from the late twelfth or eleventh century B.C.E., which is a time when Yahwistic religion was in its infancy and thus almost wholly devoid of institutionalized structures.[45] "Structures," indeed, can be taken quite literally here: although early Israelite settlements have been extensively studied by archaeologists, only domestic architecture and no public buildings—and this means no temples—have been found. Instead, there are only remains of open-air sanctuaries or small household shrines.[46] According to the model articulated by Hackett, the lack of cult centralization and bureaucratization this evidence suggests should create an environment in which it was possible to portray women as strong and forceful religious leaders.[47] She writes, "the characterization of the era as one of decentralized and ad hoc power would lead us to expect wider possibilities for women in public and powerful positions."[48] As we have seen, these expectations are indeed fulfilled: the woman Deborah can be depicted in Judg 5:1–23 as a prophet who exercises religious power publicly and independently, and Jael can likewise be imagined in Judg 5:24–27 as a religious functionary who both presides over a place of sanctuary and correctly interprets the divine mandate that requires that its guarantees of asylum be overthrown.

The case of Judges 4 is more complex but I believe it is, in many respects, analogous. Again, the crucial consideration is the issue of date. Although Judges 4 purports to describe events of the late second millennium B.C.E. and thus presents itself as contemporaneous with Judges 5, it is actually a part of the Bible's great Deuteronomistic History, which includes the books of Joshua, Judges, Samuel, and Kings and which was compiled in Jerusalem at some point during the reign of King Josiah (c. 640–609 B.C.E.), probably during the last decade of his monarchy (between c. 620–610 B.C.E.).[49] This was another period of cultic instability within the course of Israelite history. It was, first, a period of cultic instability because it was a time during which a set of major religious reforms were undertaken, inspired by a document called the "book of the *tôrâ*," usually translated the "book of the law" and probably some form of what we know today as the book of Deuteronomy.[50] According to 2 Kings 22, this proto-Deuteronomy was previously unknown in Jerusalem until it was found in the temple in c. 622 B.C.E., during the course of some repair work. When the book was brought and read to King Josiah, he was dismayed to realize his and his people's failure to adhere to its mandates. He consequently instituted a massive program of reformation in order to bring his subjects' cultic practices into line with the book's commandments.

This fact alone—that at some point following the 622 B.C.E. discovery, Josiah is described as enshrining a new version of Israel's covenant code which involves instituting a massive reform program—indicates that during at least the first three decades of the Josianic monarchy, the cult was in a state of some confusion and disorder. Also important in this regard are the biblical texts describing Josiah's predecessors, Manasseh (c. 687–642 B.C.E.) and Amon (c. 642–640 B.C.E.), as these accounts further suggest the presence of instabilities in Israelite religion during the latter half of the seventh century B.C.E. Unfortunately, however, the texts describing Manasseh's and Amon's reigns are too polemical to indicate definitively the precise nature of the disquiet. Still, we can say with confidence that during the monarchies of Manasseh and Amon, Jerusalem and Israel's southern kingdom of Judah found themselves under Assyrian hegemony. Even though, moreover, the notion that the Assyrians imposed their own religious practices upon their vassals has been discounted by scholars,[51] it is nonetheless the case that Jerusalem and Judah would have experienced some sort of contact with the theologies of their suzerain. We would expect at least some degree of disarray within the Yahwistic cult as a result.

Can it be coincidence, then, that it is during this period of cultic disarray and disorder that Judges 4 depicts both Jael and Deborah as playing a major role in Israel's religious life? Hackett's thesis would argue no, suggesting instead that the Judges 4 portrayals of Jael and Deborah as religious leaders are directly linked to the period of cultic confusion during which the Judges 4 text was composed. More specifically, what this means is that, as the prose redactors of Judges 4 reinterpreted their source for the Deborah and Jael stories, the archaic poem of Judges 5, they found themselves completely willing to follow their poetic predecessors in depicting Jael and Deborah as religious specialists. In fact,

Judges 4 is even willing to *elaborate* upon the poem's earlier descriptions by providing concrete articulation concerning the religious roles that Jael and Deborah play. Thus, while Judg 5:1–23 leaves us to intuit Deborah's prophetic role by examining her actions in calling and mustering an army to fight in God's holy war, Judg 4:4 explicitly labels her as a prophet. Similarly, in Judg 4:11 and 17–22, the oblique reference in Judges 5 to Jael as a "Kenite" is elaborated upon and refined. By providing this woman with a distinguished priestly lineage and by stationing her under a sacred tree and next to a sanctified town, Judges 4 leaves no doubt about her exalted religious status.

It is further of note that the Deuteronomists responsible for Judges 4 appear willing to assign women an exalted religious status elsewhere in their great Deuteronomistic History. The parade illustration is the aforementioned Deuteronomistic description of the finding of the "book of the law" in 2 Kings 22. This text recounts how Josiah, before instituting his sweeping program of religious reformation, seeks a consultation with a prophet in order to verify that the proto-Deuteronomy found in the temple really does represent Yahweh's requirements for Israel. The prophet in question is a woman, Huldah. She affirms that the book is indeed Yahweh's word.[52] Deuteronomistic tradition, moreover, clearly regards her prophecy as binding, as 2 Kgs 23:1–25 describes the massive crusade that Josiah undertakes in order to bring his kingdom into compliance with the description of Yahwistic tradition this woman prophet has endorsed. Huldah is thus surely to be understood as a worthy associate of her ancient compatriots, Deborah and Jael.

Nevertheless, whatever the religious instabilities of the late seventh century B.C.E. that allowed the Deuteronomistic authors of Judges 4 and 2 Kings 22 to portray Jael, Deborah, and Huldah as respected religious functionaries, Israelite religion of the seventh century B.C.E. was not the completely decentralized and destabilized cult of the eleventh. That is, while foreign domination and religious reformation meant there was a notable measure of disorder and even chaos in the Israelite cult at the time of Deuteronomistic composition, there remained a significant degree of institutionalization inherent in the traditions of that era. There was, for example, a national temple in Jerusalem and a designated line of priestly authority and descent. There was also, as the enshrining of the Deuteronomic covenant code makes obvious, an increasing sense of what constituted "orthodoxy" versus "heterodoxy" in the land. According to Hackett's thesis, what this sort of institutionalization means is that, however much Deuteronomistic texts are willing to allow for the presence and even power of female religious agents, they still impose some limitations based on their assumptions regarding culturally-appropriate gender behavior.

In particular, in their depictions of Deborah, Jael, and Huldah, the Deuteronomists show a tendency to deny these women religious functionaries a *public* voice and instead to define their cultic role as primarily manifesting itself within the *private* confines of the domestic sphere. Recall, for example, that in the Deuteronomistic retelling of Judges 5 in Judges 4, the poem's reference to Jael as a member of the *ḥeber haqqênî*, "the Kenite community" (5:24), is reinterpreted as being the proper name of Jael's husband, "Heber" (4:17). Jael's religious authority thus remains in the Deuteronomistic prose, but lost is the notion that she might have exercised that authority independent of the traditional female accoutrement of a husband. In fact, unlike Judges 5, Judges 4 insists that it is *only* through her husband and his descent from the priest Hobab that Jael can lay claim to her role as cultic functionary. Deborah, who also appears in Judges 5 without a woman's customary trappings of a husband or children, similarly seems to have been "domesticated" by the redactor in Judg 4:4 since most commentators believe that the prose's phrase describing Deborah as *'ēšet lappîdôt* should be translated as the "wife of Lappidoth."[53] Some, in addition, have suggested that "Lappidoth," whose name means "Torches" or "Flashes," is the same person as Barak, whose name means "Lightning."[54] Since, moreover, biblical tradition in 1 Sam 12:11 and Heb 11:32 remembers Barak, and not Deborah, as the *real* deliverer at the time of the battle against Sisera,[55] it can even be proposed that in Judges 4, Deborah's religious authority, like Jael's, exists only by virtue of her marital relationship.[56] As for Huldah in 2 Kings 22, it has also been argued that her prophetic authority is secondary, derived from her marriage to Shallum, son of Tikvah, who is described in verse 14 as "the keeper of the wardrobe." Shallum, this means, is some sort of royal official (if the wardrobe in question is the king's) or cultic functionary (if the wardrobe consists of the priestly vestments), and hence the argument that Huldah's prophetic stature and authority derive from her husband's position within Jerusalem's palace and/or temple bureaucracy.[57] There is, to be sure, no basis for this assumption in the text. Nevertheless, it is the case that Huldah does disappear rather quickly from the biblical account, and this despite the fact that, as noted above, the subsequent narrative in 2 Kings 23 focuses almost exclusively on the Deuteronomistic program of reform that her words were used to validate. Deuteronomistic prose, we conclude, although willing to acknowledge that women can assume positions of religious leadership, is sparing in the amount of public or permanent authority it believes these women can be assigned.

III. JEPHTHAH'S DAUGHTER, MANOAH'S WIFE, MICAH'S MOTHER

There are three other texts found in the Deuteronomistic chapters of Judges—the stories of Jephthah's daughter, Manoah's wife, and Micah's mother—that I believe should be considered alongside Judges 4 and 2 Kings 22 and interpreted in much the same way that I have just analyzed those two texts. That is, like Judges 4 and 2 Kings 22, these stories of Jephthah's daughter, Manoah's wife, and Micah's mother describe women who play a decisive role in ancient Israelite cultic matters, and, as was the case regarding Judges 4 and 2 Kings 22, I believe these portrayals of women playing a decisive cultic role are possible because they stem from the period of religious instability associated with the composition of the Deuteronomistic History. However, I also believe that, once more, these portrayals demonstrate that, for all the religious authority allowed to women in depictions that come from the Deuteronomistic era, the norms that typically constrained women's religious power within the context of a male-dominated cult are not wholly absent. Jephthah's daughter, Manoah's wife, and Micah's mother, for example, all are limited to the domestic sphere in their exercise of religious authority. Other features of these women's stories also signal the relatively circumscribed scope of their cultic influence, as I will discuss more thoroughly below.

Let us begin by examining the story of Jephthah's daughter (Judg 11:29–40). The story's prologue, in Judg 11:4–28, sets the scene: Israel is being oppressed by the Ammonites, and the elders of Gilead have commissioned the judge Jephthah to lead them in battle against this foe. In 11:29, as our tale proper begins, the elders' choice is ratified by Yahweh; as the text tells it, "the spirit of Yahweh came upon Jephthah." Then, in verses 30–31, Jephthah makes a vow to Yahweh, pledging that if the deity indeed gives the Ammonites into Jephthah's hand, Jephthah, when he returns home after the battle, will sacrifice whomever or whatever comes out of his house to meet him (the Hebrew *'ăšer* is ambiguous). As luck would have it, the one who comes forth to meet him is his daughter, performing in jubilation a postwar victory song. Her joyous celebration is thus immediately rendered tragic, as Jephthah realizes that under the terms of his vow, it is she who must be sacrificed. The tragedy is all the greater since, as verse 34 stresses, this daughter is Jephthah's only child. Jephthah rends his clothes and mourns, but there can be no reprieve. As he says, "I have opened my mouth to Yahweh, and I cannot turn back" (v 35).

This text has been much discussed by feminist scholars in the last decade and a half, especially by Mieke Bal, Peggy L. Day, J. Cheryl Exum, Esther Fuchs, Hackett, and Phyllis Trible.[58] Trible's analysis is the earliest and is perhaps the best known, in particular because it is Trible who most astutely points out that it was not necessary that Jephthah get himself into his tragic predicament in the first place. In verse 29, the spirit of Yahweh had descended upon Jephthah and with it had come the guarantee of an Israelite victory. Thus the vow in verses 30–31 is at best superfluous and, in fact, it implies a lack of faith in Yahweh's promise. Trible writes, "Jephthah desires to bind God rather than embrace the gift of the spirit."[59] Trible goes on to note that Jephthah continues to behave in ways motivated by his own self-interest even in verses 34–35, in which Jephthah's daughter comes forth to meet her father and the price of his vow becomes clear. Thus, while Jephthah does rend his garments in a traditional gesture of mourning, he indicates that his grief is for himself as the victim of a foolish vow and not for the real victim, the daughter. Jephthah even goes so far as to accuse his daughter of bringing him low and of being the cause of his calamity. In some ancient versions, he also speaks of her as a stumbling block.[60] Trible writes: "At the moment of recognition and disclosure, Jephthah thinks of himself and indicts his daughter for the predicament."[61]

By contrast, the daughter is a paragon of faithfulness. She accepts immediately the consequences of her father's act, acknowledging in verse 36 that the vow must be kept. Here, Hackett offers an analysis that is especially salient, arguing that the story at this point, while at least implicitly critical of Jephthah, shows his daughter in a positive light, as one who is loyal to the standards of the Israelite covenant community.[62] Both Hackett and Trible also suggest that the daughter's next action speaks to her faithfulness. She asks for a two-month reprieve before her death, during which time she intends to retreat into the mountains with her female companions and mourn. The story closes with the notice that there arose an Israelite custom that for four days every year, the daughters of Israel would commemorate Jephthah's daughter by going forth to lament. Jephthah's daughter is thus identified as the founder of an annual ritual event.

This is an extraordinary datum. Elsewhere in biblical tradition, annual ritual events most typically commemorate some act done on Israel's behalf by Yahweh: Passover, for example, commemorates Yahweh's delivering of the Israelites from Egypt. Israel's ritual calendar also contains festivals associated with the cycles of nature: Shavuot, or the festival of weeks, is associated with the spring harvest season. But only a few ritual observances commemorate some human activity. Hanukkah is one such holiday, as it commemorates the victory of the Maccabean army over the Syrian forces of Antiochus IV Epiphanes and the subsequent rededication of the temple in Jerusalem (c. 164 B.C.E.); Purim similarly celebrates the way in which Queen Esther and the vizier Mordecai were able to deliver the Jews from their oppressor Haman during the reign of the Persian emperor Xerxes (c. 468–465 B.C.E.). Both these holidays, however, come from Israel's postexilic period (c. 525 B.C.E. and beyond). For most of Israelite history, the ritual founded by Jephthah's daughter stands alone as an observance that commemorates a human character and her deeds.

It is equally extraordinary that the ritual Jephthah's daughter founds is a women's ritual, for the Bible in general tells us very little about the nature of women's religious lives.[63] Unfortunately, though, the text's description is so brief that we learn next to nothing about the precise nature of the ritual or about those among Israel's women who participated in it. Still, Day has effectively used comparative materials from ancient Greek tradition to argue that the ritual event in question is a female rite of passage commemorating a young woman's onset of menstruation. What the participants in this ritual are lamenting, then, is the "death" of their childhood as they prepare to leave girlhood behind and enter into the adult stage of their lives.[64]

Like Jephthah's daughter, Manoah's wife is a Judges woman who has been much discussed by feminist scholars in the last decade and a half, especially by Exum and, again, by Hackett.[65] As the story of this woman opens, in Judg 13:2, we are told that Manoah's wife is barren and that she has no children. In verse 3, though, a messenger of Yahweh appears to the woman and promises her that she will bear a son. The woman dutifully reports to her husband what has happened, telling him that a "man of God" came to her and that his appearance was awe-inspiring, like that of an angel. Manoah, however, either does not believe or is not satisfied with the information provided by his wife, and he thus entreats Yahweh to send the man of God again. Like Jephthah's vow, this entreaty seems unnecessary and even unwise. Although it is certainly the case in the Bible that messages from God can be delivered a second time, the more typical pattern is for the deity to send both the first and second revelations unprompted: Pharaoh receives two unasked-for dreams, for example, regarding the seven years of plenty and seven years of famine due to be experienced in Egypt (Gen 41:1–8), and Amos' vision of locusts devouring (7:1–3) is duplicated with no urging from him by a vision of an all-consuming fire (7:4–6).[66] For Manoah to *ask,* though, for a repeated revelation is a different matter and smacks of hubris. Still, the messenger does reappear, yet, as Exum astutely points out, it is once more only the woman who is privy to the epiphany. She then runs and fetches her husband, who returns with her to the site where the messenger waits. Exum writes, "One is tempted to ask whether Manoah would ever have seen the messenger were it not for the woman's intervention."[67] She further points out that whereas, "the messenger comes only to the woman . . . Manoah must come to the man."[68]

When the messenger and Manoah do finally meet, Manoah asks a series of questions, the intent of which is to confirm the truth of what his wife had reported earlier. He next invites the messenger to stay and eat. Here again, Exum argues, a contrast is being drawn between the piety of Manoah's wife and the bumbling faithlessness of Manoah: the wife has already guessed, according to verse 6, that their visitor is a divine emissary, but in verse 15, Manoah, by inviting the guest to eat, still assumes that the messenger is human. Verse 16 emphasizes this fact further by stating explicitly that Manoah did not know that the man was the angel of Yahweh. Only in verse 20, after the angel has refused Manoah's meal and suggests that he offer a sacrifice instead, does Manoah— as he sees the angel ascend in the sacrificial flames—realize the nature of the messenger. Yet even in the face of such awesome imagery, Manoah again shows himself to be rather like Jephthah in that he manages to think only of his own interests. "We shall surely die," he says to his wife, "for we have seen God" (v 22). The wife, by contrast, displays a theological acumen and sensitivity to Israel's covenant tradition that is reminiscent of the piety of Jephthah's daughter, pointing out that, "If Yahweh had meant to kill us, Yahweh would not have taken a holocaust offering and a cereal offering from our hands" (v 23). Hackett concludes:

> Manoah lacked faith in his wife's word and memory, was slow to figure out the identity of their divine visitor, and in the end was afraid for his life. His wife had to explain to him that Yahweh would hardly have bothered to announce the birth of a son and the grand career of that son only to kill them immediately afterward.[69]

Hackett's reference to the "grand career" of the promised son alludes to the second half of the angel's message to Manoah's wife in 13:4–5, in which the woman is told that her son will be a Nazirite dedicated to Yahweh from the moment of his birth and that therefore no razor should touch his head. I have described in Chapter 1 how the Nazirites abstained from cutting their hair as a sign of their special sanctity and how they also were required to avoid corpses, which were considered polluting and unclean, and to refrain from drinking wine and other intoxicating beverages. Curiously enough, Judges 13 does not prescribe these latter two restrictions for Samson, the son whom Manoah's wife eventually bears.[70] But the woman is told that during her pregnancy, *she* is required to abstain from wine and other strong drink (vv 4, 7, 14). It seems as if she, as she carries her son who is the Nazirite-to-be, must temporarily undertake at least this obligation of the Nazirite vow.[71]

Such a motif recalls the story of another barren woman, Hannah, found in 1 Samuel 1.[72] The setting of that story is Shiloh, where Hannah—along with her husband Elqanah, Elqanah's other wife Peninnah, and Elqanah's children by Peninnah—has gone for an annual pilgrimage festival. Judges 21:19–21 also mentions an annual pilgrimage festival at Shiloh and describes how, at it, the young women of Shiloh dance in the vineyards. As I will discuss more thoroughly in Chapter 6, this reference to vineyards, along with other evidence, suggests that Shiloh's annual festival is held in the fall when the grape harvest is being celebrated. But because of her barrenness, Hannah is in no mood to celebrate the ripening of the grapes, especially given that her fertile rival Peninnah seems intent upon tormenting her. Thus Hannah leaves her family and goes to the sanctuary at Shiloh to present herself before Yahweh.[73] According to verse 11, she asks Yahweh to give her a child and vows that if she does bear a son, "I will set him before you all the days of his life, and wine and strong beverages he will not drink, and no razor shall touch his head."[74] So before he is even born, Hannah vows that her son Samuel will be a Nazirite, just as Samson's mother is enjoined by Yahweh's divine messenger to dedicate her unborn son to Nazirite service.

The similarities with the Judges story continue. In 1 Sam 1:12–15, as Hannah prays at Shiloh's temple, she is observed by Eli, the priest at Shiloh. He sees her lips move, but because she is speaking silently, he hears nothing. Eli therefore thinks Hannah is drunk. Hannah denies his accusation, but if I have been correct above in stating that the Shiloh pilgrimage festival is the annual fall vineyard feast, a celebration that undoubtedly involved consuming large amounts of wine, then Eli's reaction to Hannah is perfectly understandable. In fact, what is difficult to understand is why Eli is wrong: Hannah, at the vineyard festival, *should* have been drinking liberally.[75] The narrator explains by telling us that Hannah's grief has caused her to abstain from the festal meal and that this accounts for her sobriety. But the parallels with the story of Manoah's wife suggest to me that, at least at some stage in the Hannah tradition, Hannah's sobriety was linked to the sobriety of her future son. Thus, as Manoah's wife was required to behave as if she were a Nazirite while pregnant with the Nazirite Samson, so, too, is Hannah required to uphold Nazirite standards of sanctity as she seeks to bear her Nazirite son. Note in this regard that Num 6:1–21, the legal document describing the Nazirites, does indicate that Nazirite service can be temporary. This text also makes clear that women, as well as men, can accept Nazirite obligations. I conclude that Judges 13 and 1 Samuel 1 assume that, for the duration of their pregnancies, Manoah's wife and Hannah have undertaken the Nazirite vow.

An act of piety similar to vowing oneself or one's child to the deity's service is to dedicate some ritual object, a cult furnishing or vessel or the like. Such an act of dedication is described in a third Judges' episode that depicts a woman's religious activities, Judg 17:1–5.[76] There, a certain man named Micah has stolen eleven hundred pieces of silver from his mother. The mother, ignorant of the fact that the thief was her son, utters a curse condemning the criminal. At this point, Micah, in danger of incurring God's wrath, confesses his guilt to his mother. In order to expiate his theft and save him from the consequences of her curse, she consecrates two hundred pieces of the silver to Yahweh, "from my hand for my son, to make an image of cast metal" (v 3). As in the stories of Jephthah's daughter and Manoah's wife, the phrase "from my hand for my son"—and, indeed, the entire episode—seems to suggest a contrast between a woman's piety and devotion and a man's failure to adhere to Israel's covenantal standards.[77]

Jephthah's daughter, Manoah's wife, and Micah's mother are thus all lauded in Judges' Deuteronomistic prose for their acts of religious piety and, moreover, for the ways in which they manifest this piety as opposed to the faithlessness exhibited by the men in their lives. One is reminded of the way the Deuteronomistic authors of Judges 4 laud the prophetic and more generally cultic roles of, respectively, Deborah and Jael and, in addition, stress that at least Deborah's piety in her prophetic role should be contrasted to the faithlessness displayed by her male counterpart, Barak. In Judg 4:6–8, he, when presented with Yahweh's mandate that he is to go forth and fight against Sisera, insists that Deborah accompany him to the field of battle, thereby demonstrating his doubts regarding Yahweh's assurances of victory. As a result, Deborah decrees in 4:9 that Barak will not be given final glory in the battle but "Yahweh will sell Sisera into the hand of a woman." This sets the stage for the murderous deed of Jael in 4:21.

Yet, while the authors of Judges 4 indicate their scorn for Barak's qualms as opposed to Deborah's faithfulness in much the same way the Deuteronomistic authors of Judges 11, 13, and 17 imply their disdain for Jephthah, Manoah, and Micah as opposed to the women in their lives, we have nonetheless seen regarding Judges 4 that Deuteronomistic tradition did not separate itself entirely from the norms that typically define women's lives within male-dominated cultures. The same is true of the Deuteronomistic portraits of Jephthah's daughter, Manoah's wife, and Micah's mother found in Judges 11, 13, and 17. I noted above, for example, that, like the depictions of both Deborah and, especially, Jael in Judges 4, the context in which all three of these women are shown exhibiting their piety is in the home and not in any public forum or arena. Moreover, for all the religious authority that Judges 11, 13, and 17 ascribe to Jephthah's daughter, Manoah's wife, and Micah's mother, the tradition does not bother to give any of these women a name. But names are important, and they are the norm for Judges' male characters.[78]

In her several articles on women in Judges, Exum has described many other points of concern regarding, especially, the portrayals of Jephthah's daughter and Manoah's wife. In the case of the former, Exum notes that, however noteworthy the actions of Jephthah's daughter in founding a women's ritual event, the narrator in Judges 11 ultimately *upholds* important aspects of male authority in the telling of her story: for example, by having the daughter raise no protest about her father's right to sacrifice her ("do to me according to what has gone forth from your mouth," she tells him [v 36]); also, by concluding the story with a note that Jephthah's daughter died without children and so suggesting that the real tragedy in the tale is the end of some man's family line (v 39); finally, by neglecting to include any information about the ritual event the daughter founds and so silencing its female participants and denying the importance of their religious expression.[79] In the case of Manoah's wife, Exum similarly argues that, despite nods to her greater piety and her more developed theological insight, the Judges 13 narrator essentially portrays the woman as acting on *behalf* of her husband's patriarchal agenda: first, by omitting any description of her background (although this is provided for Manoah [v 2]) or any description of her point of view (does she even want a child?); second, by having her subordinate herself to Manoah in the matter of questioning the messenger (compare her words in v 6 to his in vv 11–12, 17); third, by denying her any hint of sexual pleasure in her task of procreation (the text lacks the typical notice that Manoah "knew" his wife).[80] The conclusion I reached in Section II again seems to me to be operative here: the Deuteronomists are willing to ascribe religious roles to at least some of Judges' women, but they still impose limitations based on their notions of gender-appropriate behavior and gender-appropriate spheres of activity.

Because of these limitations, Deuteronomistic notions about a woman's ability to exert religious power eventually appear more transitory than real, and this suggests in turn that the degree of *actual* religious authority ancient Israelite women could exert during all but the earliest eras of the Israelite cult was very restricted indeed. For many women in ancient Israel, these restrictions must have meant that if they were to have any opportunity to assert themselves in positions of *true* religious power, they had to do so beyond the confines of what the Deuteronomists and their compatriots, the priests and the prophets, considered to be legitimate behavior for women within Yahwistic tradition. Often, this meant that women turned to other cults in addition to or even instead of the cult of Yahweh. As I will discuss in the next chapter, the historical books describe how royal women like Ma'acah, Jezebel, and Athaliah participated in the cult of the goddess Asherah alongside their worship of the Israelite God.[81] But more noteworthy here are descriptions of non-Yahwistic worship among women found in the prophetic books.[82] In Isaiah, Hosea, and Amos, for example, women are particularly cited as engaging in religious behaviors that deviate from the prescribed worship of Yahweh.[83] Also, in the book of Jeremiah, women are said to be worshiping a goddess called only the Queen of Heaven, apparently instead of the Israelite God (Jer 7:16–20; 44:15–19, 25).[84] In the cult of the Queen of Heaven, moreover, and in contradistinction to the cult of Yahweh, women seem to be able to serve as the primary ritual specialists who attend the goddess, baking cakes for the "Queen" (7:18; 44:19) and pouring out libations and burning incense to her (44:15, 19). Women are similarly described in Ezek 8:14 as being able to play a major cultic role in the worship of the Babylonian fertility god Tammuz, performing ritual lamentations on his behalf at a sacred (and quite public) space, the gates of Yahweh's temple in Jerusalem.[85]

To be sure, the biblical tradition, with its insistence on the worship of Yahweh alone, does not hesitate to condemn these women and their behavior as apostate, and most modern commentators have readily followed suit. But perhaps we should not be so quick to judge. For all but a few ancient Israelite women, opportunities for spiritual fulfillment within the male-dominated biblical tradition were sparse. Israel's women thus may have had little choice but to avail themselves of whatever religious life could be had outside the purview of Yahwistic religion. When read in this light, texts describing activities like women baking cakes for the Queen of Heaven or mourning the death of Babylonian Tammuz seem not so much evidence of female heresy as they are testimony to the fact of the heavily male orientation of biblical Yahwism. This androcentric focus of the dominant cult could have left many ancient Israelite women with no option but to seek opportunities for religious expression elsewhere.

NOTES

[1] Act III, Scene 7. The French text reads:

Hélas! Si pour venger l'opprobre d'Israël,
Nos mains ne peuvent pas, comme autrefois Jahel,
Des ennemis de Dieu percer la tête impie,
Nous lui pouvons du moins immoler notre vie.

[2] Racine's quotation was brought to my attention by M. O'Connor, "The Women in the Book of Judges," *HAR* 10 (1986), 278, n. 7.

[3] I am aware that it might be considered precarious to take the text of 5:25 quite so literally; see, for example, the cautions of Baruch Halpern, "The Resourceful Israelite Historian: The Song of Deborah and Israelite Historiography," *HTR* 76 (1983), 389, who writes, "the couplet, 'Water he asked; milk she provided,' read as poetry, carries no implication of a specific request or of a specific libation. It means, 'Sisera requested and received a drink.'" But, as Alexander Globe, "Judges V 27," *VT* 25 (1975), 363–64, n. 3, points out, the words "milk" (*ḥlb*) and "ghee/curds" (*ḥw'h*), seem to form a stock parallel in Hebrew, as well as Ugaritic poetry (see Deut 32:14 and *KTU* 1.23.1.14; see also Gen 18:8; Prov 30:33; Isa 7:22). If, moreover, it is the intent of Judges 5 to evoke this standard pair, then the third item of sustenance mentioned, "water," *does* stand out as an anomaly, and hence my sense that the poem seeks, after all, to contrast the modest nature of Sisera's request with the generous quality of Jael's response. On these parallel lines as complementary rather than synonymous, see further Robert Alter, "From Line to Story in Biblical Verse," *Poetics Today* 4 (1983), 631; idem, *The Art of Biblical Poetry* (New York: Basic Books, 1985), 44, although note that Alter, in insisting on reading the stock parallel pair of "hand" (*yd*) and "right hand" (*ymyn*) in verse 26 in a similar complementary fashion, takes his own theory too far. See again Halpern, "The Resourceful Israelite Historian," 389, and J. Blenkinsopp, "Ballad Style and Psalm Style in the Song of Deborah: A Discussion," *Bib* 42 (1961), 74.

[4] The prose, although it does not share my specific sense of the bowl's "specialness," seems to agree regarding its distinctiveness, finding it, in fact, *too* distinctive for the abode of a tent-dwelling woman and thus substituting a more appropriately pastoral (albeit mundane) wineskin. See Halpern, *The First Historians: The Hebrew Bible and History* (San Francisco: Harper & Row, 1988), 81.

[5] This *pace* Alter, "From Line to Story," who argues that the maternal imagery he believes *is* present in the prose rendition of the story is deliberately avoided in the poem, "because the poet does not want to mitigate or complicate with maternal

associations the image of Jael the triumphant slayer" (p. 635); also see idem, *Biblical Poetry*, 48.

[6]Pointed out by R. Adler, "'A Mother in Israel': Aspects of the Mother Role in Jewish Myth," *Beyond Androcentrism: New Essays on Women and Religion* (ed. R. M. Gross; Missoula, MT: Scholars Press, 1977), 248; also, L. L. Bronner, "Valorized or Vilified? The Women of Judges in Midrashic Sources," *A Feminist Companion to Judges* (ed. A. Brenner; The Feminist Companion to the Bible 4; Sheffield: Sheffield Academic Press, 1993), 89.

[7]See Halpern, "The Resourceful Israelite Historian," 379–401; idem, *The First Historians*, 76–103.

[8]"The Sanctuary of Arad and the Family of Hobab the Kenite," *JNES* 24 (1965), 297–303.

[9]See, similarly, 1 Kgs 1:50–53, where Adonijah, fearing the wrath of his rival half-brother Solomon, takes refuge by clinging to the horns of Yahweh's altar at the tent-shrine that was the predecessor of the temple in Jerusalem; also Neh 6:11. There, when persecuted by Sanballat, the governor of the province of Samaria; by Tobiah, the governor of the province of Ammon; and by Geshem the Arab, king of Qeder, Nehemiah considers (although rejects) the possibility of protecting himself by seeking sanctuary in the Jerusalem temple.

[10]"The Resourceful Israelite Historian," 379–401; *The First Historians*, 76–103.

[11]Reading "Hobab" in 1:16 with the Septuagint; the MT lacks the father-in-law's name, but it is required for the sense.

[12]Alternatively, on Reuel as a clan name, see William F. Albright, "Jethro, Hobab and Reuel in Early Hebrew Tradition (with some Comments on the Origin of 'JE')," *CBQ* 25 (1963), 1–11. Albright also proposes that, according to Num 10:29, Hobab is Moses' son-in-law (p. 7).

[13]I have discussed this phenomenon elsewhere; see "The Prayer of Nabonidus, Elijah on Mount Carmel, and Monotheism in Israel," *The Echoes of Many Texts: Reflections on Jewish and Christian Traditions, Essays in Honor of Lou H. Silberman* (ed. W. G. Dever and J. E. Wright; BJS 313; Atlanta: Scholars Press, 1997), 53–55.

[14]Mazar discounts these texts as being from "another tradition" ("The Sanctuary of Arad," 300).

[15]On the Mosaic and Aaronid priesthoods, see F. M. Cross, *Canaanite Myth and Hebrew Epic: Essays in the History of the Religion of Israel* (Cambridge, MA: Harvard University Press, 1973), 195–215.

[16]Note, for example, the sacrifices offered in the book of Judges by Gideon (6:26–27) and by Manoah (13:19–20), although on Gideon's claim to priestly authority, see B. Halpern, "The Rise of Abimelek Ben-Jerubbaal," *HAR* 2 (1978), 85–88.

[17]"The Sanctuary of Arad," 302, n. 27.

[18]Despite its brevity, this enigmatic text has occasioned much discussion. Along with the standard commentaries, add to the exhaustive bibliography collected by B. S. Childs, *The Book of Exodus: A Critical, Theological Commentary* (OTL; Philadelphia: Westminster, 1974), 90, the following works that have appeared since Childs wrote: C. Houtman, "Exodus 4:24–26 and Its Interpretation," *JNSL* 11 (1983), 81–105; L. Kaplan, "'And the Lord Sought to Kill Him' (Exod 4:24): Yet Once Again," *HAR* 5 (1981), 65–74; B. Robinson, "Zipporah to the Rescue: A Contextual Study of Exodus IV 24–6," *VT* 36 (1986), 447–61.

[19]The "him" to which the MT refers is, in fact, unclear, and some have suggested that the intended victim is Moses' son, Gershom; so, for example, Y. Blau, "Ḥătan Dāmîm," *Tarbiz* 26 (1956), 1–3 (Hebrew); M. Greenberg, *Understanding Exodus* (New York: Behrman House for the Melton Research Center of the Jewish Theological Seminary of America, 1969), 113–14, 116; H. Kosmala, "The 'Bloody Husband,'" *VT* 12 (1962), 20–23; J. Morgenstern, "The 'Bloody Husband' (?) (Exod 4:24–26) Once Again," *HUCA* 34 (1963), 45. But since Gershom has not been mentioned previously in the text, I agree with the ancient versions and with the vast majority of commentators that the intended victim of Yahweh's attack is Moses. For further discussion, see Kaplan, "'And the Lord Sought to Kill Him,'" 65–74.

[20]See above, Chapter 1, and the discussion there of the work of S. Niditch ("Eroticism and Death in the Tale of Jael," *Gender and Difference in Ancient Israel* [ed. P. L. Day; Minneapolis: Fortress, 1989], 47–48; *War in the Hebrew Bible: A Study in the Ethics of Violence* [New York and Oxford: Oxford University Press, 1993], 114), who has interpreted the reference to "feet" in Judg 5:27 similarly.

[21]Kosmala's etymology of *ḥtn*, "to circumcise," based on a cognate in Arabic, and his resulting translation of *ḥătan dāmîm* as "the blood-circumcised one" ("'Bloody Husband,'" 25–27) generally have been rejected by biblical scholars. See Childs, *Exodus*, 97–98.

[22]Robinson, "Zipporah to the Rescue," 458, goes so far as to suggest that, "by undertaking the circumcision of her son, a male role, Zipporah has taken the place of her father Jethro. Henceforth she is not only Moses' wife, but also his surrogate father-in-law" and therefore, given my discussion of Jethro's priestly status above, a surrogate priest. See, similarly, Morgenstern, "The 'Bloody Husband,'" 67, 69–70, who sees Zipporah as acting in Exod 4:24–26 on behalf of her brother and thus

again as a surrogate for a man who is a member of a priestly clan. Yet, despite my sympathies with these particular observations, I note my disagreement with both Robinson's and Morgenstern's overall interpretations.

[23]"The Sanctuary of Arad," 301.

[24]Note the related noun *tôrâ,* English "Torah," which means "teaching," "instructions," or "directions" and is the name given by the tradition to the first five books of the Hebrew Bible.

[25]Gen 13:18; 14:13; and 18:1 actually refer to "the *oaks* [plural] of Mamre" (*'ēlônê mamrē'*). However, Gen 18:4 and 8 speak only of a single "tree" (*'ēṣ*) at Mamre, and almost all the ancient authorities (the Septuagint, the Syriac, and the Vulgate) likewise take the original reference to have been to a single oak.

[26]On the translation of all these terms, see M. Zohary, *Plants of the Bible* (Cambridge: Cambridge University Press, 1982), 108; cf. BDB (Oxford: Clarendon, 1980), 18b, s. v. *'ēlôn.*

[27]BDB, 18b, s. v. *'ēlâ,* notes that there is a lack of clear distinction between *'ēlâ, 'ēlôn,* and *'allôn;* I would add the *hapax legomenon 'allâ* to this list as well.

[28]Thus Robert G. Boling, *Judges* (AB 6a; Garden City, NY: Doubleday, 1975), 95, identifies Kedesh in Judges 4 with Khirbet Qedish in the southeastern Galilee, but compare Boling's comments on p. 100 and his map on p. 91. At both these points, he retains the traditional identification of Kedesh with Tell Qades in the Upper Galilee. See also the comments of R. Arav, "Kedesh 2," and J. L. Peterson, "Kedesh 3," *ABD* 4 (ed. D. N. Freedman; New York: Doubleday, 1992), 11a and 11b, respectively.

[29]"The Resourceful Israelite Historian," 390; *The First Historians,* 91–94.

[30]Kedesh and Hazor also are listed together in Josh 15:23, but as part of the tribal allotment of the southern tribe of Judah!

[31]"The Resourceful Israelite Historian," 390, and n. 51; also n. 53 on p. 391; *The First Historians,* 85–86, 92–93.

[32]The city of refuge Shechem, for example, is also the site of a sacred oak or oaks (Gen 12:6; 35:4; Josh 24:26; and Judg 9:6, 37); the site of a sanctuary where Joshua's great covenant ceremony was held (Josh 24:1–28, especially v 26); and the site of Joseph's burial (Josh 24:32). Similarly, the city of refuge Hebron is the site of the burials of Abraham, Sarah, Isaac, and Jacob (Gen 25:9; 23:19; 35:27–29; and 50:13, respectively) and the site of David's crowning by the southern and then northern tribes (2 Sam 2:1–4 and 5:1–3), an activity which, as described above with

respect to Abimelech's crowning, is a religious ritual. See also the remarks of J. R. Spencer, "Refuge, Cities of," *ABD* 5, 657b.

[33]See, for example, Halpern, "The Resourceful Israelite Historian," 388, n. 45, and 393, n. 56; J. A. Soggin, "'Ḥeber der Qenit.' Das Ende eines biblischen Personnennamens?" *VT* 31 (1981), 89–92; idem, *Judges: A Commentary* (OTL; Philadelphia: Westminster, 1981), 74–75. Soggin prefers the translation "a woman of the Kenite group" in both 4:11 and 17 and in 5:24.

[34]"Mari and the Bible: Some Patterns of Tribal Organization and Institutions," *JAOS* 82 (1962), 144–46; see also the detailed survey of the uses of *ḥbr/ḥbr* throughout northwest Semitic in M. O'Connor, "Northwest Semitic Designations for Elective Social Affinities," *JANESCU* 18 (1986), 72–80.

[35]Gen 23:2; 35:27; Josh 14:15; 15:13, 54; 20:7; 21:11; Judg 1:10.

[36]For much of what follows, see B. Halpern, "Kenites," *ABD* 4, 17b–22b.

[37]Arabic, Syriac, and Palmyrene.

[38]In addition to Halpern, "Kenites," see in this regard R. North, "The Cain Music," *JBL* 83 (1964), 379.

[39]"Kenites," 19b.

[40]Halpern, "Kenites," 18a–b.

[41]George F. Moore, *A Critical and Exegetical Commentary on Judges* (ICC; Edinburgh: T. & T. Clark, 1903), 167, praises Bishop Lowth for justly saying that there is nothing in literature more perfect in its kind than these verses.

[42]See the similar conclusion of James S. Ackerman, "Prophecy and Warfare in Early Israel: A Study of the Deborah-Barak Story," *BASOR* 220 (1975), 9–10, although I note my disagreement with many of the specifics of Ackerman's analysis (see also in this regard D. F. Murray, "Narrative Structure and Technique in the Deborah-Barak Story (Judges IV 4–22)," *Studies in the Historical Books of the Old Testament* [VTSup 30; ed. J. A. Emerton; Leiden: Brill, 1979], 167, n. 28).

[43]See also the comment of Boling on Judg 5:7: "the title *mother in Israel* recognizes Deborah's prophetic leadership, as does the title 'father' for a male prophet" (see 2 Kgs 2:12 [Elisha addressing Elijah] and 13:14 [King Joash addressing Elisha]), quoted from "Introduction to and Annotations on Judges," *The HarperCollins Study Bible* (ed. W. A. Meeks; New York: HarperCollins Publishers, 1993), 376 (note on Judg 5:7). Similarly, Boling, *Judges,* 257; J. A. Hackett, "In the Days of Jael: Reclaiming the History of Women in Ancient Israel," *Immaculate and Powerful: The*

Female in Sacred Image and Social Reality (ed. C. W. Atkinson; C. H. Buchanan; M. R. Miles; Boston: Beacon, 1985), 28; C. Meyers, *Discovering Eve: Ancient Israelite Women in Context* (New York and Oxford: Oxford University Press, 1988), 159–60.

[44]"In the Days of Jael," 19, 25–31; idem, "Women's Studies and the Hebrew Bible," *The Future of Biblical Studies: The Hebrew Scriptures* (ed. R. E. Friedman and H. G. M. Williamson; Atlanta: Scholars Press, 1987), 149–51, 156–59.

[45]On the dating of Judges 5, see Chapter 1, n. 5.

[46]See, along with others, W. G. Dever, "The Contribution of Archaeology to the Study of Canaanite and Early Israelite Religion," *Ancient Israelite Religion: Essays in Honor of Frank Moore Cross* (ed. P. D. Miller; P. D. Hanson; S. D. McBride; Philadelphia: Fortress, 1987), 232–33; idem, *Recent Archaeological Discoveries and Biblical Research* (Seattle and London: The University of Washington Press, 1990), 128–38.

[47]See, similarly (although not identically), Meyers, *Discovering Eve,* 140, 159–64.

[48]"In the Days of Jael," 33; see likewise "Women's Studies," 161.

[49]Cross, *Canaanite Myth,* 274–89, especially 284, 287; see also R. E. Friedman, *The Exile and Biblical Narrative: The Formation of the Deuteronomistic and Priestly Works* (Chico, CA: Scholars Press, 1981), 1–26; R. D. Nelson, *The Double Redaction of the Deuteronomistic History* (Sheffield: JSOT Press, 1981), passim but especially 13–28, 119–28.

[50]On *tôrâ,* see above, n. 24.

[51]M. Cogan, *Imperialism and Religion: Assyria, Judah and Israel in the Eighth and Seventh Centuries B.C.E.* (SBLMS 19; Missoula, MT: Scholars Press, 1974); J. McKay, *Religion in Judah Under the Assyrians* (SBT [Second Series] 26; Naperville, IL: Alan R. Allenson, 1973).

[52]See further W. E. Phipps, "A Woman Was the First to Declare Scripture Holy," *Bible Review* 6/2 (April 1990), 14–15, 44.

[53]The other possible translation is "a fiery woman," from *lappîd,* "torch."

[54]See Boling, *Judges,* 95, as well as the references found in C. F. Burney, *The Book of Judges* (London: Rivingtons, 1920), 85, and in Moore, *Judges,* 113.

[55]See Chapter 1.

[56]Hackett, for example, notes this possibility (although it is not an opinion she herself shares). See "In the Days of Jael," 27; "Women's Studies," 157.

[57]This interpretation most recently has been noted by Claudia V. Camp, "1 and 2 Kings," *The Women's Bible Commentary* (ed. C. A. Newsom and S. H. Ringe; London: SPCK; Louisville, KY: Westminster/John Knox, 1992), 109, although Camp herself is not an advocate of it.

[58]M. Bal, *Death and Dissymmetry: The Politics of Coherence in the Book of Judges* (Chicago: University of Chicago Press, 1988), 41–68, 106–13; P. L. Day, "From the Child Is Born the Woman: The Story of Jephthah's Daughter," *Gender and Difference*, 58–74; J. C. Exum, "The Tragic Vision and Biblical Narrative: The Case of Jephthah," *Signs and Wonders: Biblical Texts in Literary Focus* (ed. J. C. Exum; Decatur, GA: Scholars Press, 1989), 59–83; idem, "Murder They Wrote: Ideology and the Manipulation of Female Presence in Biblical Narrative," *USQR* 43 (1989), 19–39 (reprinted in *The Pleasure of Her Text: Feminist Readings of Biblical and Historical Texts* [ed. A. Bach; Philadelphia: Trinity Press International, 1990], 45–67; slightly revised in "Murder They Wrote," Chapter 1 in *Fragmented Women: Feminist (Sub)versions of Biblical Narratives* [Valley Forge, PA: Trinity Press International, 1993], 16–41); idem, "Jephthah: the absence of God," Chapter 3 in *Tragedy and Biblical Narrative: Arrows of the Almighty* (Cambridge: Cambridge University Press, 1992), 45–69; idem, "Feminist Criticism: Whose Interests Are Being Served?" *Judges and Method: New Approaches in Biblical Studies* (ed. G. A. Yee; Minneapolis: Fortress, 1995), 75–78; E. Fuchs, "Marginalization, Ambiguity, Silencing: The Story of Jephthah's Daughter," *JFSR* 5 (1989), 35–45; Hackett, "In the Days of Jael," 29–32; idem, "Women's Studies," 158–60; P. Trible, "A Meditation in Mourning: The Sacrifice of the Daughter of Jephthah," *USQR* 36 (1981), 59–73; idem, "The Daughter of Jephthah: An Inhuman Sacrifice," Chapter 4 in *Texts of Terror: Literary-Feminist Readings of Biblical Narratives* (OBT 13; Philadelphia: Fortress, 1984), 93–116; idem, "A Daughter's Death: Feminism, Literary Criticism, and the Bible," *Backgrounds for the Bible* (ed. M. P. O'Connor and D. N. Freedman; Winona Lake, IN: Eisenbrauns, 1987), 1–14.

[59]*Texts of Terror*, 97; "A Daughter's Death," 5; "Meditation in Mourning," 61; see, similarly, Bal, *Death and Dissymmetry*, 44; D. Marcus, *Jephthah and His Vow* (Lubbock, TX: Texas Tech Press, 1986), 54–55; cf. T. W. Cartledge, *Vows in the Hebrew Bible and the Ancient Near East* (JSOTSup 147; Sheffield: JSOT Press, 1992), 179; Exum, *Tragedy and Biblical Narrative*, 49–50.

[60]As pointed out by Trible, *Texts of Terror*, 102; "A Daughter's Death," 7; "Meditation in Mourning," 63.

[61]*Texts of Terror*, 102; similarly, "A Daughter's Death," 7–8; "Meditation in Mourning," 63.

[62]"In the Days of Jael," 30; "Women's Studies," 159; cf. Fuchs, "Marginalization, Ambiguity, Silencing," 42, 45.

[63]See further the comments of P. Bird, "Women's Religion in Ancient Israel," *Women's Earliest Records From Ancient Egypt and Western Asia* (BJS 166; ed. B. S. Lesko; Atlanta: Scholars Press, 1989), 286; idem, "The Place of Women in the Israelite Cultus," *Ancient Israelite Religion,* 399.

[64]"Jephthah's Daughter," 58–74, but especially 60; see, somewhat similarly, Bal, *Death and Dissymmetry,* 46–52, especially 49 (and also 110), who also sees the daughter's ritual event as a young woman's rite of passage, although in Bal's reading, the transition in question is slightly different, having to do with the young women's impending entrance into marriage relationships. For a very different reading, see Exum, *Tragedy and Biblical Narrative,* 67–69; idem, *Fragmented Women,* 39.

[65]Exum, "Promise and Fulfillment," 43–59; idem, "'Mother in Israel': A Familiar Figure Reconsidered," *Feminist Interpretation of the Bible* (ed. L. M. Russell; Philadelphia: Westminster, 1985), 82–84; idem, "Samson's Women," Chapter 3 in *Fragmented Women,* 61–93, especially 63–68; idem, "Feminist Criticism," *Judges and Method,* 79–80; Hackett, "In the Days of Jael," 29, 32; idem, "Women's Studies," 158, 160. See also Y. Amit, "'Manoah Promptly Followed His Wife' (Judges 13.11): On the Place of the Woman in Birth Narratives," *A Feminist Companion to Judges,* 146–56; Bal, *Death and Dissymmetry,* 73–76, 104–6; D. N. Fewell, "Judges," *The Women's Bible Commentary,* 72; E. Fuchs, "The Literary Characterization of Mothers and Sexual Politics in the Hebrew Bible," *Feminist Perspectives on Biblical Scholarship* (ed. A. Y. Collins; Chico, CA: Scholars Press, 1985), 123–25; L. R. Klein, "A Spectrum of Female Characters in the Book of Judges," *A Feminist Companion to Judges,* 26–27; S. Niditch, "Samson as Culture Hero, Trickster, and Bandit: The Empowerment of the Weak," *CBQ* 52 (1990), 610–12; A. Reinhartz, "Samson's Mother: An Unnamed Protagonist," *JSOT* 55 (1992), 25–37.

[66]I am grateful to David Noel Freedman, my colleague at the University of California at San Diego, for this observation.

[67]"Promise and Fulfillment," 51.

[68]"Promise and Fulfillment," 51.

[69]"In the Days of Jael," 32; see, similarly, the conclusions of Fuchs, "Mother," 123–25 (who goes so far as to call Manoah a "schlemiel" on p. 123!) and Niditch, "Samson as Culture Hero, Trickster, and Bandit," 611 (both pointed out by Exum, *Fragmented Women,* 63); also R. Alter, "How Convention Helps Us Read: The Case of the Bible's Annunciation Type-Scene," *Prooftexts* 3 (1983), 123–24; Amit, "'Manoah Promptly Followed His Wife,'" 149–50; Bal, *Death and Dissymmetry,* 74, 105; Exum, "Feminist Criticism," 79; O'Connor, "Women in the Book of Judges," 280; Reinhartz, "Samson's Mother," 32–33; cf. J. L. Crenshaw, "The Samson Saga: Filial Devotion or Erotic Attachment," *ZAW* 86 (1974), 475.

[70]See J. Blenkinsopp, "Some Notes on the Saga of Samson and the Heroic Milieu," *Scripture* 11 (1959), 84–85; idem, "Structure and Style in Judges 13–16," *JBL* 82 (1963), 66–67; Exum, "Promise and Fulfillment," 49, n. 18, and references there; idem, "The Theological Dimension of the Samson Saga," *VT* 33 (1983), 31; E. L. Greenstein, "The Riddle of Samson," *Prooftexts* 1 (1981), 250–51; Niditch, "Samson as Culture Hero, Trickster, and Bandit," 612–13; O'Connor, "Women in the Book of Judges," 280, n. 13.

[71]See, similarly, Exum, "Promise and Fulfillment," 49; D. M. Gunn, "Samson of Sorrows: An Isaianic Gloss on Judges 13–16," *Reading Between Texts: Intertextuality and the Hebrew Bible* (ed. D. N. Fewell; Louisville, KY: Westminster/John Knox, 1992), 229; O'Connor, "Women in the Book of Judges," 280, n. 13. Blenkinsopp, moreover, in "Structure and Style," 66, seems so to assume that there is a correspondence between the abstentions required of the pregnant woman and those that will eventually be required of her Nazirite son that, without even comment, he describes the prohibitions imposed upon the mother as part of the son's Nazirite vow. Cf. R. W. Neff, *The Announcement in Old Testament Birth Stories* (unpublished Ph.D. dissertation; Yale University, 1969), 142.

[72]Much of the discussion of 1 Samuel 1 that follows has benefited greatly from conversations with my colleague Julie A. Duncan at Princeton Theological Seminary.

[73]Reading with the Septuagint in 1 Sam 1:9; the MT lacks "and she presented herself before Yahweh."

[74]The text here is quite confused, with both the Greek tradition and 4QSam[a] indicating that an original reference concerning the abstaining from wine and strong drink has fallen out of the MT. Yet both the Greek and Qumran versions otherwise seem *too* long, as both, under the influence of verse 22, have added an explicit notice concerning the unborn child's Nazirite status. See P. K. McCarter, *1 Samuel* (AB 8; Garden City, NY: Doubleday, 1980), 53–54, and also 56.

[75]Again, as in n. 72 above, I am grateful to Julie A. Duncan, my colleague at Princeton Theological Seminary, for this observation.

[76]Unlike the Jephthah's daughter and Manoah's wife stories, the Micah's mother narrative has attracted very little attention from feminist critics. See only Bal, *Death and Dissymmetry*, 203–6, and G. A. Yee, "Ideological Criticism: Judges 17–21 and the Dismembered Body," *Judges and Method*, 158.

[77]Cf. Yee, "Ideological Criticism," 158, who raises questions about the adherence of Micah's mother to the Bible's dicta prohibiting graven images (Exod 20:4) and about this woman's supposed generosity (Yee presumes that the dedication of only two hundred pieces of silver for the statue means that the mother "pockets the

rest"). To me, however, a tithe of almost twenty percent of the original eleven hundred silver coins seems plenty munificent, and the alleged "idolatry" points not so much to a particular sin on the mother's part as to a more general disjunction between the actions prohibited by ancient Israelite legal traditions and the actions actually undertaken by the practitioners of Israelite religion. See further my "Idol, Idolatry," *The Eerdmans' Dictionary of the Bible* (ed. D. N. Freedman; Grand Rapids, MI: Eerdmans, forthcoming [1998]).

[78] On the namelessness of women in Judges, see the Introduction, n. 18; Chapter 1, n. 72; and, as in both of these citations, the comments of Bal, *Death and Dissymmetry*, 43–93, 217–24; of A. Brenner, "Introduction," *A Feminist Companion to Judges*, 10–14; of Exum, "Feminist Criticism," 75–86; and of C. Meyers, "The Hannah Narrative in Feminist Perspective," *"Go to the Land I Will Show You": Studies in Honor of Dwight W. Young* (ed. J. Coleson and V. Matthews; Winona Lake, IN: Eisenbrauns, 1994), 120–22 (reprinted as "Hannah and her Sacrifice: Reclaiming Female Agency," *A Feminist Companion to Samuel and Kings* [ed. A. Brenner; The Feminist Companion to the Bible 5; Sheffield: Sheffield Academic Press, 1994], 96–99). See also my comments in Chapter 5.

[79] See Exum, *Tragedy and Biblical Narrative*, 65–69; idem, *Fragmented Women*, 18–21, 31–41; idem, "Feminist Criticism," 76–77.

[80] See Exum, *Fragmented Women*, 63–68, 89–93; idem, "Feminist Criticism," 78–83; on the asexual nature of Samson's conception, see also Bal, *Lethal Love: Feminist Literary Readings of Biblical Love Stories* (Bloomington and Indianapolis: Indiana University Press, 1987), 41.

[81] 1 Kgs 15:13; 18:19; 2 Kgs 11:18; see further Chapter 3.

[82] S. Ackerman, "Isaiah," *The Women's Bible Commentary*, 162.

[83] Isa 3:16–24; 4:1; 32:9–14; Hosea 1–3; 4:13; Amos 4:1–3.

[84] S. Ackerman, "'And the Women Knead Dough': The Worship of the Queen of Heaven in Sixth-Century Judah," *Gender and Difference*, 109–24; idem, *Under Every Green Tree: Popular Religion in Sixth-Century Judah* (HSM 46; Atlanta: Scholars Press, 1992), 5–35.

[85] Ackerman, *Under Every Green Tree*, 79–93.

Chapter 3

⚬⚬⚬

"Out of the Window She Peered"

SISERA'S MOTHER, QUEEN MOTHERS,
AND THE GODS

Allah is great, no doubt, and Juxtaposition his prophet.

FROM THE POEM *AMOURS DE VOYAGE,*
BY ARTHUR HUGH CLOUGH[1]

Juxtaposition is the stuff of which Judges 5 is made. A woman offers sanctuary and then turns to murder; a divine warrior marches forth to lead a human army into battle; a male God recruits female confederates to be his principal allies. Usually, these oppositions are presented in the course of juxtaposed verses, such as the portrayal of Jael in verses 24–25 and 26–27, or even in juxtaposed stanzas, for example, the depictions of Yahweh in Stanza 2 (vv 4–5) of Judges 5 and of Deborah in Stanza 3 (vv 6–7). But the poem's impulse to contrast is so strong that on occasion juxtapositions can be introduced with the use of only a few words or in just a few lines. For instance, verse 24, where Jael is introduced with the epithet "most blessed" because of her willingness to commit murder on behalf of Israel's God, becomes all the more evocative when compared to verse 23, where the Israelite tribes are ordered to "curse utterly" the people of Meroz because that clan failed to answer Yahweh's call to arms.

The final words describing Jael, found in verse 27, also are juxtaposed evocatively with imagery that comes from a neighboring verse,

verse 28.² The former passage ends with a description of Sisera's dead body as it lies battered and crumpled between Jael's feet:

> *Between her feet, he sunk, he fell, he lay,*
> *Between her feet he sunk, he fell,*
> *Where he sunk,*
> *He fell there, dead.*

The verse's tone here is full of tension, with each of its four short lines dominated by a series of staccato verbs: "he sunk," "he fell," "he lay." These verbs, moreover, are repeated again and again and in increasingly terse and more urgent formulations: "he sunk, he fell, he lay" (line 1); "he sunk, he fell" (line 2); "he sunk" (line 3); "he fell" (line 4). Finally, by the end of the verse, closure is achieved in the form of one word, "dead," and with it, a climactic picture of Sisera lying devastated and destroyed on Jael's tent floor. The effect on us when we read or hear this verse is likewise devastating. Just as Jael's hammer struck unrelentingly against Sisera's skull, we suffer the thrust of the verbs in verse 27 hitting us over and over, metaphorically, at least, beating our minds into a pulp. And, although unlike Sisera, we do not ultimately find that we are rendered dead, we do feel as if we have been deadened or numbed, pounded by the language and images of verse 27 into a state of stupefaction and shock.

Before, however, we can even catch our breaths, much less assimilate the portrayal of violent death that lies splayed across our imaginations, the scene shifts, and the poem's depiction of wartime chaos gives way to peaceful images of civilization and domesticity: the shepherd's tent becomes a noble's home and the woman of war becomes a matron of the hearth. This is Sisera's mother, the third major woman character of Judges 5, who stands in the window of her great house, gazing out across the countryside and toward the horizon beyond. The narrative's movement here, from manifest calamity to apparent serenity, seems disconcertingly abrupt. But, in fact, Judges 5 uses the juxtaposition of verses 27 and 28 to enhance rather than confuse our appreciation of the moment's drama. The key here is to realize that, in spite of its ostensibly halcyon veneer, the tone of verse 28, like that of verse 27, is full of tension. Anxiety consumes the mother as she stares out of her window, and she intently scans the landscape for even the least of signs that her son will return safely home at the end of the Israelite-Canaanite war:

> Out of the window she peered,
> The mother of Sisera gazed[3] through the lattice.
> "Why does his chariot tarry in coming?
> Why do the hoofbeats of his chariot corps delay?"

The cumulative effect here is almost that of a double blow, with verse 27 evoking the sort of gut-wrenching nausea that comes when we are exposed to gruesome and relentless depictions of violence, at the same time that verse 28 calls forth the sort of gut-churning butterflies that come when we are afflicted with nervousness and unease and unable to think of anything but the worst. In fact, by allowing absolutely no interlude between the description of Sisera's grisly murder in verse 27 and the depiction of his mother's anxiety in verse 28, Judges 5 leaves us with no choice but to confront feelings of both horror and dread simultaneously, layering atop our unalleviated numbness concerning the scene of Sisera's death the pain of the mother's just dawning awareness that she waits in vain for her son to come home.[4]

The agonies engendered by this juxtaposition become even more affecting if we recall the underlying eroticism of verse 27.[5] As that verse ends, Sisera lies ravaged between Jael's legs in a pose of sexual submission; in the very next line, we see Sisera's mother, the woman between whose legs Sisera as a newborn first lay. But, although Sisera lies helpless at Jael's genitalia in the same way that he once lay helpless at the mouth of his mother's womb, disjunction is once more the poem's point, for while Sisera's helplessness as an infant was the fragility of the newly living, his helplessness as he lies in Jael's tent is the impotence of the newly dead.[6] It is as if verses 27 and 28 have sung in perfect harmony until one suddenly and unexpectedly finds itself off-key. As melody turns to dissonance, the sounds of crying women clamor cacophonously beneath the poem's surface. While a seductress moans in orgasmic satisfaction, a laboring woman screams in pain and travail; while a conquering assassin shouts in exultation and triumph, a mother wails in lamentation and woe.

The pathos effected by this juxtaposition continues, moreover, in verses 29–30, as the mother finds that the only comforts available to ease her worries are the pitiful fantasies that one of her waiting women provides about the cause of her son's tarrying:[7]

> "Are they not finding and apportioning plunder?
> A maiden, two maidens for every warrior?"

But while the attendant can only fantasize that Sisera's delay is caused by the gathering of "a maiden, two maidens" for each warrior's sexual gratification, we know, from verse 27, and indeed from the twenty-six verses that precede it, that just the opposite is the case. Although it is indeed one "maiden" (Deborah), two "maidens" (Deborah and Jael) who have brought about Sisera's delay, no women will be brought home as spoil.[8] Instead, Sisera himself has been ravaged by the very women he and his army had hoped to rape. The only women who will be a part of Sisera's entourage in the future, then, are his mother and her female courtiers as they march and mourn in his funeral procession.

Judges 5 ends on this note, and Sisera's mother is mentioned nowhere else in the entire Bible, not even in the prose account of the "Song of Deborah" found in Judges 4. But, despite this woman's very brief appearance, I believe there is much that can be said about her. In Section I of this chapter, I intend to suggest that, contrary to Judges 4, Judges 5 regards Sisera as a king and thus understands his mother as fulfilling the role of queen mother within his royal court. In Section II, using comparative materials, I hope to show that, throughout the biblical world, a queen mother like Sisera's mother would have wielded enormous power within her son's monarchy. This power is most often portrayed as being economic and political in nature, but in Section III, it will be my contention that the power exercised by the queen mother is equally a matter of religious authority. More specifically, I will argue that the queen mother dedicated herself to the cult of the Canaanite mother goddess Asherah and that this dedication was an important part of the official religion of her son's court. While Judges 5 hardly makes this point explicitly regarding Sisera's mother, I will suggest in Section IV of my discussion that the description of her peering out of her window intimates strongly that, like her queen mother counterparts, she is understood by biblical tradition as an Asherah devotee.

I. SISERA'S MOTHER AS QUEEN MOTHER

Although Judg 4:2 identifies Sisera only as the "commander" (*śār*) of the army of Jabin, the Canaanite king who is said to engage Israel in battle, Judges 5 seems to believe that Israel was opposed not by one but by several Canaanite kings and that Sisera was counted as one of these monarchs.[9] This is seen especially in verses 19–21, where an elaborate poetic structure suggests Sisera's royal status. These verses can be represented schematically as follows:

COUPLET NO. 1

The kings came, they fought,
Then fought the kings of Canaan.

COUPLET NO. 2

At Ta'anach by the waters of Megiddo,
They took no spoils of silver.

COUPLET NO. 3

From heaven fought the stars,
from their courses they fought against Sisera.

COUPLET NO. 4

The Wadi Kishon swept them away.
The wadi attacked them,[10] the Wadi Kishon.

This stanza is made up of four poetic couplets, in which Couplets #1 and #3 are paired, as are Couplets #2 and #4. The first line of the first couplet thus refers to the Canaanite army ("the kings came, they fought") in the same way that the first line of the third couplet refers to a fighting force, the stars as one component of the Israelite militia ("from heaven fought the stars"). The same verb—*lhm,* "to fight"—is even used in the same form—*nilḥāmû,* "they fought"—in both lines. The first line of Couplet #2 and the first line of Couplet #4 are similarly paired, as both refer to water (Couplet #2: "the waters of Megiddo"; Couplet #4: "the Wadi Kishon"). Although less obviously parallel, the second lines of Couplets #2 and #4 also contain shared imagery, as the description of the Wadi Kishon attacking the Canaanite army in Couplet #4 makes clear *why* the kings of Canaan were not able to capture the spoils of silver mentioned in Couplet #2.

This elaborate structure suggests that the second lines of Couplets #1 and #3 should likewise be read as corresponding units. Notably, these read as paired "the kings of Canaan" and "Sisera." What the poem thus indicates is its sense that Israel was opposed in battle by a coalition of Canaanite kings and that Sisera was one of its members. Moreover, since

he is the only member of the coalition who is named, we should probably regard Sisera as being the king who serves as its leader.

Sisera's kingly status further implies that we should understand Sisera's
mother as royal. By emending one word in the last line of verse 30,
some commentators have even argued that the poem contains an explicit
reference to the mother's regal status.[11] As it stands, this verse, with its
words of comfort spoken by the mother's waiting woman, reads as
follows:

> *"Are they not finding and apportioning plunder?*
> *A maiden, two maidens for every warrior?*
> *Plunder of dyed cloth for Sisera?*
> *Plunder of patterned dyed cloth?*
> *Two patterned dyed cloths[12] for the neck of the* šālāl*?"*

The last word, *šālāl,* is left untranslated, for, as Roland de Vaux writes,
its usual meaning of "plunder" is "impossible" in this context.[13] Most
typically, commentators revocalize the word as *šōlēl,* "plunderer," indicating that Sisera delays because he is gathering elaborately embroidered
cloths that he can wear around his neck.[14] Others, myself included, prefer a slightly more radical emendation, replacing the middle *l* of *šālāl*
with a *g* and revocalizing as *šēgal,* "queen." The cause of Sisera's delay
thus becomes that he tarries to gather rich cloths for his royal mother.
Presumably this woman was queen in the court of her husband, Sisera's
father and the former king. When the old king died and Sisera inherited
his throne, she assumed a position in her son's palace as Sisera's queen
mother.

II. THE POLITICAL ROLE OF THE QUEEN MOTHER

Much of the evidence describing the role that a queen mother like Sisera's mother would have played in Canaanite society comes from the
archives found at the Late Bronze Age city-state of Ugarit (c. 1550–1200
B.C.E.). Michael Heltzer has shown, for example, that these materials
attest to the economic power wielded by the Ugaritic queen mother.[15]
Though women at Ugarit generally were not allowed to own property,
queen mothers could possess real estate and were even able to buy land
to supplement their holdings. The queen mother also owned her own

storage facilities, as can be seen in a text that speaks of the two hundred and fifty measures of oil housed in the queen mother's *gt,* a warehouse used for agricultural products. These properties seem to have been managed for the queen mother by administrative personnel under her authority. Heltzer notes that the queen mother counted among her household a chief administrative official (the *šākinu*); a chief counselor (the *mudu*); and several *mārê šarrati,* an Akkadian term that literally means "sons of the queen" but in reality refers to certain officials of high rank who were not actually related to the queen mother. Also in the queen mother's entourage was a group of courtiers described as her "dependents" (*bunušū* [Akkadian] or *bnšm* [Ugaritic]).

Other texts describe the kinds of political power accorded to the Ugaritic queen mother. This power was vast, as is especially indicated by the fact that the Ugaritic king is repeatedly seen as acknowledging the authority of his queen mother. The most vivid demonstration of this is a collection of eight "queen mother" letters, letters that were sent to a Ugaritic queen mother from her son the king.[16] In six of these letters, the Ugaritic kings describe themselves as paying homage to the authority of the queen mother by bowing at her feet.[17] In one text, the king even describes prostrating himself some fourteen times.[18] And in four of the "queen mother" letters, Ugaritic kings acknowledge their queen mothers' authority by addressing them as *adt,* a feminine form of *adn,* "lord." [19]

The power ascribed to the Ugaritic queen mother is also attested in texts that describe the activities of some specific queen mothers. One such document details the terms of a divorce between King Amistamru II (1274–1240 B.C.E.) and Piddu, the daughter of Benteshina, king of Amurru.[20] As in modern divorce cases, much of the settlement concerns the disposition of children, especially the custody of the crown prince Utrisharruma. Utrisharruma is told that he will remain Amistamru's heir after the divorce only if he allies himself with his father; if he sides with his soon-to-be-divorced mother, King Amistamru will appoint an alternate heir. Moreover, according to the agreement, even when Utrisharruma becomes king after his father's death, he cannot reestablish ties with his mother. The son is told that should he bring his mother back to Ugarit as queen mother (*SAL.LUGAL-ut-ti*), he will be forced to abdicate. Amistamru's intent here is to ensure that his former wife never will gain the kinds of economic and political power otherwise accorded to queen mothers at Ugarit. And certainly Amistamru was well aware of the kinds of power that a Ugaritic queen mother could wield since he himself was the son of another notable queen mother, Aḥat-milki. In fact, the power that Aḥat-milki was able to wield was so great that she began her tenure as queen mother by displacing her husband's rightful heir and securing the throne for Amistamru, who was her younger son.[21] Aḥat-milki also seems to have served as regent on behalf of Amistamru for the initial years of his reign since it appears that he ascended the throne while still a minor. Heltzer further suggests that even after a king comes of age, it was common for the Ugaritic queen mother to serve as her son's regent whenever he was absent from the palace.[22] The eight "queen mother" letters are again of significance here, for Heltzer believes the king sent these letters to the queen mother while he was away from court and that their purpose was to describe the ways in which the monarch wanted his queen mother to use her regency to deal with various administrative and political issues.

Queen mothers from elsewhere in the Canaanite world also seem to have served as regents in their sons' courts. The Phoenician inscription of King Eshmunazor of Sidon, for example, which dates from c. 500 B.C.E., begins by describing how King Eshmunazor is "an orphan" and "the son of a few days."[23] The implication is that Eshmunazor succeeded his father Tabnit on the throne of Sidon while still a child. The inscription also states that Eshmunazor died in the fourteenth year of his reign.[24] This suggests that Eshmunazor was still a minor upon his death or, at a minimum, that he had been a minor throughout much of his tenure upon Sidon's throne. The regent who seems to have guided the reign of this boy king was Amoʿashtart, Tabnit's widow and Eshmunazor's queen mother. In lines 14–18 of the text, in which some of the accomplishments of Eshmunazor's reign are listed, it is said that *we* (Eshmunazor and Amoʿashtart) built temples for the gods, for Astarte, for Eshmun, and for other gods of the Sidonians. Similarly, in lines 18–20, the inscription describes how *we* (again, Eshmunazor and Amoʿashtart) annexed Dor and Joppa as part of Sidonian territory. These lines show that, in matters of both domestic policy and foreign affairs, the queen mother of Eshmunazor ruled side-by-side with her son.

I have already described in Chapter 1 how the Israelites, no matter how diligently they sought to distinguish themselves from Canaanite cultures like those of Ugarit and Phoenicia, were in fact of Canaanite descent. My point there was to argue that many of Israel's *religious* traditions, and particularly traditions regarding Anat-like female military heroes, were adopted from Israel's Canaanite ancestors. It is equally the case that many of Israel's *political* institutions were derived from Canaanite antecedents. Certainly this seems to be true in discussing the office of the queen mother, for, as is particularly described in the biblical books of Kings and Chronicles, Israelite queen mothers take on many of the same responsibilities elsewhere assigned to their Canaanite counterparts.[25] For example, as the Ugaritic queen mother Aḫat-milki began her tenure by asserting herself in matters concerning the royal succession, so, too, do Israel's queen-mothers-to-be seem able to play a role in naming their husbands' heir. This can be seen most clearly in 1 Kings 1, the story of how King Solomon succeeds to the throne of his father David. As described in the text, David is on his deathbed, and his throne is about to be inherited by his oldest living son, Adonijah.[26] In fact, Adonijah's claim to the throne seems to be so secure that he is proclaimed king even before David dies, with the support of Joab, the commander of David's army, and of Abiathar, one of David's high priests.

There is, however, dissent: "the priest Zadok [David's other high priest], and Benaiah, son of Jehoiada [the commander of David's private mercenary force], and Nathan the prophet, and Shimei and Rei [two otherwise unknown officials], and David's own warriors did not side with Adonijah" (1 Kgs 1:8). As the passage continues, it is the prophet Nathan who takes the lead in challenging Adonijah's claim. What is of particular note for our purposes is Nathan's means of expressing his opposition. He approaches Bathsheba, one of David's wives and the mother of Solomon, and urges her to go to the ailing David and petition him to appoint Solomon instead of Adonijah as king. Bathsheba does this, Solomon is named the next king, and Adonijah is deposed. Bathsheba thus plays a crucial role in determining the royal succession. This role is also indicated in a text from the Song of Songs (Cant 3:11):

> *Look, O daughters of Zion,*
> *At King Solomon,*
> *At the crown with which his mother crowned him,*
> *On the day of his wedding,*
> *On the day of the gladness of his heart.*

Note especially the third line of the verse and its reference to the crown with which Solomon's *mother* crowned him.

As the story of Solomon's monarchy continues in 1 Kings 2, the text describes another important role Bathsheba plays as she assumes her position as queen mother: she acts as a counselor or adviser within her son's court. Particularly significant are verses 13–25, in which Bathsheba is depicted as a courtier to Solomon, presenting the king with a petition on behalf of the recently deposed Adonijah. Solomon, to be sure, hardly receives this particular petition with favor since in it, Adonijah asks that he be given Abishag the Shunammite, David's concubine, as his wife. Solomon takes this request to be tantamount to asking for David's kingdom.[27] Yet, despite Solomon's displeasure concerning Adonijah's petition, this in no way affects the respect the king accords to his queen mother. As she enters into the room, he rises and bows down to her (*wayyištaḥû*). I am reminded here of the eight "queen mother" letters from Ugarit and their descriptions of how Ugarit's kings are said to bow at the feet of their queen mothers. Also, in much the same way that those Ugaritic kings indicate their respect for their queen mothers by addressing them as *adt,* the feminine form of "lord," so, too, does Solomon acknowledge the authority he accords to Bathsheba by having a seat placed for her at his right hand. A comparison with Pss 80:18 (English 80:17) and 110:1, where the king is described as sitting at the right hand of God, even suggests that after the throne of the monarch himself, the chair assigned to Bathsheba is the place of highest honor on the royal dais.[28]

Another queen mother who is described as sitting on a throne at the side of her son is Nehushta, the queen mother of Jehoiachin (Jer 13:18). Moreover, when the Jerusalem monarchy first falls to its Babylonian conquerors in 597 B.C.E., the same king, Jehoiachin, and his queen mother, Nehushta, are condemned together as subject to the exile of the nation's rulers (2 Kgs 24:12; Jer 22:26). This suggests that king and queen mother are the nation's two most powerful authorities. This is similarly implied in 2 Kgs 10:13, where dignitaries from the southern kingdom of Judah visit the north after the death of Israel's King Ahab. These ambassadors mention in the same breath Ahab's sons and Ahab's widow, Jezebel, who is now serving as queen mother. The important role that the queen mother plays in her son's court is further demonstrated in 2 Chr 22:3, where Athaliah, the queen mother of King Ahaziah of Judah (841 B.C.E.), is specifically identified as a "counselor" (*yôʿeṣet*) to the king.

Biblical tradition also indicates that, like her Canaanite counterparts, the Israelite queen mother, if necessary, can serve as regent on behalf of her son. It may be, for example, that the exalted status of Nehushta, the queen mother of Jehoiachin, is due to the fact that she served as regent for her son because he was too young to rule, given that Jehoiachin was only eighteen during the three months that he held the Jerusalem throne (2 Kgs 24:8). The story of Athaliah found in 2 Kgs 11:1–20 provides a second instance of a queen mother exerting her power as regent. Admittedly, the story of Athaliah's regency is a notorious one from the point of view of the biblical writers since Athaliah is described not only as assuming the Jerusalem throne as regent following the death of her son King Ahaziah (2 Kgs 9:27), but also as scheming to secure the throne permanently by assassinating all the other male members of the royal line. According, though, to folkloristic tradition, Athaliah is foiled, as one male heir, a baby, is spirited away from her slaughter.[29] After seven years, he is presented as king and accepted by the nobles and the people; Athaliah, the queen mother, is seized and killed. Athaliah's regency is thus portrayed as a failure due to her excessive ambition, yet the fact remains that Athaliah shared with other Israelite and Canaanite queen mothers the responsibility of serving as regent when her son—for whatever reason—was unable to rule.

III. THE RELIGIOUS ROLE OF THE QUEEN MOTHER

Commentators generally agree that the kinds of economic and political power ascribed to Canaanite and Israelite queen mothers have their roots in Hittite culture (c. 2000–1180 B.C.E.), where the queen mother or *tawananna* had significant responsibilities in managing the economic and political affairs of the king's court. But the Hittite *tawananna* also had responsibilities within the cultic life of Hittite society. In the most recent study of the *tawananna,* Shoshana R. Bin-Nun has even argued that in the earliest periods of the Hittite Old Kingdom (the seventeenth to the fifteenth centuries B.C.E.), and in pre-Hittite Anatolia as well, the title *tawananna* referred *exclusively* to a religious functionary.[30] According to Bin-Nun, it was only secondarily, in the period of the Hittite Empire (c. 1425–1180 B.C.E.), that the *tawananna* assumed responsibilities within the court's political and economic life. Yet even then her cultic obligations persisted. Despite, however, this primacy of religious function in the duties of the Hittite queen mother, most scholars believe that when

the office of the *tawananna* was borrowed into Canaanite and then Israelite culture, the cultic role of the queen mother was eliminated.[31] I wish
to argue the contrary by suggesting that both Canaanite and Israelite
queen mothers fulfilled not only the socio-political roles detailed above
but also had an official function within their cultures' religious communities. This function was to devote themselves to the cult of the mother
goddess Asherah.

As Steve A. Wiggins has pointed out, the text from the Canaanite
world that most explicitly demonstrates the association of the queen
mother with Asherah comes from Ugarit and is an episode from the
Baal-Anat cycle of myths.[32] I have previously discussed parts of this cycle
in Chapter 1, describing there, for example, how Baal, the king of the
gods, finds himself threatened and ultimately deposed from his throne
by Mot, the god of death and sterility. I further discussed in Chapter 1
the ways in which Anat exerts herself to rescue her brother-consort from
Mot's underworld abode and to restore him to the throne. What I have
not previously noted, however, is a scene that is found between these
two episodes and that depicts what happens after Baal is rendered dead
but before Anat effects his rescue. In it, two of the major gods of the
pantheon, the divine patriarch El and El's consort, the mother goddess
Asherah, meet in order to determine which of Ugarit's deities might
succeed to the throne of the "dead" King Baal (*KTU* 1.6.1.44–65).[33]

The presence of the mother goddess Asherah at this divine colloquy
is suggestive, for it recalls the role that can exist on earth when queen-
mothers-to-be begin their tenures by helping to determine the royal
succession. In fact, this mythological passage explicitly indicates that, as
Bathsheba's participation, say, was integral to the naming of Solomon
as David's successor, so, too, is Asherah's part in appointing Baal's heir
crucial to the succession process. The scene opens with El crying out to
Asherah (*KTU* 1.6.1.44–46):

> *Hear, O Lady Asherah of the Sea,*
> *Give me one of your sons so that I might make him king.*

Asherah readily accepts this responsibility, nominating her son Yadi Yilhan as king. Most probably, Yadi Yilhan is proposed for the throne because of his superior wisdom (the root *ydʿ* means "to know" and *lḥn*
means "to understand"). El, though, is dubious, protesting that Yadi
Yilhan lacks the physical strength of Baal. Asherah then nominates a

second of her sons, Athtar the Terrible. As his epithet "the Terrible" suggests, Athtar seemingly does possess the physical prowess that was lacking in Yadi Yilhan. Yet when Athtar the Terrible ascends to the throne of Baal, he literally does not "measure up": his feet do not reach Baal's footstool, and his head does not reach the throne's top. There is then a relatively short break in the text (about thirty-five lines). As the narrative resumes, its focus has shifted to a description of Anat and her search for the dead Baal (*KTU* 1.6.2.4–37). This juxtaposition of scenes is telling, for it indicates that Anat embarks on her search for Baal only after Asherah's attempts to name a new king have failed. It thus seems that after Baal dies, the obvious response within the gods' royal court is to ask the mother goddess/queen-mother-to-be to help select a new heavenly king. Only when this strategy fails does Anat undertake her quest to resurrect Baal.

Yet, while this story of El and Asherah does suggest that Asherah fulfills at least the "determining succession" role in the heavens with which the queen mother can begin her tenure on earth, it need not necessarily follow that there is a more general association of the earthly queen mother and the cult of Asherah.[34] Elsewhere in Ugaritic literature, though, there are indications that the queen mother on earth was associated with the Asherah cult, even associated to the degree that the queen mother and Asherah might be described as earthly and heavenly counterparts.

The best illustrations of this are found in the Kirta Epic, a text that has as its major concern issues of the royal heir and the royal succession. As the story opens, King Kirta is depicted as bewailing the fact that he has lost his wife and all his children through a series of disasters (disease, plague, drownings, and war). In despair, Kirta undertakes a series of ritual preparations designed to induce the god El to appear to him in a dream.[35] Once El appears and learns the cause of Kirta's grief, he provides Kirta with a list of instructions that, if followed, are designed to secure the noble maiden Hurriya as Kirta's wife. When Kirta awakes, he proceeds to follow El's instructions, offering sacrifices, mustering an army, and marching forth to do battle with King Pabil of Udm, Hurriya's father. Kirta, however, deviates in one significant aspect from El's orders. On the third day of his march toward Udm, he and his forces come to a shrine of Asherah, and there Kirta makes a vow to the goddess that he will dedicate gold and silver to her if he is successful in his quest for Hurriya (*KTU* 1.14.4.32–43).

Critics have puzzled over this vow.[36] It appears unnecessary and even superfluous for Kirta to seek divine succor from Asherah given that success in his mission has already been promised by El. In fact, although the text becomes fragmentary at a crucial point, it seems that Kirta's vow ultimately brings him harm rather than good. After securing Hurriya, the king fails to dedicate the promised riches to Asherah, and consequently, she seeks revenge. The next complete scene in the text describes how Kirta is afflicted with some unspecified but seemingly mortal illness, which most commentators presume is the result of Asherah's curse.[37]

Why, then, does Kirta enter into his unnecessary and arguably foolish vow?[38] I propose that the context of his mission provides a clue. Kirta has presented himself to El as one desperate for an heir. "Grant that sons I might acquire," Kirta begs El. "Grant that children I might multiply" (*KTU* 1.14.2.4–5). For Kirta, the important point in his marriage to Hurriya is not so much the fact that she will serve him as queen but that she will become mother and eventually, upon Kirta's death, queen mother to their royal son. When she becomes queen mother, moreover, my thesis proposes, she will devote herself to the worship of Asherah within her son's court and will even be considered the earthly counterpart of the goddess. This is why Kirta is described in the epic tradition as deviating from El's instructions. Even though, as the high god of the pantheon, El's decrees normally are binding,[39] matters concerning queen mothers—and even queen-mothers-to-be—more appropriately fall within the province of Asherah. In seeking a mother for his royal heir, Kirta dare not neglect the queen mother's patron goddess.

Equally significant is a scene later in the Kirta Epic, after Hurriya has been secured as wife. There, at a banquet that celebrates the marriage, El appears and blesses Kirta and especially the son Yassib whom El predicts Hurriya will bear. This blessing reads (*KTU* 1.15.2.26–28):

He [Yassib] will suckle the milk of Asherah,
Suck at the breasts of Virgin Anat,
The two wet-nurses of the gods.

As many commentators have pointed out, this passage is reminiscent of other ancient Near Eastern texts that depict a royal infant as being suckled by a goddess. For example, the Sumerian King Lugalzaggisi is said to be "fed with holy milk by Ninḫarsag,"[40] and the Mesopotamian king of the gods Marduk nurses at the breasts of goddesses.[41] Yet, while I agree that there is a certain stereotypical quality to this language and its description of a royal suckling who has divine wet-nurses, it still seems to me significant that *Asherah* is named along with Anat as the one who gives Yassib suck. Elsewhere in the Kirta Epic, it is the goddess Astarte who is typically paired with Anat (*KTU* 1.14.3.41–42; 1.14.6.26–28). Only here does the epic substitute Asherah's name: why? The answer is that Ugaritic tradition is once more indicating its belief that the earthly queen mother—and even a woman who is at this point just a queen-mother-to-be—is the human counterpart of the goddess Asherah. Hurriya, the woman at whose breasts the royal heir Yassib will actually suck, is thus alluded to metaphorically through the poem's reference to Asherah, who will be Hurriya's divine alter ego.[42]

Given the rather unrelenting monolatry of the Hebrew Bible, which requires that all references to a deity other than Yahweh either be excised altogether or presented in a polemical and denunciatory fashion, any discussion of texts that portray an association between *Israelite* queen mothers and *Canaanite* Asherah is bound to be problematic. Yet, despite the inherent difficulties, an investigation of the biblical data is extremely important. What is revealed, first, is that, although the Bible is generally silent concerning the religious allegiances of Israel's queen mothers, in the few places where the text does offer comment, it either explicitly indicates or strongly intimates that, as in the older Canaanite materials, it is characteristically the goddess Asherah who is the object of the religious devotions of these women. Moreover, although the biblical writers tend to depict the queen mothers' devotions to Asherah in a derogatory fashion, a careful assessment of the relevant data suggests that the queen mothers' Asherah worship was an accepted part of monarchical religion. I will even argue that the queen mothers' allegiances to Asherah were an *integral* part of monarchical religion, especially as monarchical religion was construed in the southern kingdom of Judah. This latter point is crucial, for by undertaking an examination of the ideology of Judahite kingship, I will also attempt to determine the theological underpinning that informs the queen mother's role in the Asherah cult. This theological underpinning in turn will indicate that, as in the old Hittite paradigm of the *tawananna,* the cultic obligations of the Israelite queen mother stand primary among the queen mother's other socio-political responsibilities. It is even the case, I will propose, that the queen mother's identity as the earthly counterpart of Asherah is the source of the power and legitimization this woman requires in order to wield her authority elsewhere in Israelite society, particularly in the political affairs of her son's court.

The biblical text that most explicitly links an Israelite queen mother with the worship of Asherah or, indeed, with a cultic activity of any sort is 1 Kgs 15:2, 9–13. This text (along with its parallel found in 2 Chr 11:20–22; 15:16) describes the activities of Ma'acah, the queen mother of a son who is alternatively called Abijam (in Kings) and Abijah (in Chronicles).[43] Abijam/Abijah ruled for three years in Jerusalem (915–913 B.C.E.). Subsequently, Ma'acah served as queen mother for her grandson Asa, who had a forty-one year reign (913–873 B.C.E.). Already these data imply that Ma'acah as queen mother was able to exercise the kinds of political power elsewhere ascribed to her Israelite and Canaanite counterparts. For example, the very fact that Asa reigned for forty-one years suggests that he assumed the throne at an early age, and it is quite possible that Ma'acah, as queen mother, served as regent before Asa reached maturity. Also, the way in which Ma'acah was able to continue to serve Asa as queen mother after her son Abijam/Abijah had died indicates that she commanded a position of power in the royal court. She must have been powerful enough, for example, to have somehow supplanted Asa's actual mother, who is nowhere mentioned in the biblical text. To be sure, Ma'acah may have been aided in this quest by natural causes, Asa's mother's death in childbirth, perhaps, or some other illness bringing about an untimely demise; nevertheless, Ma'acah's ability to retain the position of queen mother after her own son had died indicates she can claim at least some degree of authority independent of the authority she derived by virtue of her relationship to her son.

Still, the authority of Ma'acah as queen mother is not completely independent, as can be seen in 1 Kgs 15:13 and 2 Chr 15:16, which describe how Asa becomes angry at Ma'acah and removes her from the office of queen mother. The act that angers Asa is that Ma'acah asserts her authority in a way that he feels is religiously inappropriate, for she has made what is called in 1 Kgs 15:13 a *mipleṣet lā'ăšērâ,* which I would translate as "an abominable image for Asherah." Admittedly, the translation here is a matter of some debate, in part because the word *mipleṣet,* "an abominable image," occurs only in this verse in Kings and in its parallel in Chronicles and in part because of the grammatical difficulties associated with the word *lā'ăšērâ.*[44] Rather than reading the proper name of the goddess, Asherah, as I have suggested, some scholars prefer to read a common noun, translating the entire phrase as "she made an abominable image of the asherah."[45] But whatever translation is preferred, the sense is still very much the same since commentators generally agree that the asherah image was a statue frequently erected in honor of the goddess Asherah and thus was called by her name.[46] Descriptions of the asherah image found scattered throughout the Hebrew Bible make clear that this statue was in the shape of a stylized wooden pole or tree, representing the sacred tree associated with the goddess Asherah elsewhere in Canaanite tradition.[47]

Thus Maʿacah's act that so angered Asa was that the queen mother made a statue of a stylized pole or tree that was meant to symbolize the goddess Asherah and was dedicated to her worship. In all likelihood, moreover, Maʿacah erected this cult image of Asherah in Yahweh's temple in Jerusalem. There are two reasons for suggesting this. The first is an argument based on proximity: because the palace and temple in Jerusalem stood side-by-side, the temple is the most probable place in which a member of the royal family would have erected a cult icon. More significant is the fact that the Jerusalem temple essentially functioned as a royal chapel for the king's family.[48] Kings of the southern kingdom of Judah were even considered to be the titular heads of the Jerusalem temple, reserving for themselves the right to appoint temple personnel and to determine the temple's appropriate furnishings.[49] Because of the powerful role that queen mothers played in the royal court, it is likely that they, too, would have exerted themselves in matters concerning cult officials and cult paraphernalia.[50] It follows that when Maʿacah dedicated her cult statue to Asherah, she would have erected it in the Jerusalem temple.

Asa, who deposes Maʿacah, clearly does not see her action as one that is religiously appropriate, and the biblical authors agree, lauding Asa as one who was "faithful to Yahweh all his days" (1 Kgs 15:14). Many modern commentators have also assumed that Maʿacah's worship of Asherah was heterodox, arguing that it was an alien element introduced by her from Canaanite culture and into the Jerusalem cult.[51] Their primary piece of evidence is Maʿacah's presumed foreign ancestry since elsewhere in the Hebrew Bible, the name Maʿacah does appear as the name of a non-Israelite, Maʿacah, the daughter of King Talmai of Geshur and mother of Absalom (2 Sam 3:3 and 1 Chr 3:2). Also, this Maʿacah of Geshur is apparently the grandmother of the Maʿacah of 1 Kgs 15:13

and 2 Chr 15:16 since the latter Ma'acah is identified in 1 Kgs 15:2 and 2 Chr 11:20–22 as the daughter of Absalom, who is the former Ma'acah's son:

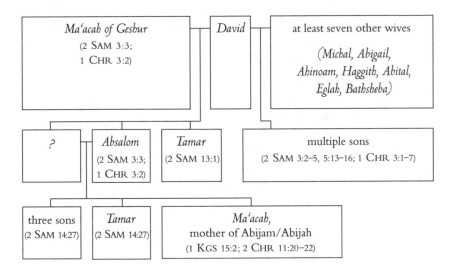

Ma'acah's presumed foreign heritage, however, need not predicate the conclusion that the Asherah cult Ma'acah promoted was foreign. Nor does the fact that King Asa and the biblical authors regarded Ma'acah's worship as heterodox necessarily imply that this was the case. Michael D. Coogan has written, "It is essential to consider biblical religion as a subset of Israelite religion and Israelite religion as a subset of Canaanite religion."[52] What this means with respect to Ma'acah is that, no matter how strenuously Asa and the biblical authors insist that the worship of the Canaanite goddess Asherah is apostasy in Jerusalem, Ma'acah, along with many in the population, may have felt that this so-called "Canaanite" cult was a perfectly legitimate part of *Israelite* religion.

Saul M. Olyan has even argued that the worship of Asherah may have been part of the *normative* Jerusalem cult, that Asherah may have been worshiped side-by-side with Yahweh in the *official* religion of the southern kingdom of Judah.[53] This is entirely consistent with my argument above that Ma'acah's image devoted to Asherah stood in all likelihood in Yahweh's temple in Jerusalem. Also important to realize is that the statue Ma'acah erected in Yahweh's temple was no anomaly. Although the worship of Asherah may have been suspended when Asa destroyed the cult statue that Ma'acah had made, Ma'acah's cult statue of Asherah was replaced in the Jerusalem temple at some point after Asa had died and his reforms had lapsed. This is indicated by 2 Kgs 18:4, in which Hezekiah (715–687 B.C.E.) removes an asherah from Jerusalem as part of his own reforms. Unfortunately, the actual location in Jerusalem where this asherah stood is not specified in the text, but I believe that, like Ma'acah's and for the same reasons, it stood in Yahweh's temple. The biblical text is explicit that a third asherah—the one that replaced the icon Hezekiah destroyed—stood in the Jerusalem temple. Thus 2 Kgs 21:7 describes how Manasseh (687–642 B.C.E.) erected an asherah in Yahweh's temple in Jerusalem. According to 2 Kgs 23:6, this asherah stood there until destroyed as a part of the cultic reforms instituted by King Josiah (640–609 B.C.E.). Josiah also removed from the Jerusalem temple the vessels made for Asherah as part of her sacrificial cult (2 Kgs 23:4) and tore down the structures within the temple compound where women wove garments to be draped as clothing over Asherah's cult statue (2 Kgs 23:7).

The fact that Asa, Hezekiah, and Josiah repeatedly found it necessary to destroy the cult image of Asherah, along with the fact that Josiah felt compelled to remove Asherah's cult paraphernalia from the temple, suggests that throughout the eras of these kings—which span the ninth, eighth, and seventh centuries B.C.E.—it was accepted practice to worship Yahweh and Asherah side-by-side in the state temple in Jerusalem. The biblical writers may have wished it were otherwise, but the zeal of the reformer kings who sought to abolish Asherah's cult appears to have been not the norm, but the exception. An important piece of archaeological evidence supports this conclusion, namely an eighth-century B.C.E. inscription that comes from a site called Khirbet el-Qom, some 10 kilometers east-southeast of the Judaean city of Lachish.[54] This inscription has been much discussed by biblical scholars, although it has proven to be difficult to read. The most satisfying attempt at translation is Patrick D. Miller's:

> Blessed is Uriyahu by Yahweh;
> Yea from his adversaries by his asherah he has saved him.[55]

As to what it means to describe Uriyahu as having been saved by "his," that is, "Yahweh's asherah" (l'šrth), commentators disagree. Is there a specific reference to the goddess Asherah? Some have suggested this, but as is indicated by Miller's translation, in which the word "asherah" is rendered with a lower-case "a," he does not see the term as being a proper name. So is the reference to the cult statue of the goddess, the asherah? Or, as Miller argues, is the asherah to be understood as a female aspect of Yahweh, here reified and given a separate identity? There are also a few commentators who propose that the term "asherah" in this inscription means "shrine."[56] The scholarly discussion is far from over. Still, almost all agree that whatever the specifics of translation, the cult of Yahweh and some allusion to the cult of Asherah are paired at Khirbet el-Qom. Thus, in the "variety" of Yahwistic religion practiced at this Judaean site, Yahweh had—at a minimum—a female aspect or symbol (an asherah) and possibly even a female consort (Asherah). If we now pair this Khirbet el-Qom evidence with the biblical texts I have already cited, the data strongly suggest that Olyan is correct and that it was common and even typical to worship Asherah side-by-side with Yahweh in Jerusalem and more generally in the official religion of the southern kingdom of Judah.

Despite the Bible's censure, then, we cannot conclude that Ma'acah as queen mother introduced an alien cult of Asherah into the Jerusalem court. Nor, I would argue, should Jezebel, another queen mother who is often regarded by commentators as introducing a foreign cult of Asherah into Israel, be so accused. Instead, I intend to suggest that, like Ma'acah, Jezebel as queen mother participated in an *official* cult of Asherah. Unlike Ma'acah, though, Jezebel was queen mother in Israel's northern kingdom, with the implication being that the worship of Asherah was a part of the state cult of the north as well as being normative in the state cult in the south.

The data concerning Jezebel's religious acts while queen mother are somewhat ambiguous, however. The first problem is that the biblical tradition tends to focus most of its attention on Jezebel's tenure as queen and as the wife of King Ahab rather than discussing her role as queen mother. But, as noted above, Jezebel is labeled queen mother at least once, by messengers sent by King Ahaziah of Judah to visit the northern court after Ahab's death (2 Kgs 10:13). Thus, at a minimum, Jezebel fills the role of queen mother in the minds of the editors who included 2 Kgs 10:13 in the biblical text. And, if 2 Kgs 10:13 is historically reliable, she was considered queen mother at least by the members of the southern royal family.

Whether, though, Jezebel as queen mother devoted herself to the cult of Asherah as did Ma'acah is a second ambiguity, as scholars even disagree on whether Jezebel while queen worshiped Asherah in addition to her oft-mentioned allegiance to the cult of Baal. The crux of the matter is 1 Kgs 18:19, where the prophet Elijah summons to Mount Carmel the "four hundred and fifty prophets of Baal and the four hundred prophets of Asherah who eat at Jezebel's table." This text seemingly does associate Jezebel with the cult of Asherah, but subsequent to this passage, the narrative turns its attention solely to the four hundred and fifty prophets of Baal. The four hundred prophets of Asherah are never mentioned again.[57] This raises doubts about whether the original version of 1 Kings 18 actually included the Asherah prophets in its description of those who enjoyed Jezebel's patronage. Most commentators believe that it did not.

Still, while this evidence does suggest that the reference to "the prophets of Asherah" in 1 Kgs 18:19 is secondary, it need not mean that Queen Jezebel did not worship the goddess Asherah. Certainly there were ample opportunities for her to do so. Most significant in this regard is 1 Kgs 16:33, which reports that her husband Ahab erected an asherah in Samaria, the capital city of the northern kingdom. Since 1 Kgs 16:33 occurs near the beginning of the long cycle of narratives concerning Ahab (1 Kgs 16:29–22:40), it seems probable that the king erected this asherah early in his reign. This means that there was an Asherah cult of some sort in Samaria during the bulk of Ahab's monarchy and that the king participated in it. Jezebel, as Ahab's wife, also may have participated in this cult as part of her obligations of marriage.

Inscriptional evidence from Kuntillet 'Ajrud in the eastern Sinai, fifty kilometers south of Kadesh Barnea, also locates a cult of Asherah contemporaneous with Ahab's reign in Samaria (the inscriptions are ninth or eighth century B.C.E.).[58] The crucial text reads, "I bless you by Yahweh of Samaria and by his Asherah/asherah."[59] As in the Khirbet el-Qom inscription described above, the interpretation of the crucial word Asherah/asherah (*l'šrth*) is a matter of some debate. But once more, whatever specific translation is embraced, scholars in general agree that the inscription demonstrates that, at least among certain religious circles in Samaria, the cult of Yahweh and the cult of Asherah were paired. This pairing of Yahweh and Asherah is also suggested by two other inscriptions found at Kuntillet 'Ajrud: "by Yahweh of the south and by his Asherah/asherah" and "I bless you by Yahweh of the south and by his Asherah/asherah. May he bless and keep you and may he be with my lord."[60]

Olyan, moreover, has again argued that this pairing of Yahweh and Asherah at Kuntillet 'Ajrud and in Samaria should not be regarded as an alien element introduced by foreigners into Israelite religion, proposing instead that the worship of Asherah was a part of the normative religion of the northern kingdom of Israel.[61] He notes several data in support of this conclusion. The first concerns the reformer King Jehu, who kills King Jehoram, son of Ahab, and Ahab's other sons and purges from Samaria and from the northern kingdom all the religious imagery that Jehu considers to be apostate within the Yahwistic cult. Notably, this purge is *not* described as destroying the asherah that Ahab had erected in Samaria. Instead, according to 2 Kgs 13:6, Ahab's asherah remained standing in Samaria even after Jehu's death. This suggests that Jehu and his followers perceived the Samaria asherah to be an acceptable cult icon within official Yahwism.[62] According to 2 Kgs 23:15, there was also an asherah in the state temple of Yahweh located in the northern city of Bethel, which likewise indicates that the asherah was considered a legitimate part of the Yahwism of the northern monarchy.[63] Olyan further suggests that, despite the virulent attacks on non-Yahwistic cult elements found in the book of the northern prophet Hosea, the cult of Asherah never is condemned, implying that Hosea had no objections to an Asherah cult as part of the official religion of the north.[64] Olyan argues that the silence of another prophet of the north, Amos, regarding Asherah worship is equally of significance.[65] He concludes, "We argue that the asherah was a legitimate part of the cult of Yahweh . . . in the north . . . in state religion and in popular religion."[66]

If Olyan is correct in pairing the cult of Asherah with the cult of Yahweh in the state religion of the northern kingdom, and if in particular the cults of Asherah and Yahweh were paired in Ahab's Samaria, then Jezebel as queen must have participated in the cult of Asherah not only because of her obligations of marriage but also as part of her obligations of state.[67] More speculative, although I believe equally probable, is that Jezebel continued to participate in an Asherah cult even after Ahab's death, when she assumed the role of queen mother. Unfortunately, the only narrative that describes the widowed Jezebel is the story of her death in 2 Kings 9. But it may be significant that Jezebel is lodged during that scene in her royal residence in Jezreel and not in Samaria. She is thus distanced from the Baal temple in Samaria that is more typically associated with her religious allegiances.[68] Consequently, her cultic attentions in Jezreel would have been primarily focused on the state religion of the northern kingdom and its pairing of the worship of Yahweh with the worship of Asherah. This means that, like Ma'acah, Jezebel as queen mother should be seen as participating in a widely accepted and even normative cult of the goddess Asherah.

It also seems to be the case that the queen mother Athaliah, the daughter of Jezebel and Ahab, participated in the cult of Asherah.[69] Athaliah was given by her parents to Jehoram, the king of Judah, as wife, presumably as part of a treaty between the northern and southern kingdoms (2 Kgs 8:18). As noted above, she became queen mother to her son Ahaziah after Jehoram was killed in battle against the Edomites (2 Kgs 8:20–24). This arrangement, however, was short lived since Ahaziah was killed as part of Jehu's bloody coup while on a visit to Jezreel (2 Kgs 9:27–28). It was then that Athaliah asserted her rights as regent, assuming the throne of Judah for six years until she was deposed in the uprising led by the high priest Jehoiada (2 Kgs 11:1–20).

One part of this uprising involved destroying the Baal temple that was in Jerusalem and killing its priesthood.[70] Although the text does not specify that it was Athaliah who was responsible for having this temple built, commentators unanimously assign it to her reign and are also unanimous in suggesting that Athaliah promoted the Baal cult in Judah under the influence of Jezebel and her patronage of the Baal cult in the north. If this is indeed the case, then one also would expect that Athaliah allied herself with other cults favored by her mother. If, moreover, I have been correct above in assuming that Jezebel both as queen and queen mother participated in the cult of Asherah, I can now suggest that Athaliah would have done the same. In fact, I would assume as much, given my earlier conclusion that devotion to Asherah was a normative aspect of Yahwistic religion in the south.[71]

In addition to Ma'acah, Jezebel, and Athaliah, the Bible records the names of another sixteen queen mothers. Of this total of nineteen, only one, Bathsheba, comes from the period of Israel's united monarchy; the other eighteen come from the period of the divided monarchy. Of these eighteen queen mothers of the divided monarchy, moreover, seventeen come from the southern kingdom of Judah. This means that, while we know the name of only Jezebel, the queen mother of Kings Ahaziah (853–852 B.C.E.) and Jehoram (852–844 B.C.E.), from the northern kingdom, we know the names of all but two of the queen mothers of the

southern kingdom (the exceptions are the queen mothers of Kings Jehoram [849–841 B.C.E.] and Ahaz [734–715 B.C.E.]). The names of the
seventeen queen mothers of the south even seem to have been preserved
as a part of the official Judaean archives, meaning that the names are
found in the formulaic notices that begin the description of the reign of
each king of Judah.[72] The archival notices for the kings of the northern
kingdom in the main parallel their southern counterparts but fail to
name a northern queen mother.[73] It is also important to recall that the
one northern queen mother whose name we do know, Jezebel, is only
assigned the title of queen mother in a passage that records the words of
southern visitors who have come to the north. There is no text that
describes her as being called "queen mother" by native northerners.

It is further the case that Jezebel, both as queen and queen mother,
reigns in a court that is much more characterized by a "southern" style
of kingship than by typical "northern" fashion.[74] For example, while in
the south, kingship from the time of David on was determined through
a principle of dynastic succession, succession in the north tended to be
much more volatile, with the mantle of kingship often falling on non-
royals who laid claim to the office solely because of their skills in charismatic leadership. Jezebel's father-in-law Omri, however, was able to
establish a southern-style dynasty that controlled the throne of Israel
through three generations (four kings). Another accomplishment of
Omri and his descendants is that they established the city of Samaria as
the capital of the northern kingdom, and notably, in doing so, they modeled their capital after the southern capital in Jerusalem. One of the
reasons, for example, that the Omride dynasty sought to move the
northern capital from its previous location in Tirzah to Samaria is that
Samaria lies in a spot that is less mountainous and that is near major
trade routes. This location allowed Omri and his descendants to establish
alliances with their neighbors, especially their Phoenician neighbors to
the north, an act that is highly reminiscent of the alliances Solomon's
court in Jerusalem established with its foreign neighbors (1 Kgs 3:1;
5:12). Also like the Solomonic monarchy (1 Kgs 3:1), the Omride court
cemented its foreign alliances with foreign marriages, including the marriage of Omri's son Ahab to the Phoenician princess Jezebel. Omri's
court also followed Solomon's lead in persecuting dissenters. According
to 1 Kgs 2:23–35, after Solomon was crowned king, he managed to have
his rival, Adonijah, and Adonijah's chief military supporter, Joab, put to
death. Adonijah's chief religious supporter, Abiathar, was also threatened

with death but ultimately was exiled from Jerusalem and sent to his ancestral home in Anathoth. In 1 Kgs 19:1–9, Queen Jezebel similarly threatens the life of her main religious critic, the prophet Elijah, and Elijah responds by fleeing the northern kingdom and descending into Judah and, eventually, into the wilderness of Sinai.

Together, what all these data imply is that, while the office of the queen mother generally does not seem to find a home in the traditional court life of the northern kingdom, it does appear to be an integral part of the southern monarchy and of the southern-styled monarchy of Omri. Yet, while commentators have frequently noted this discrepancy between northern and southern attitudes toward the queen mother,[75] none has explained the reason for this difference. I believe, however, that the clue to understanding the two nations' disparate assessments of the queen mother's office is to be found in an observation I made already above: that generally speaking, northern kingship can be defined as being "charismatic" in character, whereas southern kingship is without exception dynastic.

It was the German scholar Albrecht Alt, writing in 1951, who first distinguished carefully between these two types of kingship found in the north and the south.[76] Since that time, although Alt has been criticized for being too sweeping in his analysis and for overly dramatizing the disparities he found between the northern and southern monarchies, his basic observations have still held. In fact, in many cases they have been amplified upon. Of particular interest is the way in which Frank M. Cross has built on Alt's work by arguing that one of the features that distinguishes Alt's contrasting ideologies of northern and southern kingship is the notion of sacral kingship.[77] As Cross explains, sacral kingship is a doctrine that characterizes only the southern monarchy. Its tenets suggest that, even though the southern king really cannot be described as a god nor can he be considered to be in any way divine, it is nevertheless true that a southern monarch is thought to have a kind of filial relationship with Yahweh.[78] In describing this relationship, the Bible most frequently uses the language of adoption, suggesting that upon assuming office, the king becomes regarded as the metaphorical son of Yahweh, who is accordingly described as the king's divine father. In Ps 2:7–9, for example, the king speaks and says:

> *I will tell of the decree of Yahweh:*
> *He said to me, "You are my son,*

Today I have begotten you.
Ask of me, and I will make the nations your inheritance,
And the ends of the earth your possession.
You shall break them with an iron rod,
And shatter them like a potter's vessel."

Similar sentiments are expressed in 2 Sam 7:14a and Isa 9:5 (English 9:6). Most significant, though, is Ps 89:20–30 (English 89:19–29). Again in these verses, the king speaks to Yahweh. He begins with these words (vv 20–22):

Then you spoke in a vision to your faithful one[79] and said:
"I have set the crown[80] upon one who is mighty,
I have exalted one chosen from the people.
I have found David, my servant,
With my holy oil I have anointed him,
That my hand shall always remain with him,
That my arm shall strengthen him."

Then, in verses 27–28, Yahweh utters what is according to Cross the "ultimate statement" of the southern royal ideology:[81]

He [the king] will cry out to me [Yahweh], "You are my father,
My God and the rock of my salvation."
I surely will make him my firstborn,
The highest of the kings of the earth.

It is this motif of divine sonship found in southern royal ideology that I believe explains the role the queen mother plays in the Jerusalem monarchy. For if the Judaean royal ideology holds that Yahweh is the metaphorical father of the king, then is it not possible that the metaphorical mother of the king is to be understood as Asherah, given, as I have argued above, that Asherah was seen by many—in both the state and popular cult—as the consort of Yahweh? The southern monarchy's language of divine sonship, to put the matter more bluntly, should imply not only Yahweh, the male God, as the king's surrogate father, but also Asherah, the female consort, as the monarch's surrogate mother.

If this is so, then the implications for the southern queen mother are enormous. As the human mother of the king, the queen mother would be perceived as the earthly counterpart of Asherah, the king's heavenly mother. The queen mother might even be considered the human representative of Asherah. Such a correspondence explains why those queen mothers for whom cultic allegiances are described or hinted at in the Bible are depicted as patrons of the goddess Asherah. In fact, according to the logic I have described, it is nothing but appropriate that these women direct their homage to their divine alter ego. Because of the royal ideology of the south, the worship of Asherah could even be construed as a queen mother's *primary* cultic obligation.

I would also argue that if my hypothesis is correct, then the cultic functions undertaken by the Judaean queen mothers on behalf of the goddess Asherah stand in close relationship to the political responsibilities assigned to the queen mothers within their sons' courts. Indeed, I believe it is the queen mother's cultic functions on behalf of Asherah that give rise to this woman's political authority. For example, I suggest that the reason the queen mother can fulfill an official role as a royal adviser or counselor in her son's palace stems from the belief that she represents the goddess Asherah within the monarchy. The queen mother, that is, can claim a power and an authority that, like the king's, originate in the world of the divine. This allows the queen mother to function as the second-most powerful figure in the royal court, superseded only by her son, the king.

Such divine legitimization would also explain why the queen mother acts as the king's regent when her son is unable to rule, for, besides the king, she is the only member of the royal court who can be said to have a familiar relationship with a god. Consider as well the way the queen mother can begin her tenure by exercising authority in the matter of the royal succession. Could not the crucial role the queen-mother-to-be plays in this transition of power be derived from the cultic function I have proposed for the queen mother as devotee of Asherah? More specifically, if the woman about to become queen mother is considered the human representative of Asherah in the royal court, she should be able to legitimate her son's claim to be the son of Yahweh. Indeed, this soon-to-be queen mother, assuming she speaks as the counterpart of the goddess and thus, at least metaphorically, as Yahweh's consort, is the sole individual in the land qualified to attest to her son's divine lineage. Because of this, power in determining the royal succession would most naturally and properly fall to her.

IV. QUEEN MOTHERS IN THE WINDOW

Chronologically, the Judges 5 depiction of Sisera's queen mother, which dates from c. 1100 B.C.E., stands at the midpoint of the continuum that stretches from the culture of Late Bronze Age Ugarit (c. 1550–1200 B.C.E.) to the monarchical period of Iron Age Israel (c. 1040–586 B.C.E.).[82] I propose, moreover, that the Judges 5 representation of Sisera's mother as queen mother stands in a *political* continuum with the Ugaritic and Israelite representations of queen mothers since I believe, for example, that, like her Canaanite and biblical counterparts, Sisera's mother is most probably understood by her poetic biographers as serving as regent for Sisera while her son is away at war. I also believe that the authors of Judges 5 imply that Sisera's mother stands in a *religious* continuum with Ugaritic and Israelite queen mothers, functioning like them as the human representative of the Canaanite mother goddess Asherah. The description of how this woman stands at the window while she waits for Sisera to return home from battle suggests this possibility.

The key here is to realize the existence of a series of ninth- and eighth-century B.C.E. ivory plaques that have been found by archaeologists at four ancient Near Eastern sites, Khorsabad and Nimrud, both on the banks of the Tigris River in northern Iraq; Arslan Tash, a settlement on the Balikh River, one of the major tributaries of the Euphrates in northern Syria; and Samaria in Israel.[83] Typically described by scholars as representing the "woman in the window," these plaques, although multiply attested (nine examples at Khorsabad; thirteen at Nimrud; seventeen at Arslan Tash; and one complete plaque and several fragmentary pieces at Samaria), are practically identical:[84] each shows the head of an elegantly coiffed and attired female who stares straight ahead, looking out over a window sill from the inside of some building. The window typically has three recesses (with a few exceptions at Arslan Tash) and is supported by a balustrade of four ornately carved columns (or, in a few examples, three). This sort of elaborate architectural decoration suggests that the building represented is either a palace or a temple, and because the doorways of many Mesopotamian temples were triply recessed, most scholars believe that the identification of the building as a temple is the correct one.[85] This further implies that the plaques depict a goddess. Based on a story found in Plutarch of a young Cypriot woman called *Parakyptousa,* "the one who looks out a window," who is turned to stone as she peers through a lattice watching her spurned lover's funeral procession,[86] commentators most often assume that the ivories' gazing deity is Cyprian Aphrodite/Canaanite Astarte, who, as the goddess of eroticism and love, would have had greatest cause to punish the hard-hearted maid.[87] A reference in Ovid's *Metamorphoses* to the Cypriot temple of *Venus prospiciens,* "Venus who looks into the distance,"[88] which is said to commemorate a similarly haughty maiden who was turned to stone as she stared out a window at the funeral cortege of her rejected suitor, seemingly confirms this identification since Venus is Aphrodite's and Astarte's Roman counterpart.[89] Based, though, on references found in Herodotus and in a number of other Greek and Latin sources,[90] some scholars have suggested a slightly different interpretation: that the "woman in the window" represents not the goddess of love herself but a sacred prostitute who serves Astarte (Aphrodite/Venus) in the cult.[91]

There are problems, however, with both of these identifications. The notion that sacred prostitution ever existed in Israel or anywhere in the ancient Near East, for example, has been widely discredited,[92] and while the association of the "woman in the window" with Cypriot Aphrodite/ Venus is ostensibly more plausible, there are still certain concerns. First is the issue of date, for Plutarch's reference to *Parakyptousa* dates from the second half of the first century C.E. and Ovid's story of the cult of *Venus prospiciens* comes from only a few score years prior (8 C.E.). Both sources thus postdate the ninth- and eighth-century B.C.E. plaques depicting the "woman in the window" by almost a millennium. Admittedly, both Plutarch and Ovid claim to report legendary material, thus suggesting that their stories have roots that reach back through the centuries, and, indeed, a third reference to Cyprus' peeping goddess cult, a fragment from Hermesianax's *Leontion,* does indicate that the Aphrodite *parakyptousa* tradition has some older antecedents (Hermesianax's work dates from the first half of the third century B.C.E.).[93] Still, only with the greatest speculation can we read backwards from Hermesianax another five hundred years and into the religious idiom of the mid-Iron Age. Moreover, as I have argued in the Introduction, even if we did make so bold as to posit an old Iron Age story that had been handed down through the generations, it is methodologically a mistake to assume that such orally transmitted material could reveal historically reliable information. Given, that is, only the evidence of one Hellenistic and two Roman-era texts, we cannot in good conscience assume *even the existence* of a ninth- and eighth-century B.C.E. "gazing goddess" cult. Much less can we claim to have found in the "woman in the window" plaques a perfectly realized representation of it.

An equally serious problem in equating the "woman in the window" with the "gazing goddess" of Plutarch and other *literary* sources is the failure to understand that the identification of an artistic image is more appropriately determined by comparing *iconographical* materials. The "woman in the window"/"gazing goddess" equation also, by looking exclusively *forward* to the Hellenistic and Roman eras, fails to consider the *antecedents* of the "woman in the window" imagery. Yet these antecedents—by which I mean, I should again stress, *iconographical* antecedents—are not only very rich but also very revealing. We can begin by noting that in each locale where they were found, the "woman in the window" plaques were a part of a larger ivory assemblage, and an assemblage, moreover, that was for the most part identical at each site.[94] For example, in all four sites where "woman in the window" plaques were found, there were also found ivory representations of a human-headed sphinx. Likewise, at three of the four "woman in the window" locations (the exception is Khorsabad), there were found ivory carvings portraying an infant sitting atop a lotus. Another nearly ubiquitous image among the ivory assemblages of the "woman in the window" sites (the exception is again Khorsabad) is "the cow and the calf," a depiction of a mother cow that nuzzles a suckling calf.[95]

Although carved by Canaanite, specifically Phoenician craftsmen, each of these images was originally derived from an Egyptian prototype.[96] In the case of the human-headed sphinx, the derivation is clear. The infant atop a lotus is also an image well known from royal art of the Egyptian New Kingdom (c. 1575–1087 B.C.E.), where the child was identified with the infant pharaoh. And, in the case of "the cow and the calf," once more, the prototype seems to have been Egyptian since the Egyptian mother goddess Hathor is often represented in bovine form, giving suck to the pharaonic heir.

The imagery of the "woman in the window" ivories also is probably best described as depending on Egyptian iconography in general and, as in the case of "the cow and the calf," on the iconography of the Egyptian goddess Hathor in particular.[97] Several data suggest this. First, in all but the Samaria exemplar of the "woman in the window" ivories (which is the most crudely rendered of the collection and difficult to decipher in terms of its details), the woman is depicted as having enormous ears that have even been described by scholars as resembling the ears of a cow.[98] This intimates already an identification of the "woman in the window" with Egyptian Hathor who, as noted above, is frequently depicted in bovine form. This identification is strengthened by comparing represen-

tations of Hathor in her human guise, in which Egyptian artisans typically impose upon the image of the goddess' anthropoid body some allusion to her bovine attributes. Sometimes this means portraying an
otherwise human-looking Hathor with horns coming forth from her
head, but, in more subtle renderings, Hathor's associations with cattle
are alluded to only by depicting her with the same enormous, cow-like
ears worn by the "woman in the window." Also, when depicted in her
human guise, Hathor typically wears a distinctive coiffure, one, in fact,
that is so associated with her image that it is even called by scholars the
"Hathor headdress." It shows the goddess' hair parted in the middle and
hanging freely down to her shoulders, but pushed away from her face
and toward the back of her head so that her characteristic ears are exposed. Without exception, the "woman in the window" ivories depict
their subject as wearing a similar hairstyle.[99] Of further note is the fact
that, unlike the representations of almost all of Egypt's other gods, the
depictions of Hathor wearing her cow's ears and her distinctive wig are
presented full-face.[100] This is the same sort of frontal posture assumed by
the subject of the "woman in the window" plaques.

Eleanor F. Beach has also pointed out that, while these anthropoid
representations of Hathor generally portray her entire body, the Egyptian
artistic repertoire included as well depictions of a "framed Hathor head,"
which represent the goddess' head facing forward, cut off at the neck,
and bounded by a rectangular form.[101] As in her full-body representations described above, moreover, the goddess sports in these framed portrayals her distinctive cow's ears and wig. The similarities with the
"woman in the window" plaques are striking. Beach further observes
that the motif of the "framed Hathor head" occurs several times in
Egyptian art in conjunction with depictions of "the infant on a lotus,"
"the cow and the calf," and the human-headed sphinx. This suggests
that when we find the motifs of "the infant on a lotus," "the cow and
the calf," and the human-headed sphinx together at Samaria, Arslan
Tash, and Nimrud, we should also be on the lookout for the "framed
Hathor head." And, indeed, we do find it, rendered at these sites as the
"woman in the window."

Yet at the same time that Beach and scholars like her insist upon
identifying an Egyptian prototype for the "woman in the window" iconography and for the other iconographies of the Khorsabad, Nimrud,
Arslan Tash, and Samaria ivory assemblages, they also maintain that for
these iconographic motifs to convey meaning within the Semitic con-

texts in which they were created, their originally Egyptian imagery must be redefined so as to suggest an indigenous referent. Amihai Mazar has suggested, for example, that in Samaria, the human-headed Egyptian sphinx would have been reinterpreted as a biblical cherub.[102] Similarly, concerning the Nimrud ivories in general, Richard D. Barnett has written, "The features, forms and dresses of the gods and demigods whom the Phoenicians depict, [sic] may be unmistakeably Egyptian; but the actions in which they are depicted as engaged, [sic] will be found in most cases really to be based on the religious ideas and artistic principles of Hither Asia."[103] For us, these observations have an extremely significant implication: that the method we should adopt in interpreting the "woman in the window" iconography is *not,* recalling the discussion above, to make a giant leap backwards in both genre and time, from Hellenistic- and Roman-era *texts* to Iron Age *images,* but rather to assay a far more modest step forward, seeking to understand how the originally Egyptian representation of the "framed Hathor head" would have been reinterpreted in the religious imagination of the Iron Age Semitic world. The answer, I submit, is that the "woman in the window" imagery of the Egyptian mother goddess Hathor would most naturally and logically have been identified by its Semitic audience as a representation of the mother goddess of Canaanite mythology, Asherah. Elsewhere in Semitic tradition, in fact, these two goddesses are equated.[104] At Byblos, for example, the "Lady of Byblos" (*ba'lat gebal*), who in a Semitic context is to be understood as Asherah,[105] is in Egyptianizing texts and iconography identified as Hathor.[106] In the Sinai, too, where a Hathor and an Asherah cult each thrived during the Late Bronze Age,[107] the title *ba'lat,* "Lady," seems to have been assumed by both the Egyptian goddess and her Canaanite compatriot (the latter otherwise worshiped in this locale under the name of Qudshu).[108] Note finally in regard to the two goddesses' equivalence that, like Hathor, Asherah can be associated with bovine imagery and that the two deities share connections with snakes, lions, and sacred trees.[109]

I suggest, therefore, that in its Semitic reinterpretation, the originally Egyptian iconography of the "framed Hathor head" comes to represent the Canaanite mother goddess Asherah as the "woman in the window." Armed with this thesis, moreover, I propose to make fruitful return to the literary portrait of Sisera's mother found in Judges 5. The similarities between this poetic representation and the "woman in the window" images are manifold.[110] Like the ivories' "women," for example, Sisera's queen mother certainly should be imagined as wearing the elegant clothes and elaborate coiffure that befit her royal status. Likewise, the window from which she peers must surely have been as ornately decorated as the recessed and balustraded windows of the ivory plaques. The Judges 5 description of this woman, it follows, must be intent upon evoking the same image as do the "woman in the window" plaques, a depiction of Canaanite Asherah.[111] Or, more specifically, given its earthly setting and its mortal actor, the Judges 5 portrayal of Sisera's mother must be intent upon evoking a depiction of the Canaanite mother goddess Asherah in the deity's guise as the human queen mother. The Judges 5 description of Sisera's mother and the artistic presentations found in the "woman in the window" ivories might even be thought of as mirror images of one another. One shows a royal matron as she stands in the dormer of her son's great house and the other this matron's divine alter ego, Asherah, as the goddess gazes out of the casement of her heavenly temple.

This interpretation—to equate the description of Sisera's queen mother as she gazes out of her lattice with a portrayal of her patron goddess, Asherah, "the woman in the window"—illuminates two other biblical texts that depict a woman standing in a window. The first of these is 2 Kgs 9:30, in which Jezebel stands in the window of her palace at Jezreel, awaiting Jehu, the usurper who has dethroned her son Jehoram and killed him.[112] Jehu's act also deposes Jezebel from her office as Jehoram's queen mother, and Jehu has come to Jezreel to complete this deposition by murdering the royal matriarch. Jezebel prepares to meet her killer by beautifying herself; as the text puts it, "she painted her eyes and adorned her head." Although Simon B. Parker has seen Jezebel's actions here as implying an attempt at seduction,[113] most commentators conclude that her intent is to present herself as a woman who stands regal and even defiant in the face of her certain death.[114] Her defiance can be seen especially in the next verse, in which Jezebel taunts Jehu by addressing him as "Zimri," the name of a previous usurper of the Israelite throne. Zimri, however, was hardly the most successful of usurpers, as he was only able to hold the throne for seven days before himself being overthrown. The point of Jezebel's address is thus to insult Jehu by suggesting that his play for kingship will likewise meet a sudden and an ignominious end.

In the verse that follows, 9:31, Jezebel twists the knife even further by asking Jehu, "Is it peace?" meaning "Does all go well?" or "Is all in

order?" As Olyan has shown, the expected answer to this question, Hebrew *hăšālôm,* is *šālôm,* "All is peaceful" or "All is well."[115] But Jehu has
come to Jezreel to kill, so clearly all is *not* well. Jezebel's query thus
drips with sarcasm. She continues to speak in this contemptuous vein,
although with her final words she drops all pretense of subtlety by explicitly accusing Jehu of being the murderer of his lord. Yet even though
it lacks in subtlety, the reference to "lord" is still significant, for it returns
our attention to the royal content of these verses: it is a king whom Jehu
has already killed and a queen mother who now confronts death. The
text's portrait of Jezebel in the window, then, is ultimately a portrait of
a proud noblewoman who stands formally and regally adorned in what
was surely an ornately decorated palace window.

The parallels between this literary portrait of the queen mother Jezebel and the "woman in the window" plaques are remarkable. I have also
argued above that during her tenure as queen mother in Jezreel, Jezebel
devoted herself to the cult of the goddess Asherah. If, now, the "woman
in the window" plaques do indeed depict Asherah, as I have proposed,
and if I have also been correct in associating the queen mother Jezebel
with the mother goddess' cult, then, as in the case of Sisera's mother,
the description of Jezebel in 2 Kgs 9:30–31 seems meant to present this
queen mother who stands in her palace window as the human counterpart of Asherah.[116] Recall, moreover, that one of the exemplars of the
"woman in the window" ivory plaques comes from ninth- or eighth-
century B.C.E. Samaria, that is, from the capital city and from the era of
the Omride dynasty. This ivory, in fact, was found in a building commonly identified as the "ivory palace" of Ahab and Jezebel (1 Kgs
22:39).[117] There can thus be no question that those writers who chroni-
cled Jezebel's reign had access to the "woman in the window" iconography. They therefore could, and I believe did, make use of the image
when constructing their literary portrait of Jezebel's final moments.

The one other woman who is described in the Hebrew Bible as looking out of a window is also a royal woman, Michal, the daughter of
King Saul and one of the wives of King David.[118] The scene in question
occurs in 2 Sam 6:16, as Michal watches out of the palace window in
Jerusalem while David dances in the procession that brings the ark of
the covenant into the city. Many of the "woman in the window" elements we have come to expect are present here, especially the ornate
architectural setting and the noble woman.[119] Michal, however, while a
queen by virtue of her marriage to David, is not a queen mother. In fact,

she will never be a queen mother, for the story of the ark's entry into Jerusalem ends in 2 Sam 6:23 with a notice that Michal was barren until the day of her death.

It might thus seem that my interpretation—equating a royal woman who watches from a palace window with the queen mother in her guise as Asherah—falters here. But in actuality, although Michal is not queen mother, imagery associated with the queen mother's office lies not so far below the surface of 2 Samuel 6. After all, the point of the entire episode, as suggested by its concluding verse, is to make clear that Michal could never perform the role of queen mother because she could not bear a royal heir. It is almost as if the description of Michal looking out of the window stands ironically juxtaposed to the portraits that depict Sisera's mother and Jezebel as queen mothers who gaze out of a palace dormer. The use of similar imagery in all three passages—and the use of some strikingly similar vocabulary (for example, the use of the same verb *šqp,* "to peer," in Judg 5:28; 2 Sam 6:16; and 2 Kgs 9:30)—implies that Michal should have been what the other two women were, the queen mother who is the earthly representative of Asherah.[120] Yet because of Michal's bitter spirit—she chastises David for what she considers his vulgar cavorting before all the people—the role this woman should fill as queen mother is denied to her. The episode thus begins, in verse 16, by evoking the "woman in the window" image of the royal mother/mother goddess. But its final line, in verse 23, turns this opening depiction on its head, the fact of Michal's barrenness making a mockery of the notion that some day she would serve as the queen mother for David's son.

Michal, then, waits in her palace window in vain, for the political, economic, and religious power the office of the queen mother should bring to her will never come. To this degree, she is not unlike Sisera's mother, who also waits vainly in her great house's lattice, hoping against hope that the tarrying of her son's chariot does not mean that her tenure as his queen mother has come to an abrupt, unexpected, and humiliating end.

NOTES

[1] Canto III, part 6. *The Poems of Arthur Hugh Clough* (ed. H. F. Lowry; A. L. P. Norrington; F. L. Mulhauser; Oxford: Clarendon, 1951), 203.

[2] On this juxtaposition, see, in addition to my discussion below, S. Niditch, *War in the Hebrew Bible: A Study in the Ethics of Violence* (New York and Oxford: Oxford University Press, 1993), 115–16, and, as pointed out there, M. Levine, "The Polemic Against Rape in the Song of Deborah," *Beth Mikra* 25 (1979), 83–84 (Hebrew).

[3] Reading *wattabbēṭ*, "she gazed," with certain Greek manuscripts (Alexandrinus; Vaticanus) and with the Targumic tradition, for the MT's *hapax legomenon wattĕyabbēb*, which, based on Aramaic and Syriac cognates, presumably means "to cry out" or "to exclaim." See the discussion of C. F. Burney, *The Book of Judges* (London: Rivingtons, 1920), 154–55, and of G. F. Moore, *A Critical and Exegetical Commentary on Judges* (ICC; Edinburgh: T. & T. Clark, 1903), 167, 169.

[4] See also the catalogue of scholarly comment on the juxtaposition of these verses collected by W. J. Urbrock, "Sisera's Mother in Judges 5 and Haim Gouri's 'Immô," *HAR* 11 (1987), 423–24.

[5] On the eroticism of verse 27, see the discussion above in Chapter 1 and, as there, the comments of D. N. Fewell and D. M. Gunn, "Controlling Perspectives: Women, Men, and the Authority of Violence in Judges 4 & 5," *JAAR* 58 (1990), 404; S. Niditch, "Eroticism and Death in the Tale of Jael," *Gender and Difference in Ancient Israel* (ed. P. L. Day; Minneapolis: Fortress, 1989), 47–52; idem, *War in the Hebrew Bible*, 113–15; Y. Zakovitch, "Sisseras Tod," *ZAW* 93 (1981), 364–74.

[6] Mieke Bal, *Death and Dissymmetry: The Politics of Coherence in the Book of Judges* (Chicago: University of Chicago Press, 1988), 228, describes Sisera dead at Jael's feet as "a stillborn baby."

[7] Reading the singular *ḥakmat* for the MT plural *ḥakmôt*, as is suggested by the Syriac and Vulgate and by almost all commentators; cf. Chr. H. W. Brekelmans, "Some Translation Problems," *OTS* 15 (1970), 170–72.

[8] Whether Deborah and Jael are actually "maidens" in the technical sense of unmarried girls is, in fact, unspecified in Judges 5. But the poetic tradition's failure to assign them spouses (assuming the translation of *ḥeber* as "community" for which I argued in Chapter 2) suggests to me that Judges 5 intends to signal an ironic contrast between "maidens" as hoped-for conquests, on the one hand, and as con-

querors, on the other. Note also that the cognate of the Hebrew word used here for "maiden," *raḥam*, is used twice in Ugaritic literature as an epithet for Anat (*KTU* 1.6.2.5 [restored], 27). The "one maiden, two maidens," that is, to whom I believe verse 30 ironically alludes—Deborah and Jael—are linguistically equated with the Canaanite warrior goddess. This adds further support to my thesis of Chapter 1 that these two women are envisioned by Judges 5 as Anat-like military heroes. See, similarly, R. Alter, "From Line to Story in Biblical Verse," *Poetics Today* 4 (1983), 633; idem, *The Art of Biblical Poetry* (New York: Basic Books, 1985), 46.

[9]In addition to my discussion below on Sisera's kingly role, see B. Halpern, *The First Historians: The Hebrew Bible and History* (San Francisco: Harper & Row, 1988), 89–91.

[10]Reading *qiddĕmām* for MT *qĕdûmîm*, following the vast majority of commentators (but see M. D. Coogan, "A Structural and Literary Analysis of the Song of Deborah," *CBQ* 40 [1978], 150, n. 48).

[11]According to Burney, *Judges,* 156, and Moore, *Judges,* 168, this was originally suggested by Heinrich Ewald and widely accepted by nineteenth-century authorities. In this century, the proposal has found renewed support from R. de Vaux, *Ancient Israel* 1: *Social Institutions* (New York: McGraw Hill, 1965), 119; see also J. Gray, *Joshua, Judges, Ruth* (rev. ed.; New Century Bible Commentary; Grand Rapids: Eerdmans; Basingstoke: Marshall Morgan & Scott, 1986), 282.

[12]Reading *ṣabʿē riqmātayim,* the dual construct, for MT *ṣĕbaʿ riqmātayim.* See Coogan, "Song of Deborah," 151, n. 57, who follows F. M. Cross and D. N. Freedman, *Studies in Ancient Yahwistic Poetry* (SBLDS 21; Missoula, MT: Scholars Press, 1975), 20, n. bb.

[13]*Ancient Israel* 1, 119; see, similarly, Moore, *Judges,* 168, who calls the usual translation "absurd."

[14]For example, Coogan, "Song of Deborah," 151, n. 58, who vocalizes *laṣawwāʾrê šōlēl* for MT *lĕṣawwĕʾrê šālāl,* noting that the plural form of *ṣawwāʾr* is frequently used with a singular meaning (so Gen 27:16; 45:14; 46:29). See, similarly, R. G. Boling, *Judges* (AB 6a; Garden City, NY: Doubleday, 1975), 115; J. A. Soggin, *Judges: A Commentary* (OTL; Philadelphia: Westminster, 1981), 92.

[15]The pertinent texts are *Ugaritica* V, Nos. 159–61 (= RS 17.86 + 241 + 208; 17.102; 17.325) and *KTU* 4.143. For Heltzer's discussion, see *The Internal Organization of the Kingdom of Ugarit* (Wiesbaden: Reichert, 1982), 182–83.

[16]The pertinent texts are *KTU* 2.11; 2.12; 2.13; 2.16; 2.24; 2.30; 2.33; and 2.34, which I have discussed thoroughly in "The Queen Mother and the Cult in the Ancient Near East," *Women and Goddess Traditions: In Antiquity and Today* (Studies in

Antiquity and Christianity; ed. K. L. King with an Introduction by K. J. Torjeson; Minneapolis: Fortress, 1997), 182–83.

[17]The six letters are *KTU* 2.11; 2.12; 2.13; 2.24; 2.30; and 2.33. *KTU* 2.13 contains a particularly good example of the sort of language referred to here; see lines 5–6: *lp'n umy qlt,* "at the feet of my mother I fell."

[18]*šh'd wšb'id,* "seven and seven"; *KTU* 2.12, lines 8–9.

[19]The texts are *KTU* 2.11; 2.12; 2.24; and 2.33. For the translation of *adt,* see J. Aistleitner, *Wörterbuch der ugaritischen Sprache* (Berlin: Akademie Verlag, 1974), 8, s. v. *'dn; cf.* C. Gordon, *Ugaritic Textbook* (Rome: Pontifical Biblical Institute, 1965), 351, s. v. *ad* (#71).

[20]The text is RS 17.159; *PRU* IV, pp. 126–27, discussed by R. Yaron, "A Royal Divorce at Ugarit," *Or* 32 (1963), 21–31; see also I. Seibert, *Women in the Ancient Near East* (New York: Abner Schram, 1974), 15.

[21]The text that describes this is RS 17.352; *PRU* IV, pp. 121–22, discussed by E. Lipiński, "Aḫat-milki, reine d'Ugarit, et la guerre du Mukiš," *OLP* 12 (1981), 79–115; see also Z. Ben-Barak, "The Queen Consort and the Struggle for Succession to the Throne," *La femme dans le Proche-Orient antique* (Compte rendu de la XXXIIIe Rencontre assyriologique internationale [Paris, 7–10 juillet 1986]; ed. J.-M. Durand; Paris: Recherche sur les Civilisations, 1987), 34, 37; M. S. Drower, "Ugarit," *CAH* 2 (3d ed.; ed. I. E. S. Edwards; C. J. Gadd; N. G. L. Hammond; E. Sollberger; Cambridge: Cambridge University Press, 1975), Part 2, ch. XXI (b), 141–42; T. Ishida, *The Royal Dynasties in Ancient Israel: A Study on the Formation and Development of Royal-Dynastic Ideology* (BZAW 142; Berlin: de Gruyter, 1976), 155; A. F. Rainey, "The Kingdom of Ugarit," *BAR* 3 (Sheffield: Almond, 1970), 84–85; Seibert, *Women,* 48.

[22]*Internal Organization,* 182.

[23]The text is *KAI* 14. Eshmunazor is called "an orphan," *ytm,* in line 3 and also line 13; he is called "the son of a few days," *bn msk ymm,* in line 3 and in lines 12–13.

[24]*bšnt 'sr u' rb' 14 lmlky;* line 1.

[25]For discussions of the queen mother in Israel, see, in addition to my own articles, "The Queen Mother and the Cult in Ancient Israel," *JBL* 112 (1993), 385–401, and "The Queen Mother and the Cult in the Ancient Near East," 179–80, 184–85, 193–98: G. W. Ahlström, *Aspects of Syncretism in Israelite Religion* (Horae Soederblomianae 5; Lund: C. W. K. Gleerup, 1963), 57–88; N.-E. A. Andreasen, "The Role of the Queen Mother in Israelite Society," *CBQ* 45 (1983), 179–94; Z. Ben-Barak, "The Status and Right of the *Gĕbîrâ,*" *JBL* 110 (1991), 23–34 (reprinted

in *A Feminist Companion to Samuel and Kings* [ed. A. Brenner; The Feminist Companion to the Bible 5; Sheffield: Sheffield Academic Press, 1994], 170–85); idem, "Queen Consort," 33–40; H. Donner, "Art und Herkunft des Amtes der Königinmutter im Alten Testament," *Festschrift Johannes Friedrich zum 65. Geburtstag am 27. August gewidmet* (ed. R. von Kienle et al.; Heidelberg: Carl Winter, 1959), 105–45; Ishida, *The Royal Dynasties,* 155–60; G. Molin, "Die Stellung der Gᵉbira im Staate Juda," *TZ* 10 (1954), 161–75; K. Spanier, "The Queen Mother in the Judaean Royal Court: Maacah—A Case Study," *A Feminist Companion to Samuel and Kings,* 186–95; de Vaux, *Ancient Israel* 1, 117–19.

²⁶David had, the Bible tells us, several sons: 2 Sam 3:2–5 (see also 1 Chr 3:1–4) lists Amnon, Chileab (alternatively known as Daniel [1 Chr 3:1]), Absalom, Adonijah, Shephatiah, and Ithream, all born in the early years of David's reign, when his power was centered in Hebron. Later, in Jerusalem, he is said to have begot Shimea/Shammua, Shobab, Nathan, Solomon, Ibhar, Elishua/Elishama, Eliphelet, Nogah, Nepheg, Japhia, Elishama, Eliada, and another Eliphelet (2 Sam 5:13–16; 1 Chr 3:5–8). By all rights, the throne upon David's death should have gone to the fourth of these children, Adonijah, who was David's oldest living heir (David's first-born, Amnon, was killed by Absalom in revenge for Amnon's rape of his half-sister and Absalom's full sister, Tamar; Absalom himself was killed by David's general, Joab, in the fighting that surrounded Absalom's rebellion against his father's house; Chileab/Daniel seems to have died young, for the adult Chileab/Daniel is nowhere mentioned in our sources [moreover, the confusion over his name points to his obscurity]).

²⁷See in this regard 2 Sam 3:6–11, where King Saul's son, Ishbaal (the MT reads *ʾîš-bōšet,* Ishboshet, an artificially created name where *bōšet,* "shame," is substituted for *baʿal,* "lord," because of the latter term's associations with the Canaanite god Baal), and Saul's general, Abner, argue over Rizpah, the concubine of the dead king. But as verses 9–10 indicate, the argument is really over Saul's kingdom, which Ishbaal wishes to inherit from his father and which Abner hopes to secure for David. Concubine and kingdom are similarly equated in 2 Sam 16:20–22, where David's rebellious son Absalom goes into David's concubines as a part of his attempt to wrest the throne from his father.

²⁸J. Gray, *I and II Kings: A Commentary* (OTL; London: SCM, 1964), 104.

²⁹On the folkloristic motifs in this story, see M. Liverani, "L'Histoire de Joas," *VT* 24 (1974), 438–53.

³⁰*The Tawananna in the Hittite Kingdom* (Heidelberg: Carl Winter; Freiburg: Universitätverlag, 1975), 34–50, 107–59.

³¹See, for example, the discussion of Andreasen, "Queen Mother," 181–82, 187–94.

[32] *A Reassessment of 'Asherah': A Study According to Textual Sources of the First Two Millennia B.C.E.* (AOAT 235; Kevelaer: Butzon & Bercker; Neukirchen–Vluyn: Neukirchener Verlag, 1993), 63–66.

[33] I have briefly discussed the complementary characters of El, the divine patriarch, and Asherah, the mother goddess, in *Under Every Green Tree: Popular Religion in Sixth-Century Judah* (HSM 46; Atlanta: Scholars Press, 1992), 191–92.

[34] Using mythological texts to describe human social institutions is methodologically problematic; see R. A. Oden, Jr., "Method in the Study of Near Eastern Myths," *Religion* 9 (1973), 185–88; also idem, "Theoretical Assumptions in the Study of Ugaritic Myths," *Maarav* 2 (1979–80), 51–55.

[35] I have discussed Kirta's incubation more thoroughly in "The Deception of Isaac, Jacob's Dream at Bethel, and Incubation on an Animal Skin," *Priesthood and Cult in Ancient Israel* (JSOTSup 125; ed. G. A. Anderson and S. M. Olyan; Sheffield: JSOT Press, 1991), 110–11.

[36] Representative are the comments of Simon B. Parker, *The Pre-Biblical Narrative Tradition* (SBLRBS 24; Atlanta: Scholars Press, 1989), 159: "This raises the question in the mind of the audience, why, in a long narrative in which Keret [= Kirta] is clearly acting out El's instructions to the letter, he should now initiate this unanticipated act with reference to another deity?" and 172, "the vow is intrusive in the account of Keret's expedition. . . . the vow actually has no function in the tale of El's response to Keret's need of a family."

[37] See Parker, *Narrative Tradition,* 176; idem, "The Historical Composition of KRT and the Cult of El," *ZAW* 89 (1977), 163; M. D. Coogan, *Stories from Ancient Canaan* (Philadelphia: Westminster, 1978), 53.

[38] See, similarly, Chapter 2 concerning the unnecessary and even foolish vow of Jephthah in Judg 11:29–40 (and, as there, Bal, *Death and Dissymmetry, 44;* D. Marcus, *Jephthah and His Vow* [Lubbock, TX: Texas Tech Press, 1986], 54–55; P. Trible, "A Meditation in Mourning: The Sacrifice of the Daughter of Jephthah," *USQR* 36 [1981], 60–61; idem, "The Daughter of Jephthah: An Inhuman Sacrifice," Chapter 4 in *Texts of Terror: Literary-Feminist Readings of Biblical Narratives* [OBT 13; Philadelphia: Fortress, 1984], 96–97; idem, "A Daughter's Death: Feminism, Literary Criticism, and the Bible," *Backgrounds for the Bible* [ed. M. P. O'Connor and D. N. Freedman; Winona Lake, IN: Eisenbrauns, 1987], 5).

[39] Some have argued that El is *deus otiosus* in Ugaritic myth, his place as high god of the pantheon having been usurped by Baal. But, as Frank M. Cross has argued, El does seem to retain the supreme (although not the sole) place of authority among Ugarit's deities. See *Canaanite Myth and Hebrew Epic: Essays in the History of*

the Religion of Israel (Cambridge, MA: Harvard University Press, 1973), 22, 39–40, et passim.

[40]J. Gray, *The KRT Text in the Literature of Ras Shamra. A Social Myth of Ancient Canaan* (2d ed.; Leiden: Brill, 1964), 59; see also idem, "Sacral Kingship in Ugarit," *Ugaritica* VI (Paris: Mission Archéologique de Ras Shamra; Librairie Orientaliste Paul Geuthner, 1969), 295–96; more generally on this usage in the inscriptions of the pre-Sargonic kings of Sumer, see T. Frymer-Kensky, *In the Wake of the Goddesses: Women, Culture, and the Biblical Transformation of Pagan Myth* (New York: Fawcett Columbine, 1992), 60 and 238, n. 10.

[41]Enuma Elish I.85. See H. L. Ginsberg, *The Legend of King Keret: A Canaanite Epic of the Bronze Age* (BASOR Supplementary Studies 2–3; New Haven, CT: American Schools of Oriental Research, 1946), 41; G. R. Driver, *Canaanite Myths and Legends* (2d ed.; revised by J. C. L. Gibson; Edinburgh: T. & T. Clark, 1978), 91, n. 7. See also Parker, *Narrative Tradition,* 162, who writes, "Rulers claim to have been suckled by a goddess as early as the presargonic royal inscriptions from Lagash."

[42]Cyrus H. Gordon has pointed out one additional piece of information that may link queen mothers at Ugarit with the cult of Asherah: the fact that Ugaritic queen mothers seem to be addressed by the epithet *rbt,* "Lady," which is the same title found in the standard epithet of Asherah at Ugarit, *rbt aṯrt ym,* "Lady Asherah of the Sea." See Gordon's "Ugaritic *RBT/RABĪTU*," *Ascribe to the Lord. Biblical and Other Studies in Memory of Peter C. Craigie* (JSOTSup 67; ed. L. Eslinger and J. G. Taylor; Sheffield: JSOT Press, 1988), 127; this reference was brought to my attention by Wiggins, *'Asherah',* 65.

[43]The variant names Abijam and Abijah are most probably the result of textual confusion; see M. Noth, *Die israelitischen Personennamen im Rahmen der gemeinsemitischen Namengebung* (Hildesheim: Georg Olms, 1980), 234, #117.

[44]The noun *mipleṣet* comes from the verb *plṣ,* "to shudder." Presumably it means "a thing to be shuddered at," "a horrid thing," or, as here, "an abominable image."

[45]I have discussed this issue of translation more thoroughly in "Queen Mother and the Cult in Ancient Israel," 389.

[46]Cf. the discussions on the nature of the asherah as cult object found in E. Lipiński, "The Goddess Atirat in Ancient Arabia, in Babylon, and in Ugarit," *OLP* 3 (1972), 112–16; M. S. Smith, *The Early History of God: Yahweh and the Other Deities in Ancient Israel* (San Francisco: Harper & Row, 1990), 80–94. See also the useful survey of scholarly positions found in J. Day, "Asherah in the Hebrew Bible and in Northwest Semitic Literature," *JBL* 105 (1986), 398–404.

[47]This point is made most explicitly in Deut 16:21, which commands the Israel-

ites, "You shall not plant (*nāṭaʿ*) for yourself as an asherah any tree beside the altar of Yahweh, your God." Terminology found elsewhere in the Hebrew Bible further implies that the asherah is a stylized pole or tree by describing how the asherah can be "made" (*ʿāśâ*) or "built" (*bānâ*), "stood up" (*ʿāmad*) or "erected" (*hiṣṣîb*). When destroyed, the cult symbol is "burned" (*bīʿēr* or *śārap*), "cut down" (*kārat*), "hewn down" (*gādaʿ*), "uprooted" (*nātaš*), "overturned" (*nātaṣ*), or "broken" (*šibbēr*); for more detailed comments concerning the use of these verbs with the noun *ʾăšērâ*, see W. L. Reed, *The Asherah in the Old Testament* [Fort Worth, TX: Texas Christian University Press, 1949], 29–37). The Greek tradition also indicates that it understands the word asherah as referring to some sort of tree imagery by translating it most commonly as "grove" (*alsos*) and twice as "trees" (*dendra;* at two other points, 2 Chr 15:16 and 2 Chr 24:18, the Greek reads "Astarte" [*Astartē, Astartais*] instead of "asherah" due to textual confusion). Similarly, the Latin translation of the Hebrew Bible reads "grove" (*lucus*) or "wood" (*nemus*) for asherah (although once [Judg 3:7], the Latin reads *Astaroth* for "asherah" due to textual confusion). Further of significance is the story of the garden of Eden found in Gen 2:4b–3:24, for Howard N. Wallace has suggested that the way Eve is described in that narrative as "the mother of all the living" (3:20) mimics in some respects the characterization of Asherah as the mother goddess (*The Eden Narrative* [HSM 32; Atlanta: Scholars Press, 1985], 111–14, 158). If this is so, then the association of this Asherah-*cum*-Eve with Eden's tree of life/tree of knowledge is significant. Iconographical data lastly demonstrate that the symbol of the goddess Asherah is a stylized pole or tree. I have discussed this evidence thoroughly in "Queen Mother and the Cult in the Ancient Near East," 191–92, and also, briefly, in *Under Every Green Tree*, 190–91.

[48]See W. F. Albright, *Archaeology and the Religion of Israel* (2d ed.; Baltimore: Johns Hopkins University Press, 1946), 139, and the references there; also J. Pedersen, *Israel, Its Life and Culture* 3–4 (London: Oxford University Press; Copenhagen: Branner og Korch, 1940), 429.

[49]David, for example, appoints the two high priests Zadok and Abiathar, who minister to the ark in Jerusalem. See further Cross, *Canaanite Myth*, 208, 215, n. 74, and 232. 1 Kings 2:26–27, which describes Solomon's expulsion of Abiathar from the Jerusalem priesthood, also attests to the king's right to appoint, or in this case depose, temple personnel. Some three hundred and fifty years later, King Josiah similarly asserts himself in the matters of both appointing and deposing temple personnel by removing the priests from the shrines they tended in the towns round about Judah and bringing them to serve in the temple in Jerusalem (2 Kgs 23:8–9). At the same time, Josiah removes other cult functionaries, the *qĕdēšim*, from their temple offices (2 Kgs 23:7), and he has certain of the temple's cult furnishings burned or otherwise destroyed (2 Kgs 23:4, 6, 11–12). King Hezekiah also removes certain cult furnishings from the temple; see 2 Kgs 18:4.

[50]I have discussed this more thoroughly in "Queen Mother and the Cult in the Ancient Near East," 194–95.

[51]See, for example, Spanier, "Queen Mother," 194; also Ahlström, *Aspects of Syncretism,* 59, 61, who cites Albright, *Archaeology,* 157–59, and S. Yeivin, "Social, Religious, and Cultural Trends in Judaism Under the Davidic Dynasty," *VT* 3 (1953), 162–64. See, too, the remarks of Peter R. Ackroyd, "Goddesses, Women and Jezebel," *Images of Women in Antiquity* (ed. A. Cameron and A. Kuhrt; London and Canberra: Croom Helm, 1983), 255, although note that Ackroyd himself does not agree with the conclusions of Ahlström, Albright, and Yeivin.

[52]"Canaanite Origins and Lineage: Reflections on the Religion of Ancient Israel," *Ancient Israelite Religion: Essays in Honor of Frank Moore Cross* (ed. P. D. Miller; P. D. Hanson; S. D. McBride; Philadelphia: Fortress, 1987), 115.

[53]*Asherah and the Cult of Yahweh in Israel* (SBLMS 34; Atlanta: Scholars Press, 1988), 9.

[54]The *editio princeps* was by William G. Dever, "Iron Age Epigraphic Material from the Area of Khirbet el-Kôm," *HUCA* 40/41 (1969–70), 158–89, although Dever did not suggest in this article that the inscription had any relation to the cult of Asherah. But the inscription was restudied by André Lemaire, "Les inscriptions de Khirbet el-Qôm et l'Ashérah de Yhwh," *RB* 84 (1977), 597–608; idem, "Date et origine des inscriptiones hebraiques et pheniciennes de Kuntillet 'Ajrud," *Studi epigraphici e linguistici* 1 (1984), 131–43; idem, "Who or What Was Yahweh's Asherah?" *BARev* 10/6 (1984), 42–51, and in these reassessments, Lemaire proposed reading a reference to Asherah in the second and third lines of the text. Dever now accepts this reading: see "Asherah, Consort of Yahweh? New Evidence from Kuntillet 'Ajrûd," *BASOR* 255 (1985), 22; less completely, idem, "Recent Archaeological Confirmation of the Cult of Asherah in Ancient Israel," *Hebrew Studies* 23 (1982), 40, and "Material Remains and the Cult in Ancient Israel: An Essay in Archaeological Systematics," *The Word of the Lord Shall Go Forth. Essays in Honor of David Noel Freedman in Celebration of His Sixtieth Birthday* (ed. C. L. Meyers and M. O'Connor; Winona Lake, IN: Eisenbrauns, 1983), 570 and n. 17 on p. 583. Other studies of the el-Qom material include J. M. Hadley, "The Khirbet el-Qom Inscription," *VT* 37 (1987), 50–62; K. Jaroš, "Zur Inschrift Nr. 3 von Ḫirbet el-Qōm," *BN* 19 (1982), 31–40; W. A. Maier, *'Ašerah: Extrabiblical Evidence* (HSM 37; Atlanta: Scholars Press, 1986), 172–73; B. Margalit, "Some Observations on the Inscription and Drawing from Khirbet el-Qôm," *VT* 39 (1989), 371–78; P. D. Miller, "Psalms and Inscriptions," VTSup 32 (1981), 311–32; S. Mittman, "Die Grabinschrift des Sangers Uriahu," *ZDPV* 97 (1981), 139–52; J. Naveh, "Graffiti and Dedications," *BASOR* 235 (1979), 27–30; M. O'Connor, "The Poetic Inscription from Khirbet el-Qôm," *VT* 37 (1987), 224–29; Olyan, *Asherah,* 23–25; Smith, *Early History,* 88; Z. Zevit, "The Khirbet el-Qôm Inscription Mentioning a Goddess," *BASOR* 255 (1984), 39–47.

[55]"Psalms and Inscriptions," 317.

[56]To translate '*šrt* as "shrine," cognate with Phoenician '*šrt,* Aramaic '*trt',* and

Akkadian *aširtu,* was first proposed by Lipiński, "Atirat," 101–19. However, J. A. Emerton, "New Light on Israelite Religion: The Implications of the Inscriptions from Kuntillet ʿAjrud," *ZAW* 94 (1982), 2–20, has argued that this translation is inviable, pointing out that *ʾăšērâ* never means "shrine" in the Hebrew of the Bible and thus should not have such a meaning in the Hebrew epigraphic corpus. Emerton and others discuss instead two of the other options noted here: (1) to read *ʾšrt* as "asherah," i.e., the cult object sacred to the goddess Asherah, or (2) to read *ʾšrt* as "Asherah," the divine name. The fourth option—to understand *lʾšrth* as a hypostatized aspect of the female side of Yahweh—is discussed by Miller in "The Absence of the Goddess in Israelite Religion," *HAR* 10 (1986), 246, and also by P. K. McCarter in "Aspects of the Religion of the Israelite Monarchy: Biblical and Epigraphic Data," *Ancient Israelite Religion,* 149.

As my comments below suggest, choosing between these four options, while an important task for those concerned with the morphology of the inscription, is something that need not concern us here. For the historian of religion, the attempt to differentiate between asherah, a sacred symbol; Asherah, the goddess; or asherah, a female hypostasis of Yahweh, is to quibble over semantics. In the ancient Israelite imagination, the cult symbol of the goddess would have been perceived as Asherah herself. One has only to compare the ancient Israelite understanding of Yahweh's primary symbol during Israel's tribal period and during the time of the Jerusalem temple, the ark, to see how close the relationship between cult object and deity was in Israelite religion. Numbers 10:35–36, the so-called "Song of the Ark," illustrates perfectly the simultaneity of symbol and god in Israelite imagination: "whenever *the ark* set out, Moses said, 'Arise, O *Yahweh*'"; similarly, "when *it* [the ark] rested, he [Moses] said, 'Return, O *Yahweh*.'" We would expect that the asherah, the cult symbol, and Asherah, the goddess, likewise would have been understood by the ancient Israelites as one and the same.

[57]At least they do not reappear in the Masoretic tradition. They do appear in verse 22 of the Septuagint, but as several recent commentators have noted, the phrase *hoi prophētai tou alsous* is marked by an asterisk in Origen's Hexapla, indicating a secondary addition in the Greek. See Day, "Asherah," 400–1; Emerton, "New Light," 16; Lipiński, "Atirat," 114; these references are pointed out by Olyan, *Asherah,* 8, n. 24.

[58]The bibliography is vast. Preliminary reports can be found in Z. Meshel and C. Meyers, "The Name of God in the Wilderness of Zin," *BA* 39 (1976), 6–10; Z. Meshel, "Kuntillet ʿAjrûd—An Israelite Site from the Monarchical Period on the Sinai Border," *Qadmoniot* 9 (1976), 118–24 (Hebrew); idem, "Kuntillet ʿAjrûd—An Israelite Religious Center in Northern Sinai," *Expedition* 20 (1978), 50–54; idem, *Kuntillet ʿAjrûd: A Religious Center from the Time of the Judean Monarchy* (Israel Museum Catalogue 175; Jerusalem: Israel Museum, 1978); idem, "Did Yahweh Have a Consort? The New Religious Inscriptions from Sinai," *BARev* 5/2 (1979), 24–35. Significant studies include P. Beck, "The Drawings from Ḥorvat Teiman (Kuntillet ʿAjrûd)," *Tel Aviv* 9 (1982), 3–86; Dever, "Asherah, Consort of Yahweh?" 21–37;

idem, "Archaeological Confirmation," 37–43; Emerton, "New Light," 2–20; D. N. Freedman, "Yahweh of Samaria and His Asherah," *BA* 50 (1987), 241–49; M. Gilula, "To Yahweh Shomron and to His Asherah," *Shnaton* 3 (1978/79), 129–37 (Hebrew); J. M. Hadley, "Some Drawings and Inscriptions on Two Pithoi from Kuntillet ʿAjrud," *VT* 37 (1987), 180–211; Lemaire, "Date et origine," 131–43; idem, "Yahweh's Asherah," 42–51; Lipiński, "Aṯirat," 101–19; McCarter, "Aspects of the Religion," 137–49; Maier, *Ašerah,* 168–72; Miller, "Absence of the Goddess," 239–49; Olyan, *Asherah,* 25–37; Smith, *Early History,* 85–88; J. Tigay, "Israelite Religion: The Onomastic and Epigraphic Evidence," *Ancient Israelite Religion,* 173–75; idem, *You Shall Have No Other Gods: Israelite Religion in the Light of Hebrew Inscriptions* (HSS 31; Atlanta: Scholars Press, 1986), 26–30; M. Weinfeld, "A Sacred Site of the Monarchic Period," *Shnaton* 4 (1980), 280–84 (Hebrew); idem, "Further Remarks on the ʿAjrûd Inscription," *Shnaton* 5–6 (1981–82), 237–39 (Hebrew); idem, "Kuntillet ʿAjrud Inscriptions and Their Significance," *Studi epigraphici e linguistici* 1 (1984), 121–30.

[59]The text reads *brkt ʾtkm lyhwh šmrn wlʾšrth*. In the original announcements of the ʿAjrud materials ("Kuntillet ʿAjrûd—An Israelite Site," 118–24; "Kuntillet ʿAjrûd—An Israelite Religious Center," 50–54; *Kuntillet ʿAjrûd*), the excavator, Meshel, understood *yhwh šmrn* as "Yahweh our guardian" (*šōmĕrēnû*). But in 1979, Gilula ("Yahweh Shomron," 129–37) proposed reading instead "Yahweh of Samaria" (*šōmĕrōn*), and almost all commentators, including now Meshel ("Consort," 31), prefer this translation. See in particular Emerton, "New Light," 3–9, who points out that a second ʿAjrud inscription reading *yhwh tmn,* which can only be translated "Yahweh of the south," gives credence to the translation "Yahweh of Samaria." Emerton also assembles other evidence suggesting that our traditional understanding of Hebrew grammar, which would not permit proper names such as Yahweh to serve as the *nomen regens* in a construct phrase, is flawed.

[60]These two inscriptions read, respectively, *lyhwh htmn wlʾšrth* and *brktk lyhwh tmn wlʾšrth ybrk wyšmrk wyhy ʿm ʾdny.* However, the official publication of the Kuntillet ʿAjrud material has not yet appeared, and various commentators differ on the number of relevant inscriptions and their precise readings. I rely here on Tigay, "Israelite Religion," 173–74, and 189, n. 85. Tigay's sources are Meshel's remarks in *Kuntillet ʿAjrûd* and information provided by Meshel to M. Weinfeld and published by Weinfeld in "Further Remarks" and in "Kuntillet ʿAjrud Inscriptions."

[61]Olyan, *Asherah,* 6–8.

[62]See also on this point Ackroyd, "Goddesses, Women and Jezebel," 255–56; Ahlström, *Aspects of Syncretism,* 51; Freedman, "Yahweh of Samaria," 248.

[63]On Bethel as a state temple of Yahweh, see Amos 7:13, where the priest Amaziah calls the Bethel temple "a king's sanctuary" and "a dynastic temple" (for notes on translation, see Albright, *Archaeology,* 139).

[64]Hosea 4:13 does describe the daughters of Israel who play the harlot "under evergreen oak, styrax tree, and terebinth," but the asherah is not explicitly mentioned. Ditto Hos 4:12 and its reference to the people's attempt to "inquire of a thing of wood" for purposes of divination. Although some have interpreted this "thing of wood" to be Asherah's stylized pole or tree (e.g., P. J. King, *Amos, Hosea, Micah—An Archaeological Commentary* [Philadelphia: Westminster, 1988], 100), there is, in fact, no specific indication that this is the case.

[65]On the reference to Asherah that some have seen in Amos 8:14, see King, *Amos, Hosea, Micah*, 100–1.

[66]*Asherah*, 13.

[67]Note here that even though Jezebel is primarily remembered in the biblical tradition for introducing the cult of Baal into her husband's court, the religion of Ahab's monarchy actually remained Yahwism. This is particularly indicated by the fact that the name of Yahweh is incorporated into the names of the two sons of Jezebel and Ahab, Ahaziah and Jehoram (*'ăḥazyāhû*, "Yahweh has grasped"; *yĕhôrām*, "Yahweh is exalted"), which demonstrates that Yahweh was the parents' patron God. Ahab and Jezebel also give a Yahwistic name to their daughter, Athaliah (*'ătalyāh*, "Yahweh is great," based on Akkadian *etellu*, "to be great, exalted"; the root *'tl* is otherwise unknown in Hebrew), and Yahwistic names, in addition, are borne by others of their descendants: by Athaliah's son, Ahaziah; by her daughter, Jehosheba (*jĕhôšeba'*, "Yahweh is abundance"); and by her grandson, Joash (*yô'āš*, "Yahweh has given").

[68]On the location of this temple, cf. Y. Yadin, "'The 'House of Ba'al' of Ahab and Jezebel in Samaria, and that of Athaliah in Judah," *Archaeology in the Levant* (Kathleen Kenyon *Festschrift;* Warminster: Aris and Phillips, 1978), 127–29.

[69]There has been some debate on the relationship of Athaliah to Ahab and Jezebel; in 2 Kgs 8:26 and 2 Chr 22:2, Athaliah is called the *bat 'omrî*, "the daughter of Omri," whereas in 2 Kgs 8:18 and 2 Chr 21:6, she is called the *bat 'aḥ'āb*, "the daughter of Ahab." It is generally conceded that *bat* in *bat 'omrî* should be understood in a more general sense of female descendant; the NRSV, in fact, translates "granddaughter." But see H. J. Katzenstein, "Who Were the Parents of Athaliah?" *IEJ* 5 (1955), 194–97.

[70]The temple could possibly have been in Jerusalem's outskirts; see Yadin, "'House of Ba'al,'" 130–32.

[71]Note here that, as in the case of Jezebel (above, n. 67), the Yahwistic names of Athaliah's descendants prove she participated as required in Yahweh's state cult. Concerning Jehosheba, note that, while she is said to be the daughter of Jehoram, Athaliah's husband, according to 2 Kgs 11:2, her mother's name is not given. But

since the names of no other wives of Jehoram are known, it is reasonable to presume that Jehosheba was Athaliah's daughter.

[72]For kings who reigned before the fall of the northern kingdom of Israel in 722 B.C.E., the standard pattern reads, "In the XX year of King NN of Israel, NN began to rule over Judah. He reigned for XX years in Jerusalem; his mother's name was NN, daughter of NN" (1 Kgs 15:1–2, 9–10; 22:41–42; 2 Kgs 8:25–26; 12:1; 14:1–2; 15:1–2, 32–33; 18:1–2; similarly, 1 Kgs 14:21). After the fall of the north, the basic pattern remains, although the synchronization with the kings of Israel is eliminated (2 Kgs 21:1, 19; 22:1; 23:31, 36; 24:8, 18).

[73]1 Kgs 14:20; 15:25, 33; 16:8, 15, 23, 29; 22:51; 2 Kgs 3:1; 10:36; 13:1, 10; 14:23; 15:8, 13, 17, 23, 27; 17:1.

[74]See A. Alt, "The Monarchy in the Kingdoms of Israel and Judah," *Essays on Old Testament History and Religion* (Garden City, NY: Doubleday, 1967), 321–26.

[75]E.g., de Vaux, *Ancient Israel* 1, 118.

[76]"Das Königtum in der Reichen Israel und Juda," *VT* 1 (1951), 2–22; reprinted in *Kleine Schriften zur Geschichte des Volkes Israel* 2 (München: C. H. Beck, 1959), 116–34; English translation, "Monarchy," in *Essays,* 313–35.

[77]*Canaanite Myth,* 241–65.

[78]The debate concerning the "divine" versus the "sacral" character of Judaean kingship is an extensive one. The most radical position is that advanced by British and Scandinavian proponents of the "myth and ritual" school, who have argued for a Jerusalem ideology of a "god-king" and for associated cultic rituals involving the king's symbolic death and rebirth, followed by a sacred marriage with a priestess representing her patron goddess (*hieros gamos*). Most scholars, however, while acknowledging that the British and Scandinavian schools have correctly drawn our attention to the special place of the king in the Jerusalem cult, tend to prefer a more moderate description of the Judaean monarchy, one which would characterize Jerusalem kingship not so much as "divine" but rather as "sacral." The sacral king is not truly a "god" but has instead a unique filial relationship with Yahweh. For bibliography and for the history of the debate on "divine" versus "sacral," see P. D. Miller, "Israelite Religion," *The Hebrew Bible and its Modern Interpreters* (ed. D. A. Knight and G. M. Tucker; Philadelphia: Fortress; Chico, CA: Scholars Press, 1985), 218–20; more fully but less up-to-date, the survey of A. R. Johnson, "Hebrew Conceptions of Kingship," *Myth, Ritual, and Kingship: Essays on the Theory and Practice of Kingship in the Ancient Near East and in Israel* (ed. S. H. Hooke; Oxford: Clarendon, 1958), 204–35; idem, "Living Issues in Biblical Scholarship. Divine Kingship and the Old Testament," *ExpTim* 62 (1950–51), 36–42.

[79]Reading the singular with many of the versions instead of the plural form found in the MT.

[80]Reading *nēzer*, "crown," for Masoretic *ʿēzer*, "help."

[81]*Canaanite Myth*, 258.

[82]On the date of Judges 5, see Chapter 1, n. 5.

[83]See G. Loud and C. B. Altman, *Khorsabad, Part II: The Citadel and the Town* (Oriental Institute Publications 40; Chicago: University of Chicago Press, 1938), 96–97 and Pl. 51–52 (Nos. 29–37); R. D. Barnett, *A Catalogue of the Nimrud Ivories, with other examples of Ancient Near Eastern Ivories in the British Museum* (2d ed.; London: Trustees of the British Museum, 1975), 172–73 and Pl. IV and V (C-12 through C-16 and C-20 through C-21); F. Thureau-Dangin, A. Barrois, G. Dossin, and M. Dunard, *Arslan-Tash* (Bibliothèque archéologique et historique 16; Paris: Librairie Orientalist Paul Geuthner, 1931), 112–18 and Pl. XXXIV–XXXVI (Nos. 45–60); J. W. Crowfoot and G. M. Crowfoot, *Early Ivories from Samaria* (London: Palestine Exploration Fund, 1938), 29–30 and Pl. XIII.2.

[84]Regarding the number of exemplars at Nimrud, Barnett published ten examples in *Nimrud Ivories*, C-12 through C-21, of which six, C-16 through C-21, consisted of the head alone. The excavations of Max Mallowan, reported in "The Excavations at Nimrud (Kalḫu), 1949–1950: Ivories from the N. W. Palace," *Iraq* 14 (1952), 50 and Pl. XIII, Nos. 2, 5, and 10, revealed one more head and two more windows. See further Barnett, *Nimrud Ivories*, 111, n. 2. Regarding Samaria, Crowfoot and Crowfoot describe finding "small fragments of other window frames" in Area Qc, the same area in which the complete plaque was discovered. They also report "fragments of at least two other replicas" in Area Qk. See *Samaria*, 29.

[85]For discussion, see Barnett, *Nimrud Ivories*, 99.

[86]*Amatorius* 20.

[87]This was first proposed by R. Herbig, "Aphrodite Parakyptusa (Die Frau im Fenster)," *OLZ* 30 (1927), 917–22, and has been followed by many, for example, Barnett, *Nimrud Ivories*, 149; Crowfoot and Crowfoot, *Samaria*, 30.

[88]14.696–761, especially 760–61.

[89]On these correspondences, see Ackerman, *Under Every Green Tree*, 22.

[90]Herodotus, *Histories* 1, 199. For other ancient sources, see the catalogue found in R. A. Oden, Jr., *The Bible Without Theology: The Theological Tradition and Alterna-*

tives to It (New Voices in Biblical Studies; San Francisco: Harper & Row, 1987), 140–44.

[91] See, for example, Ackroyd, "Goddesses, Women and Jezebel," 258; S. Brown, "Perspectives on Phoenician Art," *BA* 55 (1992), 11; Dever, "Asherah, Consort of Yahweh?" 23; King, *Amos, Hosea, Micah,* 100; M. Mallowan, *The Nimrud Ivories* (London: British Museum Publications, 1978), 33; N. Robertson, "The Ritual Background of the Dying God in Cyprus and Syro-Palestine," *HTR* 75 (1982), 316; Thureau-Dangin, et al., *Arslan Tash,* 116. A related theory suggests that the "woman in the window" is the demoness "Kililu of the window," an attendant of Astarte's Mesopotamian equivalent, the goddess Ishtar. Among those who identify the "woman" as Kililu, see H. Frankfort, *The Art and Architecture of the Ancient Orient* (Harmondsworth: Penguin Books, 1954), 321 and n. 170 on p. 406; E. Strommenger, "Ivory carving of a woman in a window," *Ebla to Damascus: Art and Archaeology of Ancient Syria* (ed. H. Weiss; Washington, D.C.: Smithsonian Institution Traveling Exhibition Service, 1985), 355. For discussion, see R. D. Barnett, "The Nimrud Ivories and the Art of the Phoenicians," *Iraq* 2 (1935), 203–4; idem, *Nimrud Ivories,* 150; and, especially, W. Fauth, *Aphrodite Parakyptusa: Untersuchungen zum Erscheinungsbild der vorderasiatischen Dea Prospiciens* (Akademie der Wissenschaften und der Literatur, Abhandlungen der Geistes- und Sozialwissenschaftlichen Klasse, Jahrgang 1966, Nr. 6; Wiesbaden: Franz Steiner, 1967), 417–21.

[92] See E. J. Fisher, "Cultic Prostitution in the Ancient Near East? A Reassessment," *Biblical Theology Bulletin* 5 (1976), 225–36; Oden, "Religious Identity and the Sacred Prostitution Accusation," *Bible Without Theology,* 131–53; J. Westenholz, "Tamar, *Qĕdēšā, Qadištu,* and Sacred Prostitution in Mesopotamia," *HTR* 82 (1989), 245–65. See also the criticisms of the "woman in the window"/sacred prostitution equation in M. O'Connor, "The Women in the Book of Judges," *HAR* 10 (1986), 285, n. 25.

[93] Quoted by Antoninus Liberalis, *Metamorphoses* 39.

[94] Eleanor F. Beach, "The Samaria Ivories, *Marzeaḥ,* and Biblical Text," *BA* 56 (1993), 94, has particularly stressed the importance of considering the "woman in the window" depictions in the context of the overall assemblage of ivories.

[95] A catalogue of which of the ivories' motifs is found at each of the "woman in the window" sites has been meticulously assembled by Beach. See her chart in "Samaria Ivories, *Marzeaḥ,* and Biblical Text," 99.

[96] As pointed out by Irene Winter, "Phoenician and North Syria Ivory Carving in Historical Context: Questions of Style and Distribution," *Iraq* 38 (1976), 1–22, the identification of the ivories as Phoenician in origin yet derived from Egyptian prototypes was first advanced by Friedrich Poulsen, *Der Orient und die frühgriechische Kunst* (Leipzig: B. G. Teubner, 1912), 37–59, and was subsequently developed by

Barnett, in "The Nimrud Ivories," 185–99, and in *Nimrud Ivories,* 55–58 et passim, and, now, by Winter herself, in "Phoenician and North Syria Ivory Carving," 4–17.

[97]This *contra* Brown, "Phoenician Art," 11, who sees the "woman in the window" images as "distinctively Phoenician," as opposed to the other representations of the ivory assemblage, which she does regard as "wholly Egyptian in origin." See, similarly, Frankfort, *Art and Architecture,* 321; Robertson, "Ritual Background," 316–17, n. 13, and 320; and Thureau-Dangin, et al., *Arslan Tash,* 115–16.

[98]Crowfoot and Crowfoot, *Samaria,* 29.

[99]See, for example, the comments of Barnett, *Nimrud Ivories,* 172, who writes of the woman's "Egyptian wig and dress" (also, p. 145, her "Egyptian sort of wig," and p. 147, her "Egyptian type of wig"); similarly, Thureau-Dangin, et al., *Arslan Tash,* 112, "La chevelure frisée est rendue à l'égyptienne." Moreover, Dever, "Asherah, Consort of Yahweh?" 23, notes that the distinctive coiffure worn by the lyre-playing female in the drawings from Kuntillet 'Ajrud, "recalls . . . the 'Lady-at-the-Window.'" Note also that this lyre player wears a dress decorated with polka dots, which is the same sort of decoration that adorns the neck of the garment worn by at least the Nimrud exemplars of the "woman in the window" (so Barnett, *Nimrud Ivories,* 147). In his article, Dever goes on to identify the 'Ajrud lyre player-*cum*-"woman in the window" with Asherah, which is entirely consistent with the argument I will make below that in the Semitic world, the Hathor imagery of the "woman in the window" is reinterpreted as being the imagery of Hathor's Canaanite counterpart, Asherah.

[100]C. J. Bleeker, *Hathor and Thoth: Two Key Figures of the Ancient Egyptian Religion* (Leiden: Brill, 1973), 22. According to Bleeker, the only other Egyptian god that is usually presented frontally is Bes.

[101]"Samaria Ivories, *Marzeah̬,* and Biblical Text," 98, 101.

[102]*Archaeology of the Land of the Bible, 10,000–586 B.C.E.* (Anchor Bible Reference Library; New York: Doubleday, 1990), 505; similarly, King, *Amos, Hosea, Micah,* 146.

[103]Barnett, *Nimrud Ivories,* 137. Barnett makes a similar claim on p. 138: "Phoenician artists in the type of scenes we describe are utilizing Egyptian figures, even Egyptian divinities, to illustrate purely Phoenician themes"; still on p. 138, he also notes, "Phoenician artists adapt Egyptian groups and figures . . . using them to represent subjects of Phoenician mythology and worship." See also p. 56, "The deities wearing quasi-Egyptian costumes . . . on Phoenician seals and ivories are not just Egyptian gods misrepresented, but are local deities partially adapted to their Egyptian equivalents." Similarly, see Barnett, "The Nimrud Ivories," 199, where, simultaneous with admitting the imagery's Egyptian prototypes, he claims "it may be

submitted that for its own creators it was actually full of content" (similarly, p. 200); also see idem, "Syria and Phoenicia in the Iron Age," Chapter 8 in *Ancient Ivories in the Middle East and Adjacent Countries* (Qedem 14; Jerusalem: Hebrew University Institute of Archaeology, 1982), 54.

[104]Although it is true that in the *Greek* world, Hathor was equated with Aphrodite (= Astarte); see Maier, *'Ašerah,* 96, who cites as evidence Lucian, *De Dea Syria* 6.

[105]A crucial text here is Eusebius, *Praeparatio evangelica* 1.10.35, which describes how Kronos (= El) gives the city of Byblos "to the goddess Baaltis who is also Dione" (for translation, see H. W. Attridge and R. A. Oden, Jr., *Philo of Byblos: The Phoenician History, Introduction, Critical Text, Translation, Notes* [CBQMS 9; Washington, D.C.: The Catholic Biblical Association of America, 1981], 57 and n. 126 on p. 91). Dione, however, is not only Baaltis (i.e., *ba'lat gebal*), she is to be equated also with Asherah (see Cross, *Canaanite Myth,* 28; Attridge and Oden, *Philo of Byblos,* 91–92, n. 132). Thus the *ba'alat gebal* is Asherah. Note further in this regard Byblos' role as a maritime city and the chief epithet of Asherah at Ugarit, "Lady Asherah of the *Sea*" (emphasis mine); moreover, Asherah's attendant *dgy,* "Fisherman," mentioned twice in the Baal-Anat cycle (*KTU* 1.3.6.10; 4.2.31). These references brought to my attention by Maier, *'Ašerah,* 96.

[106]See, for example, the stele of King Yehawmilk of Byblos, which pictures the king presenting a libation to the "Lady of Byblos." She, given her portrayal with horns embracing a sun disk, is undoubtedly to be identified as Hathor (*ANEP* [ed. J. B. Pritchard; Princeton: Princeton University Press, 1954], #477).

[107]On the Sinai's Hathor cult, see Bleeker, *Hathor and Thoth,* 72–73; on Asherah in the Sinai, see Cross, *Canaanite Myth,* 33, who in particular discusses the epithet *dt bṭn,* "Lady of the Serpent," used of Asherah in the fifteenth-century B.C.E. proto-Sinaitic texts from Serabit el-Khadim, a site which, not coincidentally, was the location of a Hathor temple; for references, see Maier, *'Ašerah,* 88 and 135, n. 63.

[108]Cross, *Canaanite Myth,* 28–29, n. 90; see also Maier, *'Ašerah,* 88–90, 93–94.

[109]The evidence for Hathor's and Asherah's shared association with sacred trees has been assembled most thoroughly by Ruth Hestrin, "The Lachish Ewer and the 'Asherah," *IEJ* 37 (1987), 215–20, especially 219–20. See also idem, "The Cult Stand from Ta'anach and Its Religious Background," *Studia Phoenicia 5: Phoenicia and the East Mediterranean in the First Millennium B.C.* (Orientalia Lovaniensia Analecta 23; ed. E. Lipiński; Leuven: Uitgeverij Peeters, 1987), 68–71, where Hestrin discusses less completely Asherah's and Hathor's shared association with sacred trees yet supplements with a discussion of the two goddesses' shared associations with lions and snakes. See also, on Hathor's association with sacred trees, Bleeker, *Hathor and Thoth,* 34–37; for Asherah's association with lions and snakes, see Ackerman, "Queen

Mother and the Cult in Ancient Israel," 396–98, and, for Asherah's association with lions, idem, *Under Every Green Tree,* 190–91. Finally, on Hathor's association with bovine imagery, see Bleeker, *Hathor and Thoth,* 22–24 and, especially, 30–34; for the reflection of this bovine imagery in the Asherah cult, note that in both Ugarit and Israel, Asherah's consort—whether El (in Ugarit) or Yahweh (in Israel)—can be called "Bull," implying that she is "Cow" (on "Bull El," see Ackerman, *Under Every Green Tree,* 156; on Yahweh as bull, see Gen 49:24; Isa 1:24; 49:26; 60:16; Ps 132:2, 5; and the comments on translation found in Cross, *Canaanite Myth,* 4, n. 6; also, on the bull as an icon of Yahweh at the shrines of Bethel and Dan, see Cross, *Canaanite Myth,* 73–75). Note, moreover, that the iconography of Kuntillet 'Ajrud, which Dever has argued is replete with Asherah imagery ("Asherah, Consort of Yahweh?" 26–29), includes the Hathor icon of the cow and the suckling calf.

[110]Although the argument I will make below concerning the nature of the relationship between the imagery of the "woman in the window" plaques and the role of Sisera's mother as queen mother in Judg 5:28 is mine alone, I am hardly the first to point out the general similarity between these artistic and literary depictions. See, for example, Barnett, *Nimrud Ivories,* 147; King, *Amos, Hosea, Micah,* 146–48; O'Connor, "Women in the Book of Judges," 284–85, n. 25 (although note O'Connor's insistence, contrary to most commentators, that the biblical and artistic sources should be considered separately).

[111]Note also in this regard that, although the "woman in the window" *ivories* postdate the Judges 5 text by at least two hundred years, the "woman in the window" *motif* is known in the Syro-Phoenician world almost two hundred years prior to the composition of Judges 5; see, for example, a thirteenth-century B.C.E. bronze stand from Enkomi, Cyprus, reproduced in Barnett, *Nimrud Ivories,* 148 (Fig. 54), and in U. Winter, *Frau und Göttin: Exegetische und ikonographische Studien zum weiblichen Gottesbild im Alten Israel und in dessen Umwelt* (Freiburg: Universitätsverlag; Göttingen: Vandenhoeck & Ruprecht, 1983), Abb. 313.

[112]Again, as in n. 110 above, I should point out that I am hardly the first to point out the similarities between the artistic representation of the "woman in the window" and the biblical portrait of Jezebel in 2 Kgs 9:30. See, for example, Ackroyd, "Goddesses, Women and Jezebel," 258; Beach, "Samaria Ivories, *Marzeaḥ,* and Biblical Text," 101; King, *Amos, Hosea, Micah,* 146; O'Connor, "Women in the Book of Judges," 284–85, n. 25. The argument I will advance below concerning the connection between Asherah, the "woman in the window," and Jezebel as queen mother, however, is mine alone (excepting only the oblique comments of Tina Pippin, "Jezebel Re-Vamped," *A Feminist Companion to Samuel and Kings,* 199, who asserts without documentation that Jezebel's "adorned face peering through the lattice" represents "the face of the goddess Asherah").

[113]"Jezebel's Reception of Jehu," *Maarav* 1 (1978), 67–78.

[114]See the references in Parker, "Jezebel's Reception," 74, n. 1, and add S. M. Olyan, "2 Kings 9:31—Jehu as Zimri," *HTR* 78 (1985), 203–7.

[115]*"Hăšālôm:* Some Literary Considerations of 2 Kings 9," *CBQ* 46 (1984), 666.

[116]Parker, "Jezebel's Reception," 69–70, drawing upon the work of Fauth, *Aphrodite Parakyptusa,* 47–48, 51, 54, 91, considers also the possibility that Jezebel may be meant to represent Asherah here, although Parker rejects this notion because he correctly realizes that the specifics of Fauth's proposal—Jezebel/Asherah as the bride of the king in the *hieros gamos*—do not fit the passage's context, which focuses on the king's *mother,* not his wife, and on *death,* not on sexual union.

[117]But see Barnett, *Ancient Ivories,* 49 and n. 64 on p. 88; also King, *Amos, Hosea, Micah,* 143–44; Winter, "Phoenician and North Syrian Ivory Carving," 16, all of whom argue for an eighth-century B.C.E. date for the Samaria ivories, that is, a date post-Ahab and Jezebel.

[118]Proverbs 5:8; 7:6–9; and 9:14–18 also are often cited as "woman in the window" texts, but the reference is not at all clear: 5:8 and 9:14–18 speak of the "strange" (or "loose") woman who stands enticingly in the *door* of her house; conversely, while 7:6–9 does describe how the speaker looks out the window "of my house," this person seems to be male, having been identified in 4:3 as a "son." A text some cite in the Song of Songs is also problematic. Canticles 2:9 does describe how the young male lover gazes up at the windows of his beloved's house, and since it is she who provides this observation, we can presume she is looking out of one of those same windows down at him. Yet this is not explicitly stated.

[119]Once again, as in nn. 110 and 112 above, the arguments here concerning the constellation of Asherah, woman in the window, and queen mother are mine alone, but the observation comparing the artistic image of the "woman in the window" and the biblical portrait of Michal has frequently been made. See, for example, King, *Amos, Hosea, Micah,* 148; O'Connor, "Women in the Book of Judges," 284–85, n. 25.

[120]The connection between Judg 5:28, which reads *bĕ'ad hahallôn nišqĕpâ,* and 2 Sam 6:16, *nišqĕpâ bĕ'ad hahallôn,* is particularly clear.

Chapter 4

⦿⦿⦿⦿⦿

"You Shall Conceive and Bear a Son"

MANOAH'S WIFE, BARREN WOMEN,
AND THE STORY OF THE VIRGIN BIRTH

Long ago, at the end of Deborah's song,
I heard the silence of Sisera's chariot, which was late in coming,
I looked at Sisera's mother peering out of the window,
A woman with a streak of silver in her hair . . .

For forty years the land was calm. For forty years
Horses did not gallop, dead riders did not stare with glassy eyes.
But she died shortly after her son was killed.

FROM THE POEM "'*IMMÔ*" ("HIS MOTHER"),
BY HAIM GOURI[1]

Who lives in sorrows many as are mine
How shall he not be glad to gain his death?

ANTIGONE SPEAKING TO CREON,
FROM THE PLAY *ANTIGONE,*
BY SOPHOCLES[2]

The Song of Deborah is a poem permeated by images of tumult, chaos, and, ultimately, death. The tumult is that of the trembling earth and of the shaking heavens, both reduced to a mass of quivering jelly by the forceful steps of Yahweh, the divine warrior, marching forth to do battle from Sinai's mountain abode (vv 4–5). The chaos is of Yahweh's torrential rains and the Wadi Kishon's rampaging flood, which sweeps up the Canaanites' chariots as if they were straw and tosses them tumbling into the depths of roiling, raucous waves (vv 20–21). The deaths are those, first, of the Canaanite army and its coalition of kingly leaders at Ta'a-nach, by the waters of Megiddo (v 19), and, then, of Sisera, the king who marched at the head of this mighty host, his skull pummeled into a pulpy mire by Jael's tent-peg and hammer when he sought sanctuary inside her canopied abode (vv 24–27).

From the poem's point of view, this violent upheaval of nature and the massacre of the Canaanites seems a cause for celebration: "Thus may all your enemies perish, O Yahweh!" the last verse of Judges 5 exults (v 31). For us, however, the poem's modern audience, the mayhem can be disquieting. We are disconcerted by the notion that "a good woman can murder," disturbed by the idea that a religious asylum can become a house of slaughter, and agonized by the juxtaposition that describes one woman triumphant over her murder victim while depicting another as a victim herself, a prisoner of a window from which she sees and hears nothing and so can only anticipate the worst. In fact, so discomfited by this final image is the Israeli poet Haim Gouri that he concludes "'*Immô*" ("His Mother"), his 1960 meditation on the Song of Deborah, by imag-ining how devastating the climactic scene of Judges 5 must have been for Sisera's mother. As Gouri envisions it, this woman, shortly after the death of Sisera, also dies, the despair generated by her experience of loss so overwhelming that existence becomes for her, as it did for the Greek maid Antigone, an ordeal that she can no longer endure. It is al-most as if the regal streak of silver that Gouri sees shot through the mother's hair in his poem's first stanza, as she still holds out hope that Sisera will return, is transformed by his text's end into a tattered shroud of wispy grey strands, so few in number that they barely cover the scalp of a woman utterly beaten down by the vicissitudes of life. This trans-mutation renders the mother more corpse-like than not, so much so that nothing remains but for her to complete her metamorphosis and to turn dejected, literally dispirited, into the cold but beckoning arms of death.

Yet, despite the focus on death that is the climax of his poem, Gouri does not choose for his title "Her Demise," or "Her End," or some designation of the sort. Rather, he calls his composition "'*Immô*," "His Mother," and in so doing, Gouri draws our attention to a second set of images that is just as deeply rooted in his Judges 5 source as is the imagery of chaos and destruction. This is the imagery of maternity. Indeed, a closer look at the motif of maternity in Judges 5 suggests that the Song of Deborah itself, despite its closing gloat, is not wholly comfortable with its seemingly unrelenting concatenation of violent language. The poetic tradition, that is, appears to realize that an unmitigated stress on the taking of life might be unbearable to even its ancient Israelite audience and that there thus must be some hope proffered that new life will be given in return. Mothers are the obvious instruments with which to effect such rebirth, and so Judges 5 uses motherhood as a motif that holds its otherwise cataclysmic imagery in check. Motherhood, in this sense, becomes the theme that keeps the poem sane, stitching a thread of faith in the future through the Judges 5 fabric of bloodthirstiness and gore. The seam motherhood sews, moreover, passes through each of the poem's three main woman characters, who, although Israelite as opposed to Canaanite, tent dweller as opposed to palace habitant, and peasant as opposed to noble, are bound together by maternity into a unity.[3] Their unitedness in turn gives us a sense of coherence, that the fragmentation of a world seemingly consumed by chaos can once again be made whole.

Motherhood is first explicitly evoked by the poem in verse 7, where, although by all indications it is inaccurate as a biological reference, the tradition chooses the epithet "mother" to bestow upon Deborah its greatest praise. I have already discussed in Chapter 1 the multiple aspects of the maternal role Judges 5 seeks to evoke with this one word, a mother's attributes of wisdom or, as I termed it previously, her skills in persuasive counseling; a mother's fidelity and loyalty to the covenant of Yahweh; and, above all, a mother's fierce sense of protectiveness and her utter devotion to the well-being of her offspring, understood here as the "children of Israel" or even more generally as the "heritage of Yahweh." The poem presents still more attributes manifest in the maternal ideal in its description of Jael in verses 24–27, in particular, in depicting Jael's offering of milk and ghee to Sisera, lauding qualities such as a mother's instinctive wish to provide nurture and compassion to those in need of sustenance and support (and recall here the Jewish midrash that imagines that the milk Jael offers to Sisera was suckled by him from her breast). Yet, while a consummate giver of kindness, Jael in her role as mother is also, just as is Mother Deborah, unyielding in her devotion to the heritage of Yahweh, so absolute in this commitment, in fact, that she is willing to perform cold-blooded murder on behalf of the children of Israel.

Still, this one mother's triumph on behalf of Yahweh's progeny is another mother's tragedy regarding hers, and the last mother of Judges 5 is the mother bereaved, this woman's fierce sense of maternal protectiveness forced to confront the unthinkable reality that the child of her womb has died and that Sisera will come home to her no more. Here, it might seem, as it seemed at the end of Gouri's poem, that the imagery of death and destruction has final triumph over the motherhood motif. But, in fact, as was Gouri's, the biblical text's point is somewhat more subtle, for even in a moment of death, Judges 5 still aims to describe the maternal ideal, or, better, the paradox this ideal can coerce. Although she knows that if she is to mother well, she should assay everything in her power to protect her child, Sisera's mother also realizes that she must eventually allow Sisera to face the world on his own if he is to become fully an adult. Facilitating this process of maturation, in fact, is the ultimate goal of the maternal enterprise. Thus, as deeply as she must despair for not keeping her son safe within her home, Sisera's mother teaches us through her grief the poem's final lesson about the mother's role: that the ideal mother must be prepared to let go, even if this means coming to terms with the practically unendurable pain that will ensue if her offspring's ventures into the wider world fail.

Further meditations on the nature of motherhood—on its nature both idealized and real—are found elsewhere in the book of Judges. Motherhood thus might be described not only as a unifying motif that binds Judges 5 together but also as a theme that binds Judges 5 to Judges 1–4 and 6–21. The theme of motherhood, moreover, can help bind individual chapters within Judges 1–4 and 6–21 to one another. Michael O'Connor has pointed out, for example, that, although seemingly unrelated, the stories of Abimelech in Judges 9 and Jephthah in Judges 11 are joined by the theme of motherhood. In both stories, O'Connor explains, the tragic flaw that brings down the male protagonists stems to some degree from the irregular status of their mothers: Abimelech's mother is a secondary wife (8:31) and Jephthah's mother is a prostitute (11:1).[4] These two stories also can be contrasted profitably to a third and seemingly unrelated tale, the story of Micah in Judg 17:1–6. There, it is the "regularized" status of Micah's mother that is crucial, for it allows this woman to redeem her son from his own imperfections of character. She does this by dedicating two hundred pieces of silver to God and so mitigating Micah's thieving nature that otherwise had put him in danger of standing cursed before Yahweh.

It is in Judges 13, though, that the theme of motherhood that runs through Judges is at its most pronounced, and it is also in this chapter that the book's motif of mothering achieves its greatest poignancy. This is because the story's main character, Manoah's wife, is introduced in verse 2 as a woman who cannot even try to fulfill Israel's maternal ideal because she is barren and can have no child. In the narrative that follows, however, the tragedy of this "mother's" unrealized potential turns into an experience of joy, as a messenger of Yahweh appears and promises the woman that her barrenness will be ended and that she will bear a son. She is further told that this miracle child will be one extraordinary in character, a Nazirite consecrated to God from the day of his birth and one who will deliver Israel from the oppressions of the Philistines (vv 3–5). There is next the lengthy interlude I have described in Chapter 2, which depicts Manoah's dubious reaction to his wife's news and his failure to recognize the otherworldly origin of the messenger or his oracle (vv 6–23). Finally, though, Manoah does understand that he and his wife have been privy to a divine epiphany, and God's promise is fulfilled in verse 24, where "the woman bore a son and named him Samson."

The story of a barren woman whose tragic fate is reversed by the miraculous acts of a merciful God is found five other times in the Hebrew Bible: in the stories of Sarah, Abraham's wife and Isaac's mother; Rebekah, Isaac's wife and Jacob's and Esau's mother; Rachel, Jacob's wife and Joseph's and Benjamin's mother; Hannah, Elqanah's wife and Samuel's mother; and the Shunammite woman.[5] In Section I of this chapter, I wish to compare Judges 13 to these five tales. As we will see, all five share the same basic pattern of the story of Manoah's wife. More important, we will see that quite frequently, the climactic moment of each story, the promised son's miraculous birth, is closely followed by a story describing that son's near death. Yet in two examples—the stories of Manoah's wife and Hannah—this near-death episode is missing, and what is found instead is the consecration of the son to divine service under the terms of the Nazirite vow. My intent is to suggest that, although seemingly different, these motifs of near death and of Nazirite consecration both stem from a common ideological underpinning. This underpinning, I will argue in Sections II and III, illuminates other ancient Near Eastern stories of barren women, including some New Testament materials. The most obviously parallel New Testament text is Luke's story of the birth of John the Baptist, who is born to the barren Elizabeth. I will describe, however, my belief that Luke's and Matthew's stories of Mary, the mother of Jesus, also fit within the overall context of the Bible's barren women stories. Even though she is technically "virgin" and not "barren," for example, Mary is still like a barren woman in being an "empty vessel"[6] who has not yet borne a son. Also like a barren woman, Mary, as a virgin, cannot give birth except through the miraculous intervention of God.

I. MANOAH'S WIFE AND BARREN WOMEN

In a 1983 article analyzing the six barren women narratives found in the Hebrew Bible,[7] Robert Alter borrowed the term "type-scene" from Homeric scholarship and used it to demonstrate that, in the same way that Homer's *Iliad* and *Odyssey* use standard formats and outlines to describe set "types" of scenes (scenes that describe a wedding, or the arrival of a messenger, or preparations for a battle, for example), the Bible's barren women stories all share a basic tripartite structure.[8] Each begins with an indication of the woman's barrenness;[9] followed by a promise that the woman's barrenness shall be ended, given by divine messenger, by oracle, or by a man of God;[10] and concluding with the conception and birth of the promised son.[11]

Alter further noted that this basic tripartite structure can be elaborated upon in various ways in different versions of the barren woman type-scene. For example, the initial notice of the woman's barrenness can be expanded through the inclusion of her husband's name and his ethnic identification. Thus in the Judges story of Manoah's wife, we read in 13:2, "And there was a certain man of Zorah of the tribe of Dan whose name was Manoah, and his wife was barren and had no children." Also in this initial section, a description of some aspect of the wife's background can be added, most commonly information concerning her relationship to her husband and to her husband's other wives. In lengthier versions of the barren woman story, this information can provide the basis for a subplot that depicts a conflict between the barren wife and her fertile rival. This can be seen in Gen 30:1–21, the story of Rachel and her fertile sister, Leah; in 1 Sam 1:6, the story of Hannah and her husband's fertile wife, Peninnah; and—in its most elaborate rendition—in the Genesis story of Sarah. Sarah's rival is her maid, Hagar, whom the barren Sarah had given to Abraham in the hope that she might have a child through her. In one version of the Sarah story, Hagar taunts her mistress when the maid becomes pregnant while Sarah cannot (Gen 16:4–6). In another, Hagar provokes Sarah by presuming herself to be Sarah's equal and allowing Ishmael, her son by Abraham, to play with Isaac, the child Sarah eventually bears (Gen 21:8–10).[12]

The second element of the type-scene is the divine annunciation, and, according to Alter, this likewise can be elaborated upon, often by describing doubts the husband or wife or both have about the truth of the divine message.[13] In Judg 13:6–23, we have seen how Manoah manifests such doubt by refusing to accept the news his wife brings to him about the promise she has received from Yahweh's angel. Abraham and Sarah also express doubts concerning God's promise of a child. In one version of the Abraham-Sarah story, in Genesis 17, Abraham laughs at the ludicrousness of the idea that he and Sarah will bear a child at the ages of one hundred and ninety, respectively. In an alternate version, in Genesis 18, it is Sarah who laughs at the absurdity since the text tells us that it had "ceased to be with her after the manner of women" (Gen 18:11).[14]

Elaborations of the third major section of the story, the conception and birth, may include some mention of the extraordinary nature of the child in question, his role, for example, as an ancestor to the covenant community Israel; or as a redeemer; or as a man vowed as a Nazirite to God. The story of Manoah's wife thus ends by describing how, as Samson grows up, Yahweh blesses the boy and how Yahweh's spirit began to incite the young Samson to act (Judg 13:24–25). In the Abraham-Sarah tale, a variant type of elaboration is found whereby the act of naming the infant Isaac is particularly stressed. This is because the Hebrew word for Isaac, *yiṣḥāq,* is derived from the verb *ṣāḥaq,* "to laugh," recalling the reaction that both Abraham and Sarah had when confronted with the seemingly ludicrous idea that Sarah might bear a son.

In the story of the Shunammite's son, however, the elaboration of the childbirth section has what Alter terms a "salient peculiarity" when compared to the sorts of elaborations otherwise seen in the third part of the barren woman type-scene.[15] This peculiar development is found in 2 Kgs 4:18–37. The previous narrative, in 2 Kgs 4:8–17, has followed Alter's pattern perfectly by first introducing us to the Shunammite woman (that is, a woman who lives in the vicinity of Shunem) and by describing at least one aspect of her background, the way in which she serves as a patron for the prophet Elisha, feeding him and even persuading her husband to build for him a small apartment atop their house in which the prophet could lodge whenever he was in their vicinity. Elisha is clearly touched by these many kindnesses and wishes to repay the woman, and as he casts about for an appropriate gift, he learns from his servant that "she has no son and her husband is old" (2 Kgs 4:14). Elisha, the man of God, then pronounces the divine promise typically found in the second part of the barren woman type-scene: "In this season, at the appointed time, you shall embrace a son" (2 Kgs 4:16). The woman responds with the same doubt that characters like Abraham, Sarah, and Manoah elsewhere express, but as Alter's analysis leads us to expect, the doubt is unjustified since "the woman conceived, and she bore a son in that season, at the appointed time, as Elisha had said to her" (2 Kgs 4:17).

In verses 18–37, as the story continues, the Shunammite's son, who is now some years older, is working in the fields when an injury befalls him and he is rendered unconscious. He is brought back to the house of the Shunammite woman, where he lies in a coma in his mother's lap until he dies. But he is not buried. Instead, the Shunammite woman goes forth from her home in search of Elisha, the man of God who had originally promised her that she would give birth to the child. She finds him at Mount Carmel and eventually persuades the prophet to return with her to Shunem. Once there, he closets himself in his small apartment with the body of the dead boy. He prays to God and conducts what appears to be a ritual of sympathetic magic, in which he lies on top of the boy, mouth to mouth, eyes to eyes, and hands to hands, until the boy lives again. The narrative then ends, and the Shunammite's son appears no more in the biblical text. As Alter notes, this is in striking contrast to his counterparts from the other barren women tales—Sarah's son, Isaac; Rebekah's favored son, Jacob; Rachel's firstborn son, Joseph; the son of Manoah's wife, Samson; and Hannah's son, Samuel—all of whom go on to lead heroic lives after being born to barren women. This prompts Alter to comment, "the type-scene does not signal the birth of a hero at all but rather of an anonymous peasant boy whose sole functions in the narrative are to be born and then to be brought back from the brink of death."[16] Alter characterizes the part of the narrative describing how the Shunammite's son is brought back to life as a second type-scene, the scene of the life-threatening trial in the wilderness, which he compares to the trials undergone by Hagar's son Ishmael, after Sarah orders mother and child thrown out of her house (Gen 21:8–21), and by Moses' son Gershom, during Yahweh's murderous attack at the "lodging place" on the way between Midian and Egypt (Exod 4:24–

26).[17] Alter then argues that the purpose of these two juxtaposed type-scenes of annunciation and trial is to provide a commentary on Elisha's miraculous abilities to give and to restore life.

I have no doubt that Alter is correct in concluding that the crucial point of both parts of the Shunammite story is to focus attention on Elisha and especially to engender wonder as we contemplate Elisha's gifts as a servant of God.[18] In this respect, the Shunammite annunciation *does* differ from the other barren women stories, for in them the focus is the child of the annunciation and not the divine agency of the annunciator. Still, I am not convinced that this different focus makes the Shunammite story as distinctive as Alter might suggest. If one considers the larger context of all the annunciation stories, it becomes clear that the same pattern found in the Shunammite tale frequently occurs: the child of promise, very shortly after the narrative describing his birth, is faced with the threat of death in much the same way that the Shunammite's son is threatened. I think particularly of Sarah's son, Isaac; of Rebekah's favored son, Jacob; and of Rachel's firstborn son, Joseph.

The case of Isaac is particularly instructive. Isaac's birth and his earliest childhood (through weaning) are described in Gen 21:1–8. Following this episode, there are two narratives that concern Isaac's half-brother Ishmael and his father Abraham, but the next scene that involves Isaac himself is Gen 22:1–19. This is the well-known story of the *akedah*, in which God puts Abraham to the test by ordering him to take his son to a mountain in the land of Moriah and to sacrifice him there. In this episode, Isaac is pictured as significantly older than he was in Gen 21:1–8. He is at least old enough to know the normal practices of sacrificial ritual and so questions why he and his father do not carry with them the animal required for the burnt offering. Isaac also is pictured as being mature enough physically to carry the load of wood required for the holocaust to the top of the mountain. With respect to age, then, Isaac is described in Genesis 21–22 in a way that parallels almost exactly the way in which 2 Kings 4 describes the Shunammite's son. That boy, at the end of the scene of annunciation in 2 Kgs 4:17, is said to be an infant, yet in 2 Kgs 4:18, as the scene of his death and resuscitation begins, he is old enough to work in the fields. Isaac's life story likewise begins by describing the infant days of the child of promise and then turns immediately to describe a near-death experience this child faces as a much older boy or as a teen.[19]

It is somewhat more difficult to discern this pattern in the stories of

Jacob and Joseph, but I believe that it is there. Following the description of his birth "holding onto the heel of Esau" in Gen 25:26, Jacob is faced with near death in Gen 27:41, when Esau seeks to kill him because Jacob has deceived their father Isaac into giving Jacob the blessing of the firstborn. In this near-death scene, Jacob is pictured as a fully mature character. But since he has not yet married, I presume that the narrator intends for us to envision him as a younger rather than older man. Like the narratives of Isaac and the Shunammite's son, therefore, the story concerning Jacob as the child of promise describes first his infancy and then quickly turns to consider a death threat that he faces in the first decades of his life. Unlike the Isaac and Shunammite stories, however, there is a narrative concerning Jacob that intervenes between birth and threat. But because this narrative, Gen 25:29–34, which describes Jacob's purchase of Esau's birthright for a bowl of lentils, is a thematic doublet of the story of Jacob's deception of Isaac, I propose to read 25:29–34 as still within the context of threat. This suggests that, as in the Isaac and Shunammite stories, there is, after all, an immediate movement in Jacob's life story from the experience of birth to the threat of near death during the course of his teenage or young adult years.

Joseph, the elder son of the previously barren Rachel, also faces a threat of near death as a young man. According to Gen 37:12–28, his jealous older brothers plot to kill him, and his demise is only averted when traders carry him into Egypt, either after hauling his body up out of the pit where his brothers had left him (Gen 37:28) or after buying him from his brothers when they opt for profit rather than revenge (Gen 37:26–27).[20] Like the previous actors I have considered, Joseph is understood by the narrator to be an adolescent or young man when this incident occurs, as Gen 37:2 observes that Joseph was seventeen years of age "when he tended the flocks of his brothers." It is also important to note that, although the announcement of Joseph's birth in Gen 30:23–24 and the threat to his life in Gen 37:12–28 are narratives widely separated in the biblical text, there is no story concerning Joseph that intervenes between the account of his birth and the tale of threat. That is, like the life story of the Shunammite's son, of Isaac, and of Jacob, the life story of Joseph proceeds directly from a description of his birth as the child of promise to the specter of his near death some decade and a half or two decades later.

Upon closer reflection, then, the "salient peculiarity" that Alter saw in the Shunammite woman's story does not seem so peculiar at all. Rather, the motif by which a child of promise is threatened with death before reaching full adulthood appears more common than not in the Bible's barren women stories. Yet what of the barren woman story that is the focal point of this chapter, the story of Manoah's wife in Judges 13? In it, although Samson, the miracle son, does meet with menacing situations in his life, he is unlike his counterparts in Genesis and in 2 Kings in that he is not faced with such challenges while still a boy or adolescent. Instead, his confrontations come only after he is fully an adult, first, around the time of his wedding to his Timnite wife (Judg 14:1–20), and, later, after his marriage has broken up (15:1–20) and he has taken the Gazite prostitute and then Delilah as his mistresses (Judg 16:1–31).

A second difference between the Samson story and the four other stories' recountings of the miracle child's near death concerns the role God plays in these narratives. In the Samson story, when Samson as an adult does encounter threats of near death, he again and again delivers himself with the aid of Yahweh. For example, when brought before the Philistines bound with ropes in Judg 15:14, Samson is seized by the spirit of Yahweh so that "his bonds melted off his hands." Somewhat later, after being betrayed by Delilah, Samson is shorn of the hair that was his power and is blinded and imprisoned by the Philistines. When they bring him to the temple of Dagan to celebrate their triumph, he stands between the two pillars of the vestibule. Calling out, "O Lord Yahweh, remember me and strengthen me only this once, O God, so that with this one act of revenge I may pay back the Philistines for my two eyes," Samson topples the pillars of the temple. With God's help, Samson thus brings death to the thousands of Philistines who lie crushed beneath the collapsed building (Judg 16:28–30). Contrast, especially, the story of Isaac, where it is Yahweh who *provokes* the near death of the hero by requiring that the child of promise be sacrificed.

Finally among this list of differences, note that the story of Samson *adds* an element that the near-death stories of Isaac, Jacob, Joseph, and the Shunammite do not have, the dedication of the extraordinary child as a Nazirite. Only the story of Samuel, the son of Hannah, also includes this Nazirite vow. The Samuel tale, moreover, like only the story of Samson, does *not* describe a boyhood threat of near death faced by the miracle child.

I contend that these distinctive elements shared by the Manoah's wife and Hannah stories—the lack of a boyhood death threat that must be faced by Samson and Samuel and the dedication of the two babies as

Nazirites—are related. I further believe that together, these elements make the same point as does the description of near death found in the four other barren women stories. That is to say: while the *narrative* details in the near-death versions of the barren women stories do differ from those found in the stories of Manoah's wife and Hannah, the underlying *ideological* motif is the same. That ideological motif is the Israelite understanding that a child given to a barren woman is a gift of Yahweh. Yahweh might even be understood to be the child's metaphorical father. But because Yahweh is the "father" who has given life to the child in the first place, Yahweh has a right to ask for the life of the offspring in return. Yahweh thus can demand that the child be offered up as a sacrifice, as the deity asks of Isaac; Yahweh can allow contention between the child of promise and a brother or brothers, as the deity does in the cases of Jacob and Joseph; Yahweh can threaten the child with a natural but premature death, as the deity inflicts upon the Shunammite's son. Or, Yahweh can command that the child be dedicated to God as a Nazirite, as the deity requires of Samson and Samuel. The specifics of the narratives *will* vary, but the motif that holds together all the barren women stories is still the same. If Yahweh fills the womb, then Yahweh has a particular claim on all that comes forth from it.[21]

To be sure, in all the Bible's barren women stories, even though it is Yahweh's right to claim the life of the miracle child, Yahweh never once requires that the child actually die. Instead, the tradition somehow allows for the redemption of the threatened boy. The child, for example, can be redeemed by substituting an animal sacrifice, which is exactly what happens in Genesis 22, where Isaac, the child of the barren Sarah, faces what I would now suggest is an expected ordeal of near death but is redeemed at the last minute when a ram is offered to God. So, too, are Jacob, Joseph, and the Shunammite woman's son delivered from death by a God who ultimately chooses not to exercise the option of taking the progeny previously granted. Samson and Samuel are also redeemed, by their mothers' dedication of them to divine service before their births. In fact, in these two stories, the boys' commissions as Nazirites so inexorably require of them lifetimes devoted to the deity's cult that Yahweh's need even to threaten them with death is forestalled. Instead, and in contradistinction to the near-death stories, Yahweh can be presented throughout their narratives as these two heroes' ally.

The Bible's stories of its barren women are thus narratives in two acts. The first act climaxes with the birth of the promised child, and the second describes some way in which Yahweh exercises God's rightful claim upon the life of that child. Yahweh's ways of exercising this claim can vary in the different stories. But, although the narrative details diverge, I would again insist that all the barren women stories reflect one theme. The God who fills a woman's womb has the right to demand, in some fashion, the life that comes forth from it.

II. THE EPIC OF AQHAT

While Alter does not discuss these variations between the stories' near-death threat and the Nazirite vow in his analysis of the Bible's barren woman type-scene, he does describe some other ways in which the six renditions of the barren woman tale vary in their use of the type-scene's basic motifs.[22] Concerning the story of Manoah's wife, for example, Alter argues that this tale's particular stress on the husband's "repeated failures of perception" as compared to the theological acumen displayed by his wife is meant to foreshadow the career of the couple's son, Samson, a man who will constantly be outwitted by women—in particular, by Delilah—and whose "formidable brawn will not be matched by brain, or even by a saving modicum of common sense."[23] Similarly, in the story of Abraham and Sarah, Alter suggests that between the annunciation (Genesis 18) and Isaac's birth (Genesis 21), the Bible's authors interpose two narratives—the story of the destruction of Sodom and Gomorrah (Genesis 19) and the story of the barrenness that inflicts all the women of Gerar (Genesis 20)—in order to demonstrate what a fragile thing life is in the world of Genesis. This point in turn underscores the truly miraculous nature of Isaac's birth. Alter also notes that in the Abraham-Sarah story, the annunciation from God is delivered, atypically, to the husband rather than to the wife. He argues that the point of this variation is to emphasize the importance of *patriarchal* descent since it was Abraham's bloodline from which the entire nation of Israel eventually would stem.[24]

This last observation regarding patriarchal descent is particularly helpful in illuminating a story from elsewhere in the ancient Near East that I believe should be compared to the Bible's barren woman type-scenes. This is the story of Danil and Danataya with which the Ugaritic Epic of Aqhat begins. The parallel between the Bible's barren women tales and this Danil-Danataya story, however, is not immediately obvious since it is indicated explicitly in the Aqhat Epic that, although like their biblical counterparts, Danil and Danataya are childless,[25] the cause of the couple's infertility is not, as in the Bible, attributed to the woman, Danataya. Rather, barrenness is ascribed to the husband, Danil.[26] Yet I would still argue that the paradigm of the barren "woman" type-scene stands in the background here. The crucial piece of evidence is the story's royal context: Danil is a king who lacks an heir.[27] Thus at issue are the same motifs of patriarchal descent and male bloodline that Alter identified as being present in the Abraham-Sarah barren woman story.

Still, in the Abraham-Sarah story, this patriarchal emphasis means only that Abraham, atypically, receives the divine annunciation; it does not mean that Abraham himself is identified as barren. This is because the barrenness of his "correct" or "legitimate" wife Sarah is enough to threaten the future of his line.[28] But in a royal context such as the Aqhat Epic's, a wife's barrenness is usually *not* enough to threaten the continuation of the line since an ancient Near Eastern king typically had many wives and could father an heir simply by mating with some other fertile woman in his harem. This is clearly indicated in the Bible's story of the barren Queen Michal, who, despite her lifelong infertility (2 Sam 6:23),[29] does not endanger the royal line of her husband David since David is able to father many other children by Abigail, Ahinoam, Ma'acah, Haggith, Abital, Eglah, Bathsheba, and other wives unnamed in the biblical text.[30] Had David been infertile, though, patriarchal descent and the male bloodline would have been in peril. This is precisely the problem that confronts Danil and Danataya. I thus propose that what we have in the Epic of Aqhat is a permutation of the barren "woman" type-scene whereby the king is rendered as the couple's barren member in order to highlight the dangers that male infertility can bring to a royal house. In fact, as the David-Michal example demonstrates, it is *only* by rendering the king as infertile that the story's narrative tension can have its desired effect. While highly atypical, then, the Epic of Aqhat represents a Ugaritic version of the Bible's barren "woman" tale in which the focus on royal descent necessarily requires that the man be depicted as the infertile member of the couple.

Notably, though, except for this rather dramatic change in the barren one's gender, the structure of the Epic of Aqhat conforms perfectly to the tripartite outline of the barren woman type-scene. Thus the story begins by introducing the plight of childlessness that inflicts Danil and also describes the measures he undertakes in order to overcome his fate.

These measures include Danil's going for seven days, presumably to a temple, to make offerings to the gods and then to lie down to sleep.[31] The point of these actions is not explicitly stated, but commentators have generally and correctly assumed that the purpose of Danil's sacrifices and of his reposing in a sacred space is to induce some deity to appear to him in a dream. Danil then can petition that deity for the gift of a child. In many respects, one is reminded here of 1 Samuel 1, the story of Hannah's barrenness. Like Danil, she, too, goes to a temple, the sanctuary at Shiloh, to bemoan her childless state and to ask Yahweh for the gift of a child. The story of the barren Rebekah, found in Gen 25:19–26, is also of note, for although a specific temple setting is not mentioned, the text does describe how Isaac prays to Yahweh that Rebekah's barrenness might be reversed.

In the story of Danil, moreover, as in the stories of Hannah and Rebekah, the divine response to the childless one's petition is the element that is typical of the second part of the barren woman type-scene, the annunciation promising that a child shall be born. In Danil's case, his dreamtime prayer is first heard by the god Baal, who then brings Danil's distress to the attention of El and the rest of Ugarit's divine assembly. El responds by blessing Danil and promising that his "spirit" and "vigor" shall revive (*KTU* 1.17.1.36–38). Next, a band of goddesses called the Kotharot appear at Danil's palace. As their name—from the root *ktr,* meaning "skillful" or "crafty"—implies, these female deities are goddesses skillful and crafty in the ways of conception and childbirth. The text also describes them as wise "in the pleasures of the bed" and "in the delights of the bed" (*KTU* 1.17.2.41–42). Given such expertise, it should come as no surprise to learn that after the Kotharot have been in Danil's house for only seven days, Danil begins to "count the months" (*KTU* 1.17.2.43), the nine months, that is, before the now-pregnant Danataya will bear a child.

Unfortunately, following this scene, there is quite a lengthy break in the tablets on which the Aqhat Epic is inscribed, meaning that the third and final element expected in the barren woman type-scene—the announcement of the birth of the promised son—is missing. Still, we can be sure that the expected birth took place, as can be inferred from the next complete scene preserved in the epic. In it, the craftsman god Kothar-wa-Hasis brings to Danil the mighty bow and arrows that eventually wind up in the hands of Aqhat, who is elsewhere in the epic identified as Danil's son.[32] Undoubtedly, then, Aqhat is the child given in response to Danil's entreaties for an heir. Indeed, it is not too far-fetched to suggest that the bow and arrows fashioned by Kothar are brought to Danil as a present for Aqhat at the time of the child's birth. It only makes sense, after all, that Kothar would extend divine favor to a child whose conception was effected through the actions of his female counterparts, the Kotharot.

The analysis I proposed in Section I next suggests that, as in the Bible's six versions of the barren woman type-scene, the story of Danil and Danataya's son Aqhat should proceed directly from the description of the child's miraculous birth to an account of how the divine realm exerts some claim upon the life of the child. Most commonly, as we have seen, this claim is exercised by a threat of near death, and, in fact, in the scene that immediately follows Kothar's presentation of his birthing gift, the promised child Aqhat does face a deity's murderous challenge. I have previously described this incident, how the goddess Anat, jealous of Aqhat's magnificent bow and arrows, attempts to persuade the youth to give her the weapons. When her initial overtures fail, she and her henchman Yatpan mount an attack against the hero.

Yet there are two problems in interpreting Anat's attack as conforming to the paradigm that I put forward in Section I in regard to the Bible's barren woman type-scenes. First, I earlier argued that according to the biblical materials, Yahweh had a right to lay claim to the life of the child of promise because Yahweh was the one who had granted the child life in the first place. In the Epic of Aqhat, though, Anat has not seemed to be involved in the begetting of Aqhat. It should thus not be she who can threaten the life of the hero. I have also earlier proposed that in the Bible, although Yahweh had the right to lay claim to the life of the miracle child, Yahweh in fact relinquished that claim, by substituting a sacrificial animal for the life of the child, for example, or by demanding of the child the Nazirite vow. In the Epic of Aqhat, however, Anat never retreats. She and Yatpan not only plot to attack Aqhat, they kill him.

While these very significant deviations from the biblical paradigm might suggest that the assumptions with which I introduced this section were wrong and that the pattern of the Bible's barren woman type-scene does not hold in the Aqhat Epic, I believe that a careful analysis of the Ugaritic text does indicate that the model I have identified is present. Consider first the problem of the divine agent who seeks the hero's life, the god who, according to the pattern of the Israelite materials, should be the same as the deity who originally facilitated the child's begetting. Yet who, precisely, is this child-granting deity in the Aqhat Epic? Multiple deities seem to be involved. It is Baal who first hears Danil's dreamtime plea for a child and in response carries Danil's request to the divine patriarch El. El agrees to act upon Danil's request by decreeing that Danil's "spirit" and "vigor" will revive. Then, at some point soon after, the Kotharot step to the fore, coming to Danil's palace and enabling Danataya to conceive and eventually to bear Aqhat.

That the Aqhat Epic insists on the participation of these multiple divine agents in bringing about Aqhat's conception paints a fascinating picture of the nature of polytheistic religions and the way in which these traditions assign to every deity of the pantheon a certain area of expertise. We have already seen, for example, that the Kotharot are depicted as attending Danil and Danataya while they try to conceive because these goddesses have particular talents in matters of lovemaking. Logic also dictates that El be involved when Danil and Danataya's childlessness is to be reversed, given that El is the progenitor god *par excellence* in the Canaanite pantheon. Throughout Ugaritic mythology, for example, the deities of the pantheon are identified as "the children of El" and "the generation of El." He, correspondingly, is called by them "father," as in the epithets "father of years"[33] and "father of the gods." He is also called "patriarch"[34] and "creator." In addition, Ugaritic tradition describes El as the "father of humanity." I have discussed one example of this in Chapter 3, describing how El, according to epic, promises and provides progeny to the human king Kirta when Kirta finds himself without an heir.[35]

What, though, of Baal, the deity first identified as coming to the aid of Danil? Here, we seem to find a god who acts on Danil's behalf voluntarily, out of genuine compassion and concern and not because religious logic dictates that he must be present in the narrative if a solution to the problem of barrenness is to be found. In fact, the narrative is quite emphatic that, although Baal bemoans Danil's lack of a child, he is basically powerless when it comes to reversing the king's infertility. That prerogative, the epic insists, belongs to El and to the Kotharot. Still, while impotent to respond to Danil's request on his own, Baal is hardly uninvolved in effecting Danataya's pregnancy: it is Baal who first hears Danil's plea and is compelled by it; it is Baal who carries Danil's request to El; it is Baal who acts as Danil's advocate in El's assembly, arguing that since Danil has observed the gods' cults and has offered food and libations, he seems not to deserve his childless state. It is Baal, in short, who really presents himself as Danil's benefactor, prodding El and, eventually, the Kotharot to action. Although he cannot himself give children, Baal is the god ultimately responsible for the end of Danil's childlessness.

The logic of my proposed paradigm thus suggests that if any deity has the right to ask for the life of Danil's son, it is Baal. Yet this seemingly brings me no closer to addressing the problem I raised above, for it is Anat, not Baal, who threatens Aqhat and eventually takes his life. We must remember, however, how Anat is conceived of in Ugaritic mythology, especially in the stories of the Baal-Anat cycle. This mythological complex is unequivocal in describing Anat as Baal's counterpart and even as his alter ego. I believe this conception also holds in the Epic of Aqhat. Thus, when Anat threatens the child that Baal has caused to be given, it is as if the same deity has both granted a child and then laid claim to his life. Indeed, if we do not see Anat here as exercising on behalf of Baal his right to the child, the role of the goddess in the narrative becomes somewhat incomprehensible. Typically in Ugaritic myth, Anat is pictured as working in conjunction with Baal and in sympathy with his aims. How can it be that in the Aqhat Epic she works against him? In my interpretation, she does not. Her murder of the child Baal has given is perfectly consistent with the logic of the second act found in the barren woman type-scene.

Yet in the barren woman type-scene as found in the Hebrew Bible, the child of promise, while claimed or challenged in some way by the deity, is never ultimately rendered dead. In Aqhat, though, the prince is killed. Many commentators have been bothered by this outcome, arguing that such an ending is unsatisfactory and leaves the epic unresolved. They thus posit that there is another part of the tale, now lost, that clarifies this matter. Michael D. Coogan, for example, suggests that "the Aqhat cycle presumably continued with his restoration to life."[36] As we have seen, such a return to life *is* possible within the genre of the barren woman type-scene: witness the story of the Shunammite's son. But, although possible, there is no compelling evidence that argues for this resolution, either in the Epic of Aqhat itself or in the one other text from Ugarit that mentions Danil.[37] All available data instead indicate that the narrative ends with Aqhat dead, presumably for good.

The most complete and compelling analysis of Aqhat's death scene has been offered by Ronald S. Hendel.[38] Hendel's study focuses on the character of Pughat, Aqhat's sister, who seeks revenge against her brother's killers and, although the text is broken, apparently succeeds in killing Yatpan, Anat's henchman. In much the same way that I argued in Chapter 1 that the Bible's female military heroes are modeled after Ugarit's warrior goddess Anat, Hendel argues that Pughat in her role as Yatpan's murderer is cast as an Anat figure. First, he notes, Pughat is a sister who initially mourns and then seeks to avenge the murder of her brother Aqhat. So, too, in the Baal-Anat cycle does Anat initially mourn after her brother Baal is rendered dead by Mot and then exacts revenge by confronting Mot and dismembering him. Hendel next points out that Pughat's plan in attacking Yatpan involves dressing outwardly as a woman while concealing a man's weapons under her clothes, which should be compared to the Nineteenth Dynasty Egyptian text cited in Chapter 1 that describes Anat as "a woman acting (as) a warrior, clad as a male and girt as a female."[39] Finally, Pughat's female garb, donned after she bathes and applies rouge, seems designed to seduce Yatpan and lull him into incautious behavior, which Hendel compares to the sexual overtones Delbert Hillers has found in Anat's speech propositioning Aqhat for his bow.[40] Hendel concludes, "Both figures [Anat and Pughat] exact vengeance on their adversary; sexual undercurrents may be at play in both encounters; and in both the woman acts as a warrior."[41]

Hendel goes on to comment on the setting of Pughat's encounter with Yatpan. Yatpan is pictured in his pavilion, and Pughat, having come to this tent, acts as a maidservant, pouring him wine. As already noted, however, Pughat's maiden clothes and her solicitous behavior are a disguise that conceal her murderous intent. Hendel compares this to the fact that Anat and Yatpan disguise themselves as vultures before attacking Aqhat. Anat and Yatpan, moreover, disguise themselves and attack Aqhat while he sits in a pavilion, eating, just as the disguised Pughat attacks Yatpan while he sits eating in his pavilion. Also Hendel notes that the pavilion in which Aqhat sits is located in Qarit Abilim, which, according to a broken passage, may be the city of Yatpan.[42] Thus, just as Pughat "becomes" the warrior Anat as she sets out to exact revenge, Yatpan "becomes" the assassinated Aqhat as he encounters death while eating in a tent. Hendel concludes, "Pughat's murder of Yatpan mirrors Anat's and Yatpan's murder of Aqhat."[43]

Hendel's understanding of Pughat as an Anat figure can now be coupled with the point I have made several times concerning Anat as the counterpart and the alter ego of Baal. I suggest that, as Anat is the counterpart of her brother Baal, so, too, is Pughat, in her role as a humanized Anat, also the counterpart of Baal. Or, more accurately, Pughat is the counterpart of Baal's earthly protégé, who is Pughat's brother Aqhat. Pughat, in short, is the "new" Aqhat. Indeed, although not saying so explicitly, the text does hint rather strongly that this is the case. Thus, after Aqhat's death, Pughat is described as saddling an ass and lifting her father upon it so he can ride through his domain, a responsibility we might otherwise have expected to find assigned to Aqhat.[44] Similarly, in the last tablet of the epic, Pughat asks for and receives her father's blessing and favor, a blessing and favor presumably previously given to Aqhat.[45] Finally, the text describes Pughat as donning "hero's clothes" (*nps ġzr*), and implicit here is an understanding of Pughat as a hero (*ġzr*). Yet the title "hero" elsewhere in the epic has been reserved for Aqhat (and for Danil). Pughat has become the hero her brother was. As Hendel succinctly notes, she is her brother's successor.[46] Thus, although Aqhat himself is dead, all that seemed promised through his miraculous birth cannot really be said to have come to an end. As in the Bible's exemplars of the barren woman type-scene, the hero—in the person of Aqhat's alter ego, Pughat—can be said to have overcome the characteristic threat of death administered by the deity.

Such an interpretation suggests, moreover, that there is an elaborate chiastic structure at work in the Epic of Aqhat, whereby the permutations of the type-scene's gender roles that characterized the story in its beginning come back into play at its end. This can be seen by comparing once more the biblical materials, in which the barren women stories' initial focus on a barren *woman* gives way, in the end, to the recounting of a heroic event in the life of the *son*. As the Aqhat Epic, though, countered the typical depiction of a barren *female* by rendering the *husband* as infertile, so, too, does the epic defy the type-scene's conventions by replacing the *male* hero with whom the story should conclude with a *female* protagonist. The change in gender roles with which the story opened is, in this sense, an elaborate foreshadowing of the reversal found at its end, quite similar, for example, to the kind of foreshadowing Alter argued was present in the "expression of doubt" section of the Manoah's wife story.

III. THE STORY OF THE VIRGIN BIRTH

Two other points where the Hebrew Bible's conventions of the barren woman type-scene are altered in order to enhance the story's overall narrative effect are found in the New Testament annunciation tales of Matthew and Luke. The most obvious of the permutations found in these narratives is that the woman receiving the annunciation, Mary, is cast as a virgin rather than as barren. Yet, as I noted in the introductory comments to this chapter, virginity is in many respects a condition analogous to barrenness since both states concern an empty womb that has not as yet fulfilled a woman's obligation to beget a son who will continue her husband's patriarchal line. Both these types of empty wombs, moreover, can only be filled through God's miraculous intervention. In the same way, then, that Danil's tale of childlessness is an example of the barren "woman" type-scene, despite the fact that the infertile one is a man, so, too, is the Mary narrative—despite its stress on virginity—an illustration of the "barren" woman tale.[47]

In Matthew's version of Mary's tale, this change from "barren" to "virgin" engenders a further permutation in the type-scene paradigm, namely, that the normal order of annunciation followed by conception is reversed, so that the story begins by describing how Mary, although a virgin, is with child (1:18). Only when Joseph, her betrothed, plans to break their engagement because of her presumed infidelity, does an angel of God appear and declare that it is God who miraculously has filled Mary's womb (1:20–24). In verse 25, though, the type-scene's expected pattern is restored, as Mary bears a son and he is named Jesus. This verse is then followed by a particularly good example of the kind of elaboration sometimes found in this third part of the barren woman type-scene, a description of the extraordinary nature of the child who has just been born. This elaboration is found in Matt 2:1–12, in which the wise men from the east visit the baby Jesus and pay him homage.

As my analysis predicts, the Matthew narrative next turns immediately to describe a threat of near death faced by the child of promise. This threat, intimated already in 2:1–12 and detailed especially in 2:13–18, is brought about by the acts of Judaea's King Herod, who seeks to kill the miracle child because his future role as the "king of the Jews" compromises Herod's royal authority. This threat from Herod, however, is twice averted, first, when the wise men from the east avoid reporting to Herod that they have found the baby Jesus in a house in Bethlehem, and, second, when Joseph and Mary flee into Egypt with their infant son in order to escape Herod's massacre of all of Bethlehem's newborns.

Yet unlike the case of, say, the near sacrifice of Isaac, in neither of these instances does the boy Jesus face death head-on. Matthew thus seems to believe that the life of the miracle child must in some other way be dedicated to God. This is the point of 2:19–23, in which Jesus' family returns from Egypt after Herod's death and goes to settle in the town of Nazareth in the Galilee. According to 2:23, this was done "so that what had been spoken through the prophets might be fulfilled, 'He will be called a Nazorean'" (NRSV translation). There is, however, no known prophetic statement identifying the future messiah as a "Nazorean," and commentators have thus debated about the specific messianic attribute that Matthew intends to evoke here. One possibility is that "Nazorean" is derived from Hebrew *nāzîr*, "Nazirite."[48] Such an interpretation is entirely consistent with my thesis in this chapter. Because in 2:1–18, Jesus did not confront death directly, as the second act of the barren woman type-scene requires, the boy must give his life to God in some other way. Matthew thus closes his story of Jesus' birth with the otherwise obscure description of Jesus as a Nazorean/Nazirite in order to signal that the boy's life is thereby dedicated to God's service. Not coincidentally, the stories that immediately follow are of John the Baptist, Jesus' baptism, and the temptation (Matt 3:1–4:11), all of which culminate with the beginning of Jesus' public ministry and his devoting of himself to the doing of God's work on earth (4:12–25).

An even more intriguing New Testament variation upon the Hebrew Bible's barren woman type-scene is found in the annunciation scene depicted in chapters 1–2 of the gospel of Luke. The most striking permutation of the expected paradigm found there is that there are *two* annunciations, one to Mary, the mother of Jesus, and one to Elizabeth, the mother of John the Baptist. Elizabeth's story of infertility and its reversal, moreover, is intricately interwoven with Mary's, meaning that Luke's barren woman type-scene is not really a "scene" at all, but two "scenes" that are elaborately intermingled.

This interwoven narrative begins in Luke 1:5, with the story of Elizabeth. This story, at least in its opening verses, closely follows the expected barren woman paradigm. For example, like all the barren women exemplars, the story of Elizabeth first introduces the narrative's two major actors, Elizabeth and her husband Zechariah. We also are told certain background information, that Zechariah is a priest belonging to the order of Abijah and that Elizabeth, too, is of priestly descent and is even from the highly distinguished line of Aaron, Moses' brother. The story's most important background data, though, are revealed in verse 7, which describes how Elizabeth is barren and how both she and her husband are getting on in years.

Verses 8–23 continue to follow the expected pattern of the barren woman type-scene, as the angel Gabriel appears to Zechariah and reveals that Elizabeth will bear a son called John. In verse 15, the angel also reveals, as in the Manoah's wife story, that John will never drink wine or strong drink. Unlike Judges 13, the word Nazirite is not used explicitly here, probably omitted by Luke because this Hebrew word would not have been understood by the evangelist's primarily gentile audience. Still, the Nazirite vow required of Samson is clearly the image Luke has in mind.[49] The similarities with the Manoah's wife story continue, in verse 18, as Zechariah expresses the same sorts of doubts Manoah expressed about the annunciation. In Judges 13, the narrator's point in depicting these doubts was to describe the bumbling faithlessness of Manoah. Luke also seems to want to make this point. In fact, Luke's scorn for the bumbling faithlessness manifest by Zechariah is so great that he has the angel Gabriel curse Zechariah with muteness until the time of the promised son's birth (1:20).

Luke further evokes his Judges 13 predecessor by contrasting the piety of the barren wife to the faithlessness of the husband. In 1:24, Elizabeth, as expected in the barren woman type-scene, conceives, but before the story concludes with the birth of John, Luke interposes the story of the annunciation to Mary. As Athalaya Brenner has pointed out, the introduction of this second story of a mother-to-be recalls the motif of the barren woman and her fertile rival found in the Hebrew Bible stories of Sarah, Rachel, and Hannah.[50] But because this story of a second woman is introduced in the third part of the barren woman type-scene—after Elizabeth has conceived but before she gives birth—rather than in the first part of the story—before the barren woman becomes pregnant—the threat of rivalry that is so prominent in the Hebrew Bible narratives is defused. It is further defused in verses 39–45, when Mary and Elizabeth meet. Elizabeth is older and, by virtue of her marriage to a priest and her own priestly lineage, is of greater social standing. But these human accomplishments seem to mean nothing to Elizabeth, and hence she defers to Mary and to the son she will bear, acknowledging that the child in Mary's womb will be greater than hers.[51] Elizabeth, moreover, utters this pronouncement while "filled with the Holy Spirit" (v 41; NRSV translation). The contrast drawn here between the barren wife and her doubting husband is pointed. Zechariah's impiety has ren-

dered him mute so that he cannot speak, while Elizabeth's faith empow-
ers her to speak with the voice of God. Note also that in Gabriel's annunciation in verse 15, the angel declares that even before John is born,
he will be "filled with the Holy Spirit" (NRSV translation). Elizabeth,
during her pregnancy, thus speaks as will her future son. Again, one is
reminded of the Manoah's wife story, where, by refraining from wine
and other strong drink while she was pregnant, that woman assumed the
Nazirite vow that eventually would be undertaken by her miracle child.

The story of the annunciation to Mary in Luke 1:26–56 and 2:1–7
also resembles the Judges 13 story of Manoah's wife, as well as recalling
the stories of Sarah found in Genesis and of Hannah found in 1 Samuel
1.[52] Even though, as in Matthew, a crucial element is different—Mary
is not barren, but a virgin—the same basic pattern of these barren
woman type-scenes still holds.[53] The woman is introduced in verse 27;
in verses 28–33, a divine messenger appears and promises that she will
bear a son; in verses 34–38, the woman expresses doubt about the truth
of the message; but in 2:1–7, she gives birth. Moreover, Gabriel's annunciation to Mary in 1:31—"you shall conceive in your womb and bear a
son" (NRSV translation)—is reminiscent of the angel's promise that
"you shall conceive and bear a son," found in verses 3, 5, and 7 of the
Manoah's wife story.[54] Also, as James A. Sanders (among others) has
pointed out,[55] Gabriel's words chiding Mary for her dubiety in verse 37
are essentially identical to the words spoken by the angel who chides
Sarah in Gen 18:14 (the only difference being that the Genesis passage
is in the interrogative—"is anything impossible for God?"—whereas the
Lukan passage is in the declarative—"nothing is impossible for God").

As for the similarities between the Hannah and Mary stories, the
crucial passages are found in Luke 1:46–55, where Mary utters a prayer
of thanksgiving (traditionally called the "Magnificat") that is, to cite
Sanders again, "a bare reworking of the Song of Hannah" (sung by Hannah in thanksgiving in 1 Samuel 2).[56] This parallel demonstrates once
more that even though Mary is technically a virgin and not barren, she
is imagined in the tradition as if she were like Hannah and the Bible's
other barren women. But there is one crucial difference between Mary
and Hannah. Mary does *not* vow her unborn son to Nazirite service.
Neither does a Nazirite vow—nor even Matthew's rather oblique description of Jesus as a "Nazorean"—show up later in the story, after
Jesus' birth. And the Lukan story does not contain the Herodian threat
stories found in Matthew that intimate Jesus' near death. There are, in

short, *none* of the motifs we have come to expect in the second act of the barren woman type-scene whereby God exercises some claim upon the life of the child of promise. Even the text that comes the closest to fulfilling the paradigm, Luke 2:22–24, ultimately fails to satisfy, for although these verses do describe how Mary and Joseph bring the baby Jesus to Jerusalem and consecrate this firstborn son—as Exod 13:2 requires—as "holy to the Lord" (v 23; NRSV translation), the text does not indicate that Jesus' parents accompanied this dedication with the animal sacrifice that is needed in order to redeem the miracle child. They do offer, according to verse 24, "a pair of turtledoves or two young pigeons" (NRSV translation), but as Lev 12:8 tells us, this is the purification offering required of a woman who has recently given birth but who cannot afford a sheep. Thus this sacrifice, while it ends Mary's postpartum period of ritual impurity, does not address the redemption of Jesus.[57]

Yet according to the paradigm of the barren woman type-scene that I have proposed, the life of a child of divine promise *must* be redeemed through some sort of confrontation with death—as in the stories of Isaac, Jacob, Joseph, and the Shunammite's son—or there *must* be a Nazirite vow—as in the stories of Samson and Samuel and also as in Luke's story of John the Baptist. In fact, Luke's understanding of the Baptist's story is particularly telling in this regard, as can be seen later on in the gospel, where Luke deviates from his source, the gospel of Mark, in depicting John's death. Mark's account (6:14–29), which also is found in the gospel of Matthew (14:1–12), recounts in detail the events that lead to John's beheading by King Herod Antipas, describing how the king agrees to have John killed because of a promise he makes to the daughter of Herodias after being pleased by the girl's dancing.[58] But in Luke, although Herod's beheading of John is mentioned (9:7–9), the gospel writer omits Mark's elaborate portrayal of the act. This suggests that Luke, while he cannot totally ignore such a major event as John's execution, wishes to minimize the significance assigned to this episode. I believe this is because Luke, and only Luke among the evangelists, depicts John both as a child born to a barren woman and as a Nazirite.[59] Thus only Luke tells the story of John's life as if it follows the paradigm of the barren woman type-scene, first indicating that John is a child of promise and then proposing that the deity has a right to make a claim upon John's life by demanding John's devotion as a Nazirite. But what of John's subsequent beheading by Herod? For Luke, this second sacrifice on the part of the miracle child is unrequired in the paradigm of the barren woman story, and, indeed, it is an unwelcome deviation. Consequently, although it is an important enough event in Luke's source that it cannot be omitted, the event in Luke's gospel is downplayed.

In Luke's account of the birth story of Jesus, however, because there is no sacrificial offering or Nazirite vow, Luke understands that, according to the barren woman paradigm, God will make some future claim upon the life of this child. Such an interpretation suggests that the crucifixion in Luke 23 is the inevitable result of the failure of Mary and Joseph to act in Luke 1–2.[60] Especially to be noted in this regard is the overwhelming sense in Luke—as opposed to Matthew and Mark—that the crucifixion *is* inevitable. Only Luke, for example, describes an oracle uttered by Simeon immediately after the scene of Jesus' designation in the temple (2:29–35) that contains both the expected language acknowledging Jesus as Israel's future savior as well as words of ominous foreboding that describe the ways in which Jesus will be opposed during his life. Luke's sense of Jesus' inevitable death is further seen in his recounting of the first episode of Jesus' public ministry, in Luke 4, in which Jesus' teachings are rejected by the people of Nazareth. This famous scene, centered around the maxim that a prophet has no honor in his own country, is moved from its later position in Luke's source, the gospel of Mark (6:1–6), in order that it might become a programmatic statement in Luke on the necessity of suffering as a part of Jesus' ministry. Similarly, only Luke among the synoptic gospels structures his gospel as a long travel narrative directed toward Jerusalem (Luke 9–19) because, as Jesus says about his going there, "it is impossible for a prophet to be killed outside of Jerusalem" (Luke 13:33; NRSV translation). The key word here is "killed"; Luke's Jesus goes to Jerusalem purposely and knowingly to die. Luke 24:25–26 and 46 further insist that Jesus' sufferings were necessary and inevitable.[61]

Yet no matter how inevitable it was for Luke that the crucifixion eventually claim the life of Jesus as the child of divine promise, the paradigm of the barren woman type-scene suggests that, ultimately, God does not demand the unrequited death of the child of annunciation. Instead, there is some sort of redemption. In Luke, therefore, God resurrects the son and so allows Jesus to transcend the death that he would otherwise have had to endure forever. Note in this regard that the resurrection receives a special emphasis in Luke, as the scenes describing this event are much longer and more extensive than the comparable narratives found in Luke's counterpart, Matthew. Only in Luke, moreover, is there a description of the ascension of Jesus into the heavens (24:50–51). In the end, then, Luke's God does redeem the promised child from the claims of death, bringing Jesus to live alongside the divine father in the heavenly realm for eternity.

NOTES

[1]The Hebrew text reads:

> *lipnê šānîm, běsôp šîrat děbôrâ,*
> *šāmaʿtî ʾet dûmiyyat rekeb sîsěrāʾ ʾăšer bôšěš lābôʾ,*
> *mabbît běʾimmô šel sîsěrāʾ hannišqepet bahallôn,*
> *ʾiššâ šepas kesep biśʿārāh . . .*
>
> *ʾarbāʿîm šānâ šāqěṭâ hāʾāreṣ. ʾarbāʿîm šānâ*
> *lōʾ dāhărû sûsîm ûpārāšîm mētîm lōʾ nāʿāṣû ʿênê zěkûkît.*
> *ʾăbāl hîʾ mētāh, zěman qāṣār ʾaḥar môt běnāh.*

The poem was first brought to my attention by William J. Urbrock, "Sisera's Mother in Judges 5 and Haim Gouri's ʾImmô," *HAR* 11 (1987), 433–34, who reproduces the Hebrew text and a translation by Dan Pagis from S. Burnshaw, T. Carmi, and E. Spicehandler, *The Modern Hebrew Poem Itself* (New York, Chicago, and San Francisco: Holt, Rinehart and Winston, 1965), 158–59. In my own translation, I have been more influenced by the essays of Ruth Finer Mintz (*Modern Hebrew Poetry: A Bilingual Anthology* [Berkeley and Los Angeles: University of California Press, 1966], 288–90) and of Warren Bargad and Stanley F. Chyet (*Israeli Poetry: A Contemporary Anthology* [Bloomington: Indiana University Press, 1986], 61).

[2]Lines 463–64. The Greek text reads:

> *hostis gar en polloisin hōs egō kakois*
> *zē. pōs hod' ouchi katthanōn kerdos pherei;*

The translation is by E. Wyckoff in *Sophocles I: Oedipus the King, Oedipus at Colonus, and Antigone* (ed. D. Grene and R. Lattimore; New York: Washington Square Press, 1967), 178.

[3]This same general point about the "mothers" of Judges 5 is made by M. Bal, *Death and Dissymmetry: The Politics of Coherence in the Book of Judges* (Chicago: University of Chicago Press, 1988), 206–17, 227–29; A. Brenner, "A Triangle and a Rhombus in Narrative Structure: A Proposed Integrative Reading of Judges 4 and 5," *A Feminist Companion to Judges* (ed. A. Brenner; The Feminist Companion to the Bible 4; Sheffield: Sheffield Academic Press, 1993), 102–3; J. C. Exum, "Feminist Criticism: Whose Interests Are Being Served?" *Judges and Method: New Approaches in Biblical Studies* (ed. G. A. Yee; Minneapolis: Fortress, 1995), 72–75; D. N. Fewell and D. M. Gunn, *Gender, Power, and Promise: The Subject of the Bible's First Story* (Nashville: Abingdon, 1993), 125–26; and by F. Gottlieb, "Three Mothers," *Judaism* 30 (1981), 194–203. In all these cases, however, the specific understanding of the

way "motherhood" imagery is used in Judges 5 differs from the one I will describe below.

4"The Women in the Book of Judges," *HAR* 10 (1986), 280.

5The pertinent references are: Gen 18:9–15 and 21:1–7 (Sarah); Gen 25:19–25 (Rebekah); Gen 30:1–8, 22–24 (Rachel); 1 Sam 1:1–28 (Hannah); 2 Kgs 4:8–17 (the Shunammite woman).

6See on this usage Nehama Aschkenasy, "The Empty Vessel: Woman as Mother," Chapter 3 in *Eve's Journey: Feminine Images in Hebraic Literary Tradition* (Philadelphia: University of Pennsylvania Press, 1986), 79–105, who borrows the term "empty vessel" from Ruth 1:21.

7"How Convention Helps Us Read: The Case of the Bible's Annunciation Type-Scene," *Prooftexts* 3 (1983), 115–30; also see Alter, "Biblical Type-Scenes and the Uses of Convention," *Critical Inquiry* 5 (1978), 355–68, revised in *The Art of Biblical Narrative* (New York: Basic Books, 1981), 47–62, on the appropriation of the Homeric notion of "type-scene" in the study of the Hebrew Bible. In *Biblical Narrative,* 81–87, Alter also comments briefly on the Bible's annunciation type-scene. The discussions of Esther Fuchs, "The Literary Characterization of Mothers and Sexual Politics in the Hebrew Bible," *Feminist Perspectives on Biblical Scholarship* (ed. A. Y. Collins; Chico, CA: Scholars Press, 1985), 117–36; of James G. Williams, "The Beautiful and the Barren: Conventions in Biblical Type-Scenes," *JSOT* 17 (1980), 107–19, especially 110; and the brief comments of Walter Brueggemann, "I Samuel 1: A Sense of a Beginning," *ZAW* 102 (1990), 34, are of note as well, as all adumbrate Alter's 1983 article on the annunciation type-scene by borrowing from his earlier (1978) work on type-scenes in general and seeking to apply the type-scene model to the Bible's annunciation stories.

8On type-scenes in Homer, see W. Arend, *Die typischen Scenen bei Homer* (Problemata 7; Berlin: Weidmann, 1933); B. Fenik, *Typical Battle Scenes in the Iliad. Studies in the Narrative Techniques of Homeric Battle Description* (Hermes Einzelschriften 21; Wiesbaden: Franz Steiner, 1968); most recently, M. W. Edwards, *Homer: Poet of the Iliad* (Baltimore and London: Johns Hopkins University Press, 1987), 71–77, with further bibliography on p. 77.

9Gen 18:11 (Sarah; see also Gen 11:30 and 17:17); Gen 25:21 (Rebekah); Gen 29:31 (Rachel); Judg 13:2 (Manoah's wife); 1 Sam 1:2 (Hannah); 2 Kgs 4:14 (the Shunammite woman).

10Divine messenger: Gen 18:10 (Sarah); Judg 13:3 (Manoah's wife); oracle: Gen 25:23 (Rebekah); man of God: 1 Sam 1:17 (Hannah); 2 Kgs 4:16 (the Shunammite woman).

[11]Gen 21:2 (Sarah); Gen 25:24–26 (Rebekah); Gen 30:23 (Rachel); Judg 13:24 (Manoah's wife); 1 Sam 1:20 (Hannah); 2 Kgs 4:17 (the Shunammite woman).

[12]In the standard source critical analysis of the Genesis narratives, Gen 16:4–6 is J; Gen 21:8–10 is E.

[13]In addition to the examples of Sarah and Manoah's wife discussed below, see the tale of the Shunammite woman (2 Kgs 4:16) and also, to some degree, the story of Rebekah (Gen 25:22). Although raising no doubts about the promise that she will conceive, Rebekah does wonder, when she begins to sense mighty strugglings in her womb (the twins Esau and Jacob fighting), whether the divine promise will be fulfilled and the offspring carried to term.

[14]In the standard source critical analysis of the Genesis narratives, Genesis 17 is P; Genesis 18 is J.

[15]Alter, "Convention," 126.

[16]Alter, "Convention," 126.

[17]See Chapter 2.

[18]See also Williams, "The Beautiful and the Barren," 110.

[19]I make this claim concerning the larger pattern of the life story of Isaac even though Gen 21:1–8 and Gen 22:1–19 come, according to standard source critical analysis, from different authors (Gen 21:1–8 contains elements of J, E, and P; Gen 22:1–19 is E). For my point, it is enough that, whoever the original authors, the final redactor of Genesis thought to juxtapose the stories.

[20]In the standard source critical analysis of the Genesis narratives, Gen 37:26–27 is J; Gen 37:28 is E.

[21]See, similarly, the very brief comments of Brueggemann in "I Samuel 1," 38, n. 10, regarding the stories of Sarah and Hannah.

[22]Williams, "The Beautiful and the Barren," 111, makes a similar point, writing:

> Conventions provide a stylized set of expectations that an audience can anticipate. A complex of information is presented compactly "at a glance" or "in a word" through the use of formal scenes, images and symbols. However, when the convention becomes highly predictable it ceases to give information that seems important and we cease to look or listen. There is therefore a dialectical tension between conventions, which maintain continuity with the past, and

those elaborations and variations that present a new dramatic emphasis or a new insight.

[23] Alter, "Convention," 124; see also the catalogue of other scholars' unflattering descriptions of Samson collected by D. M. Gunn, "Samson of Sorrows: An Isaianic Gloss on Judges 13–16," *Reading Between Texts: Intertextuality and the Hebrew Bible* (ed. D. N. Fewell; Louisville, KY: Westminster/John Knox, 1992), 225.

[24] Alter, "Convention," 120–21. Fuchs, "Literary Characterization of Mothers," 119–22, similarly points out that in this annunciation type-scene, Abraham occupies center stage, and she also, like Alter, sees underlying this a concern with patriarchal ideology.

[25] Or, at least, they have been unable to bear a son; a daughter, Pughat, appears later in the text, but whether she is younger or older than Aqhat, the son Danataya eventually bears, is unspecified.

[26] See *KTU* 1.17.1.36–42.

[27] While monarchical status never is explicitly claimed for Danil, the assumption that Danil is a king is implicit throughout the Epic of Aqhat. This is suggested by several data. Like a king, Danil lives in a palace (*bt // hkl; KTU* 1.17.1.25–26, 43; 17.2.24–25; 19.4.8–9, 10). Also, Danil and the son he eventually sires, Aqhat, fulfill kingly functions. For example, Danil is described as sitting in the gate, judging the cases of widows and orphans (*KTU* 1.17.5.6–8; 19.1.21–25). This is an attribute elsewhere ascribed to the typical ancient Near Eastern king. From Mesopotamia, see the Code of Hammurapi, col. I, 37–38 (Prologue), and col. XLVII (Rs. XXIV), 59–75 (Epilogue); in these lines, Hammurapi describes his intention to keep the rich from oppressing the poor and to procure justice for the orphan and the widow. From Ugarit, see *KTU* 1.16.6.33–34, in which King Kirta is described as neglecting his kingly duties by failing to judge on behalf of widows and the oppressed. From the Hebrew Bible, see 2 Sam 15:2, in which Absalom is depicted sitting and judging in the gate in an attempt to usurp King David's royal prerogatives; 2 Sam 19:9 (English 19:8), in which King David sits and judges in the gate; Isa 11:4a, which is Isaiah's description of the messianic king as one who will judge with righteousness for the poor and the meek of the earth; Jer 22:1–3, which is Jeremiah's oracle to the king of Judah, requiring justice for the oppressed, the alien, the orphan, the widow, and the innocent. Finally, for all of the ancient Near East, see F. C. Fensham, "Widow, Orphan, and the Poor in Ancient Near Eastern Legal and Wisdom Literature," *JNES* 21 (1962), 129–39.

[28] The terminology of "correct" and "legitimate" wife is that of Mara E. Donaldson, "Kinship Theory in the Patriarchal Narratives: The Case of the Barren Wife," *JAAR* 49 (1989), 83.

[29] See Chapter 3.

[30] 1 Sam 25:42 (Abigail); 25:43 (Ahinoam); 1 Chr 3:2 (Ma'acah and Haggith); 3:3,5 (Abital; Eglah; Bathsheba). Abigail was the mother of Chileab/Daniel (1 Chr 3:1); Ahinoam was the mother of Amnon (1 Chr 3:1); Ma'acah was the mother of Absalom (1 Chr 3:2); Haggith was the mother of Adonijah (1 Chr 3:2); Abital was the mother of Shephatiah (1 Chr 3:3); Eglah was the mother of Ithream (1 Chr 3:3); Bathsheba was the mother of Shimea/Shammua, Shobab, Nathan, and Solomon (2 Sam 5:14; 1 Chr 3:5). According to 2 Sam 5:15 and 1 Chr 3:5–7, David had nine other sons whose mothers are unnamed.

[31] I have discussed the location where Danil receives his dream more thoroughly in "The Deception of Isaac, Jacob's Dream at Bethel, and Incubation on an Animal Skin," *Priesthood and Cult in Ancient Israel* (JSOTSup 125; ed. G. A. Anderson and S. M. Olyan; Sheffield: JSOT Press, 1991), 111. In this article, I point out that, while Danil's location during his dream is, in fact, unspecified, we can be sure that he is not in his own bedchamber since after Danil visions Baal in a dream, he is described as returning to his house (*bt // hkl*). That Danil's sleeping place is a temple is more speculative, but I believe likely since throughout the ancient Mediterranean world, the kind of incubation dream Danil receives typically takes place in a sacred space.

[32] *KTU* 1.17.6.52 (restored); 19.4.12, 16–17.

[33] Ugaritic *ab šnm*. On this epithet, see W. F. Albright, *Archaeology and the Religion of Israel* (2d ed.; Baltimore: Johns Hopkins University Press, 1946), 72; F. M. Cross, "'ēl," *TDOT* 1 (ed. J. G. Botterweck and H. Ringgren; Grand Rapids, MI: Eerdmans, 1974), 245. For other possibilities for *šnm*, see U. Oldenburg, *The Conflict Between El and Ba'al in Canaanite Religion* (Leiden: Brill, 1969), 17, and M. Pope, *'El in the Ugaritic Texts* (Leiden: Brill, 1955), 32–34.

[34] On *ḥtk*, "patriarch," see F. M. Cross, "The Canaanite Cuneiform Tablet from Taanach," *BASOR* 190 (1968), 45, n. 24.

[35] Note, however, that, while the tradition finds it mandatory that the progenitor El be involved in the Epic of Kirta if Kirta is to acquire a son and heir, the Kotharot do not make an appearance in Kirta. I would suggest that this is consistent with the logic I have described: Kirta's problem is not barrenness but the lack of a wife. He thus has no use for goddesses like the Kotharot, whose skill is in aiding in conception and childbirth. As I also have suggested in Chapter 3, if Kirta does have any need of a deity besides El, it is Asherah, who, I have argued, is the patron of queen mothers, the role Kirta's new wife, Hurriya, eventually will assume. Thus Kirta, in his march to Udm to secure Hurriya as wife, deviates from El's instructions by offering a vow to Asherah.

[36] *Stories from Ancient Canaan* (Philadelphia: Westminster, 1978), 31; see, similarly, H. L. Ginsberg, "The Tale of Aqhat," *ANET* (3d ed.; ed. J. B. Pritchard; Princeton: Princeton University Press, 1969), 155; idem, "The North-Canaanite Myth of Anath and Aqhat," *BASOR* 97 (1945), 7; idem, "The North-Canaanite Myth of Anath and Aqhat, II" *BASOR* 98 (1945), 23; J. Obermann, *How Danil Was Blessed with a Son: An Incubation Scene in Ugaritic* (Supplement to *JAOS* 6; Baltimore: American Oriental Society, 1946), 2; C. H. Gordon, *Ugaritic Literature: A Comprehensive Translation of the Poetic and Prose Texts* (Rome: Pontificium Institutum Biblicum, 1949), 85; T. II. Gaster, *Thespis: Ritual, Myth, and Drama in the Ancient Near East* (2d ed.; Garden City, NY: Doubleday, 1961), 320 et passim; G. R. Driver, *Canaanite Myths and Legends* (2d ed.; ed. J. C. L. Gibson; Edinburgh: T. & T. Clark, 1978), 27.

[37] The text in question is *KTU* 1.20.2.7. Conrad L'Heureux, in *Rank Among the Canaanite Gods: El, Ba'al, and the Repha'im* (HSM 21; Missoula, MT: Scholars Press, 1979), 137, points out, however, that Danil's presence in *KTU* 1.20 does not necessarily mean that *KTU* 1.20 is to be read in conjunction with the Aqhat cycle. L'Heureux compares the Adapa myth from Mesopotamia, in which Dumuzi appears as one of Anu's gatekeepers even though the tale of Adapa otherwise has no connection with the Dumuzi mythic cycle.

[38] *The Epic of the Patriarch: The Jacob Cycle and the Narrative Traditions of Canaan and Israel* (HSM 42; Atlanta: Scholars Press, 1987), 89–94.

[39] Papyrus Chester Beatty VII, verso i, 8–9. For text and translation, see *Hieratic Papyri in the British Museum. Third Series. Chester Beatty Gift* 1 (ed. A. H. Gardiner; London: British Museum, 1935), 62–63; see also *ANET,* 250a, n. 18, and W. F. Albright, *Yahweh and the Gods of Canaan: A Historical Analysis of Two Contrasting Faiths* (Winona Lake, IN: Eisenbrauns, 1968), 129.

[40] "The Bow of Aqhat: The Meaning of a Mythological Theme," *Orient and Occident. Essays Presented to Cyrus H. Gordon on the Occasion of His Sixty-Fifth Birthday* (AOAT 22; ed. H. A. Hoffner; Neukirchen-Vluyn: Neukirchener Verlag; Kevelaer: Butzon & Berker, 1973), 71–80.

[41] Hendel, *Epic,* 92.

[42] *KTU* 1.18.4.7–8.

[43] Hendel, *Epic,* 94.

[44] In something like the catalogue of the "Duties of the Ideal Son" with which the epic begins, for example.

[45] Reading as Pughat's request to her father (*KTU* 1.19.4.32–33):

> *Bless me that I may go blessed,*
> *Favor me that I may go with your favor.*

Cf. the translation of G. R. Driver, who understands Pughat's request as directed to the gods. See Driver, *Canaanite Myths,* 120.

[46]Hendel, *Epic,* 94.

[47]Williams, "The Beautiful and the Barren," 110, 113.

[48]The other two possibilities are, first, that "Nazorean" simply might indicate a geographical reference, someone from Nazareth, and second, that "Nazorean" might be derived from Hebrew *nēṣer,* "branch," which in Isa 11:1 is used to describe the messiah who will blossom forth from the "root" of David. See Raymond E. Brown, *The Birth of the Messiah: A Commentary on the Infancy Narratives in Matthew and Luke* (Garden City, NY: Doubleday, 1977), 209–13. In further comment on pp. 218–19, Brown suggests that Matthew's use of "Nazorean" alludes to all three meanings, although he is equally insistent, on pp. 223–25, that it is the designation "Nazirite" that Matthew has primarily in mind.

[49]As is commonly noted by commentators; see, for example, Brown, *Birth of the Messiah,* 268, 273–74.

[50]"Female social behaviour: two descriptive patterns within the 'birth of the hero' paradigm," *VT* 36 (1986), 269–70; reprinted in *A Feminist Companion to Genesis* (ed. A. Brenner; The Feminist Companion to the Bible 2; Sheffield: Sheffield Academic Press, 1993), 217–18.

[51]Brenner, "Female social behaviour," 269–70.

[52]James A. Sanders makes a similar point, stating, "Luke's two annunciations in chapter 1 follow, in detail, the great annunciations in Genesis 16–18 [Sarah], 1 Samuel 1 [Hannah], and Judges 13 [Manoah's wife]." See "Isaiah in Luke," *Interpreting the Prophets* (ed. J. L. Mays and P. J. Achtemeier; Philadelphia: Fortress, 1987), 78.

[53]Williams, "The Beautiful and the Barren," 110.

[54]Note, moreover, that the Greek version of Judges 13 that Luke would have been using adds in all three verses the same phrase, *en gastri,* "in the womb," that is found in Luke 1:31.

[55]"Isaiah in Luke," 79; see also, in addition to most of the commentaries, W. Brueggemann, "'Impossibility' and Epistemology in the Faith Tradition of Abraham and Sarah (Gen 18 1–15)," *ZAW* 94 (1982), 626.

[56]"Isaiah in Luke," 78; further on the "Song of Hannah," see Chapter 6.

[57]Note also the comments of Brown, *Birth of the Messiah,* 448, who argues that in 2:22–24, Luke is thinking *primarily* of the custom of a mother's purification after the birth of her child.

[58]Mark 6:22 actually reads "his daughter Herodias," thus identifying the dancer as Herodias herself and further describing her as the daughter of Herod. However, several ancient manuscripts of Mark read "the daughter of Herodias" instead, and this is consistent with the reading found in the rest of the Markan story, with Matt 14:6, and with the genealogy of the Herods found in Josephus (*Antiquities* 17.14).

[59]In addition to the designation of John as a Nazirite in Luke's annunciation story, see also Luke 7:33, where John is identified again as one who does not drink wine. Notably, in the parallel to this verse in Matthew (11:18), while it is said that John has been neither eating nor drinking, the abstention from wine specific to John's commission as a Nazirite is not mentioned.

[60]Hans Conzelmann, in his influential study of Luke-Acts, *The Theology of Saint Luke* (New York: Harper & Row, 1961), has virtually ignored Luke 1–2 in his discussion of the gospel, thus indicating his belief that the birth narratives are not an integral part of Luke's gospel and so can be disregarded in any interpretation ("the authenticity of these first two chapters is questionable" [p. 118]). My analysis, however, suggests the birth stories must be taken seriously in any exegesis of the text. This point is also made most forcefully by P. S. Minear, "Luke's Use of the Birth Stories," *Studies in Luke-Acts* (Paul Schubert *Festschrift;* ed. L. E. Keck and J. L. Martyn; Nashville: Abingdon, 1966), 111–30; H. H. Oliver, "The Lucan Birth Stories and the Purpose of Luke-Acts," *NTS* 10 (1963–64), 202–26, especially 215–26; W. B. Tatum, "The Epoch of Israel: Luke I–II and the Theological Plan of Luke-Acts," *NTS* 13 (1966–67), 184–95. See also the brief comments of Brueggemann, "I Samuel 1," 44, n. 20, and of R. E. Brown, "Luke's Method in the Annunciation Narrative of Chapter One," *No Famine in the Land: Studies in Honor of John L. McKenzie* (ed. J. W. Flanagan and A. W. Robinson; Missoula, MT: Scholars Press [for the Institute for Antiquity and Christianity, Claremont], 1975), 181.

[61]On all this, see D. Tiede, *Prophecy and History in Luke-Acts* (Philadelphia: Fortress, 1980), 19–63, 70–78, 97–103.

Chapter 5

❦

"Ravish Them and Do to Them Whatever You Want"

DELILAH, THE LEVITE'S CONCUBINE,

AND DETERMINING THE STATUS OF

MEN'S LOVERS AND WIVES

At the end of the gospel of Luke, Jesus is resurrected and ascends into the heavens, leaving behind his disciples to complete his work on earth. Presumably, he also leaves behind his mother Mary. But where is she? In the second volume of Luke's history of the early church, the book of Acts, Mary shows up in 1:14, where, along with Jesus' disciples, Jesus' brothers, and certain other women, she is said to be constantly devoting herself to prayer. This brief notice, however, marks the final mention of Mary in the combined Luke-Acts account, and it is, moreover, her first appearance in the text since Luke 8:19–21, when she had come early in Jesus' ministry, along with Jesus' brothers, to see Jesus as he preached to a crowd of his followers. Before that episode, Mary last had been present in Luke 2:41–52, when she and her husband Joseph had brought Jesus, then a twelve-year-old boy, on their annual Passover pilgrimage to Jerusalem.

According to Luke, then, Mary, after giving birth to Jesus and appearing in the single scene that concerns his youth, interacts with her son only once during his adult years before disappearing from Jesus' ministry entirely. She is not even present at the crucifixion, the climactic event of Jesus' life, and this despite the fact that Luke, like the other three gospels, generally assumes that women play a central role in the cross account. The evangelist reports, for example, that it is women who keep watch as Jesus dies, who prepare Jesus' body for interment, and who sit in vigil outside his burial chamber (23:49, 55–56, and 24:1). It is also women—Mary Magdalene; Mary, the mother of James; Joanna;

and "the other women with them" (24:10; NRSV translation)—who are said to bring word of Jesus' empty tomb to the disciples. Luke further notes that Mary Magdalene and Joanna, as well as the other women present at the cross, have been in Jesus' entourage for a long time, since the beginnings of his ministry in the Galilee (8:2–3; 23:49, 55).

Luke elsewhere describes Jesus as welcoming these sorts of women, even preferring that they listen to his teachings rather than attend to their usual domestic chores (10:38–42). Yet Luke simultaneously portrays Jesus as rebuffing his mother Mary. In Luke 8, for example, when Jesus is told by his followers that his mother and brothers await him, he refuses to see them, declaring instead, "My mother and my brothers are those who hear the word of God and do it" (v 21; NRSV translation). Luke's Jesus expresses a similar sentiment a few chapters later, in 11:27. This passage describes how a nameless woman lauds Mary by crying out to Jesus, "Blessed is the womb that bore you and the breasts that nursed you." Jesus, however, again rejects the ties of kinship by replying, "Blessed rather are those who hear the word of God and obey it!" (NRSV translation). This text is also significant because, unlike the chapter 8 pericope, it is unique to Luke. This indicates that the motif of Jesus' distancing himself from his mother is not just something that Luke borrows unthinkingly from his source, the gospel of Mark.[1] Instead, it is a theme Luke himself seeks to put forward.[2]

This "distancing" theme is also put forward in Matthew, the gospel most akin to Luke. There, Mary's sole appearance after the infancy narratives of 1:18–2:25 is the scene described above in which she comes to see Jesus when he preaches to the crowds early in his ministry (12:46–50).[3] As in Luke 8, moreover, Jesus' response to her and to his brothers— "Here," he says, pointing to his disciples, "are my mother and my brothers!" (v 49; NRSV translation)—repudiates the notion that Mary's maternal role allows her to claim any special place in her son's life. Matthew also resembles Luke in depicting Mary as absent at the crucifixion and resurrection, again despite the fact that Matthew shares with Luke a sense that women are otherwise intimately associated with these events (Matt 27:55–56, 61; 28:1–8).[4] In fact, in Matthew, women assume such an important role in the cross narrative that the first resurrection appearance is to women, to Mary, the mother of James and Joseph, and to Mary Magdalene (28:9–10).[5] Still, Mary, the mother of Jesus, is not mentioned.

Why Mary's absence? As in Chapter 4, comparing the Mary story to the Hebrew Bible's barren woman type-scenes can prove instructive, for typically in the barren women narratives, the mother of the child of

promise also vanishes from the story almost immediately after her miracle son's birth and childhood. Sarah, for example, essentially disappears
from the Isaac narrative after a description in Gen 21:1–8 of how the
child Isaac is, in short order, conceived, born, named, circumcised, suckled, and weaned. Like Mary, Sarah is even depicted as missing during
the climactic event of her son's life, the *akedah,* Abraham's near sacrifice
of Isaac in Genesis 22. Then, shortly after the *akedah* story has ended,
and without ever being said to interact with Isaac again, Sarah dies (Gen
23:1–2). When we are subsequently told that Isaac, upon marrying Rebekah, found comfort after his mother's death (Gen 24:67), our natural
impulse to empathize is thus tempered by confusion since as far as we
know, Isaac has had no special ties to Sarah during his young adult life
and, indeed, has not even seen his mother since he was a very small child.

The formerly barren Rebekah similarly makes her last appearance in
the life story of her favored son Jacob while he is still a young man,
when, in Gen 27:46, she arranges with her husband Isaac to send Jacob
away to Paddan-aram to find a wife. Then, except for a notice describing
her burial site (Gen 49:31), she never shows up in the Bible again. She
is not even mentioned when Jacob is reunited with Isaac upon the former's return from Paddan-aram (Gen 35:27), not even to the extent that
Jacob makes inquiries about her absence or that Isaac offers comment
about where she might be. As for Manoah's wife, she, like Rebekah, is
said to work along with Manoah to arrange Samson's marriage to his
Timnite wife (Judg 14:1–9), but once Samson is wed, she disappears
from the story for good. After Samson's marriage falls apart, for example,
he is said to return home to "his father's house" (14:19) but whether his
mother is there or not gets no notice, and, as in the Genesis story of
Jacob's return to Isaac, no questions are asked or answers provided about
where the mother might have gone.[6] Even the burial place of Manoah's
wife goes unremarked in the Judges text, and this despite the fact that
Manoah's tomb is described (Judg 16:31). Hannah, too, disappears from
the Samuel narrative once her son reaches adulthood, although before
that time, she is said to visit him annually when she and Elqanah make
their autumnal pilgrimage to Shiloh (1 Sam 2:19). Finally, note the most
dramatic disappearance of a child of promise's mother, found in the story
of Rachel, who dies giving birth to her second son, Benjamin (Gen
35:16–20), while her firstborn son, Joseph, is still a young boy.[7]

In the same way, then, that Matthew and Luke seem to derive other
aspects of their Mary narratives from the Hebrew Bible's barren woman

type-scene, it also appears that these two gospels share the type-scene's sense that Mary, as the mother of the child of promise, must disappear from the story of her son at some point early on in his life. Still, it just as easily might have been the case that this "disappearing" element would *not* have been included in the Mary version of the "barren" woman tale, given, as Henri Cazelles has proposed, that there is another set of Hebrew Bible narratives that help structure Matthew's and Luke's characterizations of Mary.[8] These are the stories discussed in Chapter 3, the accounts of ancient Israel's queen mothers. In these materials, as I have previously shown, the queen mother character can hardly be described as a woman who disappears during her son's adult life. Rather, she is the exact opposite, someone who wields considerable influence in her son's royal court and, indeed, in all of Israelite society. Thus, if Cazelles' thesis is correct—and as I will discuss in Section I below, I believe that it is—we might well have expected that the New Testament's "queen mother" Mary, rather than disappearing almost entirely from Jesus' life story, would have been depicted as having a prominent place within it, playing at least some of the same sorts of roles in her son's ministry as did her ancient Israelite counterparts in the lives of Jerusalem's kings.

The question that prompts me first in this chapter is thus the question of why Mary, although cast as both "barren" woman and "queen mother," is rendered only according to the pattern of the disappearing barren one. Then, more generally, as Section I continues, I want to ask why, as a group, some of the Bible's women, like the previously barren mothers of a child of promise, are easily brushed aside by the biblical authors, while others, like queen mothers, are more typically depicted as women able to assert themselves in their society's affairs. The answer, I will argue, has to do with the biblical tradition's attitudes toward male hegemony. A woman whom the Bible's authors imagine to be in a relationship under the control of a man—whether it be her father, brother, or husband—is generally overshadowed by this man in the biblical text, subsumed under the authority of his patriarchal household. Conversely, women who are envisioned as somehow divorced in their lives from the domination of men can more readily be portrayed as acting independently and autonomously. This thesis will in turn illuminate the stories of two of the more memorable women characters of Judges. In Section II, I will discuss Delilah, the lover of Samson, whose story is told in Judges 16, and will explore the ways in which Delilah's status as Samson's mistress rather than his wife allows her to exercise considerable power in the conduct of their relationship. Then, in Section III, I will consider the Levite's concubine of Judges 19, describing the way concubinage is defined in terms of marriage in that story and explaining how the restrictions implicit in this definition dictate the woman's subordination to the Levite—and, in fact, to all the men in her life.

I. WIDOWS

Cazelles' suggestion that Mary is depicted in Matthew and Luke, at least figuratively, as the counterpart of an ancient Israelite queen mother depends primarily on these two gospels' efforts to proclaim Jesus as the "king of the Jews."[9] In Matthew, this understanding of Jesus as Israel's royal messiah, the new King David, is made evident already in the first verse of the gospel (1:1), where the evangelist introduces Jesus' genealogy by identifying him as "the son of *David,* the son of Abraham" (NRSV translation; emphasis mine). The genealogy that follows then divides Jesus' lineage into three periods, the first two of which consist of fourteen generations, as the gospel itself points out (1:17); Matt 1:17 erroneously counts fourteen generations (instead of the thirteen actually listed) in the third period as well. Since such a highly schematized lineage hardly can be taken as literal history, scholars instead assume that it has some symbolic significance, and several commentators have noted in this regard that the numerical value of *dwd,* the name of David in Hebrew, is fourteen ($d = 4$; $w = 6$; $d = 4$).[10] Matthew, they thus suggest, has deliberately structured his genealogy by "fourteens" in order to portray its final member, Jesus, as the new King David.

Matthew's understanding of Jesus as the new King David manifests itself also in 2:2–6, where the evangelist insists on Jesus' birth in Bethlehem, the town where David was born (1 Sam 17:12) and also the town from which, according to Mic 5:1 (English: 5:2), the ideal Davidic ruler will come. Luke, too, insists on Jesus' birth in Bethlehem, "because he was descended from the house and family of David" (2:4; NRSV translation). Luke's description of the annunciation to Mary is also replete with language of the Davidic monarchy, especially in 1:32–33, where the angel Gabriel promises to Mary that her child will be called Son of the Most High, that he will sit on the throne of David, that he will reign over the house of Jacob, and that his kingdom will be without end. All these phrases appear in the Hebrew Bible in texts describing the ideal Davidic king.[11] Luke elsewhere uses similar messianic language from the Hebrew Bible to speak of Jesus as the redeemer of Israel (24:21; see also Acts 1:6) and the redeemer of Jerusalem (2:38).

Cazelles' thesis next suggests that because Matthew and Luke regard Jesus as the new King David, Matthew's and Luke's Mary is to be understood, at least figuratively, as a reflection of the ancient Israelite queen mother. One of the most important pieces of evidence in support of this thesis is found in Matt 1:23, where the evangelist, in his story of Jesus' virgin birth, quotes the well-known "Immanuel" prophecy found in Isa 7:14. There, Isaiah predicts that a young woman soon will give birth to a son whom she will name Immanuel (which means "God is with us"). Relying on the Greek translation of the Hebrew Bible, which mistakenly renders the Hebrew word for "young woman" (*'almâ*) as "virgin" (*parthenos*), Matthew applies this text to Mary and to her divine son Jesus. Most commentators, however, understand that in its original context, the "young woman" of Isa 7:14 was Abi, the wife of Judah's King Ahaz, who subsequently became the queen mother of King Hezekiah.[12] Matthew's use of this "queen mother" text in reference to Mary thereby intimates an understanding that Mary should be regarded, again at least figuratively, as Jesus' "queen mother."

Another text crucial in this regard is Matt 1:1–17, the genealogy of Jesus, in which one of the four women who appears in Jesus' lineage is Bathsheba, who, as discussed in Chapter 3, is in many respects the most fully articulated and most memorable of the Hebrew Bible's queen mothers.[13] The other three women of the genealogy, moreover, while not actual queen mothers in ancient Israel (given that their stories are set during Israel's premonarchical period), are nevertheless like the Bible's queen mothers in that they are described as playing a crucial role in engendering Jerusalem's royal line. For example, the first woman mentioned, Tamar, bears Perez and Zerah by Judah, the son of Jacob who is said, in Gen 49:10, to bear the "scepter" and the "ruler's staff." The imagery of monarchy invoked here is overt. Indeed, since Judah is the eponymous ancestor of David's tribe, his wife Tamar might even be considered the archetypal "queen mother" of the Davidic house. The second woman who appears in Matthew's genealogy, Rahab, is an equally prominent ancestor of David since she is said to be the mother of Boaz,[14] and Boaz is the father of David's grandfather, Obed. Obed's mother, and thus David's great-grandmother, is Ruth, and she, not coincidentally, is the third woman named in Matthew's genealogy.[15] Then, after citing its fourth woman, Bathsheba, in verse 6, the genealogy ends in verse 16 with Mary, who, as the counterpart of these ancient Israelite "queen mothers," will bear the new David.

As "queen mother," however, even as a figurative one, we would expect Mary to wield a considerable amount of power in her son's life. In particular, given Jesus' religious mission, we might well expect that Mary would wield some of the same sorts of cultic authority that, as discussed in Chapter 3, are ascribed to her ancient counterparts in Ugaritic sources and in the Hebrew Bible. To be sure, it would be a mistake to posit too precise a parallel here since none of the more blatant Asherah imagery associated with the queen mothers of Ugarit and the Hebrew Bible is likely to be found in the uncompromisingly patriarchal and monotheistic language of the New Testament. Still, the notion that Jesus' true parents are Mary and God closely resembles the older Hebrew Bible motif whereby the queen mother represents the mother goddess, who in turn is believed to be the consort of Yahweh, the king's divine father. This correspondence prompts us to imagine a portrayal of Mary in which she, like the ancient Israelite queen mother, manifests some special association with the divine.[16] Consequently, we can conceive of an account of Jesus' life where she plays the typical queen mother role of a trusted spiritual adviser to her son. We can even envision a depiction of Mary as her son's *most* trusted spiritual adviser, given the place the ancient Israelite queen mother assumed as the second-most powerful authority in her son's royal court.

As I have already described, however, the "queen mother" Mary is depicted in the New Testament as anything but Jesus' most valued religious counselor, and this is because of a crucial difference between the New Testament conception of Mary and the Hebrew Bible's depictions of its queen mothers. In the Hebrew Bible, the queen mother's son, in addition to his divine sire Yahweh, had a human father, the king who was queen mother's husband. It was, moreover, only when this old king died that the queen mother assumed a position of power and authority in her son's court. But the New Testament "king" Jesus does not have a human father to speak of (only his adopted parent, Joseph), and his divine father, God, is eternal. Thus Mary, in contradistinction to the queen mothers of the Hebrew Bible, does not become—*and can never become*—a royal widow. Hence she cannot be depicted similarly to her Hebrew Bible predecessors, as a queen mother who exercises power and authority during the course of her son's adult life.

But why is widowhood so crucial? At issue is the biblical ideal concerning the organization and the operation of the patriarchal family unit. According to this ideal, women in the biblical tradition, during both the Hebrew Bible and New Testament periods, were conceived of as subject to their closest male kin. Hebrew Bible law even goes so far as to mandate this sort of arrangement, thus giving it the imprimatur of divine command. Israel's God, the legal texts of the Bible proclaim, requires of a young girl that she submit to the authority of her father before she is married or, if her father is deceased, to the authority of her brothers. In particular, a father and brothers are ordered to restrain a young woman's sexual activities in order to ensure that her virginity is safeguarded until the time of her marriage (Deut 22:13–21, 28–29). Then, with marriage, when a woman moves into the home of her husband, the legal traditions insist that she assume a place under this man's hegemony, a hegemony that also is said to concern itself primarily with restricting "improper" sexual behavior. Numbers 5:11–31 illustrates by describing how a wife "under her husband's authority" (*taḥat 'îšāh*) is said to "go astray" (*śāṭāh*) and to "defile herself" (*niṭmā'*) if she commits adultery.

A widow, however, is a woman perceived of by the tradition as living outside these strictures of the patriarchal household, having long since left the hegemony of her father and brothers behind, yet no longer having a husband who keeps her bound to his authority. The Bible's authors thus can and do imagine such women as acting with an independence and autonomy not readily available to Israel's daughters, sisters, and wives.[17] A small, but telling example comes again from the Bible's legal codes, in Num 30:3–15. This text concerns the role of women in Israel's religious life and in particular addresses the validity of a woman's religious vow. For the most part, the passage describes how a vow or a pledge made by a woman who is either a daughter or a wife is not inevitably binding, but, if deemed necessary, it can be nullified by the woman's father or by her husband, respectively. According to verse 9, though, a vow made by a widow always remains her obligation, for the widowed woman acts as an autonomous religious agent, independent of male supervision. She thus is held accountable for her own decisions.[18]

The case of the queen mother illustrates the same point even more dramatically. Because she is widowed, the tradition can envision this woman as able to exercise a significant amount of independence and autonomy and thus able to exert considerable influence in managing the political, economic, and religious affairs of her son's court. Note, however, that this ability is *not* depicted as available to a queen before she is widowed. Bathsheba, for example, although described in the Bible as an especially influential queen mother, is not portrayed as wielding any sort of public power before her husband David's death.[19] In fact, Gale A. Yee has argued that quite the opposite is the case, that whenever Bathsheba appears in the narrative before the scene of David's death found in I Kings 1–2, she is a character completely shrouded in ambiguity.[20] Even 2 Samuel 11, the infamous episode of Bathsheba's and David's adulterous affair, offers no comment about Bathsheba's nature or concerning her feelings or motivations. Adele Berlin goes so far as to describe Bathsheba in this scene as a "complete non-person,"[21] merely an "agent" necessary for plot development rather than being a character in her own right.[22] Only when she is widowed in I Kings 1–2 does Bathsheba emerge as a full-fledged personality.[23]

Nor is Bathsheba unique in this regard. Strikingly, while the archival records of all but two of the kings of Judah record the name of the king's queen mother as part of the royal annals,[24] none mentions the name of a queen.[25] This suggests that the pattern implied in the Bathsheba story holds throughout the biblical period. Only when widowhood frees a royal woman from the authority of her husband the king can the tradition describe for her a position of public responsibility and public power in her son's court.[26] For the "queen mother" Mary, however, this sort of widowhood never happens. Hence her narrators leave her in the background throughout their accounts of her son's career rather than allowing her to step forward and act in the public arena of Jesus' ministry.

II. PROSTITUTES AND DELILAH

In the Hebrew Bible, in addition to the widow, there are a few other types of women who are imagined as being able to act independently of the hegemony of a father, brothers, or husband. The divorced woman, for example, is a woman who, like the widow, is understood to have left the household of her father and brothers behind but who, with the dissolution of her marriage, is no longer seen as subject to the authority of her husband.[27] She thus can be described as acting autonomously, and, notably, in Num 30:3–15, the law code describing the validity of women's religious vows, the divorced woman is the one woman in addition to the widow of whom it is said that her vow cannot be nullified by the decree of a man. Rather, it always remains her obligation (v 9). The legal tradition also seems to believe that a divorced woman who enters into a second marriage can be allowed to arrange this on her own, without relying on the mediation of her father or brothers. This is at least hinted at in Deut 24:1–3, where a law concerning the divorced woman's taking of a second husband makes no mention of any man being involved in the arrangements. Conversely, in the case of a first marriage, a woman's nuptials are routinely depicted as arranged for her by her father or, if he is dead or otherwise unable to act, by her brothers.[28]

Yet at the same time that Deut 24:1–3 hints at the autonomy accorded to the divorced woman in the arranging of her second marriage, the text also acknowledges—simply by admitting the possibility of these subsequent nuptials—that a divorced woman might voluntarily put aside her postmarital status of autonomy and willingly reenter a situation of male hegemony. Leviticus 22:13 testifies to much the same, describing how a priest's daughter who is divorced, or one who has been widowed, might voluntarily rejoin the household of her father. The notion that a widowed daughter might voluntarily put aside autonomy in order to rejoin the household of her father is also found in the book of Ruth. There, the two widowed daughters-in-law of Naomi, Ruth and Orpah, appear to gain considerable independence after the deaths of their husbands Mahlon and Chilion (they seem free to move from place to place according to their own desires, for example, and Ruth is eventually able to court her second husband Boaz in ways impossible for a woman under the control of a man). Nevertheless, in Ruth 1:8, Naomi urges these two women to forgo their freedom to return to their childhood homes.[29] Naomi, too, who has also been widowed, chooses to return to her hometown of Bethlehem after her husband's death, despite the fact that this brings her back into her family's orbit and thus potentially back into her male kin's control.

What underlies these various accounts is an issue that, from our point of view, might even be described as the paradox of the Bible's widowed and divorced women's traditions: that, while a woman who is widowed or divorced can be imagined by the biblical authors as being freed from the hegemony of her husband, father, and brothers, she is also often envisioned by the tradition as suffering from the lack of financial support that her husband, father, and/or brothers were previously able to provide.[30] This means that the economic situations of the widow and the divorcée are perceived to be precarious, and hence the portrayals in Leviticus, Deuteronomy, and Ruth of widowed and divorced women who rejoin the houses of their fathers or find new husbands in order to ensure their financial security. This is particularly indicated in the Lev 22:13 passage, where the point of the law mentioning the priest's widowed or divorced daughter is to describe how this daughter, if she returns to her childhood home, reacquires access to a food source that had been available to her prior to her marriage, the sacrificial offerings that are the sustenance of her father. The author of Ruth also seems to be thinking of the financial needs of Naomi's daughters-in-law by having her urge Orpah and Ruth to return to their childhood homes and to seek, through these homes, new marriages. The text's choice of words is the crucial datum here: "May Yahweh grant that you find *security*," Naomi says, "each of you in the house of her husband" (Ruth 1:9; emphasis mine).[31] As the story goes, though, Ruth resists Naomi's urgings and instead returns with her mother-in-law to Judah. Yet this does not mean that the narrative's concern in regard to Ruth's financial well-being is eased. In Ruth 3:1, Naomi again announces that it is necessary to seek "security" for Ruth,[32] and so begin the mother-in-law's machinations that end with the marriage of Ruth and Boaz.[33]

Thus, while widowhood and divorce were believed theoretically to release women from the strictures of patriarchal supervision that had previously dominated their lives, the tradition simultaneously suggests that the realities of sustenance and need could so constrain many of these women that they must be depicted as voluntarily reentering the household of a male authority. In fact, it is only widowed and divorced women with some source of independent financial support at hand who can be portrayed in the Bible as fully able to avail themselves of the opportunity to act outside the purview of male hegemony.[34] A perfect example of this is found, again, in the accounts of ancient Israel's queen mothers, whose elevated economic status is an obvious corollary of their royal rank. The widow Judith is likewise described in Judith 8 as wealthy (v 7), and consequently, I would argue, she is depicted in Judith 9–16 as a woman who is able over and over again to assert herself autonomously and independent of male authority. As discussed in Chapter 1, this means she is able to engage the elders of her town about her plan to save Bethulia (8:9–36) and go forth on her own to wage her one-woman battle against Holofernes (9:1–15:7). Also, according to Judith 16, it is within her rights to dedicate her portion of this battle's booty in whatever way she sees fit (v 19); to free her maid (v 23); and to determine by herself how her estate is to be distributed after her death (v 24). Note, moreover, that according to 16:22, although many men desired to marry Judith subsequent to her victory over the Assyrians, she refused them all. This is a luxury allowed her by her affluence. Contrast the depictions of Orpah and Ruth, who, lacking such riches, are urged by Naomi to return to their birth families and to seek through them new husbands—and renewed security.

There is one more sort of woman whom the biblical tradition depicts both as living outside the strictures of a patriarchal household and as able to sustain herself financially while doing so: the prostitute.[35] The way Rahab, the prostitute (*zōnâ*) of Joshua 2 and 6, is described by the biblical authors is particularly telling in this regard.

Joshua 2:1 sets the scene. The tribes of Israel are encamped at Shittim, a site across the Jordan River from Jericho, preparing to attack the city. As part of his initial reconnaissance before mounting this offensive, Joshua, the commander of the Israelite army, sends two spies to Jericho to scout out the lay of the land. They house themselves at the brothel of Rahab, the prostitute, and, even though the king of Jericho gets wind of their presence and demands of Rahab that she turn the spies over to him (vv 2–3), Rahab protects the two Israelites, hiding them on the rooftop of her house and then lowering them down through a window so that they can escape from the city (vv 6, 15).[36] She exacts from them a vow, however, that when Israel returns to conquer Jericho, she and her family will be spared (vv 12–14). The two spies agree, and, in Josh 6:22–25, although Jericho has been taken and completely destroyed, Rahab and her family are brought forth from the city to live among the Israelite people.

For the biblical authors, the point of this story has to do with Rahab's faithfulness to Israel's God: she accepts and acknowledges that it is Yahweh's will that Israel take Jericho and so she works for Joshua and against her king in order to bring about an Israelite victory.[37] For our purposes, however, what is important to note is the story's depiction of the prostitute Rahab as a woman able to function autonomously within Jericho's society. For example, Rahab is said to have her own house (2:1, 3, 18, 19; 6:17, 22), and, since the point is made that she must gather her family there when the Israelites attack (2:18), the text seems to imagine that she normally lives in this house independent of the company—and of the authority—of her father and/or brothers. Her ability to function

independently also is indicated in 2:3, where the representatives of the
king of Jericho who seek the Israelite spies are said to deal directly with
Rahab rather than through a male intermediary. Finally, note that, as she
enters into her agreement—or what might even be called a treaty—
with the two Israelites whom she shelters, Rahab is envisioned as able
to act as an equal partner in this transaction, trading, as the men say,
"Our life for yours" (2:14).[38]

A second text that indicates the way in which the Bible's authors
assume the prostitute's ability to act independent of male authority is
found in Genesis 38, the story of Tamar. In fact, this story is particularly
interesting given my concerns in this chapter since Tamar, in addition
to being depicted in the guise of a prostitute in verses 12–19, is elsewhere
in the text (vv 7–11 and 20–26) said to embody one of the other major
categories of an independent woman I have been considering, the
widow. Tamar's widowed status, however, is not fully analogous to
the examples of, say, the biblical queen mothers, for Tamar belongs to a
special category of widow, the widow constrained by levirate law.[39]

The levirate law concerning widowhood addresses a very specific
problem: the widow who did not, during her marriage, bear a son to
her husband. There is thus no heir to preserve the husband's chain of
patrilineal descent, although in Israelite society, this is a concern of para-
mount importance.[40] Levirate law responds by requiring that a sonless
widow marry her deceased husband's brother so that through him she
might bear a child to carry on the dead man's name (Deut 25:5–6). In
the case of Tamar, levirate law requires that she mate with Onan, who
is the next-oldest brother of her dead husband Er. Onan, however, resists
begetting a child who would continue his brother's bloodline rather than
his own and so refuses to impregnate Tamar. As a consequence, he is
put to death by Yahweh. The brothers' father, Judah, then commands
Tamar to "remain a widow" until his third son, Shelah, grows up and is
old enough to marry and get Tamar with child (Gen 38:11).[41]

The fact that Tamar is to "remain a widow" for only a circumscribed
period of time, and a period of time, moreover, that is defined by a man,
already indicates the text's assumption that because she did not bear a
son to Er, Tamar is not a widow of the ilk of Judith, say, and so cannot
be allowed to go forth and act with the same sorts of autonomy and
independence that the tradition elsewhere allows widows to exercise. In
fact, Judah continues his dictum to Tamar by very specifically telling her
that she should remain a widow "in her father's house" (v 11), thus

conveying the narrative's insistence that as a widow whose levirate obligations are unfulfilled, Tamar must continue to be subject to male authority. Judah, however, is also described as having no intention of ever resolving the "betwixt and between" status that Tamar's levirate widowhood implies, for, as verses 12–14 of the story make clear, even when years have passed and Shelah has grown up, Tamar is still not given to him in marriage. Male authority thus has failed in its responsibility to provide for Tamar the means by which she can fulfill her levirate obligations. Tamar is consequently placed in a position where she must take matters into her own hands.

What basis of power, however, can Tamar have on which to act? Not that of an autonomous widow since her widowhood is constrained by the requirements of levirate law. The narrative thus has her assume the guise of one of the few other sorts of women who can be depicted as exercising independence within Israelite society, the prostitute. Her goal is to seduce Judah and so become impregnated by him, using his child to fulfill her levirate responsibilities and to preserve Er's patriarchal line. The strategy works: Judah, deceived by her disguise, believes her to be a prostitute and "comes in to her" (v 18) to receive her sexual favors. Tamar then becomes pregnant by Judah and eventually bears twins, Perez and Zerah, the ancestors of David whom I mentioned above.

What is notable for our purposes here is the considerable autonomy the narrator has Judah accord Tamar during his encounter with her as a prostitute. Judah, for example, acknowledges Tamar to be his equal in a business transaction, thus agreeing to deposit with her a pledge—his signet, cord, and staff—until he can send the agreed-upon payment for her services, a kid from his flock. The parallel to the bargaining scene in the Rahab story is most striking. Also striking is to compare this passage to a verse earlier in the Tamar story, Gen 38:14. In that text, in which Tamar is presented as a powerless levirate widow, Judah seems to feel he has no obligation to honor his promise to her concerning Shelah. But when he subsequently deals with her in her guise as a prostitute, Judah appears to believe that Tamar is worthy of his respect and that he must be true to his word. Consequently, in verse 20, Judah sends to Tamar the contracted-upon kid.[42]

As the story goes, though, Tamar does not linger to receive her fee; instead, once pregnant, she trades her prostitute's veil for her widow's garb and, simultaneously, from the story's perspective, discards a prostitute's autonomy to reassume the encumbrances placed upon her as a levirate widow.[43] Not coincidentally, Judah's interactions with her once this switch takes place are depicted as they were in the story's earlier "widowhood" scenes. He treats her as subservient, requiring her to submit to the authority he wields as her father-in-law. Indeed, the text explicitly labels Tamar as Judah's "daughter-in-law" at this point (v 24) and by so doing leaves no doubts about her return to an inferior status.[44] Judah's response, once Tamar's pregnancy is discovered, also leaves no doubts about Tamar's resumption of a subordinate role, as Judah prepares to kill Tamar by burning, so incensed is he by her apparent defiance of his right to regulate her sexual activities. It is only when Judah discovers that he is the father of Tamar's child and that Tamar had schemed to become pregnant by him in order to preserve her husband's patriarchal line that he admits that the woman's actions were justified and that her death sentence is revoked.

Note, moreover, the respect with which Judah is said to address Tamar in this final scene of revocation, as he proclaims, "she is more righteous than I" (v 26). His tone of voice here has shifted yet again and now recalls the respect Judah was said to accord Tamar when she was disguised as a prostitute. This, it turns out, is only proper. Since Tamar is pregnant, the levirate responsibilities that have restricted her in her widowhood are well underway to being fulfilled. Tamar is thus on the verge of moving forward from her position of constraint to being able to exercise the independence available to her as an unencumbered widow. The narrator uses Judah's respect-filled words to signal the imminence of this transition.[45] Signaling this transition is also what underlies the concluding half-verse of the story, "And he did not lie with her again." At first glance, this line, which comes just after Judah's earnest evocation of Tamar's righteousness, might seem anticlimactic. But its point is that Tamar, having now fulfilled her obligations to Judah's family, can move beyond the orbit (and the beds) of that family's men. She prepares, that is, to assume for good the autonomy already adumbrated in her prostitution scene.[46]

In the book of Judges, two women are identified as prostitutes, the mother of Jephthah, who is mentioned in Judg 11:1, and the Gazaite prostitute, with whom Samson lies in Judg 16:1–3. Unfortunately, however, neither of these women is described at length. The Gazaite prostitute in particular is overshadowed by Samson's two other women companions, Samson's Timnite wife, who appears in 14:1–20, and Delilah, whose story is told in 16:4–22.

Still, even though the language of prostitution is never applied to either of these two women, the second of them, Delilah, in her role as Samson's mistress, is depicted in the text as very prostitute-like in her behavior. John B. Vickery even goes so far as to call her "a whore at heart."[47] This is because, like a prostitute, she uses her sexuality and a man's desire for her in order to ensure her own well-being.[48] More specifically, Delilah entices Samson to reveal to her that it is his uncut hair that is the secret of his godlike strength.[49] She then sells this information to his Philistine enemies in exchange for eleven hundred pieces of silver from each of their hands. Delilah's actions here should be compared both to the acts of the "prostitute" Tamar as she seduces Judah in order to achieve her desired state of pregnancy and, especially, to those of the prostitute Rahab, who exacts her bargain with the Israelite spies after they "enter" (*bôʾ*) her brothel and "spend the night" (*šākab*). As discussed in Chapter 1, both these verbs have a sexual connotation, indicating that Rahab, like Delilah, barters sexual pleasures for her own well-being and security.[50]

Other data also suggest the similarities between Delilah's role as Samson's mistress and Rahab's role as a prostitute. First, note that Judges 16 provides very little identifying information about Delilah. For example, although she works in conjunction with Samson's Philistine enemies, the text does not specify whether she herself is Philistine or Israelite. More important, it does not describe her family allegiances. While it may seem that the effect of this silence is to disempower Delilah by rendering her nearly anonymous, the text's lack of genealogical data in fact is meant to stress exactly the opposite: Delilah is a woman who is not defined by a relationship to a man. Instead, Delilah has her own name and, consequently, an independent identity. In the Rahab story, Rahab also has her own name and, as we have seen, an independent identity. In fact, in the Rahab story, Rahab's identity so dominates that, in striking contrast to the biblical norm, the men of Rahab's family are identified solely by their relationship to *her:* they are "*her* father" and "*her* brothers" (Josh 6:23; similarly, 2:13, 18; emphasis mine). The text's point here has to do with control: through her actions, Rahab controls her own destiny as well as that of her family members. She alone thus bears a name. While in the Delilah story, this delineation between "named" female protagonist and "nameless" male kin is not so clearly articulated, it is still the case that Delilah is the *only* woman of the four in the Samson saga who bears a name rather than being identified as Samson's mother (13:2–24), wife (14:1–20), or object of his sexual desire (16:1–3).[51] Through this language of identification versus anonymity, the tradition signals its sense of Delilah's autonomous status. The text thereby recognizes her ability to function outside the strictures of male authority.[52]

Delilah's ability to function outside patriarchal strictures is even more vividly illustrated by contrasting the actions of Delilah in Judg 16:4–22 to those attributed to one of the saga's unnamed women, Samson's Timnite wife, described in 14:1–20. This comparison is especially telling for, as is frequently noted, the plots of these two stories are transparently the same:[53] women beguile Samson into revealing a secret in order that the Philistines can use this information in their fight against him. Delilah, as I have already noted, persuades Samson to reveal the secret of his godlike strength; the Timnite woman similarly induces Samson to divulge the answer to his enigmatic lion-and-honey riddle. Both then share their privy knowledge with Samson's Philistine enemies so that the Philistines might entrap him.

There are, in addition, several quite specific parallels between the two stories. The story of the Timnite wife opens with a setting in the "vineyards of Timnah" (14:5); the Delilah story similarly commences by setting the scene in the "Valley of Sorek" or the "Valley of Choice Vines" (16:4). As the main action of the two stories begins, both women are urged by the Philistines to "coax" (*pattî*) Samson's secret from him (14:15; 16:5), and both use almost identical arguments about love in order to weaken Samson's resolve ("You do not love me," says the Timnite wife in 14:16; "How can you say that you love me?" asks Delilah in 16:15).[54] When these arguments seem to have no effect, both subsequently "nag" or "press upon" Samson in order to get the information they want (*hĕṣîqathû* in 14:17; *hēṣîqâ lô* in 16:16), and in response in both cases, he finally "tells" them the secret they had sought to uncover (*wayyagged-lāh:* 14:17; 16:17).[55] Both women, moreover, suffer three failed attempts before provoking this revelation. In the case of the Timnite wife, the Philistines are said to come to her on the fourth day of her wedding feast and set her on her task of enticement (14:15).[56] Yet according to 14:17, Samson does not reveal the answer to his riddle until the seventh day of the banqueting, implying that the wife tried to persuade him to speak on days four, five, and six but was rebuffed. The Delilah story is more explicit: Samson lied to Delilah three times before finally divulging the secret of his great strength. He first told her his might could be overcome if he were bound by seven fresh bowstrings (16:7), then claimed he could be subdued if bound with new ropes (16:11), and next suggested he could be overpowered if seven locks of his hair were tightly woven and pinned into the fabric of her loom (16:13).[57] Only after all these statements are proved false does Samson finally reveal to Delilah the true secret of his Nazirite vow (16:17).

The biblical tradition's point in amassing all these parallels is essentially to *force* us to read the stories of the Timnite wife and of Delilah as paired. Yet, as is often the case in the Bible's narratives, the text's ultimate aim in drawing our attention to the two stories' similarities is to highlight all the more vividly the differences between them.[58] In particular, Judges 14 and 16 seek to stress the ways in which they crucially diverge in their characterizations of their two women actors. Because the Timnite woman is a wife, a woman who operates very much within a world of male hegemony, Judges 14 treats her almost as incidental in the telling of her tale. She functions in the story's action primarily as an object. She is first the object of Samson's desire (14:1–4), then the object of an arranged marriage (implied in 14:2, 3, and 10), and finally the object of her countrymen's stratagem to entrap Samson (14:15). She is only subject—that is, one who speaks and takes action in the narrative—in two verses (14:16–17). Delilah, however, is a woman who is unmarried and who otherwise lives a life independent of male authority. Consequently, she can be depicted as the primary subject of 16:4–22. It is Delilah, then, who binds Samson with bowstrings and then with new ropes, it is she who weaves seven locks of his hair into her loom, and it is she who has his head shaved as he lies in her lap, all in an effort to overcome his God-given strength.[59] The man, Samson, is the object in this account, so much a passive agent that he is presented almost as a mannequin, making no response when Delilah binds him with bowstrings and ropes and sleeping soundly through first the weaving and then the shaving of his hair.[60]

We can further appreciate the empowered position of Delilah in Judges 16 by comparing her story to another of the stories of Samson's women, the Judges 13 tale of Manoah's wife.[61] Indeed, the authors of Judges again seem to intend for us to read these two narratives as paired. Danna Nolan Fewell has pointed out the crucial piece of evidence in this regard, the words with which Samson reveals the secret of his uncut hair to Delilah, "No razor has touched my head, for I have been a Nazirite to God from the womb of my *mother*" (Judg 16:17; emphasis mine).[62] This statement—almost a verbatim repetition of the words the angel spoke to Manoah's wife in 13:5[63]—ties together the mother, who first cradled the newborn Samson, bald, between her legs, and the lover, who ultimately betrays Samson as he lies, balded, between hers.[64] Note also the way in which Judg 16:16–17, which reports that Samson eventually told Delilah his Nazirite secret after her nagging had "tired him to death," evokes memories of 13:7, where his mother reports to her husband the messenger's promise that Samson would be a Nazirite "until the day of his death." Particularly significant here is that "death" in Judg 13:7 is language associated with the *mother* only. That is, in his proclamation in verse 5, the divine messenger had decreed only that Samson should be a Nazirite "from the womb"; the mother takes it upon herself to add in verse 7 that Samson's Nazirite vow shall endure until he dies.

As was the case in comparing the Timnite woman and Delilah stories, however, it is the *differences* between the depictions of Manoah's wife and Delilah in their twinned tales that are ultimately more significant than are the motifs that bind the two narratives together. Once more, what we see are divergences over issues of autonomy and over the exercise of power. I have already discussed in Chapter 2 how this matter is addressed in Judges 13: that, while the text does describe some intimations of power for Manoah's wife, it eventually, by confining her to the domestic sphere, by rendering her nameless, by having her defer to the authority of her husband, and by co-opting her participation in an agenda of patrilineal descent, subsumes whatever autonomy she may possess under the hegemony of Manoah. Delilah, conversely, unconstrained by a relationship with a man, is able both to assume a position of authority from the very beginning of her story and, by its end, to accrue even more power to herself.

In fact, when we read the tales of Judges 13 and 16 in tandem, they almost suggest a transfer of power, so that whatever power Manoah's wife was able to claim temporarily in Judges 13 is, by the climactic scene of Judges 16, delivered into the hands of her son's mistress. The key here is to realize that the power Delilah is able to acquire in Judges 16 comes from her taking from Samson the secret of his uncut hair. Yet previously in the Samson saga, the only person other than Samson who had been said to know of this privy matter was his mother. Note in particular that in the Judges 13 birth narrative, when Manoah's wife reports to her husband the original words of the angel's annunciation in verse 7, she tells him only—as the angel had said to her in verse 4—that she is to drink no wine nor strong drink nor is she to eat anything unclean while she is pregnant. She does not, however, repeat the angel's injunction of verse 5, that no razor is to touch Samson's head once he has been born. Also the angel, when he speaks directly to Manoah in verse 14, mentions only the prohibitions against the wife's consuming wine, strong drink, and unclean food. The uncut hair goes unremarked, a secret articulated only to Manoah's wife and presumably, as he grows up, to Samson.[65]

Furthermore, although the terms of the Nazirite vow outlined in Num 6:1–21 suggest that Samson, like his mother, should have been required to abstain from strong drink, and that he should also have avoided coming into contact with a corpse, it is the uncut hair that must be understood as the crucial element of Samson's Nazirite strength. In fact, the uncut hair seems to be the *only* Nazirite element that really matters in the Samson saga since Samson is repeatedly depicted as breaking the other dicta presumably required of him: he seems to drink wine (which surely was served at the festal banquet celebrating his marriage; 14:10–17),[66] and, in his multiple slaughterings of his Philistine enemies, he must have come into contact with a corpse (14:19 and 15:15). In addition, he engages in other clearly unorthodox behavior, eating unclean food (honey that came from a lion's carcass; 14:9) and entering into multiple liaisons with "foreign" women (his Timnite wife, the Gazaite prostitute, and, possibly, Delilah). None of this seems to matter, however, for as long as Samson keeps his hair unshorn, God stays with him throughout his adventures.[67]

Knowledge, Judges 16 implies, is power. As long as the secret of his uncut hair was safe with his mother, so was Samson. But when Delilah solves the mystery of Samson's might, she is able to claim his great strength for herself. In the end, then, the man who previously had been the master of all challenges is mastered by a woman, and the Philistines whom Samson theretofore had conquered become his conquerors.[68]

III. THE LEVITE'S CONCUBINE

In Judg 19:1, we are introduced to a woman described as a *pîlegeš*, usually translated as a "concubine" of a Levite who lives in the isolated reaches of the tribal territory of Ephraim. What the text means, though, when it identifies this woman as a "concubine" is not necessarily clear, for elsewhere in the Bible the term "concubine" either can mean a woman who is a part of a man's harem but is not one of his actual wives, or it can mean a woman who is married to a man as a secondary wife.[69] Only in verse 3, where we are told that the Levite is the woman's husband (*'îšāh*), and also in verses 4, 7, and 9, where the woman's father is called the Levite's father-in-law (*ḥōtĕnô*), does it become clear that the "concubine" of verse 1 is the Levite's secondary wife.[70]

Understanding this distinction is important, for my thesis in this chapter suggests that if the Levite's woman companion were envisioned by the biblical tradition as the other sort of concubine—a woman who was unmarried but in a mistress-type relationship with a man—she could be depicted in her story as assuming a considerable amount of autonomy and authority. Such is the case, for example, in 2 Sam 15:16, when King David, forced to flee from Jerusalem because of the coup being mounted by his son, Absalom, took his entire entourage with him except for ten concubines. These women—who were presumably not counted among David's wives (see 2 Sam 5:13 and 19:6 [English 19:5], where David's concubines and wives are distinguished)[71]—were left behind to oversee the palace. This suggests a very powerful position for them in the royal court, recalling as it does the role of regent that the queen mother, the woman otherwise most powerful in the king's court, is said to fill when her son is away from his throne. Note also in this regard 2 Sam 21:10–14, where Rizpah, the "concubine" (but presumably not "wife") of King Saul (Saul's wife, according to 1 Sam 14:50, was Ahinoam, daughter of Ahimaaz), was able to bring about the proper burial of Saul's bones and of those of his son Jonathan after these two men had died. Again, what is suggested is a concubine who commands a significant degree of power.

In a narrative like Judges 19, however, where the concubine is depicted as a wife, and even more so as a wife of secondary rank, we would expect her to be described much differently: as a woman subject to her husband's control and as answerable to his directives. And, in fact, indications of the concubine's subservient status are found throughout the Judges 19 text. This woman, for example, is not given a name by the tradition, and as I now have had occasion to mention several times—in both this chapter, for instance, and in my discussions in Chapter 2 of Jephthah's daughter, of Manoah's wife, and of Micah's mother—namelessness is a significant marker of a woman's subordination in the biblical text.[72] Moreover, in striking distinction to, say, Delilah, whose more autonomous, mistress-type relationship with Samson I discussed in Section II above, the Levite's concubine does not *once* utter a word in her story.[73] Even the Levite's servant, who is said to address his master in verse 11, is treated by the biblical authors better than this. The narrative's point is clear: despite the initial ambiguities raised by the use of the word "concubine" in Judg 19:1, the Levite's woman companion is meant to be understood throughout Judges 19 as a concubine who is a secondary wife, bound to the Levite through ties of marriage. Biblical tradition consequently resists portraying her as having any ability to act independently and autonomously.

Indeed, as the Judges 19 story unfolds, we find that its entire plot concerns the concubine's inability to exert any control over her own fate. In verse 2, immediately following the introduction of the Levite and the woman in verse 1, the narrative describes how the woman spurns the Levite, leaving his home in Ephraim to return to the house of her father in Bethlehem in the tribal territory of Judah.[74] This may seem an act of autonomy,[75] but the woman quickly finds that she is answerable to men for her actions, as her husband, according to verse 3, comes to Bethlehem at the end of four months to fetch her.[76] The concubine's father, moreover, raises no objections to the Levite's mission; indeed, he greets his son-in-law with joy. As the story continues, the two men are portrayed as getting along famously, sharing food and drink aplenty for three days, and then for a fourth day and a fifth, as the Levite is urged by his father-in-law to stay and to enjoy himself further. The woman is entirely absent during this feast, reappearing only at the end of the fifth day, when the Levite finally takes her and his servant and leaves. Does she want to go? It does not seem to matter. Her husband has appeared in Bethlehem to claim his right to her, and her father graciously, and by all indications willingly, sends her along.[77] Whatever autonomy she had sought to manifest in running away in the first place is easily quashed.

The next scene in the story is no happier for the concubine. Because the Levite's party has left Bethlehem late in the day, they come only as far as the village of Gibeah in the tribal territory of Benjamin before it is time to stop for the night. Initially, the group has trouble finding lodging in Gibeah, but eventually, an old man from Ephraim who is sojourning among the Benjaminites takes them in. What follows is a variation on the well-known Sodom and Gomorrah story of Genesis 19.[78] The Benjaminites come to the house of the Ephraimite and demand that the Levite be sent out into the streets so that they can "know him," that is, so that they can subject him to homosexual rape.[79] The old Ephraimite, adhering to the rules of Near Eastern hospitality, refuses to send the man forth, but he does offer the Benjaminites his virgin daughter and the Levite's concubine instead. "Ravish them," he says, "and do to them whatever you want" (19:24). The theme of male authority exerts itself here once more: as one father had already sent his daughter forth from his house and back to a marriage of which she evidently did not want to be a part, the old Ephraimite father now volunteers to send his virgin daughter into the Benjaminites' hands to be raped. He also volunteers to send forth his guest's secondary wife, indicating that the stress on male hegemony is so pervasive in this story that even a woman who is not directly under the authority of this particular man can still be subject to his will.[80] The Levite, note, raises no objection when the Ephraimite makes his offer.

Instead, in the next verse, when the Benjaminites refuse to take the women and presumably begin pressuring the Ephraimite again to send out the Levite, the Levite himself takes his concubine and thrusts her out into the street. From our point of view, this seems a rather incomprehensible action since the Levite has, after all, just gone to a significant amount of trouble to recover this woman from her father's house. But the episode demonstrates vividly the completely subservient character of the woman in this story. She is a pawn in the hands of men, and, like a pawn on a chess board, she is valuable only up to a point.[81] If it becomes necessary, the man in control of her movements is willing to sacrifice her in the interest of protecting his more important pieces, in this case, himself.[82]

The sacrifice is a bloody one. According to verses 25–26, the Benjaminites rape and abuse the woman all the night and let her go only with the dawn, at which point she collapses at the door of the Ephraimite's house. The text describes the place as "the door of the house of the man where her master was," and the words "her master" (*'ădōnêhâ*) are significant since they almost embody in shorthand the point of this story: men's mastery over the women who are under their control.[83] This mastery, moreover, seems to continue even once a woman is deceased, for in verses 28–30, after the Levite finds his wife dead on the doorstoop, he still finds a way to use her to suit his own purposes.[84] He slings her body onto his donkey and continues on his journey to Ephraim. When he gets to his home, however, he does not—as one might expect—bury the woman but rather cuts up her body into twelve pieces and sends a piece to each of the twelve tribes of Israel. His point is to use these cut-up body parts to signal to the tribes that they should gather in assembly. There, the Levite hopes, all Israel will decree a punishment against the Benjaminites because of that tribe's heinous acts. And, according to Judg 20:1, all of the tribes of Israel, excepting Benjamin, do gather at the town of Mizpah to hear the Levite's charge.

For those of us who know the story of Judges 19, however, the charge presented at Mizpah is a little unexpected, for as Judg 20:4–5 make clear, the Levite, when he spells out to the assembly the nature of Benjamin's atrocity, views the issue primarily in terms of his own self-interest.[85] *His* life was threatened, he claims (which is not true: it was his right to consensual sex that was threatened),[86] and *his* concubine was raped until she died. Any culpability the Levite himself has in sending the woman out the door goes unmentioned, for in the mind-set that defines the patriarchal family unit, no culpability is there. The Levite has been threatened, and what we might even think of as his "property rights"—his right to control the sexual activities of his wife—have been violated. The Benjaminites deserve punishment not for what was done to the woman, but for the acts they undertook against the rights of the man.[87]

Two of Judges' longer stories about women thus stand ironically juxta-posed. Both describe women—Delilah and the Levite's concubine—who wish to assume power for themselves in their relationships with their male lovers. Both stories begin, moreover, with hints that these women's goals may be accomplished. By presenting Delilah, Samson's mistress, as Vickery's "whore at heart," Judges 16 allows us to imagine her as able to exert the sorts of autonomy available to prostitutes else-where in the Hebrew Bible and so able to render her will supreme in her relationship with Samson. The introduction of the Levite's woman companion as a "concubine" in Judg 19:1 similarly permits us to con-sider the possibility that this woman could exploit the mistress-like inde-pendence available to an unmarried concubine in order to take herself up and away from the Levite's domination. But, as the description of the concubine's leave-taking in Judg 19:2 turns in verses 3, 4, 7, and 9 to specify that this woman's status as concubine is that of secondary wife, any expectations we might have had about her exercising a right to self-determination disappear. The Levite's concubine, that is, is introduced in verse 1 with intimations about her possible role as an unmarried mistress only to make clear the degree to which she will in fact be mastered over by men. By the third verse of her story, we learn that she is really the Levite's wife and thus lacks the ability to take control of her own life. Instead, she is captive to the men who surround her, first her Levite husband, then her Judahite father, and next her Ephraimite host. Finally, she is captive to the Benjaminites, who signal her subservient status within their society by leaving her body ravaged and dead in the midst of their streets.

NOTES

[1] Mark 3:31–35.

[2] Commentators, in fact, often claim that of the three synoptic gospels, Luke is the *most* neglectful of Mary. See, for example, Hans Conzelmann, *The Theology of Saint Luke* (New York: Harper & Row, 1961), 172, who writes, "Mary disappears to a greater extent in Luke than in Mark and Matthew," and W. Barnes Tatum, "The Epoch of Israel: Luke I–II and the Theological Plan of Luke-Acts," *NTS* 13 (1966–67), 184: "St Luke pushes Mary further into the background than do the other synoptic evangelists."

[3] Mary is named as the mother of Jesus in Matt 13:55, but she does not appear as a character in that pericope.

[4] Matthew also shares with Luke the sense that these women present at the crucifixion had been a part of Jesus' entourage for a long time, since the beginnings of his ministry in the Galilee (27:55). This sentiment is found in Mark, too (15:41), and, in addition, Mark reports that women are well represented at the cross events in general (15:40–41, 47; 16:1–8). This tradition similarly appears in John (19:25–27; 20:1–10). John, moreover, contrary to Matthew, Mark, and Luke, depicts Mary as being present at the crucifixion, and he even describes Jesus as speaking with her (19:25–27). Still, John basically suggests for Mary the same minor role envisioned elsewhere. For example, although John describes numerous resurrection appearances of Jesus to the disciples and to Jesus' other devoted followers, he is silent when it comes to describing whether the resurrected Jesus appeared to his mother. Furthermore, Jesus' last words to Mary at the cross—in which he commits Mary to the care of one of his disciples by saying to her, "Woman, here is your son!" (19:26; NRSV translation)—have the effect of relegating Mary to membership in the unnamed disciple's family and thus divorcing her from her rightful biological relationship with Jesus.

[5] See also John 20:11–18, where the first resurrection appearance is to Mary Magdalene.

[6] The absence of Samson's mother in this scene was brought to my attention by M. Bal, *Death and Dissymmetry: The Politics of Coherence in the Book of Judges* (Chicago: University of Chicago Press, 1988), 201.

[7] He is only seventeen years of age one-and-one-half chapters later, in Gen 37:2.

[8] H. Cazelles, "La Mere du Roi-Messie dans l'Ancien Testament," *Maria et ecclesia* 5: *Acta Congressus Mariologici-Mariani in civitate Lourdes anno 1958 celebrati* (Romae: Academie Mariana Internationalis, 1959), 39–56.

[9]Matt 2:2; 27:11, 29, 37; Luke 23:3, 37, 38.

[10]E.g., R. E. Brown, *The Birth of the Messiah. A Commentary on the Infancy Narratives in Matthew and Luke* (Garden City, NY: Doubleday, 1977), 80, and n. 38 on that page; N. Perrin, *The New Testament: An Introduction* (2d ed.; revised by D. C. Duling; New York: Harcourt Brace Jovanovich, 1982), 275; see further the references listed in M. D. Johnson, *The Purpose of the Biblical Genealogies with Special Reference to the Setting of the Genealogies of Jesus* (SNTSMS 8; 2d ed.; Cambridge: Cambridge University Press, 1988), 192, nn. 1–8.

[11]2 Sam 7:12–16; Isa 9:5–6 (English 9:6–7); Ps 89:27–30 (English 89:26–29); Dan 2:44; 7:14, 27.

[12]E.g., Cazelles, "La Mere du Roi-Messie," 40, 51–53; J. H. Hayes and S. A. Irvine, *Isaiah. The Eighth-Century Prophet: His Times and His Preaching* (Nashville: Abingdon, 1987), 132, 135–36; cf. N. Gottwald, "Immanuel as the Prophet's Son," *VT* 8 (1958), 36–47; J. J. M. Roberts, "Isaiah and His Children," *Biblical and Related Studies Presented to Samuel Iwry* (ed. A. Kort and S. Morschauser; Winona Lake, IN: Eisenbrauns, 1985), 198.

[13]Bathsheba is not cited by name but is called the "wife of Uriah," her first husband whom David had killed so that by marrying Bathsheba after Uriah's death and thus claiming the child in her womb as legitimately conceived, he could conceal the fact of their adulterous relationship (2 Sam 11:14–27).

[14]This tradition is found only in Matt 1:5 and is not recounted anywhere in the Hebrew Bible.

[15]The Bible itself makes explicit this connection between the royal line as descended from Judah to Perez and as descended from Boaz to Obed and then to Jesse, David's father: see Ruth 4:12.

[16]I have elsewhere discussed briefly some of the ways in which this notion, implicit in Matthew and Luke, is made more explicit in later Christian texts. In the *Gospel of Philip,* for example, a collection of Valentinian Gnostic meditations with its roots in the second century C.E., Mary is interpreted simultaneously both as Jesus' mother and as a female heavenly power, the Holy Spirit (55:23; 59:6). See S. Ackerman, "The Queen Mother and the Cult in the Ancient Near East," *Women and Goddess Traditions: In Antiquity and Today* (Studies in Antiquity and Christianity; ed. K. L. King with an Introduction by K. J. Torjeson; Minneapolis: Fortress, 1997), 198.

[17]I say "not readily available" here because, as always, there are exceptions that might be cited. But, in fact, these exceptions may turn out to be those that, as the proverb predicts, "prove the rule." Esther Fuchs, for example, has demonstrated

that, despite our initial impressions of women like Rebekah and Potiphar's wife as strong-willed and powerful wives and of Rachel, in her stealing of her father's *tĕrāpîm,* as a resourceful and clever daughter, all have to resort to trickery and deception to have their way in their relationships with men. This is because, in a world of male power and authority, straightforward means by which these women can work their will are unavailable. See Fuchs, "Who is Hiding the Truth? Deceptive Women and Biblical Androcentrism," *Feminist Perspectives on Biblical Scholarship* (ed. A. Y. Collins; Chico, CA: Scholars Press, 1985), 137–44.

[18]This point concerning the autonomy of widows has been made by others regarding women elsewhere in the ancient Near East: in particular, regarding widows in Mesopotamia, see R. Harris, "Women (Mesopotamia)," *ABD* 6 (ed. D. N. Freedman; New York: Doubleday, 1992), 949a; K. van der Toorn, "Torn Between Vice and Virtue: Stereotypes of the Widow in Israel and Mesopotamia," *Female Stereotypes in Religious Traditions* (ed. R. Kloppenborg and W. J. Hanegraaff; Leiden: Brill, 1995), 1–13; cf. I. M. Diakonoff, "Women in Old Babylonia Not Under Patriarchal Authority," *Journal of the Economic and Social History of the Orient* 29 (1986), 225–26; and, regarding widows in the Mishnah, see Judith R. Wegner, *Chattel or Person? The Status of Women in the Mishnah* (New York and Oxford: Oxford University Press, 1988), 138–43 et passim. Wegner also comments briefly on the ways in which the Mishnaic traditions about widows draw on the earlier biblical materials (pp. 12–14 et passim). Excepting only the short article of van der Toorn cited above, however, the materials concerning widowhood in the Bible have not been thoroughly worked out. Phyllis Bird's remarks ("Women [OT]," *ABD* 6, 954b) rather miss the mark, as she associates women's autonomy and independence with age rather than widowed status ("normally a woman gained authority with age . . . many of the specialized roles and activities of women outside the home or involving public recognition and action . . . were performed by older women no longer burdened by the care of small children"). But the matter is more complex. To take just two examples, Sarah, although quite aged, is still depicted as a woman tied to the domestic sphere because she has not yet fulfilled her obligation to bear a son to Abraham. Judith, however, although seemingly envisioned in her story as relatively young (she is beautiful, a youthful attribute [8:7], and she is said to "grow old" only long after the events of the Israelite-Assyrian war [16:23]), is able to act with great independence and autonomy because of her widowed status. See further my discussion below.

[19]*Pace* R. C. Bailey, *David in Love and War: The Pursuit of Power in 2 Samuel 10–12* (JSOTSup 75; Sheffield: JSOT Press, 1989), 86–90.

[20]"'Fraught with Background': Literary Ambiguity in II Samuel 11," *Int* 42 (1988), 240–53; idem, "Bathsheba," *ABD* 1, 627b.

[21]"Characterization in Biblical Narrative: David's Wives," *JSOT* 23 (1982), 73; idem, *Poetics and Interpretation of Biblical Narrative* (Sheffield: JSOT Press, 1983), 27; this latter reference pointed out by Yee, "Bathsheba," 627b.

[22]Berlin borrows the term "agent" from Aristotle, who uses it to describe the performance of an action necessary to the plot. See "Characterization in Biblical Narrative," 73; idem, *Poetics and Interpretation,* 27.

[23]Berlin, "Characterization in Biblical Narrative," 74–76; idem, *Poetics and Interpretation,* 27–30.

[24]As noted in Chapter 3, the office of the queen mother is far more prominent in the southern kingdom of Judah than it is in Israel in the north. As also noted there, the names of queen mothers of Kings Ahaz and Jehoram were, for some reason, not preserved in the archival records.

[25]1 Kgs 15:1–2, 9–10; 22:41–42; 2 Kgs 8:25–26; 12:1; 14:1–2; 15:1–2, 32–33; 18:1–2; 21:1, 19; 22:1; 23:31, 36; 24:8, 18; similarly, 1 Kgs 14:21.

[26]See further my entry "Queens, Biblical," *Encyclopedia of Women and World Religion* (ed. S. Young; New York: Macmillan, forthcoming [1998]).

[27]Wegner, *Chattel or Person?* 129–38 et passim, similarly discusses the divorced woman as an autonomous agent in the Mishnah.

[28]See, for example, Gen 24:34–51 (Rebekah's father Bethuel and brother Laban arranging her marriage); Gen 29:15–30 (Laban arranging the marriages of his daughters Rachel and Leah); Exod 2:21 (Reuel arranging the marriage of his daughter Zipporah); Judg 1:11–15 (Caleb arranging the marriage of his daughter Achsah); and 1 Sam 18:17–29 (Saul arranging the marriage of his daughters Merab and Michal).

[29]On the usage *bêt 'ēm,* "mother's house," rather than the usual *bêt 'āb,* "father's house," in this verse, see Carol Meyers, "'To Her Mother's House'—Considering a Counterpart to the Israelite *Bêt 'āb,*" *The Bible and the Politics of Exegesis: Essays in Honor of Norman K. Gottwald on His Sixty-Fifth Birthday* (ed. D. Jobling; P. L. Day; G. T. Sheppard; Cleveland, OH: Pilgrim, 1991), 39–51; idem, "Returning Home: Ruth 1:8 and the Gendering of the Book of Ruth," *A Feminist Companion to Ruth* (ed. A. Brenner; The Feminist Companion to the Bible 3; Sheffield: Sheffield Academic Press, 1993), 85–114.

[30]See, similarly, regarding widows, van der Toorn, "Torn Between Vice and Virtue," 2–4.

[31]On translating Hebrew *měnûḥâ,* which normally means "resting place" or "rest," as "security," and, more specifically, as the "condition of rest and security attained by marriage," see BDB (Oxford: Clarendon, 1980), 630a, s. v. *měnûḥâ,* and also BDB, 629b, s. v. *mānôaḥ.*

[32]The Hebrew word here is *mānôaḥ;* on the translation, see above, n. 31, and, as there, BDB, 629b, s. v. *mānôaḥ.*

[33]See also my comments in the Introduction on the single-mindedness with which the women of Ruth pursue their goal of finding male providers.

[34]Similarly, van der Toorn, "Torn Between Vice and Virtue," 4–6. Wegner also makes much the same points about widows and divorced women in the Mishnah; see *Chattel or Person?* 144.

[35]In addition to my discussion of prostitutes below, see P. Bird, "The Harlot as Heroine: Narrative Art and Social Presupposition in Three Old Testament Texts," *Narrative Research on the Hebrew Bible* (*Semeia* 46; ed. M. Amihai; G. W. Coats; A. M. Solomon; 1989), 120–21; idem, "'To Play the Harlot': An Inquiry into an Old Testament Metaphor," *Gender and Difference in Ancient Israel* (ed. P. L. Day; Minneapolis: Fortress, 1989), 77; S. Niditch, "The Wronged Woman Righted: An Analysis of Genesis 38," *HTR* 72 (1979), 147.

[36]On Rahab's "house" as a brothel, see Bird, "Harlot as Heroine," 127-28 and 135–36, n. 27.

[37]On this, see F. M. Cross, "A Response to Zakovitch's 'Successful Failure of Israelite Intelligence,'" *Text and Tradition: The Hebrew Bible and Folklore* (ed. S. Niditch; Atlanta: Scholars Press, 1990), 100.

[38]On the almost "covenantal" nature of this agreement, see further the discussion and reservations of Bird, "Harlot as Heroine," 129, and n. 33 on p. 136.

[39]The contrast between widowhood in general and the specific case of the levirate widow is also drawn by Wegner in *Chattel or Person?* 97–113 and 138–41.

[40]In fact, it is because they are so passionately committed to preserving this descent that the fathers, brothers, and husbands described above in Section I pursue their control of a woman's sexual activity with such zeal. By doing so, these men guarantee that any son a woman bears will undoubtedly be of her husband's patriarchal line. This boy thus can continue his father's lineage with no one needing to fear that the bloodline has been blemished.

[41]Deuteronomy 25:5–6 requires that a dead man's brother *marry* the sonless widow. Genesis 38 is less clear. Regarding Onan, the text describes only how he should mate with Tamar and makes no mention that he has an obligation to marry her. Nor does Tamar end up marrying Judah, the man with whom she eventually fulfills her levirate responsibilities (see below). Yet verse 14 assumes that the levirate widow Tamar is to marry Shelah. This passage, however, seems the anomaly, meaning that the assumption of Genesis 38 is that the issue in a levirate union is concep-

tion and not marriage. This also can be seen in the book of Ruth. There, the line of Elimelech, the husband of Naomi, is threatened with extinction because of the deaths, in short order, of Elimelech and his two sons, Mahlon and Chilion (1:3–5). It thus becomes Naomi's obligation to bear a child to carry on Elimelech's line, but, because she is postmenopausal ("Do I still have sons in my womb?" she says, "I am too old to have a husband" [1:11–12; see also 1:21]), she cannot fulfill her levirate responsibilities on her own. Ruth's marriage to Elimelech's kinsman Boaz, in addition to ensuring security for Ruth (see my discussion above), thus becomes the means by which Naomi conceives and Elimelech's lineage is preserved. That the point of this marriage is to give Naomi a child and to preserve Elimelech's patriarchal line is brought into clear focus in Ruth 4:17, where it is said of Obed, the son eventually born to Boaz and Ruth, "A son has been born to Naomi." Biologically this statement is false: Ruth is the mother of the child. But within the context of the story's focus on Naomi's need to bear a child, the assertion is true: the birth of Obed preserves the line of Elimelech and thus brings Naomi fulfillment in her levirate obligations. Marriage for Naomi, however, is never mentioned. See further G. W. Coats, "Widow's Rights: A Crux in the Structure of Genesis 38," *CBQ* 34 (1972), 461–66, and, on the overall similarities between Genesis 38 and the book of Ruth, H. Fisch, "Ruth and the Structure of Covenant History," *VT* 32 (1982), 425–37.

[42]See, similarly, N. Furman, "His Story Versus Her Story: Male Genealogy and Female Strategy in the Jacob Cycle," *Feminist Perspectives on Biblical Scholarship,* 111.

[43]On the notion that there is a distinctive garb for prostitutes in ancient Near Eastern societies, see Bird, "Harlot as Heroine," 134, n. 5, and 135, n. 15. In these two notes, Bird cites evidence indicating that, unlike a married woman, the Mesopotamian prostitute went unveiled, yet she also cautions that since, in Genesis, Tamar is specifically described as veiled in her guise as prostitute, we cannot assume Mesopotamian customs were universal across the ancient Near East.

[44]As pointed out by Bird, "'To Play the Harlot,'" 90, n. 14.

[45]Johanna W. H. Bos, "Out of the Shadows: Genesis 38; Judges 4:17–22; Ruth 3," *Reasoning with the Foxes: Female Wit in a World of Male Power* (Semeia 42; ed. J. C. Exum and J. W. H. Bos; 1988), 43, similarly points out how *Tamar's* words indicate that she begins to claim the same autonomy in this scene of revocation that she enjoyed earlier in her guise as a prostitute. The crucial datum here is that it is *only* at these two points in the narrative (vv 16–18 and v 25) that Tamar speaks and thus it is only at these points that Tamar is envisioned as independent subject in the text rather than as an object that is acted upon.

[46]Cf. Gerhard von Rad, *Genesis: A Commentary* (OTL; Philadelphia: Westminster, 1961), 356: "The conclusion to the narrative, however, is somewhat unsatisfac-

tory. . . . Strangely it concludes without telling whose wife Tamar finally became" (this quote brought to my attention by Coats, "Widow's Rights," 461).

[47]J. B. Vickery, "In Strange Ways: The Story of Samson," *Images of God and Man: Old Testament Short Stories in Literary Focus* (ed. B. O. Long; Sheffield: Almond, 1981), 69; cf. M. Bal, *Lethal Love: Feminist Literary Readings of Biblical Love Stories* (Bloomington and Indianapolis: Indiana University Press, 1987), 50–51.

[48]Note in this regard that of Samson's three sexual companions described in Judges 14–16 (his Timnite wife, the Gazaite prostitute, and Delilah), Delilah is the only one he is said to love (Judg 16:4; also 16:15). See further Vickery, "In Strange Ways," 69, and J. M. Sasson, "Who Cut Samson's Hair? (And Other Trifling Issues Raised by Judges 16)," *Prooftexts* 8 (1988), 334.

[49]This "revelation" scene is redolent with sexual imagery, as Samson is said to sleep with his head between Delilah's knees (*birkêhâ*) while his hair is shaved. As in Judg 5:27, where the description of the "feet" of Jael (*raglêhâ*) between which Sisera lies is a sexual euphemism, a reference to the woman's genitalia, so, too, should we understand Delilah's "knees" here as signifying her sexual organs (see Gen 30:3; 50:23; and Job 3:12, which describe a child's coming forth from his mother's womb as being "born upon knees").

[50]For a catalogue of passages in which *bô'* is used in a sexual sense, see, as in Chapter 1, O. Margalith, "More Samson Legends," *VT* 36 (1986), 400; also, R. Alter, "From Line to Story in Biblical Verse," *Poetics Today* 4 (1983), 635; idem, *The Art of Biblical Poetry* (New York: Basic Books, 1985), 49; A. Reinhartz, "Samson's Mother: An Unnamed Protagonist," *JSOT* 55 (1992), 34, and n. 37 on that page. For *šākab,* see, again as in Chapter 1, D. N. Fewell and D. M. Gunn, "Controlling Perspectives: Women, Men, and the Authority of Violence in Judges 4 & 5," *JAAR* 58 (1990), 404; S. Niditch, "Eroticism and Death in the Tale of Jael," *Gender and Difference,* 49; Yair Zakovitch, "Sisseras Tod," *ZAW* 93 (1981), 367. Zakovitch, however, in "Humor and Theology or the Successful Failure of Israelite Intelligence: A Literary-Folkloric Approach to Joshua 2," *Text and Tradition,* 82–83, denies that *škb* has a sexual sense in the Rahab story. Cf. Cross, "Response to Zakovitch," 102.

[51]See further my discussion on names in Chapter 2, and, as there, Bal, *Death and Dissymmetry,* 43–93, 217–24; A. Brenner, "Introduction," *A Feminist Companion to Judges* (ed. A. Brenner; The Feminist Companion to the Bible 4; Sheffield: Sheffield Academic Press, 1993), 10–14; J. C. Exum, "Feminist Criticism: Whose Interests Are Being Served?" *Judges and Method: New Approaches in Biblical Studies* (ed. G. A. Yee; Minneapolis: Fortress, 1995), 75–86; C. Meyers, "The Hannah Narrative in Feminist Perspective," *"Go to the Land I Will Show You": Studies in Honor of Dwight W. Young* (ed. J. Coleson and V. Matthews; Winona Lake, IN: Eisenbrauns, 1994), 120–22 (reprinted as "Hannah and her Sacrifice: Reclaiming Female

Agency," *A Feminist Companion to Samuel and Kings* [ed. A. Brenner; The Feminist Companion to the Bible 5; Sheffield: Sheffield Academic Press, 1994], 96–99).

[52]Although not as clearly delineated, a similar argument could also be made regarding the characters in the Tamar story. While in that story, almost every character does have a name, it is still the case that Tamar alone is described by "no genealogy, no background, no point of identification" (Coats, "Widow's Rights," 461). This, as in the Rahab and Delilah stories, is a signal of her autonomy. Note in particular in this regard that, as was the case in the Rahab story, the men of her family are identified solely by their relationship to *her:* "*her* father" (Gen 38:11; emphasis mine) otherwise bears no name. Contrast in this regard the way in which the truly marginalized woman of Genesis 38, Judah's wife, is treated. In her case, it is she who is nameless, while her father, Shua, although he plays *absolutely* no role in the narrative, is given a name.

[53]The most thorough description of the two stories' similarities is that of J. C. Exum, "Aspects of Symmetry and Balance in the Samson Saga," *JSOT* 19 (1981), 3–9.

[54]Exum, "Aspects of Symmetry and Balance," 5.

[55]Exum, "Aspects of Symmetry and Balance," 4–5. On *ngd,* see also J. L. Crenshaw, "The Samson Saga: Filial Devotion or Erotic Attachment?" *ZAW* 86 (1974), 486–87; idem, *Samson: A Secret Betrayed, a Vow Ignored* (Atlanta: John Knox, 1978), 66–69.

[56]Reading "fourth" with the Greek and Syriac traditions rather than with the Hebrew, which reads "on the seventh day."

[57]The Hebrew text of 16:13–14 is widely recognized to be defective, and, following a suggestion originally made by George F. Moore, *A Critical and Exegetical Commentary on Judges* (ICC; Edinburgh: T. & T. Clark, 1903), 353–54, and embraced by most subsequent commentators, I have relied on the Greek tradition for the correct reading.

[58]See, similarly, my discussion at the beginning of Section II of Chapter 4, where I followed Robert Alter in suggesting that, despite the many similarities between the six barren woman type-scenes, "what is finally more significant is the inventive freshness with which formulas are recast and redeployed in each new instance" ("How Convention Helps Us Read: The Case of the Bible's Annunciation Type-Scene," *Prooftexts* 3 [1983], 119); "variations in the handling of the repeated motifs are never random . . . on the contrary, these variations are finely tuned to the special thematic and structural requirements of each particular narrative and

protagonist" ("Convention," 127). See, similarly, idem, "Biblical Type-Scenes and the Use of Convention," *Critical Inquiry* 5 (1978), 360, revised in idem, *The Art of Biblical Narrative* (New York: Basic Books, 1981), 52: "what is really interesting is not the schema of convention but what is done in each individual application of the schema to give it a sudden tilt of innovation or even to refashion it radically for the imaginative purposes at hand"; also, "much of art lies in the shifting aperture between the shadowy foreimage in the anticipating mind of the observer and the realized revelatory image in the work itself" ("Biblical Type-Scenes," 368; *Biblical Narrative,* 62). Finally, note the quote of J. G. Williams, "The Beautiful and the Barren: Conventions in Biblical Type-Scenes," *JSOT* 17 (1980), 111, cited in n. 22 of Chapter 4.

[59]There is debate in the literature about who actually shaved Samson: some barber whom Delilah is said to summon or Delilah herself? The issue need not concern us here. For the two sides of the question, see F. C. Fensham, "The Shaving of Samson: A Note on Judges 16:19," *EvQ* 31 (1959), 97–98, and Sasson, "Who Cut Samson's Hair?" 333–39.

[60]See also Bal, *Lethal Love,* 39–40.

[61]Although commentators frequently assert that the birth narrative in Judges 13 and the stories of Samson's heroic exploits in Judges 14–16 were originally separate compositions, I have already implied in Chapter 4 my assumption that, at least in the form in which they have come down to us, they need to be considered as an editorial whole. See, similarly, J. Blenkinsopp, "Structure and Style in Judges 13–16," *JBL* 82 (1963), 66–69; Crenshaw, "The Samson Saga," 476 et passim; Exum, "Aspects of Symmetry and Balance," 25, n. 2; idem, "The Theological Dimension of the Samson Saga," *VT* 33 (1983), 34–45; Reinhartz, "Samson's Mother," 25. This perspective, while not articulated, also is assumed by Crenshaw, *Samson,* passim; by S. Niditch, "Samson as Culture Hero, Trickster, and Bandit: The Empowerment of the Weak," *CBQ* 52 (1990), 608–24; by J. A. Wharton, "The Secret of Yahweh: Story and Affirmation in Judges 13–16," *Int* 27 (1973), 48–65; and, wholly predictably, by R. Alter, "Samson Without Folklore," *Text and Tradition,* 47–56.

[62]"Judges," *The Women's Bible Commentary* (ed. C. A. Newsom and S. H. Ringe; London: SPCK; Louisville, KY: Westminster/John Knox, 1992), 73–74; similarly, Alter, "Samson Without Folklore," 54. See also the parallels adduced by Crenshaw, "The Samson Saga," 474–75, 486–88; idem, *Samson,* 66–69; finally, Alter's analysis of the root *p'm* in 13:25 and 16:15, 18, and 20 ("Samson Without Folklore," 49–50).

[63]Pointed out by Alter, "Samson Without Folklore," 54.

[64]Bal, *Death and Dissymmetry,* 202–3, 224–27, similarly argues that motifs of motherhood tie Judges 13 and Judges 16 together; see also her comments in *Lethal Love,* 59.

[65]See, similarly, Alter, "Samson Without Folklore," 54–55; J. C. Exum, "Promise and Fulfillment: Narrative Art in Judges 13," *JBL* 99 (1980), 49, 52; idem, "'Mother in Israel': A Familiar Figure Reconsidered," *Feminist Interpretation of the Bible* (ed. L. M. Russell; Philadelphia: Westminster, 1985), 82–83; idem, *Fragmented Women: Feminist (Sub)versions of Biblical Narratives* (Valley Forge, PA: Trinity Press International, 1993), 63–64; Fewell, "Judges," 72; E. L. Greenstein, "The Riddle of Samson," *Prooftexts* 1 (1981), 250. Reinhartz, "Samson's Mother," realizes that the mother has "unusual, and considerable, foreknowledge concerning her son" (p. 32), but fails to include in her catalogue the mother's privy knowledge concerning Samson's uncut hair.

[66]Note in this regard that the Hebrew term for "feast," *mišteh,* comes from the Hebrew verb "to drink," *šātâ.* Charles F. Burney, *The Book of Judges* (London: Rivingtons, 1920), 344, even goes so far as to translate *mišteh* here as "a drinking bout." Note also, regarding Samson's implied drinking, that he spends a great deal of his adult life in "wine country," in the vineyards of Timnah (14:5) and in the "Valley of Choice Vines" (16:4). See Fewell, "Judges," 72.

[67]I have remarked upon this briefly in Chapter 2; see, as there, the comments of J. Blenkinsopp, "Some Notes on the Saga of Samson and the Heroic Milieu," *Scripture* 11 (1959), 84–85; idem, "Structure and Style," 66–67; Exum, "Promise and Fulfillment," 49, n. 18; idem, "The Theological Dimension," 31; Greenstein, "Riddle of Samson," 250–52; Niditch, "Samson as Culture Hero, Trickster, and Bandit," 610–12; M. O'Connor, "The Women in the Book of Judges," *HAR* 10 (1986), 280, n. 13. Here, I add only that I agree with Blenkinsopp, "Structure and Style," 65–76; Greenstein, "Riddle of Samson," 250–52; and Niditch, "Samson as Culture Hero, Trickster, and Bandit," 612–13 et passim (against Crenshaw, *Samson,* 73–74, 84, 95–96, 129–30; Exum, "The Theological Dimension," 30–45; and Wharton, "The Secret of Yahweh," 59–61) in seeing the Nazirite vow in general, and the proscription against the cutting of hair in particular, as a central motif throughout the Samson saga.

[68]On the subjugation of Samson at the end of Judges 16, see further Niditch, "Samson as Culture Hero, Trickster, and Bandit," 616–17, who cogently describes how the defeated Samson is rendered as a sexually subdued woman; also, Bal, *Lethal Love,* 51–52, and finally, as pointed out by Niditch, K. van der Toorn, "Judges XVI 21 in the Light of the Akkadian Sources," *VT* 36 (1986), 248–53.

[69]This *contra* O'Connor, "Women in the Book of Judges," 278, n. 5, and others, who argue that *pîlegeš* in the Bible always means "secondary wife." But, at least in royal contexts, this meaning does not seem to hold. Thus, while concubines are frequently mentioned as dwelling among the king's harem (2 Sam 5:13; 15:16; 19:6 [English 19:5]; 1 Kgs 11:3; 1 Chr 3:9; 2 Chr 11:21; Cant 6:8, 9; Esth 2:14), in almost all these cases (the exception is 1 Kgs 11:3), they are distinguished from the king's actual wives. 2 Chronicles 11:21, for example, considers Rehoboam's "wives and

concubines" (*nāšāyw ûpîlagšāyw*) to be two separate groups of women. Cf. Bal, *Death and Dissymmetry,* 80–93.

[70]See Fewell, "Judges," 75.

[71]Above, n. 69.

[72]Above, n. 51.

[73]Fewell, "Judges," 75; S. Lasine, "Guest and Host in Judges 19: Lot's Hospitality in an Inverted World," *JSOT* 29 (1984), 47; P. Trible, "An Unnamed Woman: The Extravagance of Violence," Chapter 3 in *Texts of Terror: Literary-Feminist Readings of Biblical Narratives* (OBT 13; Philadelphia: Fortress, 1984), 66. See also n. 45 above, which describes how Tamar speaks in the Genesis 38 text *only* at those two points where she is envisioned as a prostitute and as a widow who has fulfilled her levirate responsibilities, that is, only at those two points where she is imagined as assuming the sorts of autonomy the prostitute and the widow can claim.

[74]Reading with the Greek and Latin traditions "she spurned him" (Hebrew *wattiznaḥ*) for MT *wattizneh,* "she prostituted herself against him."

[75]Exum's comments, in "Feminist Criticism," 83–85, are particularly interesting in this regard; see also G. A. Yee, "Ideological Criticism: Judges 17–21 and the Dismembered Body," *Judges and Method,* 162.

[76]Reading the *Qĕrē' lhšybh* for the *Kĕtîb lhšybw.*

[77]Cf. K. Jones-Warsaw, "Toward a Womanist Hermeneutic: A Reading of Judges 19–21," *A Feminist Companion to Judges,* 175–76, 180–81; P. Kamuf, "Author of a Crime," *A Feminist Companion to Judges,* 192, 194.

[78]Lasine, "Guest and Host in Judges 19," 37–59; S. Niditch, "The 'Sodomite' Theme in Judges 19–20: Family, Community, and Social Disintegration," *CBQ* 44 (1982), 375–78; and D. Penchansky, "Staying the Night: Intertextuality in Genesis and Judges," *Reading Between Texts: Intertextuality and the Hebrew Bible* (ed. D. N. Fewell; Louisville, KY: Westminster/John Knox, 1992), 77–88, provide the most recent analyses.

[79]See Niditch, "'Sodomite' Theme in Judges 19–20," 367–69.

[80]Lasine, "Guest and Host in Judges 19," 39, perceptively points out the difference here with the Genesis 19 story, where both the women that Lot offers to the angry mob of Sodom are his daughters and thus females under his immediate jurisdiction.

[81]I have used this language of "pawn" previously, in the Introduction, to speak of Achsah. Further on comparisons between Achsah and the Levite's concubine, see Trible, *Texts of Terror,* 90, n. 52.

[82]As in n. 77 above, cf. Jones-Warsaw, "Toward a Womanist Hermeneutic," 177, n. 2.

[83]See, similarly, Trible, *Texts of Terror,* 88, n. 11; Yee, "Ideological Criticism," 162; cf. Jones-Warsaw, "Toward a Womanist Hermeneutic," 177, n. 3.

[84]Although verse 28 does not say so explicitly, it is clearly its presumption that the woman has died (*pace* R. Polzin, *Moses and the Deuteronomist: A Literary Study of the Deuteronomistic History,* Part 1 [New York: Seabury, 1980], 200–2; Trible, *Texts of Terror,* 79–82; see Lasine, "Guest and Host in Judges 19," 45–46). In fact, a notice of the woman's death was probably originally included in the Hebrew text and is missing only because of scribal error. Both of the major Greek witnesses state unambiguously that when the Levite found the woman on the Ephraimite's doorstoop in the morning, she was dead (LXX^A: *alla tethnēkei;* LXX^B *hoti ēn nekra*). This suggests a Hebrew original of *ky mth,* probably lost in the process of transmission because of haplography induced by homeoteleuton from the preceding '*nh.* I am grateful to David Noel Freedman, my colleague at the University of California at San Diego, for this observation. See also R. G. Boling, *Judges* (AB 6a; Garden City, NY: Doubleday, 1975), 38–42 (on the textual traditions of Judges) and 276 (on Judg 19:28).

[85]As Lasine, "Guest and Host in Judges 19," 49, points out, "His speech stresses the emphatic pronouns 'I' and 'me' . . . in contrast, he mentions the murdered woman herself only three times."

[86]See M. Bal, "A Body of Writing: Judges 19," *A Feminist Companion to Judges,* 218.

[87]See also Trible, *Texts of Terror,* 82.

Chapter 6

⸺◈⸺

"When the Daughters of Shiloh Come Out to Dance in the Dances"

WINE, WOMEN, AND SONG

Maiden! Your lips so fresh and red
Must with paleness overspread;
You've danced with boys in joy and glee;
Now comes the time to dance with me.

DEATH SPEAKING TO THE MAIDEN,
FROM THE POEM "DIE JUNGFRAU,"
NUMBER 25 IN THE CYCLE "TOTENTANZ VON BASEL"[1]

Your first big reception, duckie, shall be a Totentanz.

HER INTERIOR DECORATOR AND SOCIAL CONFIDANT
GUY RICE SPEAKING TO MRS. ISOBEL CAPPER,
FROM THE SHORT STORY "TOTENTANZ,"
BY ANGUS WILSON[2]

The crisis that is provoked in Judges 19 by the murder of the Levite's concubine is finally resolved by the end of Judges 21 with the restoration of peaceful relations between the offending Benjaminites and the rest of the Israelite tribes. Between these two events, however, much turmoil and bloodshed occur. As I noted in the last chapter, the Israelites initiate the process of reprisal in Judg 20:1–7, when, after the Gibeah assault, all of the tribes excepting Benjamin gather at Mizpah in order to sit in judgment against their wayward compatriots. At first, in determining Benjamin's proper punishment, the assembly decides to prosecute only the "good-for-nothings" or "ne'er-do-wells" (*běnê běliyya'al*) who actually participated in the assault at Gibeah (20:13). But, when their fellow Benjaminites refuse to give these men up for execution, war is declared against the entire tribe (20:17). Judges 21:1 reports that also at Mizpah, the colloquy's participants pronounce an additional penalty: that they will not give any of the women of their tribes to the Benjaminites in marriage.

As described in 21:2–7, however, this latter punishment only produces a new set of problems, for after the war against Benjamin has been fought and the Benjaminites defeated, the rebuilding and repeopling of the formerly ostracized tribe is stymied by a lack of women, especially women of childbearing age. At first, in 21:8–14, this problem is addressed by giving the Benjaminites four hundred virgins from Jabesh-Gilead, for it turns out that the people of that city had not participated in the assembly at Mizpah and so were not bound by the tribes' collective oath. The four hundred virgins, though, are not sufficient enough in number to satisfy the Benjaminites' marital needs, so, in 21:15–25, a second strategy is devised.

This second plan bases itself upon the fact that the Israelites soon were to gather at the cult site of Shiloh to keep the yearly fall festival celebrating the harvest of the grapes and the pressing of the new wine.[3] The Benjaminites are told that at that festival, they should lie in wait in Shiloh's vineyards. Then, "when the daughters of Shiloh come out to dance in the dances" (21:21), the Benjaminites should emerge from their hiding places and seize the maidens, each carrying off for himself one of the women to be his wife. Ironic juxtaposition is redolent here. In 19:1–20:48, Benjamin's taking of the Levite's wife for sexual purposes was deemed to be criminal, but in 21:15–25, these same Benjaminites are encouraged to go forth and take sexual partners-*cum*-wives from the gathering of Shiloh's young women. The tribal allegiances of those victimized by the Benjaminites in these two episodes, moreover, are much the same: the Levite of Judges 19–20 resides in Ephraimite tribal territory, just as Shiloh, the setting of Judg 21:15–25, lies within Ephraim's borders. Yet, while the Levite of Ephraim denounces the sexual abuse of his wife in 20:4–5, the premise of 21:21 is that the Ephraimites of Shiloh will accept the sexual attack on their young maids. What we have, then, in Judg 19:1–20:48 and 21:15–25 is a paradox, where two episodes stand paralleled within the telling of the larger Judges 19–21 tale, yet stand paralleled in a manner curiously askew. The result is outcomes disconcertingly "out of sync," whereby a story that begins by condemning Benjamin's assault of an Ephraimite's woman concludes by condoning the Benjaminites' ravaging of the Ephraimites' women.[4]

The skewed nature of this parallelism manifests itself further in the way that specific narrative details are handled in the two parts of the Judges 19–21 tale. Judges 19:1, for example, describes how the Levite's home in Ephraim is in the region's more remote reaches, and this verse finds its complement in 21:19, where Shiloh is treated as a remote and out-of-the-way site, so unfamiliar to the narrative's audience that its location—"north of Bethel, on the east of the highway that goes up from Bethel to Shechem, and south of Lebonah"—must be painstakingly described. Yet this notion of unfamiliarity is patently absurd, for elsewhere in the Bible, Shiloh is portrayed as a well-known city of early Israel, the site, indeed, where the tent of meeting that held the ark of the covenant was housed. Thus the city typically is referred to in texts describing Israel's premonarchical period with little or no identifying information (see, for example, Josh 18:1; 22:12; 1 Sam 1:3; 3:21; and, especially, in the book of Judges, Judg 18:31). In fact, even someone like the seventh-century B.C.E. prophet Jeremiah was able to treat the whereabouts of Shiloh as common knowledge, so much so that, although Shiloh had been destroyed several centuries prior to Jeremiah's ministry, the prophet could mention the city in his oracles without offering any commentary at all regarding Shiloh's setting or significance (Jer 7:12–14; 26:6–9). The elaborate description of Shiloh's backwoods location in Judg 21:19 is thus an out-of-kilter twist in the telling of the story, totally at odds with what the rest of biblical literature would lead us to expect. It is present in the text only to accentuate the peculiar parallelism that ties Judg 19:1–20:48 and 21:15–25 together.[5]

Similarly at odds with our expectations—and another indication of the peculiar parallelism uniting Judg 19:1–20:48 and 21:15–25—is the treatment of the "elders" in the two tales. As Barry G. Webb has noted, "elders" play a crucial role in both episodes: in 21:16–21, it is the "elders" of the tribal assembly (*ziqnê hā'ēdâ*) who direct the Benjaminites to seize Shiloh's young women, just as in 19:16–24, it is an "elderly man" (*'îš zāqēn*) in Gibeah who offers his virgin daughter and the Levite's concubine to the Benjaminites for their sexual use.[6] Yet in both cases, we might more readily have assumed that the mandate of these community elders would be to *protect* their fellow citizens rather than to facilitate their countrymen's sexual assaults. The way the Ephraimite's virgin daughter is treated as a character in Judg 19:24 is also, in terms of our expectations, a surprise since, although it initially seems as if she is going to be an important actor—or at least victim—in the Judges 19 tale, she disappears without a trace after her father offers her to the Benjaminites.[7] Webb again provides the datum crucial for interpretation by pointing out that the old man's "daughter" functions in Judg 19:24 only as a foreshadowing device, prefiguring the reference to Shiloh's "daughters" in 21:21.[8]

Odd parallels between the two stories continue to exert themselves in Judg 21:22, where it is acknowledged that there may be a problem inherent in the plan put forward in 21:21, for after the Benjaminites seize Shiloh's young women, the fathers and brothers of Shiloh should have every right to bring the same sort of complaint as did the Levite in 20:4–5. These men, that is, should be able to argue that the Benjaminites' seizing of the female members of their households compromises what we can again—as in Chapter 5—think of in terms of their "property rights," their rights to control the sexual activities of women under their hegemony. In this instance, however, the elders urge the fathers and brothers to overlook the Benjaminites' violations of the Shilonites' "property," for otherwise, Benjamin will have no wives. Yet note what this means: that principles that were so important at the beginning of Judges 20 that they could provoke an Israelite civil war are so incidental by the end of Judges 21 that they can easily be brushed aside and ignored. Similarly, note that, although in Judg 21:8–14, the vow made in 21:1 concerning the giving of the Israelite women to Benjamin seems of such inviolable stature that four hundred virgins must be plundered from Jabesh-Gilead rather than breach its terms, by Judg 21:15–25 this oath readily erodes away into insignificance. Or, at least, the oath can be disingenuously gotten around, as the fathers and brothers of Shiloh are assured that no guilt will be incurred by them in allowing the daughters' abduction, for they are not willingly *giving* these young women to the Benjaminites and so are not violating the terms of their pledge. Technically, this is correct since the daughters are taken, not bestowed, but the argument is surely sheer casuistry, blatantly disregarding the spirit of the vow in favor of its letter.

Whatever concerns, however, we modern readers may raise, Shiloh's citizens are depicted as having none, so that, according to 21:23, all goes as planned, and the Benjaminites take wives from the women whom they abduct in the vineyards. With them, they return to their tribal territory to restore and rebuild it. The chapter, and indeed the entire book of Judges, then ends in verse 25 with the notice that, "in those days there was no king in Israel; everyone did what was right in his eyes." Scholars generally assume that this formulation, which is found in a similar format elsewhere in the book of Judges, is an editorial comment and not a part of the original story.[9] Important to note, however, is that one of the three other points where a version of this notice occurs is in Judg 19:1. The editor's point in inserting the phrase there is to make explicit the same argument I have just advanced, that the story of the Levite's concubine and the story of the dancing young women are stories that stand paralleled, albeit paralleled in such a way that they stand disconcertingly askance. Indeed, by repeating almost verbatim the sinisterly foreboding words that introduce the narrative cycle, "in those days, when there was no king in Israel" (19:1), in the verse that comes at its end, "in those days, there was no king in Israel," the editor signals that the whole Judges 19–21 complex depicts a world gone grossly awry, where God's cult site is so hidden in the hinterlands that it almost has been forgotten, in which elders have come to perpetuate evil and oaths have lost any sense of obligation, and where rape—whatever the rhetoric of retaliation and revenge in Judges 20 may suggest—is an act whose perpetrators are ultimately recompensed and rewarded.[10]

I. WOMEN'S MUSIC AT THE VINEYARD FESTIVAL

To be sure, it is hardly the intent of the Deuteronomistic redactors of Judges to have the bleak assessment of Israel's moral condition in 21:25 be the last word in Israelite history. Rather, although this is obscured in Christian Bibles, which interpose the book of Ruth, the Deuteronomistic History, which succeeds Judges 19–21 with the books of Samuel and Kings, immediately seeks to offer an antidote to Judges' conditions of anarchy and chaos by describing the inauguration of the Israelite monarchy. More pertinent for our purposes, however, is not this Deuteronomistic juxtaposition of whole books, but again the editors' pairing of two short episodes. Once more, what we see is that, as Judg 21:15–25 was purposely paralleled with the narrative of the rape that preceded it in Judg 19:1–20:48, it is also deliberately coupled with the story of Hannah and the birth of her son Samuel that follows in 1 Sam 1:1–2:10. Both Judg 21:15–25 and 1 Sam 1:1–2:10, for example, are set in Shiloh, and both describe the celebration in Shiloh of the fall vineyard festival.[11]

This paralleled setting in terms of place and time may seem like little more than coincidence, but, in fact, the narrators of Judg 21:15–25 and 1 Sam 1:1–2:10 take great care to ensure that we view these two texts in tandem. Thus, not only are both set during celebrations that take place in Shiloh, and not only do both indicate that these celebrations occur at the time of the annual grape harvest feast, but both describe the annual nature of their festivals by using the exact same phrase, *miyyāmîm yāmîmâ,* "year by year" (Judg 21:19; 1 Sam 1:3; 2:19), a locution, notably, that is otherwise very rare, found only at two other points in the entire Hebrew Bible (Exod 13:10 and Judg 11:40). Judges 21:15–25 and 1 Sam 1:1–2:10 also both stress that their respective festivals are pilgrimage feasts. In 1 Sam 1:3 (see also 1 Sam 2:19), Hannah and her husband Elqanah are said to come *up* to Shiloh annually, which is typical language used of a pilgrimage,[12] and Judg 21:19 explicitly describes its celebration as a *hag,* which, although often just translated as "festival" or the like,[13] is actually a technical term meaning "pilgrimage festival" or "pilgrimage feast" (as in the Arabic cognate *hajj,* the term used to describe the Muslim pilgrimage to Mecca).[14] The Shiloh festival described in 1 Sam 1:1–2:10, moreover, seems to involve the same copious amounts of eating and drinking that are elsewhere, in Judg 9:27, for example, associated with the fall vintage celebration.[15] As I stressed in Chapter 2, the priest Eli's query to Hannah as he watches her pray—asking if she were drunk—especially indicates this, for Eli naturally assumes that Hannah, as a celebrant at the feast of the new wine, would have been drinking liberally.[16]

In Chapter 2—and also somewhat in Chapter 4—I have discussed Hannah's role at this vintage festival extensively, focusing primarily on 1 Sam 1:1–20, the tale of Hannah's barrenness and its resolution, in verse 20, with the birth of Samuel. As I have previously described, a key element in these verses is Hannah's vow pledging to dedicate her unborn child to Nazirite service. Verses 21–28 describe how Hannah fulfills this vow, how she remains at home with her infant son until he is weaned and then, according to 1 Sam 1:24, she goes to Shiloh to present him to Yahweh. In the Hebrew text as it stands, it is not specifically stated whether Elqanah accompanies Hannah on this journey, nor is it made clear at what point during the year this trip takes place. But verse 25,

which describes how "they" presented the child to the priest Eli, presumes that Elqanah accompanied Hannah, and, as originally observed by
Julius Wellhausen, the ancient Greek translation of the Hebrew Bible
similarly assumes that Elqanah went to Shiloh with Hannah and her
son.[17] The Greek text, moreover, assumes that the occasion prompting
this journey was Elqanah's and Hannah's annual pilgrimage at the time
of the vineyard festival. Unfortunately, our other major textual witness
from the ancient period, the largest of the Samuel scrolls found among
the texts from the Dead Sea (4QSam[a]), is fragmentary at this crucial
point, but the gap in the scroll's leather is large enough to suggest that
it contained the longer Greek reading. In his commentary on 1 Samuel,
P. Kyle McCarter thus proposes that the original text read, "Then she
[that is, Hannah] went up with him [the boy Samuel] to Shiloh when
her husband went up to sacrifice at Shiloh." In the handing down of the
Hebrew text as we have it, some scribe's eye inadvertently jumped from
the first mention of "Shiloh" to the second. Hence the intervening
"when" clause mentioning Elqanah's presence and setting the scene at
the time of the fall vintage feast was lost.[18]

This textual confusion rampant in verses 24–25 continues in verse
28, as the received Hebrew text reads, "So he [presumably Eli] worshiped Yahweh there," while the Samuel manuscript from the Dead Sea
records, "And she [Hannah] left him [Samuel] there, and she worshiped
Yahweh." As for the Greek tradition, one of its versions has nothing at
all at this point but does read in 2:11, "And she left him there before
Yahweh." The other major Greek version follows the received Hebrew
tradition in 1:28 by reading, "So he worshiped Yahweh there," but then,
in 2:11, it sides with its Greek counterpart by reading, "And they left
him there before Yahweh." It then adds, "And they worshiped Yahweh
there."[19]

Why all this variation among the ancient manuscripts? As McCarter
notes, it is because the original narrative of Samuel's dedication was disturbed at a later point in its transmission when some editor added to it
the so-called "Song of Hannah" in 1 Sam 2:1–10.[20] With this assessment,
almost all commentators agree,[21] arguing that the hymn of praise and
thanksgiving found in 1 Samuel 2, although attributed to Hannah in
verse 1, must have been only secondarily attached to her story.[22] These
scholars point in particular to verse 10 of the "Song," which presumes
the existence of the monarchy, an institution that is otherwise not a
part of the Samuel narrative until Samuel's secret anointing of Saul in

1 Sam 10:1 and the public proclamation of Saul's kingship that follows in 10:17–27.[23]

Yet, at the same time scholars acknowledge that the hymn is anachronistic, many simultaneously suggest that it was not inappropriate that an ancient editor gave Hannah this song of jubilation to sing, given that her prayer for a child has been fulfilled. The mention in 2:5 of the "song" of the barren woman who, through God's gift, bears seven children, as well as the entire poem's sense that Yahweh can bring about great reversals in the natural order, particularly indicates to commentators that the ancient curators of the Samuel text acted in a reasonable—albeit inaccurate—fashion in putting this song into Hannah's mouth.[24] But this explanation does not satisfy me completely, for, as discussed in Chapter 4, there are, including Hannah, six women in the Hebrew Bible who find that their barrenness has been miraculously and unexpectedly reversed by a God who has given them the gift of a child. Arguably, moreover, the reversal of at least some of these women's barrenness is more miraculous than was the reversal of Hannah's: Sarah, after all, is said to be ninety years of age (Gen 17:17) and to have ceased to menstruate (Gen 18:11) before she finally becomes pregnant; Rebekah also, according to Gen 25:20 and 26, is barren for a prolonged period—twenty years—before eventually giving birth; and Rachel, too, must have been infertile for many years before bearing, given that her sister Leah is able to deliver six sons and a daughter in the interim. But despite the fact that these women receive a gift of fertility from God that must be regarded—after such long delays—as wholly unexpected, and despite the command in Isa 54:1 to the barren one to "sing," the Bible's redactors place a song of thanksgiving *only* on the lips of Hannah.

Why just her? I believe that the cultic context of 1 Sam 1:21–2:10— the annual celebration of the vineyard festival—provides the crucial clue. Also crucial is for us to look once more to the parallel tale of the vineyard festival's celebration in Judg 21:15–25. There, too, recall that music is made, by the daughters of Shiloh who dance. In both stories, moreover, it is women who are specifically identified as the music-makers. Indeed, in the Judg 21:15–25 story, male musicians are curiously absent, and this despite the fact that in most other texts in the Bible describing music at cultic revelries,[25] male musicians not only are present but could even be said to dominate.[26] My proposal, then, is that, while the singing, dancing, and related activities of music-making typical of ancient Israelite cultic celebrations were generally not restricted either to men exclusively or to women, biblical tradition did regard the musicianship associated with the grape harvest festival to be the special province and responsibility of women.[27] Hannah's song is thus *not,* according to this thesis, a specific response to her experience of barrenness reversed, but rather an example of the kind of ritual musicianship typically undertaken by all women when they come to the grape harvest feast. The reason why the Bible's editors give Hannah, but no other barren woman, a song to sing is because they expect her, as a woman participating in the vineyard celebration, to make some sort of music.

Several other texts that suggest women's role as music-makers at Israel's annual vintage feast are found in the prophetic books. In Jer 31:10–14, for example, Jeremiah expresses his hope that Israel will return from its exile in Babylon to experience once more God's goodness and munificence in Jerusalem.[28] In particular, the prophet speaks, according to the NRSV translation, of the abundance of "the grain, the wine, and the oil . . . the young of the flock and the herd" that the returnees will find on God's holy mountain (v 12). This translation, however, obscures an important nuance in the text, for the Hebrew word used for "wine" is in fact not the generic term *yayin* that the NRSV implies, but instead is *tîrōš,* which carries the specific meaning of "must" or "fresh wine."[29] This suggests that the prophet envisions that the occasion of Israel's return coincides with the fall harvest festival at which the new vintage is pressed. The mention of "oil" in the text also indicates this, for again, although the NRSV translation obscures, the Hebrew uses a specialized rather than generic term, *yiṣhār,* which refers specifically to the "new" or "fresh oil" that was pressed from the olives harvested along with the grapes at the time of the fall ingathering feast. The word used for "grain," *dāgān,* likewise seems to refer to a particular kind of cereal crop harvested in conjunction with the autumn vineyard celebration.[30] Recognizing such a temporal setting gives the next verse of Jeremiah's oracle (v 13) a whole new significance:

Then the young women will rejoice in the dance,
The young men and the old will be merry.[31]

The young women, that is, will rejoice in the dance of the vineyard festival, undoubtedly the same sort of dance described in Judg 21:15–25.

What we see in this Jeremiah text, as in Judg 21:15–25 and in 1 Sam 1:1–2:10, is evidence that women played a special role in the musical performance that is part of the vintage celebration.

The special place of women as musicians at the grape harvest festival is further indicated in Isa 5:1–7, a composition that is indeed often called the "Song of the Vineyard." As it stands, this text is a parable,[32] in which the "vineyard" represents the two nations of Israel and Judah, both of which have been lovingly tended by their "vintner," who is identified as God (v 7). Yet, despite God's care, the "vineyard" has failed, yielding only what verses 2 and 4 describe as "wild grapes," otherwise defined, in verse 7, as "bloodshed" and "outcries." For the prophet Isaiah, the "Song of the Vineyard" thus serves as a means by which he can comment on how Judah and Israel have failed to live up to God's expectations, even though God has treated the two nations with mercy and compassion and thus should deserve their fidelity.

My interest here, though, is in the tradition that stands behind this parable, for many scholars believe that Isaiah, in shaping his polemic against God's people, quotes, especially in verses 1–2, an actual song of the vintage feast.[33] What scholars have not agreed upon, however, is the identity of the underlying song's anonymous bard.[34] But, given my thesis regarding Judg 21:15–25; 1 Sam 1:1–2:10; and Jer 31:10–14, an obvious answer is at hand. Verse 1 addresses a male "beloved":

> *Let me sing a song for my beloved;*
> *A song for my lover concerning his vineyard:*
> *My beloved had a vineyard on a very fertile hill.*

Within the context of the song's original festal setting, such words must have come from a female's mouth.[35] The basis for this verse, and by extension all of Isa 5:1–7, is thus a woman's song of the vintage feast, a song that, again, is representative of women's special role in generating and executing the music of the vineyard celebration.

Isaiah 5:1–7 is significant for another reason, for unlike our other vineyard festival song, the "Song of Hannah," which the Bible's editors only secondarily put into Hannah's mouth, the "Song of the Vineyard," and again especially verses 1–2, seems to quote an actual vintage song. Isaiah 5:1–7 thus not only confirms the role of women as musicians at the fall harvest celebration; it provides an example of the *kinds* of songs women would have sung at the vintage feast. Verse 1 suggests, moreover, that a preferred topic is matters of love and fertility. This is most explicitly indicated in the second line quoted above, where the singer announces that the song she intends to sing is a *šîrat dôdî*. The key term in this passage is *dôd*, which, although it can have a nonerotic meaning that some scholars prefer,[36] more obviously means either "lover" (in the singular) or the abstract noun "love" (in the plural).[37] Hence my translation "a song for [or "to"] my lover" or, as the NRSV prefers, "my lovesong."[38] A similar argument pertains in the case of the term "beloved," *yādîd*, in lines 1 and 3 of verse 1. While this word also can be used in a nonerotic sense,[39] in this passage, it is most logical to assign it sexual connotations.[40] This is particularly suggested by the poem's juxtaposition of *yādîd*, as well as *dôd*, with the term *kerem*, "vineyard," in the last two lines of verse 1. In the Bible's most erotic composition, the Song of Songs, *kerem* is repeatedly used in a metaphorical fashion to refer to that poem's young lovers and in particular to the beloved woman. An especially clear example is found in Cant 8:12, in which the young man calls his beloved, "my vineyard, my very own."[41]

The word "vineyard," and the related terms "garden," and, more generically, "field," are also used elsewhere in ancient Near Eastern love poetry to refer metaphorically to a beloved young woman.[42] In the original vintage song of Isa 5:1–7, then, the "vineyard" that the male "beloved" tends in verse 1 should be understood as his young woman lover or, more probably, as the young wife whom he has recently married. Verse 2 then describes the man's work in "digging," "clearing," and "planting" his newlywed "vineyard":

> *He dug it and cleared it of stones,*
> *And planted it with choice vines;*
> *He built a watchtower in the midst of it,*
> *And hewed out a wine vat in it.*

These are the couple's acts of lovemaking. Their goal is to produce, by the end of verse 2, fine "cultivated grapes" or children.

Unfortunately, the sexual imagery found in Isa 5:1–7 in general and verses 1–2 in particular is not explicitly paralleled in any of our other three texts of women's vintage musicianship, Judg 21:15–25; 1 Sam 1:1–2:10; and Jer 31:10–14. Yet it should still be noted that the notion that sees eroticism as the focus of women's music-making at the vineyard festival lies very close to the surface of at least the Judges 21 and 1 Samuel

1–2 tales. Hannah's entire concern at the vintage festival described in 1 Sam 1:1–20 is, for example, a matter of fertility: she prays that her barrenness will be reversed and that she will become pregnant. Also in 1 Sam 1:21–2:10, when Hannah attends the vintage festival again after Samuel has been weaned, the song she ostensibly sings is presented as a hymn inspired by a matter of fertility, in this case the capability to bear a child that she has recently been granted. In Judg 21:15–25, the young women's dance also suggests eroticized music-making since the daughters' performance must have been enticing enough to the Benjaminite men that they are willing to risk the wrath of Shiloh's fathers and brothers in order to take these women as wives. Note, moreover, that the verb that describes how these daughters will "dance"—lāḥûl in verse 21; mĕḥōlĕlôt in verse 23—is found only in Judges 21 with this specific meaning.[43] More commonly, this verb means "to writhe," and it especially can refer to the writhing done by a woman during labor. This suggests that implicit in Judg 21:15–25 is a play on words, whereby the description of the way in which Shiloh's daughters dance is meant to evoke both the imagery of seduction and that of pregnancy and birth. What is erotic about these women's dance is, in fact, its foreshadowing of their future fertility, fertility that will be made manifest soon after their dance has come to an end, once they have conceived by their Benjaminite abductors and have borne for them children.

II. WOMEN'S MUSIC IN TIMES OF LAMENT

There are, in addition to the "Song of the Vineyard," three other texts from the book of Isaiah that allude to music made at the annual celebration of the vineyard feast.[44] The first, in Isa 16:10, begins by describing the general joy and gladness that accompany the treading of the new wine and then specifically mentions the "songs" and "vintage shout" that mark this event. Isaiah 24:7–13 similarly describes the joyous musicianship of the vintage feast by cataloguing "the mirth of the handdrum,"[45] "the noise of the jubilant," and "the mirth of the lyre" that celebrate the pressing of the freshly harvested grapes. Unfortunately, neither of these texts uses any gender-specific language to identify the sex of the festival's singers or its other musicians. Still, the evidence of Judg 21:15–25; 1 Sam 1:1–2:10; Jer 31:10–14; and Isa 5:1–7 suggests that had gender been ascribed to these festal music-makers, they would have been identified as women.

Even more interesting in this regard is Isa 32:9–14. Unlike Isa 16:10 and Isa 24:7–13, this oracle does associate women with the celebration of the annual vineyard festival. What is unmentioned in Isaiah 32, however, is the joyous music the women should make at the time of the harvest. Instead, the oracle describes how the women whom it addresses have become so "at ease" and "complacent"—having neglected their music-making responsibilities at the vintage feast?—that Yahweh intends to declare a terrible punishment in which the "vintage will fail" and "the gathering of the harvest will not come" (v 10). The women are consequently ordered to engage in typical Israelite mourning rituals, to strip and make themselves bare, to gird sackcloth upon their loins, and to beat their breasts, wailing in lamentation.[46] Isaiah 16:11 similarly describes how the joyous music it associates with the vineyard festival in verse 10 will be replaced by mourning as God laments over the imminent destruction of the nation of Moab (see also Jer 48:33, 36). Likewise, in Isa 24:7–13, as Yahweh declares judgment on all the sinful people of the earth, the new wine, it is said, will dry up and the vine will languish, the mirth of the hand-drums and the lyres will be stilled, and the singing of the jubilant will cease. Then, according to verse 7, those formerly "merry-hearted" will *ne'enḥû,* usually translated as "they will sigh" or "they will groan." More accurately, though, we should render, "they will lament," as is indicated by the fact that the verb used here, *'nḥ,* is often used in texts describing the ritual process of mourning.[47] It is found, for example, four times in the five chapters of the book of Lamentations.

By pairing the vineyard festival's joyful music with the music of lamentation, what all these texts suggest is that there is another arena in Israelite cultic life in which women play a special role as musicians: in situations of mourning.[48] References to women as the singers of laments are also found elsewhere, both in prophetic texts and in the historical books. In 2 Sam 1:24, for example, as a part of the dirge David sings after the deaths of King Saul and his son Jonathan, the daughters of Israel are commanded to weep over Saul. 2 Chronicles 35:25 similarly describes how the prophet Jeremiah, along with men and women singers, sings laments after the death of King Josiah. Note that in both these instances, men as well as women lament, indicating that the responsibility of music-making at times of mourning is not limited to women. Still,

2 Chr 35:25, which refers to *the* female singers, suggests that at least for some women, the singing of laments is their specific and even professional responsibility. This is confirmed in Jer 9:16–20 (English 9:17–21), where in verse 16 (English v 17), Yahweh, as part of the lament over the forthcoming devastation of Jerusalem, commands that *the* mourning women should be summoned. The use of the definite article again suggests a group of women specializing in lamentation, and this is also indicated in the passage's next line, in which these women are identified as being "skilled" or "learned" (*ḥăkāmôt*)—that is, specially trained—in their craft. In verse 19 (English v 20), moreover, these female mourners are commanded to teach their daughters a dirge, possibly suggesting that the profession of the lament singer was handed down by women from one generation to the next.

Phyllis A. Bird further points out that in other ancient Mediterranean cultures, women played a prominent role in mourning.[49] The Bible itself, in Ezek 32:16, describes how Egypt's demise will be lamented by "the women of the nations," presumably referring to the women who specialized in mourning in the west Asian civilizations coexistent with Israel. This role of the ancient Near East's mourning women is again attested in Nah 2:7, where the slave women of Nineveh who are led away captured from that city "moan like doves" and "beat their breasts."[50] The Bible further, in Ezek 8:14, attests to a specific role women fulfilled as mourners in Mesopotamian religion. According to that text, some of Israel's women gather at the northern entrance of the temple courtyard to "wail over Tammuz."[51] Tammuz, as is well known from Mesopotamian sources, is a young fertility god who, after courting and marrying the fertility goddess Ishtar, dies an untimely death. According to myth, this death was lamented primarily by the women of Tammuz's family, his young bride, Ishtar; his sister, Geshtinanna; and his mother, who is called both Sirtur and Ninsun.[52] This mythological tradition of women's lamentation is reflected in Mesopotamian cultic observance, where women—including those found in Ezek 8:14—imitate their mythic prototypes by engaging in ritual mourning.

Women mourners are attested in Egyptian sources as well and are especially represented iconographically in various Egyptian tomb paintings.[53] They similarly appear in Canaanite tradition, in both the Epic of Kirta and the Epic of Aqhat from Ugarit, for example,[54] and in Phoenician art, on the sarcophagus of King Ahiram of Byblos.[55] Also in Greece, women were called upon to sing songs of lamentation. At the funeral games of Hektor in *Iliad* 24, for example, the women of Troy are led in such laments, first, by Hektor's wife, Andromache; second, by his mother, Hekabe; and, finally, by his sister-in-law Helen.[56] Greek funerary art also attests to the special role of women in the performance of dirges.[57]

III. WOMEN'S MUSIC IN GREECE—AND SHILOH

Indeed, although my reference to Greece may seem to lead us dangerously far afield from the world of Israel and of the ancient Near East, a more thorough discussion of women's musicianship as depicted in Greek culture—and also as depicted in the kindred civilization of Rome—is essential for our understanding of the story of Shiloh's dancing daughters that is my focus in this chapter. Parallels are plentiful and strikingly close. Already at the beginning of this century, for example, George F. Moore, writing in 1903,[58] as well as Charles F. Burney, writing in 1920,[59] compared the Judg 21:15–25 story to the Roman legend of the rape of the Sabine women, which describes how Rome's eponymous ancestor and founder Romulus, desperate for wives for the band of undesirable ruffians who had assembled around him in Rome, proclaimed a celebration in honor of Equestrian Neptune. Many of the neighboring peoples came, including the men of the Sabine community, who brought with them their women and children. In doing so, however, they played unwittingly into Romulus' hands, for, as the festival games were about to begin and when the people were distracted by excitement and anticipation, he sent his young Romans darting into the crowd to seize the Sabine women and to take them away for themselves as wives.[60]

Theodor H. Gaster has also discussed Rome's Sabine women story as a parallel to Judg 21:15–25, as well as citing a Greek counterpart to the Judges tale.[61] This is a quasi-historical account found in Pausanias that recounts how the hero Aristomenes abducted young women who were performing dances in honor of Artemis Caryae at Sparta.[62] Aristomenes subsequently brought these maidens to a village in Messenia, where he put them under the protection of the young men in his entourage. These young men, however, became drunk and sought to rape the maids, prompting Aristomenes to kill the most unruly among his soldiers and to release his female captives unharmed.

More recently, Claude Calame has catalogued and Steven H. Lonsdale has analyzed several other Greek versions of this "abduction of dancing maidens" story.[63] Perhaps the best known of the examples given by Calame and Lonsdale is the myth of Kore, also known as Persephone, found in the Homeric Hymn to Demeter.[64] Lines 407–34 of that text describe how Demeter's daughter Kore/Persephone is dancing in a meadow with her female companions when the ground below her opens up and Hades, the god of the underworld, bursts forth to carry her off to his kingdom and to make her his queen. Also of note is the story of Theseus' abduction of Helen, which takes place while the maiden is dancing, as in Pausanias' Aristomenes story, in a precinct sacred to the goddess Artemis.[65] The "abduction of dancing maidens" motif occurs again in *Iliad* 16,[66] in a story embedded in the catalogue of the Myrmidon warriors. This tale recounts how the mother of the Myrmidon hero Eudoros, a mortal named Polymele, was a young maid dancing, again in a precinct of Artemis, when she was abducted by the god Hermes. A second story of Hermes' abducting of a young maid who dances in honor of Artemis is found in the Homeric Hymn to Aphrodite, where Aphrodite—fearful that her mortal lover Anchises will discover that she is really a goddess—fabricates a tale describing her own abduction from Artemis' dancing ground in order to explain to Anchises how she came to arrive so unexpectedly and unescorted at his abode.[67]

As is obvious, all these Greek stories share the same basic motif of maidens abducted while performing dances that is found in Judg 21:15–25.[68] It is further of note that, as in Judg 21:15–25, the context of all the Greek stories—and also of Rome's Sabine women tradition—is cultic: the women of Sparta dance in honor of Artemis Caryae; Helen, Polymele, and Aphrodite, according to her lying tale, all dance in a precinct sacred to Artemis; and, while in the Kore story, the cultic context is not immediately obvious, Lonsdale points out that Kore, in listing for her mother the names of the twenty-some companions who danced with her in the meadow, ends her recital with Artemis.[69] Note, moreover, that according to Pausanias, Artemis herself was once threatened with an abduction while dancing, as she was stalked by the river god Alpheus while she frolicked in an all-night revelry with her nymphs.[70]

It is, moreover, the case that in both the Greek corpus of abduction stories and in Judg 21:15–25, there is typically a stress on the abducted women's youth. But, while young, these dancers should not be regarded as mere girls. They are rather postpubescents who, although of marriageable age, are not yet married. Lonsdale describes such female figures as liminal,[71] adolescent women who are sexually able but not yet sexually active. In the Kore story, this is indicated by the woman's name, which means "Girl" or "Daughter" and thus signals that she is a young woman who is just reaching or has only recently reached physical maturity. Pausanias' story of Aristomenes makes this same point in a slightly different fashion by telling us that when Aristomenes released his women captives after the attempted rape, they were still virgins. In Judg 21:15–25, the virginity of the young women of Shiloh is not as directly commented upon, but it is certainly presumed, for it is precisely their virgin status that places Shiloh's daughters under their fathers' and brothers' protection and that makes them acceptable to the Benjaminites as wives. It is also probable that these Shilonite virgins, like Kore, just recently have crossed the threshold of puberty. Note in this regard that in Jer 31:10–14, the biblical text that most closely parallels Judg 21:15–25 in terms of describing women's *dancing* at the vineyard festival, the dancers are specifically called *bĕtûlâ*, a term that, although often translated as "virgin," more specifically describes a young woman who has reached puberty but who has not yet borne a child.[72]

Lonsdale's analysis of the Greek materials also suggests three more themes that, although not so immediately obvious, further connect the Hellenic corpus of abduction stories and Judg 21:15–25. The first is the notion that the abductors' actions include an element of prurience.[73] Often, this has to do with issues of pedophilia, a much older man kidnapping a young woman. In the Kore story, for example, the abductor Hades is envisioned as much Kore's senior since he, as the brother of Zeus and Poseidon, is of the age of Greece's Olympian patriarchs, whereas Kore, as the daughter of the matriarch Demeter, belongs to the next generation. In fact, according to Hesiod, Zeus is Kore's father,[74] which means she is Hades' young niece. Similarly, in the tale of Helen's abduction, Theseus is said to be fifty, while Helen is only a child, "not yet ripe for marriage."[75] A variant form of this pruriency motif is found in *Iliad* 16, where Hermes' attention is drawn to Polymele because he finds her to be the most beautiful of the girls dancing when he "watched her with his eyes."[76] According to Lonsdale, this act of gazing suggests voyeurism and also hints at predation. This theme of predation is made explicit in the abduction story found in the Homeric Hymn to Aphrodite. As Lonsdale points out, the verb for seizing used twice in that story to describe Hermes' deed ([an-]*harpazō*) is used elsewhere in early Greek poetry to characterize the acts of lions and other carnivores who plunder the flocks.

These prurient motifs of pedophilia and predation also seem to be present in Judg 21:15–25. Concerning pedophilia, we can note that according to Judg 20:47 and then Judg 21:13, it was the six hundred Benjaminite soldiers who took refuge at the rock of Rimmon in the wilderness of Judah who were summoned to the Israelite assembly in order that wives might be found for them. These soldiers are presumably adult men, their status as warriors suggesting that they are comparable in age to the heroic and even the divine abductors who dominate in the various Greek stories. But, as discussed above, the daughters of Shiloh whom they kidnap are young women who, as in Greece, only recently have passed through puberty. Regarding predation and voyeurism, consider especially verses 20–21 of the Judges 21 tale. There, the Benjaminites are instructed to lie in wait in the vineyards and to watch for the young girls as they come out to dance. The instruction to "lie in wait" (*wa'ărab-tem*) is particularly telling, for elsewhere in the Hebrew Bible, and especially in the book of Judges, this verb *'ārab* carries connotations of lying in ambush. In Judg 9:30–45, for example, *'ārab* is used four times to describe Abimelech's ambush of the people of Shechem. Judges 20:29–48, in which *'ārab* six times describes the Israelites' ambush of the Benjaminites at Gibeah, is even more significant since this text is a part of the larger Judges 19–21 narrative complex. Indeed, the presence of *'ārab* in Judg 20:29–48 provides another example of the way in which ironic twists and reversals are at play in Judg 19:1–20:48 and 21:15–25. While the Israelites in Judges 20 ambush the Benjaminites in order to subdue them, the Benjaminites themselves become the liers-in-wait in Judges 21, as they prey upon Shiloh's daughters in hope of sexual conquest.

The second additional theme Lonsdale finds in the Greek materials that is paralleled in Judg 21:15–25 comes from *Iliad* 16 and the Homeric Hymn to Aphrodite. Both these tales share a notion that the abducting of a young woman for sexual purposes stands in structural opposition to the expected pattern of the marriage ritual.[77] Typically, in Greek custom, a bridegroom gives to his prospective father-in-law a bride-price of cattle in order to compensate him for the loss of his daughter. This, indeed, is precisely what happens as we read on in the story of Eudoros' mother, Polymele, in *Iliad* 16. After her fleeting sexual encounter with Hermes, Polymele is wooed by a human suitor, Echekles, who secures the woman's hand by giving to her father a substantial gift of kine. In the abduction stories, however, this pattern of giving and taking is reversed, so that an abductor like Hermes gives to Polymele's father no cattle but simply takes the maiden who pleases his eye. We can easily compare the

Judg 21:15–25 story, where the whole strategy of abduction is concocted precisely because normal marriage practices cannot be observed. In fact, although Israelite notions of bride-price and dowry differ significantly from those found in Greece, the same opposition of "give" and "take" that defines the Greek abduction stories structures the Judges narrative: because the Israelites have vowed not to give (*nātan*) their daughters to the Benjaminites in marriage, they must be taken (*lāqaḥ*) or seized (*ḥāṭap*).

Lonsdale's third theme of significance in his discussion of the Greek stories concerns the dancing ground where the abducted young maidens dance. He argues that, as the young dancing girls subject to abduction are liminal figures, so, too, is their dancing arena typically liminal space.[78] The precincts of Artemis, where so many of the Greek narratives are set, were usually located in a space Lonsdale calls "marginal," between the city and the fields beyond.[79] A variation is found in the myth of Kore, whose meadowlands dancing ground is "marginal" in the sense that it is a place where the earth can open up, allowing the denizens of the under-world to intrude into a region that otherwise is reserved for human domain. In Judg 21:15–25, the matter is slightly more complex, for as my thesis in this chapter suggests, the tradition's decision to locate the dance of Judges 21 in a vineyard is motivated by a particularly Israelite cultic concern, the belief that women's music-making is a distinctive and perhaps even central component in the celebration of the fall vintage festival.[80] The vineyard setting of Judges 21, that is, is a distinctively Israelite adaptation in that culture's recounting of the eastern Mediterranean's "abduction of dancing maidens" story, reflecting Israel's under-standing that it is in a vineyard at the time of the vintage festival when Israelite young maidens most naturally would dance.

Nevertheless, although cultic concerns override in determining the choice of setting for Judg 21:15–25, it is still the case that the Greek motif of a marginalized dancing ground may be present.[81] Although the archaeological evidence from Shiloh itself is not conclusive (because of extensive erosion and Roman-Byzantine period rebuilding at the site), the archaeology of other early Israelite villages suggests that the vineyards of Judges 21 should be envisioned as lying outside Shiloh proper (consisting of two-and-one-half to three acres in the Iron Age) but still located on terraces easily accessible to the settlement's inhabitants.[82] They thus sit on the boundary, so to speak, between the worlds of "culture" and "nature."[83] Indeed, in Shiloh's particular case, true "wilderness" really does appear beyond the terraces, as the east, north, and west slopes of the mound fall off steeply into the valley below.[84]

Lonsdale's analysis of Greece's "abduction of dancing maidens" stories is a part of a larger study he has undertaken on the role of dance and dance-like movements within Greek religion. In it, he follows his discussion of the various abduction narratives with a chapter on choral processions in Greek funerary ritual. In explaining this transition, he notes that Hellenic scholars have commented often on, "basic similarities between wedding and funerary ritual revolving around the abduction of the bride or the snatching of the body and responses to loss by the family of the loved one" and cites especially the ways in which the "abduction of dancing maidens" stories in general and the myth of Kore in particular came to be understood in classical Greece as examples of the "tragic wedding."[85] Such a marriage, because it is born in rape, is as much an occasion for lamentation as it is for celebration.

Indeed, in Greek tradition, this sense of marriage as, in part, a "tragedy" is so pronounced that even weddings not conceived in rape can incorporate into their celebration the language of lamentation.[86] This is particularly seen in the words young women sing in Greek marriage hymns. The bride, or the young women's chorus that speaks for her, expresses profound ambivalence about her approaching nuptials. On the one hand, she acknowledges her wedding as marking her entry into maturity and adulthood. On the other hand, she expresses dread regarding her abandonment of childhood security and her journey into the unknown, both the unknown world of a new husband's home and the unknown experiences of sexual intimacy, pregnancy, and childbirth. A fragment from a marriage hymn of Sappho speaks especially to the young woman's misgivings:

> *Virginity, virginity, deserting me, where have you gone?*
> *No longer will I come to you, no longer will I come.*[87]

Catullus 62, a marriage hymn that is generally acknowledged to owe much to Sappho,[88] similarly suggests the apprehension young women feel upon the occasion of their marriage.[89] In this poem, two choruses, one of young men, one of young women, sing back and forth to each other in teasing and even flirtatious tones. Yet for the young women, the levity of the performance is hardly absolute, as they speak in Stanza 4 of the brutal severance of a daughter from her mother and in Stanza 8 of the bride as a beautiful flower that wilts and sheds its bloom after it is plucked by the groom. One commentator has even located allusions to rape within the young women's performance, thus documenting the persistent way in which the motifs of Kore's rape and the "tragic wedding" that results permeate Greco-Roman marriage traditions.[90]

I shall return to this language of rape in Catullus 62 in my concluding comments below, but before I do so, let me consider the end of Catullus' marriage hymn in Stanza 9 and also some points of comparison with Israelite materials that this stanza suggests. In Catullus' ultimate stanza, the young men's chorus responds to the young women's previously articulated apprehensions by evoking the metaphor of an ungrafted vine in a vineyard. The point of their words is to argue that a "vine," that is, the prospective bride, can only bear "rich grapes," that is, children, if she becomes "grafted," that is, joined in wedlock, to a groom. If she does not, in a culture where a woman's value is defined almost exclusively by her ability to bear children, the maiden is branded as a failure, a disappointment to both her family and her community at large. As we have seen in Chapter 4, in considering the lengths to which the Bible's barren women will go to become pregnant, Israel shares with Greek and Roman culture this general conviction that childbearing is the primary and almost exclusive measure of a woman's worth. Noteworthy, then, is the degree to which Catullus' more specific imagery of a fertile "vine" and the "rich grapes" it will bear, found within the context of a song about marriage and the subsequent experiences of lovemaking and, for the woman, pregnancy and childbirth, is reminiscent of the images found in a poem such as Isaiah's "Song of the Vineyard" in Isa 5:1–7. Note especially in Isaiah 5 the thinly veiled language of lovemaking in verses 1–2, where the beloved husband "digs," "clears," and "plants" his newlywed "vineyard," that is, his wife, with the expectation that she will yield a harvest of cultivated fruit, that is, their children.

Equally noteworthy, however, is that Isa 5:1–7 shares the sense of foreboding found in Catullus 62. In the last word of Isa 5:2, the tone of joyous celebration that up until that point has marked the poem comes abruptly to an end, as the vintner's expectations that his cherished vineyard will bear bounteously give way to a disappointing harvest of only wild grapes. This sets the stage for a change in voice in verse 3, as the woman singer's lyrics are abruptly replaced by the words of God, who speaks in condemnation and judgment of the people of Israel and Judah. It is also important to note that the series of oracles that follow the "Song of the Vineyard" in Isaiah all begin with the word *hôy*, "Ah" (Isa 5:8, 11, 18, 20, 21, 22). This interjection typically is used, especially in the book of Isaiah, to introduce a lament.[91] Originally in the prophet's message, these laments were discrete from the "Song of the Vineyard," uttered at a different time and place. Nevertheless, it is still significant that in the editorial process that collected the oracles of Isaiah together, it was perceived as appropriate to pair an oracle that begins with a jubilant love song (Isa 5:1–2), first, with a message of judgment (5:3–7) and, then, with a series of lamentations (5:8–24).

To be sure, I must hasten to add, the *content* of the laments uttered on behalf of God in Isa 5:3–7 and 8–24 is hardly the same as the *content* of the lamenting choruses that the young women perform in Catullus 62. My point is only that the same basic pairing of joyous celebration and ominous foreboding found in the young women's choruses in Catullus 62, and in Greek wedding songs more generally, is attested in an Israelite song that similarly concerns marriage and childbirth and that originally came from a young woman's mouth. This same pairing of jubilation and lamentation in conjunction with a young woman's song concerning, at least, matters of childbirth is found in 1 Sam 1:1–2:10 (although there the order of Isa 5:1–7 is reversed, as Hannah's mourning as that passage begins subsequently gives way to her song of exultation in 2:1–10). Indeed, it is the case that in *all* the Bible's grape harvest texts that I have compared to Judg 21:15–25 in this chapter—1 Sam 1:1–2:10; Jer 31:10–14; Isa 5:1–7; 16:10–11; 24:7–13; and 32:9–14—the joyous music women make as part of the vintage festival is paired with motifs of mourning and lamentation.

This observation leads me to suspect that the duality of celebration and lamentation inherent in the Greek marriage hymns is also an intrinsic part of Israel's vintage song genre. Yet what about the dance of the daughters of Shiloh on which I have focused in this chapter? Is lamentation incorporated there?

At first glance, the answer appears to be "no" since the Judges text seems to speak only of the eroticized—and thus presumably the joyous—character of the maidens' dance. Yet, as I have noted in Section II above, the verb used to describe the women's writhing dance in Judg 21:21 and 23 is more commonly found in the Bible to describe a woman's writhing during labor. In those earlier comments, I focused on the

ways such allusions to pregnancy and childbirth suggest the fertility motifs I believe dominate in the music of Israel's vintage celebration, but
given the context of my discussion here, we should consider as well
how "writhing in labor" evokes imagery of pain and suffering. While,
moreover, allusions to the pain and suffering of childbirth are not, perhaps, in and of themselves examples of the sorts of mourning and lamentation I have located in Israel's other grape harvest texts, they surely
introduce a somber note into a dance that heretofore has seemed marked
only by gaiety and jubilation. More important, these allusions to the
pain and suffering of labor recall the apprehensions regarding the unknown world of pregnancy and childbirth that are found in the young
women's choruses of the Greek marriage hymns. The Greek hymns'
more general sense of apprehension and foreboding is also present in the
larger context of the Judg 21:15–25 tale, given that the ultimate fate of
the dancing young women is to be abducted by the Benjaminites for
sexual purposes or, to put the matter another way, to be forced into
marriage through rape.

Which brings us back to the description of marriage as rape in Catullus 62. As we begin to hear in the music of Judg 21:15–25 the same
juxtaposition of dread and celebration found in that marriage hymn, can
we imagine how Catullus' meditations on the duality of marriage could
be transposed into the mouths of Israel's women? Can we imagine, that
is, that coupled with the joys of the daughters of Shiloh's whirling dances
are words of lamentation chanted as part of an accompanying song? And,
as we remember the elaborate interlocking structures of Judg 19:1–20:48
and 21:15–25, can we also imagine what the content of these lamentations might have been, that the daughters of Shiloh would have mourned
not only the tragedy of rape that was about to produce their own marriages but also the tragedy of a woman whom a Levite from Ephraim
sent forth to be raped and murdered by their soon-to-be husbands' kin?

The themes and melodies that tie the narrative complex of Judges
19–21 together are in this sense the music of a round, circling back from
the revels of the daughters abducted from an Ephraimite vineyard to
the daughter of a Judahite who got up and took herself away from the
Ephraimite hills. Or, perhaps better, we might hear in the songs that
hum beneath the surface of Judges 19–21 the tones and tempos of a
circle dance, in which women spiral round and round, whirling from
the story of daughters seized for sexual assault to the tale of a wife and
daughter sent forth to be sexually abused. Indeed, if we look and listen

just carefully enough, we will see how Shiloh's dancing women twist and gyre with such swiftness and speed that their bodies blur together to collapse into one, the body of a woman who lies collapsed and crumpled on Gibeah's streets. In their role as sexual objects, then, the daughters of Shiloh ultimately become identical to the Levite's concubine, and molestation and murder become the pillars between which Judges 19–21 stands. Within them, the story, and its macabre dance with death, spins itself out.

NOTES

[1] The German text reads:

Auch Jungkfraw ewer roter Mund
Wird bleich jetzund zu dieser Stund:
Ihr sprungen gern mit jungen Knaben,
Mit mir must ihr ein Vortantz haben.

Taken from H. Grieshaber, *Totentanz von Basel* (Dresden: VEB Verlag der Kunst, 1968); see also H. Hess, *Totentanz der Stadt Basel* (Basle: Alb. Sattler, n. d.).

[2] The story can be found in Wilson's collection, *Such Darling Dodos and Other Stories* (London: Secker & Warburg, 1959), 144–69; the quote is from p. 163.

[3] The text does not state explicitly that the festival in question is the fall vintage feast, but as all commentators recognize, its vineyard setting undoubtedly indicates such. See, most specifically, W. O. E. Oesterley, *The Sacred Dance: A Study in Comparative Folklore* (New York: Macmillan, 1923), 142.

[4] See, similarly, P. Kamuf, "Author of a Crime," *A Feminist Companion to Judges* (ed. A. Brenner; The Feminist Companion to the Bible 4; Sheffield: Sheffield Academic Press, 1993), 193–94.

[5] As should be obvious from the above discussion, the more standard explanation—that some redactor added the careful definition of Shiloh's location as a gloss at a time when Shiloh had all but been forgotten by the ancient Israelites—seems to me misinformed. See, though, the various comments of C. F. Burney, *The Book of Judges* (London: Rivingtons, 1920), 492; G. F. Moore, *A Critical and Exegetical Commentary on Judges* (ICC; Edinburgh: T. & T. Clark, 1903), 451; and J. A. Soggin, *Judges: A Commentary* (OTL; Philadelphia: Westminster, 1981), 299. More appealing, given the argument I will advance in Section I below concerning the relationship between Judg 21:15–25 and 1 Sam 1:1–2:10, is the analysis of Robert G. Boling, *Judges* (AB 6a; Garden City, NY: Doubleday, 1975), 293, who suggests there is a deliberate and satiric comparison suggested here, contrasting the behaviors of the elders of Judg 21:19, who, despite the obligations of the Yahwistic cult, seem not to have been to Shiloh to keep the vintage festival for a good long while, and those of Elqanah, the good Yahwist of 1 Sam 1:3, who is said to go to Shiloh every year to sacrifice.

[6] *The Book of the Judges: An Integrated Reading* (JSOTSup 46; Sheffield: JSOT Press, 1987), 196.

[7]This sense of foiled expectations is intensified, moreover, if we contrast the kindred Sodom and Gomorrah tale in Genesis 19 and the role there of Lot's virgin daughters, the counterparts of the virgin daughter of Judges 19. Unlike the Judges 19 daughter, Lot's daughters do reappear in a dramatic way at the end of the story as they engage in an incestuous union with their father. The contrast with the virgin daughter who disappears completely is striking. And the contrast becomes even more evocative if we follow Stuart Lasine, "Guest and Host in Judges 19: Lot's Hospitality in an Inverted World," *JSOT* 29 (1984), 38–41, in seeing Judges 19 as mimicking Genesis 19 in the telling of its tale and thus insisting that a virgin daughter be present in the Gibeah episode because that element was a part of the Sodom narrative. If this is so, then, like the virgin daughters of Genesis 19, we would expect the Gibeah daughter to do anything but disappear. However, the question of chronological priority between Genesis 19 and Judges 19 is far from settled; see S. Niditch, "The 'Sodomite' Theme in Judges 19–20: Family, Community, and Social Disintegration," *CBQ* 44 (1982), 375–78.

[8]*The Book of the Judges,* 263, n. 37.

[9]This observation is to be found in all the standard commentaries; for example, Boling, *Judges,* 293; Burney, *Judges,* 410; Moore, *Judges,* 453; Soggin, *Judges,* 300.

[10]As is undoubtedly clear, I fail to see the reasons for Boling's claim (*Judges,* 293) that in Judg 21:25, "the statement ["there was no king in Israel"] has a positive thrust after the ingenious solution of problems in the final scenes."

[11]On the reasons for associating 1 Sam 1:1–2:10 with the fall grape harvest festival, see, in addition to my discussion in Chapter 2, D. J. A. Clines, "The Evidence for an Autumnal New Year in Pre-Exilic Israel Reconsidered," *JBL* 93 (1974), 28, and Menahem Haran, "Zebah Hayyamîm," *VT* 19 (1969), 12, n. 2. Note, however, that Haran himself disputes the association of the 1 Sam 1:1–2:10 feasts with the fall vintage festival, regarding them instead as private family or clan observances. See, similarly, C. L. Seow, *Myth, Drama, and the Politics of David's Dance* (HSM 44; Atlanta: Scholars Press, 1989), 23–25.

[12]See, for example, Exod 34:24, where it is commanded in the covenant code that the Israelites shall "go up" to appear before Yahweh three times a year.

[13]As it is, for example, in the NRSV, the JB, the NAB, the KJV, and the NJPS, all of which translate "feast"; cf. the REB, "pilgrimage."

[14]See further Burney, *Judges,* 492; Soggin, *Judges,* 299.

[15]Copious eating and drinking are not specifically mentioned in Judg 21:15–25, although surely this was a part of the celebration described there. Once we realize this, moreover, we again see an example of the ironic parallelism that exists between

Judg 19:1–20:48 and 21:15–25, for in the former text there is also much eating and drinking, the eating and drinking done by the Levite and his wife's father during the five days the Levite spends at his father-in-law's house. Furthermore, in both Judg 19:1–20:48 and 21:15–25, these gluttonous orgies of food and drink are succeeded by orgies of sex: the Benjaminites' rape of the Levite's companion and these same men's seizing of the daughters of Shiloh.

[16]Again, as in Chapter 2, nn. 72 and 75, I am grateful to Julie A. Duncan, my colleague at Princeton Theological Seminary, for this observation.

[17]See Wellhausen's *Der Text der Bücher Samuelis untersucht* (Göttingen: Vandenhoeck und Ruprecht, 1871), 41; this citation pointed out by F. M. Cross, Jr., "A New Qumran Biblical Fragment Related to the Original Hebrew Underlying the Septuagint," *BASOR* 132 (1953), 19, n. 6; P. K. McCarter, *I Samuel* (AB 8; Garden City, NY: Doubleday, 1980), 56.

[18]McCarter, *I Samuel,* 56; for a similar conclusion, see Cross, "Qumran Biblical Fragment," 19–20.

[19]For these readings and for discussion, see McCarter, *I Samuel,* 57–58.

[20]*I Samuel,* 57.

[21]General scholarly opinion is exhaustively catalogued in J. T. Willis, "The Song of Hannah and Psalm 113," *CBQ* 35 (1973), 139–40, nn. 8–9.

[22]Compare the hymn of thanksgiving secondarily inserted into the Jonah story in Jonah 2.

[23]Scholars also suggest that (1) the military metaphor found in verse 4a is difficult to imagine as coming from Hannah's mouth; (2) that the reference in verse 5 to the *seven* children of the barren woman cannot refer to Hannah, who, according to 1 Sam 2:21, had only six offspring; and (3) that the overall tone of the poem is nationalistic rather than the sort of personal hymn of thanksgiving Hannah might be expected to sing. Also, the "Song" is located in slightly different places in the Hebrew and Greek versions of the Bible, which often indicates secondary material. See further R. W. Klein, "The Song of Hannah," *CTM* 41 (1970), 676–77, n. 4.

[24]Klein also adds that verses 1 and 3 express well the difficulties Hannah had suffered at the hands of Peninnah, Elqanah's other wife. See "Hannah," *CTM* 41, 677, n. 4.

[25]The only exception is texts that describe the celebration of Yahweh's victories in battle, in which music-making seems to be the exclusive province of women.

See E. B. Poethig, *The Victory Song Tradition of the Women of Israel* (unpublished Ph.D. dissertation; Union Theological Seminary, 1985); also Chapter 1, n. 17.

[26]The clearest examples are Exod 32:6, 17–18, and 19, where *Aaron* leads the Israelites in the revelries and dancing that celebrate the worship of the golden calf (cogently discussed by J. M. Sasson, "The Worship of the Golden Calf," *Orient and Occident: Essays Presented to Cyrus H. Gordon on the Occasion of His Sixty-Fifth Birthday* [AOAT 22; ed. H. A. Hoffner; Neukirchen-Vluyn: Neukirchener Verlag; Kevelaer: Butzon & Bercker, 1973], 151–59); also, 2 Sam 6:5, the description of the bringing of the ark into Jerusalem. The leader of the dancing and general musicianship associated with this cultic revel is King David. See, too, Ps 81:3–4 (English 81:2–3), where the verbs commanding the people to "raise a song," "sound the hand-drum, the sweet lyre, and the harp," and to "blow the trumpet" at the feast of the new moon are rendered in masculine plural forms, indicating, at a minimum, that men and women make music together at this festival and suggesting, perhaps, that it was men alone who are the holiday's musicians. Similarly, in Isa 30:29, masculine forms are used to describe the song Israel will raise at Yahweh's "holy festival" (otherwise unspecified); likewise, in Amos 5:21–24, the prophet uses masculine forms to speak to the Israelites of the "songs" and "harp melodies" performed at God's festivals.

[27]I have commented on this briefly elsewhere; see "Isaiah," *The Women's Bible Commentary* (ed. C. A. Newsom and S. H. Ringe; London: SPCK; Louisville, KY: Westminster/John Knox, 1992), 163; see also the brief comments of S. D. Goitein, "Women as Creators of Biblical Genres," *Prooftexts* 8 (1988), 16–18.

[28]Originally brought to my attention by J. H. Eaton, "Dancing in the Old Testament," *ExpTim* 86 (1975), 137.

[29]As in n. 13 above, it is the REB that comes closest to capturing the specifics of the Hebrew, translating, "the grain, the new wine, and the oil, the young of flock and herd." Note also the NJPS, "new grain and wine and oil . . . sheep and cattle."

[30]As is indicated by the fact that *dāgān* most typically is mentioned in the Bible in conjunction with the fall crops of *tîrôš* and *yiṣhār*. See Num 18:12; Deut 7:13; 11:14; 12:17; 14:23; 18:4; 28:51; 2 Kgs 18:32; Hos 2:10, 24 (English 2:8, 22); Joel 1:10; 2:19; Hag 1:11; Neh 5:11; 10:39 (English 10:40).

[31]Reading *yaḥĕdû*, "they will be merry," with the Greek for MT *yaḥdāw*, "together."

[32]There has been much discussion in the literature about the form of this "Song." The genres "love song," "lawsuit," "fable," "parable," and "allegory" have all been proposed (see the summary found in A. Graffy, "The Literary Genre of Isaiah 5, 1–7," *Bib* 60 [1979], 401–4; in M. C. A. Korpel, "The Literary Genre of the Song of the Vineyard (Isa. 5:1–7)," *The Structural Analysis of Biblical and Canaanite*

Poetry [JSOTSup 74; ed. W. van der Meer and J. C. de Moor; Sheffield: JSOT Press, 1988], 119–23; and in H. Niehr, "Zur Gattung von Jes 5, 1–7," *BZ* 30 [1986], 99–100, nn. 1–6). As Korpel notes, most scholars today follow John T. Willis in regarding the passage as a parable (J. T. Willis, "The Genre of Isa 5:1–7," *JBL* 96 [1977], 337–62), although many accept the refinement proposed by Gale A. Yee in seeing the text as a juridical parable (G. A. Yee, "The Form Critical Study of Isaiah 5:1–7 as a Song and a Juridical Parable," *CBQ* 43 [1981], 30–40; see also G. T. Sheppard, "More on Isaiah 5:1–7 as a Juridical Parable," *CBQ* 44 [1982], 45–47).

[33]References are collected by Willis, "Genre of Isa 5:1–7," 362, n. 116.

[34]Most assume that the "beloved" of verses 1–2 is a close friend of the prophet on whose behalf he sings; then, in verse 3, as the parabolic language of the poem begins to reveal itself, it is made clear that this "beloved friend" is Yahweh: so, for example, Robert B. Y. Scott, "Introduction and Exegesis: The Book of Isaiah, Chapters 1–39," *IB* 5 (Nashville: Abingdon, 1956), 197, who translates, "Now hear me sing on behalf of my friend, my friend's song about his vineyard." But, as will be discussed further below, this interpretation, while it is correct in its analysis of verse 3 and the verses that follow, ignores the sexual connotations elsewhere associated with the term used in verse 1 for "beloved," *yādîd*. It also ignores, as will be discussed below as well, the description of the song as a "love song" (*šîrat dôdî*) and the juxtaposition of the terms *yādîd* and *dôd*, both meaning "beloved," with the term *kerem*, "vineyard," in the last two lines of verse 1. Frequently in ancient Near Eastern poetry, *kerem* designates lovers. See further G. R. Williams, "Frustrated Expectations in Isaiah V 1–7: A Literary Interpretation," *VT* 35 (1985), 460–61.

[35]Goitein, "Women as Creators," 17–18, also briefly makes this point and suggests as well that there is a reference to women's vintage songs in Hos 2:17 (English 2:15), where God promises Israel, pictured in the text as Yahweh's bride, that she will be given vineyards as a wedding gift. Israel, the prophetic oracle goes on to say, will "respond," according to standard translations, but the verb used in this verse, *'ānâ*, can also mean "to sing," and, in particular, "to sing responsively" or "antiphonally." Sasson, "Golden Calf," 157, in fact suggests that the distinction standard lexica draw between *'ānâ*, "to respond," and *'ānâ*, "to sing," is unnecessary, that the type of antiphonal or responsive singing which *'ānâ*, "to sing," describes is fully a part of the larger context of *'ānâ*, "to respond."

[36]See, for example, Scott, "Isaiah," 196–97, "It is not easy to discern the exact shade of meaning of these words, which in the Song of Songs have an erotic sense unsuitable here . . . by no stretch of the imagination can the song be called a love song."

[37]The consonantal Hebrew text could support either reading.

[38]See further, on the meaning of *dôd,* Joaquín Sanmartín-Ascaso, *"dôdh,"* *TDOT* 3 (ed. G. J. Botterweck and H. Ringgren; Grand Rapids, MI: Eerdmans, 1978), 150–51. He is emphatic that it is only in the Pentateuch that *dôd* has a non-erotic meaning; in fact, speaking specifically of Isa 5:1, he comments on its "erotic sense" (p. 150).

[39]See Williams, "Frustrated Expectations," 459, n. 4.

[40]Again, as in n. 38 above, see Sanmartín-Ascaso, *"dôdh,"* 150.

[41]See M. L. Folmer, "A Literary Analysis of the 'Song of the Vineyard' (Is. 5:1–7)," *JEOL* 29 (1985–86), 108; Korpel, "Literary Genre," 124; Williams, "Frustrated Expectations," 460, n. 7; and Willis, "Genre of Isa 5:1–7," 345.

[42]See M. V. Fox, *The Song of Songs and the Ancient Egyptian Love Songs* (Madison: University of Wisconsin Press, 1985), 286–87, in addition to the references assembled by Korpel, "Literary Genre," 124–25, nn. 34–36; by Williams, "Frustrated Expectations," 460, n. 7; and by Willis, "Genre of Isa 5:1–7," 345–46.

[43]The noun *māḥôl* derived from this verb is, however, quite common, indeed, the most frequently used term for "dance" found in the Hebrew Bible (M. Gruber, "Ten Dance-Derived Expressions in the Hebrew Bible," *Bib* 62 [1981], 341; reprinted in *Dance as Religious Studies* [ed. D. Adams and D. Apostolos-Cappadona; New York: Crossroad, 1990], 56). Also note that some find two other occurrences of the verb *ḥwl,* "to dance," by reading the Polel participle *měḥōlělôt* for the noun *měḥōlôt* in 1 Sam 18:6 and, similarly, the Polel participle *měḥōlălîm* for the Qal participle of *ḥll, ḥōlělîm,* in Ps 87:7. See BDB (Oxford: Clarendon, 1980), 297a, s. v. *ḥwl.*

[44]I have discussed these three texts further, and especially their association with women's music at the vineyard feast, in "Isaiah," 163.

[45]On the translation "hand-drum" for Hebrew *tōp* (plural *tuppîm*), see C. L. Meyers, "Of Drums and Damsels: Women's Performance in Ancient Israel," *BA* 54 (1991), 16–27, especially 21–23.

[46]See elsewhere, for the stripping and baring of oneself and the girding on of sackcloth, Jer 6:26; 25:34; 48:37; Ezek 27:30; Amos 8:10; Mic 1:10; Joel 1:13; for the beating of the breast, Nah 2:7; Luke 23:48; for the wailing of laments, the discussion below.

[47]See further G. A. Anderson, *A Time to Mourn, A Time to Dance: The Expression of Grief and Joy in Israelite Religion* (University Park, PA: The Pennsylvania State University Press, 1991), 70–71.

[48] Isaiah 24:7–13 is particularly interesting in this regard, for although there is no specific reference to women, much of the music referred to in that text is arguably women's music. Regarding the reference in verse 8 to "the mirth of the hand-drum," for example, my colleague Nancy Bowen at Earlham College reminds me that Meyers has shown that this instrument is often (although not exclusively) played by female musicians (Meyers, "Of Drums and Damsels," 21–22). The other instrument referred to, the lyre, is not as extensively attested as a women's instrument, but women lyre players are known. One of the most famous examples is the woman lyre player pictured on Pithos A from Kuntillet ʿAjrud. See P. Beck, "The Drawings from Horvat Teiman (Kuntillet ʿAjrud)," *Tel Aviv* 9 (1982), Fig. 5, Motif U, and Pl. 5.2, with discussion on pp. 31–36; W. G. Dever, "Asherah, Consort of Yahweh? New Evidence from Kuntillet ʿAjrûd," *BASOR* 255 (1985), Fig. 1 with discussion on p. 24; J. M. Hadley, "Some Drawings and Inscriptions on Two Pithoi from Kuntillet ʿAjrud," *VT* 37 (1987), 201–3. Women lyre players also are known in Phoenicia; see the photograph in Meyers, "Of Drums and Damsels," 22 (= A. Sendrey, *Music in the Social and Religious Life of Antiquity* [Rutherford, Madison, and Teaneck: Fairleigh Dickinson University Press, 1974], Illus. 68). Finally, from Egypt, see the female lyre player depicted in the Eighteenth Dynasty tomb of Nakht, reproduced in M. Werbrouck and B. van de Walle, *La Tombe de Nakht* (Bruxelles: Fondation Egyptologique, 1929), 8; the female lyre player depicted in the Tomb of Wah from Thebes, dating from the reign of Thutmose III, pictured in C. Aldred, *New Kingdom Art in Ancient Egypt During the Eighteenth Dynasty, 1590–1315 B.C.* (London: Alec Tiranti, 1951), Pl. 29 with commentary on pp. 49–50; the female lyre player depicted in Thebes Tomb 38 from the reign of Thutmose IV, found in Sendrey, *Music in the Social and Religious Life of Antiquity,* Illus. 16, and in *ANEP* (ed. J. B. Pritchard; Princeton: Princeton University Press, 1954), #208; finally, the female lyre player depicted in another Theban tomb, again reproduced in Sendrey, *Music in the Social and Religious Life of Antiquity,* Illus. 24.

[49] "Israelite Religion and the Faith of Israel's Daughters: Reflections on Gender and Religious Definition," *The Bible and the Politics of Exegesis: Essays in Honor of Norman K. Gottwald on His Sixty-Fifth Birthday* (ed. D. Jobling; P. L. Day; G. T. Sheppard; Cleveland, OH: Pilgrim, 1991), 106; see also the artistic representations pictured in E. Jacobs, "Mourning," *IDB* 3 (ed. G. A. Butterick; Nashville: Abingdon, 1962), 453a, pointed out by Bird, "Faith of Israel's Daughters," 316, n. 38.

[50] On beating the breast as a mourning gesture, see above, n. 46.

[51] I have discussed the geographical layout of Ezekiel 8 thoroughly in *Under Every Green Tree: Popular Religion in Sixth-Century Judah* (Atlanta: Scholars Press, 1992), 53–55.

[52] Note, for example, the laments of lover, sister, and mother wailing over Tammuz that have been collected by T. Jacobsen, *The Treasures of Darkness. A History of Mesopotamian Religion* (New Haven and London: Yale University Press, 1976),

49–55; also see Jacobsen's comments in "Toward the Image of Tammuz," *Toward the Image of Tammuz and Other Essays on Mesopotamian History and Culture* (ed. W. L. Moran; Cambridge, MA: Harvard University Press, 1970), 77–78; S. N. Kramer, "The Weeping Goddess: Sumerian Prototypes of the *Mater Dolorosa*," *BA* 46 (1983), especially pp. 76–79.

[53] See, for example, the representation from a fourteenth-century B.C.E. Theban tomb reproduced in Jacobs, "Mourning," 453a, and in *ANEP*, #638; a similar fourteenth- or thirteenth-century B.C.E. relief (Nineteenth Dynasty) from Saqqara (Sendrey, *Music in the Social and Religious Life of Antiquity*, Illus. 39); and the various fourth-, third-, and second-millennium B.C.E. images collected by I. Lexora, *Ancient Egyptian Dances* (Praha, Czechoslovakia: Oriental Institute, 1935), Obr. 1–2, 66, and 72 (with regard to Obr. 1–2, see also *Nofret—Die Schöne: Die Frau im Alten Ägypten, "Wahrheit" und Wirklichkeit* [Mainz: Philipp von Zabern; Hildesheim: Roemer- und Pelizaeus-Museum, 1985], Nos. 97–99, and, on the pulling out of hair as a mourning gesture in the ancient Near East, Ackerman, *Under Every Green Tree*, 86, n. 143).

[54] The pertinent texts are *KTU* 1.16.1.5 (Kirta) and 1.19.4.9–11 (Aqhat).

[55] Conveniently reproduced in Jacobs, "Mourning," 453a; also *ANEP*, #459.

[56] Lines 723–75.

[57] Generally, on the role of Greek women as singers of lament, see M. Alexiou, *The Ritual Lament in Greek Tradition* (Cambridge: Cambridge University Press, 1974), passim; D. C. Kurtz and J. Boardman, *Greek Burial Customs* (Ithaca, NY: Cornell University Press, 1971); 143–44; S. H. Lonsdale, *Dance and Ritual Play in Greek Religion* (Baltimore and London: Johns Hopkins University Press, 1993), 234–60; E. Vermule, *Aspects of Death in Early Greek Art and Poetry* (Berkeley, Los Angeles, and London: University of California Press, 1979), 11–23.

[58] *Judges*, 451.

[59] *Judges*, 494.

[60] The tale is found in Livy, 1.9.6–11, and in Plutarch, *Romulus*, 14.1–7.

[61] *Myth, Legend, and Custom in the Old Testament: A Comparative Study with Chapters from Sir James G. Frazer's Folklore in the Old Testament* (New York and Evanston: Harper & Row, 1969), 444–45.

[62] Pausanias, 4.16.9–10.

[63] C. Calame, *Les choeurs de jeunes filles en Grèce archaïque* I: *Morphologie, fonction religieuse et sociale* (Filologia e critica 20; Roma: Edizioni dell'Ateneo & Bizzarri, 1977), 176–77; Lonsdale, *Dance and Ritual Play*, 222–33.

[64]Gaster, *Myth, Legend, and Custom*, 445, also mentions the Kore myth as a possible counterpart to Judg 21:15–24, but because he assigns to that myth a cultic context unparalleled in Israel—a spring festival involving a ceremonial gathering of flowers—he ultimately does not see the tale as significant.

[65]Plutarch, *Theseus*, 31.1–4.

[66]Lines 179–92.

[67]Lines 117–25.

[68]Two other Greek examples of the "abduction of dancing maidens" story come from plays of Menander. *Samai* begins with a speech made by one of the main characters, Moschion, in which he confesses that he kidnapped the Samian woman Plangon while she and her companions were dancing in the Adonis festival and then impregnated her (Act 1, lines 5–55). In *Epitrepontes*, lines 451–53, Menander also mentions a girl who was raped at the festival of Artemis Tauropolos, celebrated at Halai Araphenides, a coastal village eighteen miles east of Athens.

[69]*Dance and Ritual Play*, 222.

[70]Pausanias, 6.22.9.

[71]*Dance and Ritual Play*, 223; see, similarly, Calame, *Les choeurs de jeunes filles*, 176, 189–90; C. Sourvinou-Inwood, "A Series of Erotic Pursuits: Images and Meanings," *JHS* 107 (1987), 144–46.

[72]On the definition of *bĕtûlâ*, see further P. L. Day, "From the Child Is Born the Woman: The Story of Jephthah's Daughter," *Gender and Difference in Ancient Israel* (ed. P. L. Day; Minneapolis: Fortress, 1989), 59.

[73]*Dance and Ritual Play*, 223–28.

[74]*Theogony*, 912–13.

[75]Plutarch, *Theseus*, 31.3; translation, B. Perrin, *Plutarch's Lives* I (LCL; Cambridge, MA: Harvard University Press, 1914), 73.

[76]Line 182; translation, R. Lattimore, *The Iliad of Homer* (Chicago and London: University of Chicago Press, 1951), 335.

[77]*Dance and Ritual Play*, 224–26; see also Sourvinou-Inwood, "Erotic Pursuits," 136–47; I. Jenkins, "Is There Life After Marriage? A Study of the Abduction Motif in Vase Paintings of the Athenian Wedding Ceremony," *Bulletin of the Institute of Classical Studies* 30 (1983), 137–45.

[78] *Dance and Ritual Play,* 223–24.

[79] Similarly, Sourvinou-Inwood, "Erotic Pursuits," 144–46.

[80] Both Bathja Bayer, "Dance in the Bible: The Possibilities and Limitations of the Evidence," *Papers of the International Seminar on the Bible in Dance* (Jerusalem, August 5–9, 1979; Jerusalem: The Seminar on the Bible in Dance, 1979), 4, and Goitein, "Women as Creators," 16, point out that Judg 21:20–21 does not specify that the women dance in the vineyards *per se* but only that their Benjaminite abductors conceal themselves there. But, as Goitein notes, the women were surely, if not dancing right *in* the vineyards, dancing nearby. Gruber, "Ten Dance-Derived Expressions," 345, cites in this regard the suggestion of Julian Morgenstern, "The Etymological History of the Three Hebrew Synonyms for 'to Dance,' HGG, HLL and KRR, and their Cultural Significance," *JAOS* 36 (1917), 324, who, based on the reference in M. Ta'anit 4:8 to the girls of Jerusalem who danced in the vineyards between the 15th of Av and the Day of Atonement and the discussion of the "circumference of the vineyard" found in M. Kilayim 4:1–2, argues that, at least in Mishnaic times, there was an open space surrounding every vineyard in which Jerusalem's young women danced during the nights between the grape harvest and the beginning of the New Year. On M. Ta'anit 4:8, see also A. Brenner and F. van Dijk-Hemmes, *On Gendering Texts: Female and Male Voices in the Hebrew Bible* (Leiden: Brill, 1993), 72; Goitein, "Women as Creators," 16–17; and R. de Vaux, *Ancient Israel 2: Religious Institutions* (New York: McGraw Hill, 1965), 496.

[81] This Greek motif, moreover, may manifest itself more directly elsewhere in the biblical text. Compare with Kore's meadowed dancing ground the biblical Abel-meholah, literally, "the meadow of dancing," mentioned in Judg 7:22; 1 Kgs 4:12; 19:16.

[82] Note that, despite the claim of Lawrence E. Stager that viticulture is not generally a part of early Iron Age village economies ("Archaeology, Ecology, and Social History: Background Themes to the Song of Deborah," VTSup 40 [Jerusalem Congress Volume, 1986; ed. J. A. Emerton; Leiden: Brill, 1988], 222), the cache of carbonized raisins found by archaeologists in the Iron I remains of Area C at Shiloh (in the northern side unit of the courtyard of Building 335) does suggest grape production. See S. Bunimovitz, "Area C: The Iron Age I Buildings and Other Remains" in "Excavations at Shiloh 1981–1984: Preliminary Report," *Tel Aviv* 12 (1985), 135 and Pl. 19.2.

[83] The best attested examples of this phenomenon are at Ai and Raddana. See L. E. Stager, "The Archaeology of the Family in Ancient Israel," *BASOR* 260 (1985), 6, and the copious references there.

[84] On the archaeology of Shiloh, see I. Finkelstein, "Organization, Method and History of the Excavations" in "Excavations at Shiloh 1981–1984," 123–29; idem,

"Shiloh Yields Some, But Not All, of Its Secrets: Location of Tabernacle Still Uncertain," *BARev* 12/1 (January/February 1986), 22–41; idem, "Seilun, Khirbet," *ABD* 5 (ed. D. N. Freedman; New York: Doubleday, 1992), 1069a–72b; idem, "Shiloh, Renewed Excavations," *The New Encyclopedia of Archaeological Excavations in the Holy Land* 4 (ed. E. Stern; Jerusalem: The Israel Exploration Society and Carta; New York: Simon and Schuster, 1993), 1366–70.

[85] *Dance and Ritual Play*, 234. For similar comments on the similarities between Greek weddings and funerals, see, among the references cited elsewhere in this chapter, Jenkins, "Is There Life After Marriage?" 142; J. Redfield, "Notes on the Greek Wedding," *Arethusa* 15 (1982), 188–91; R. Seaford, "The Tragic Wedding," *JHS* 107 (1987), 106–30; Sourvinou-Inwood, "Erotic Pursuits," 139.

[86] Redfield, "Notes on the Greek Wedding," 181–201, especially 181–82, 190–93; Seaford, "The Tragic Wedding," 106–30, especially 110–19.

[87] Fragment 114. The Greek text reads:

parthenia, parthenia, poi me lipoisa oichēi;
ouketi ēxō pros se, ouketi ēxō.

The translation is that of my colleague in the Classics Department at Dartmouth College, Phyllis B. Katz, who also brought this quotation to my attention. I am additionally in Katz's debt for much of the discussion on Greek marriage hymns that follows.

[88] See e.g., C. R. Haines, *Sappho: The Poems and Fragments* (London: Routledge; New York: E. P. Dutton, 1926), 151; J. Ferguson, *Catullus* (Lawrence, KS: Coronado Press, 1985), 183; E. Fraenkel, "Vesper adest," *JRS* 45 (1955), 5–6.

[89] By far the most complete study of Catullus 62 is O. Thomsen, *Ritual and Desire: Catullus 61 and 62 and other Ancient Documents on Wedding and Marriage* (Aarhus, Denmark: Aarhus University Press, 1992), 151–230 (this reference brought to my attention by my colleague in the Classics Department at Dartmouth College, Phyllis B. Katz). See also Fraenkel, "Vesper adest," 1–8; D. A. Kidd, "Hesperus and Catullus LXII," *Latomus* 33 (1974), 22–33; Ferguson, *Catullus*, 181–84.

[90] Thomsen, *Catullus 61 and 62*, 181–82, 261–72.

[91] Isa 1:4, 24; 10:1, 5; 17:12; 28:1; 29:1, 15; 30:1; 31:1; 33:1; 45:9, 10; 55:1.

AFTERWORD

In 1973, Phyllis Trible published her ground-breaking article, "Depatri-archalizing in Biblical Interpretation,"[1] which in many senses inaugurated the modern enterprise of feminist biblical scholarship. In this article, Trible begins by describing what she sees as the "hermeneutical challenge . . . to translate biblical faith without sexism,"[2] and goes on to describe two strategies of what she calls "a depatriarchalizing principle."[3] The second of these has received by far the most attention. It comprises Trible's exegetical attempts to reread "passages specifically concerned with female and male,"[4] especially passages that have traditionally been seen to support a mandate of male supremacy, "with the conviction, indeed the realization, that the Bible can be redeemed from bondage to patriarchy; that redemption is already at work in the text; and that the articulation of it is desirable and beneficial."[5] Trible's most famous example is her rereading of the Garden of Eden story in Genesis 2–3, in which she argues, for example, that man is not, contrary to the more usual exegesis, created first (and thus, presumably, superior) in that story but that the 'ādām, or "adam," created in 2:7 is a sexually undifferentiated earth creature (created from the earth or 'ădāmâ) who only becomes male *and* female, simultaneously, in 2:21–23 when "divine surgery"[6] divides the one into two. The woman's status as 'ēzer, "helper," Trible similarly argues, does not necessarily connote subordination, as is traditionally assumed, unless, that is, God, who is often called 'ēzer in the Hebrew Bible, is subordinate to the humans who need the deity's help.[7] And why, Trible asks, does the serpent talk to the woman in persuading the humans to eat from the fruit of the forbidden tree? Because she is weaker, more gullible, more easily tempted, as traditional interpretations suggest? Or because she is more thoughtful, more intelligent, more capable of sustaining the sort of theological conversation in which the serpent wishes to engage?

This sort of detailed, word-by-word, verse-by-verse rereading of a

biblical text in an attempt to redeem it from a traditionally sexist interpretation stands side-by-side with and indeed serves to complement the
other depatriarchalizing principle Trible advances in her article, in which
she undertakes a more comprehensive look at the entire corpus of the
Hebrew Bible. Her goal in so doing is to find overarching themes of
redemption that manage to disavow sexism and so contradict the male-
dominated nature of the tradition. For example, Trible cites numerous
biblical verses where God, although typically understood in the Bible as
male, is given female attributes, suggesting an Israelite understanding of
a deity that is *both* male and female and thus a deity that should embrace
equally both sexes.[8] Trible likewise describes the thematic force of the
Exodus story as being liberation from bondage. Although the specifics
of that story concern a liberation that is not her particular concern—
the liberation of the Hebrew slaves from their bondage in Egypt—she
nevertheless argues that the general theme of a God who works to bring
about redemption from oppression suggests a deity who favors liberation
for women rather than subjugation.

Yet in almost the same year that Trible first argued for the Exodus
theme of liberation as a redemptive motif for feminism, another feminist
scholar of religion, Mary Daly, preached a sermon in Harvard's Memorial Church in which she evoked the biblical theme of Exodus in a very
different way.[9] For Daly, whose sermon is as famous in certain circles as
Trible's "Depatriarchalizing" article is among feminist biblical scholars,
Exodus did not offer a thematic entrée back into a religious tradition
for women who have otherwise found themselves disaffected by biblical
patriarchy. Exodus instead offered, and even mandated, a way *out* of
biblically-based religious traditions, especially Christianity, and Roman
Catholic Christianity, which is where Daly's original faith commitment
lay. Daly's sermon called upon the women's community to leave the
church behind, to go to war with "sexist religion as *sexist*,"[10] and to seek
"alternative expressions to those available in institutional religions."[11]
These "alternative expressions," Daly went on to say, included "sisterhood" as a church unto itself since sisterhood, like a church, was characterized as "a space set apart," as a charismatic community, and as a
community with a mission.[12] More important, she proclaimed:

> . . . sisterhood is an *exodus* community that goes away from the land of
> our fathers—leaving that behind because of the promise to women that
> is still unfulfilled. It is an exodus community that, perhaps for the first

time in history, is putting our own cause—the liberation of women—
first.[13]

Daly then called upon members of the audience to demonstrate their
rejection of sexist religion by rising and walking out of Memorial
Church together, thus physically signaling their exodus from the same
faith traditions that Trible, who, ironically enough, was also teaching in
Boston at that time, was drawing on the themes of Exodus to redeem.

To be sure, my focus in this volume has not been Exodus; my concern
has been the book of Judges. Nor are the sorts of interpretive enterprises
undertaken by Trible and Daly, which are essentially theological in nature, seeking to bring biblical faith into some sort of dialogue with contemporary, biblically-based religious traditions (in Daly's case, hostile
dialogue), identical to the sorts of history-of-religions questions I have
addressed. Unlike Trible and Daly, that is, my interest has been to ask
about the biblical materials within the context of their own time and
not within the context of ours. Nevertheless, I do believe that if we
consider the kinds of results that can be obtained, the theological approaches of Trible and Daly are not really so far removed from the
history-of-religions methodology I have employed. Indeed, I believe
that one of the reasons Trible and Daly are able to come to their radically
different understandings about what the Exodus tradition in particular
and the biblical teachings about women in general mean for women
today is because, as a history-of-religions investigation shows, there was
no consensus about the role and status of women in the biblical community itself. The diversity of modern feminist theology thus, at least to
some degree, is deeply rooted in the diversity of traditions about women
that a study of ancient Israelite religion can reveal.

   Certainly we have seen this diversity of traditions in this study of the
women of Judges. That book ends in much the same way that it began,
with a tale of women becoming victims to men's wartime games of "give
and take." Thus Caleb, in Judg 1:12, and the men of Israel, in Judg 21:1,
decide whether to give, or, in the case of Judges 21, not to give, their
daughters as brides; then warriors step forward to take these women as
booty. Othniel claims Achsah as the trophy of war that accompanies his
capture of Debir, and the Benjaminites seize the young women of Shiloh
in the same way prey is seized after a successful hunt. Still, I have earlier

argued that Achsah eventually "gives as good as she gets," so to speak, asserting herself in Judg 1:14–15 as the dominant partner in her nuptials by assuming the responsibility of petitioning her father for a marriage gift of land; she also provides the "brains" of the marital relationship by seeking through her request a source of water, which she and her husband will require if they are to prosper in their work as small-scale agriculturalists in Israel's semiarid climate. The daughters of Shiloh, too, although unlike Achsah in that they never are given the opportunity to speak, nevertheless are afforded a significant means of self-expression. After all, I have suggested, they are Israel's "singers of tales" according to Judg 21:15–25, assigned the role of ritual musicians at the annual celebration of the vineyard feast. Whatever autonomy, then, their story of abduction ultimately denies them, Judges still admits the important place these women occupy within at least this aspect of the practice of Israelite religious life.[14]

In a word, the traditions reflected in Judges are ambivalent: Judg 1:11–15 is ambivalent about whether Achsah is pawn or predominant; Judg 21:15–25 is ambivalent about whether Shiloh's daughters are the story's actors or merely characters who are acted upon. Elsewhere in Judges this same ambivalence is also present: is Deborah a war leader whom we should credit with Sisera's and the Canaanite army's military defeat or is she merely a sideline cheerleader who urges on the story's real—and male—hero, Barak? It depends on whether one reads her tale in Judges 4 or Judges 5. And Jael, is she a ruthless assassin or an exploitative seductress? Again, it depends what part of Judges one reads. Or what of Sisera's mother, is she a queen mother imbued with the same sorts of socio-political and religious power enjoyed by her counterparts elsewhere in the west Semitic world or is she as impotent as David's Queen Michal, staring out of a window in despair? Jephthah's daughter is dead by her own father's hand, yet she founds a young women's religious retreat; Manoah's wife is nameless and subordinate to an agenda of patrilineal descent, but she recognizes theophany when she sees it and understands the word of God and what it means. Women can be passive instruments in Samson's hands yet otherwise hold his life in theirs. A woman's rape is in one instance proscribed, but in another set of circumstances, the violation is permitted.

In the end, then, there is no easy categorizing of Judges: it is neither a handbook of patriarchy nor a celebration of matriarchy; it can neither be condemned as a remorseless portrait of unrelenting misogyny nor be

heralded as an archaic precursor of twentieth-century feminism. It paints
no picture of a world of men alone, but it portrays no women's garden
of paradise instead. It is, if anything, a book not of "either/or" but of
"both/and," a book that both glorifies the deeds of men and embraces
the tales of women. Perhaps, moreover, this multidimensionality is just
as it should be, for multiple dimensions are surely a hallmark of all religious traditions, including the Israelite religious traditions from which
the book of Judges stems. Indeed, this, in a nutshell, is the point of my
entire examination: that when the book of Judges in general and its
women characters in particular are studied from the point of view of a
history-of-religions methodology and when the full weight of the comparative enterprise is brought to bear on these materials, what *must*
emerge is not one conclusion but many. There is enormous wealth and
diversity in the theological and ideological presuppositions that underlie
even the shortest and simplest of any of the tales of Judges' women. As
a result, there is enormous wealth and diversity found in the recounting
of these tales as they appear throughout this biblical book.

NOTES

[1] *JAAR* 41 (1973), 30–48.

[2] "Depatriarchalizing," 31.

[3] "Depatriarchalizing," 47.

[4] "Depatriarchalizing," 35.

[5] P. Trible, "Eve and Miriam: From the Margins to the Center," *Feminist Approaches to the Bible* (ed. H. Shanks; Washington, D.C.: Biblical Archaeology Society, 1995), 8.

[6] Trible, "Eve and Miriam," 12.

[7] See the references assembled by Trible in "Depatriarchalizing," 36, n. 34.

[8] See the references assembled by Trible in "Depatriarchalizing," 34.

[9] "The Women's Movement: An Exodus Community," *Religious Education* 67 (September/October 1972), 327–33; reprinted in *Women and Religion: A Feminist Sourcebook of Christian Thought* (ed. E. Clark and H. Richardson; New York, Hagerstown, San Francisco, London: Harper & Row, 1977), 265–71. All quotations come from the reprinted publication.

[10] "An Exodus Community," 270; the emphasis in the quote is Daly's.

[11] "An Exodus Community," 270.

[12] "An Exodus Community," 270.

[13] "An Exodus Community," 270; the emphases in the quote are Daly's.

[14] Lillian R. Klein, *The Triumph of Irony in the Book of Judges* (Sheffield: Almond, 1988), 190, similarly compares the tales of Achsah and daughters of Shiloh, but her conclusions are very different from mine. See also D. N. Fewell, "Judges," *The Women's Bible Commentary* (ed. C. A. Newsom and S. H. Ringe; London: SPCK; Louisville, KY: Westminster/John Knox, 1992), 76, and G. A. Yee, "Introduction: Why Judges?" *Judges and Method: New Approaches in Biblical Studies* (ed. G. A. Yee; Minneapolis: Fortress, 1995), 10. Phyllis Trible, *Texts of Terror: Literary Feminist Readings of Biblical Narratives* (OBT 13; Philadelphia: Fortress, 1984), 90, n. 52, compares Achsah to the Levite's concubine.

BIBLIOGRAPHY

Ackerman, J. S. "Prophecy and Warfare in Early Israel: A Study of the Deborah-Barak Story," *BASOR* 220 (1975), 5–13.

Ackerman, S. "'And the Women Knead Dough': The Worship of the Queen of Heaven in Sixth-Century Judah," *Gender and Difference in Ancient Israel*. Ed. P. L. Day. Minneapolis: Fortress, 1989, 109–24.

———. "The Deception of Isaac, Jacob's Dream at Bethel, and Incubation on an Animal Skin," *Priesthood and Cult in Ancient Israel*. JSOTSup 125. Ed. G. A. Anderson and S. M. Olyan. Sheffield: JSOT Press, 1991, 92–120.

———. *Under Every Green Tree: Popular Religion in Sixth-Century Judah*. HSM 46. Atlanta: Scholars Press, 1992.

———. "Isaiah," *The Women's Bible Commentary*. Ed. C. A. Newsom and S. H. Ringe. London: SPCK; Louisville, KY: Westminster/John Knox, 1992, 161–68.

———. "The Queen Mother and the Cult in Ancient Israel," *JBL* 112 (1993), 385–401.

———. "The Prayer of Nabonidus, Elijah on Mount Carmel, and Monotheism in Israel," *The Echoes of Many Texts: Reflections on Jewish and Christian Traditions, Essays in Honor of Lou H. Silberman*. Ed. W. G. Dever and J. E. Wright. BJS 313. Atlanta: Scholars Press, 1997, 51–65.

———. "The Queen Mother and the Cult in the Ancient Near East," *Women and Goddess Traditions: In Antiquity and Today*. Studies in Antiquity and Christianity. Ed. K. L. King with an introduction by K. J. Torjeson. Minneapolis: Fortress, 1997, 179–209.

———. "Idol, Idolatry," *The Eerdmans' Dictionary of the Bible*. Ed. D. N. Freedman. Grand Rapids, MI: Eerdmans, forthcoming (1998).

———. "Queens, Biblical," *Encyclopedia of Women and World Religion*. Ed. S. Young. New York: Macmillan, forthcoming (1998).

Ackroyd, P. R. "Goddesses, Women and Jezebel," *Images of Women in Antiquity*. Ed. A. Cameron and A. Kuhrt. London and Canberra: Croom Helm, 1983, 245–59.

Adler, R. "'A Mother in Israel': Aspects of the Mother Role in Jewish Myth," *Beyond Androcentrism: New Essays on Women and Religion*. Ed. R. M. Gross. Missoula, MT: Scholars Press, 1977, 237–55.

Ahlström, G. W. *Aspects of Syncretism in Israelite Religion*. Horae Soederblomianae 5. Lund: C. W. K. Gleerup, 1963.

———. "Judges 5:20 f. and History," *JNES* 36 (1977), 287–88.

———. *The History of Ancient Palestine*. Minneapolis: Fortress; Sheffield: Sheffield Academic Press, 1993.

Aistleitner, J. *Wörterbuch der ugaritischen Sprache*. Berlin: Akademie Verlag, 1974.

Albright, W. F. "The Evolution of the West Semitic Deity 'An-'Anat-'Attâ," *AJSL* 41 (1925), 73–101.

———. *Archaeology and the Religion of Israel*. 2d ed. Baltimore: Johns Hopkins University Press, 1946.

———. "A Catalogue of Early Hebrew Lyric Poems (Psalm LXVIII)," *HUCA* 33 (1950–51), 1–39.

———. "Jethro, Hobab and Reuel in Early Hebrew Tradition (with some Comments on the Origin of 'JE')," *CBQ* 25 (1963), 1–11.

———. *Yahweh and the Gods of Canaan: A Historical Analysis of Two Contrasting Faiths*. Winona Lake, IN: Eisenbrauns, 1968.

Aldred, C. *New Kingdom Art in Ancient Egypt During the Eighteenth Dynasty, 1590–1315 B.C.* London: Alec Tiranti, 1951.

Alexiou, M. *The Ritual Lament in Greek Tradition*. Cambridge: Cambridge University Press, 1974.

Alonso-Schökel, L. "Narrative Structures in the Book of Judith," *Protocol Series of the Eleventh Colloquy of the Center for Hermeneutical Studies in Hellenistic and Modern Culture*. Ed. W. Wuellner. Berkeley, CA: Center for Hermeneutical Studies in Hellenistic and Modern Culture, 1975, 1–20.

Alt, A. "Das Königtum in der Reichen Israel und Juda," *VT* 1 (1951), 2–22. Reprinted in *Kleine Schriften zur Geschichte des Volkes Israel* 2. München: C. H. Beck,

1959, 116–34. English translation: "The Monarchy in the Kingdoms of Israel and Judah," *Essays on Old Testament History and Religion*. Garden City, NY: Doubleday, 1967, 313–35.

Alter, R. "Biblical Type-Scenes and the Uses of Convention," *Critical Inquiry* 5 (1978), 355–68.

———. *The Art of Biblical Narrative*. New York: Basic Books, 1981.

———. "How Convention Helps Us Read: The Case of the Bible's Annunciation Type-Scene," *Prooftexts* 3 (1983), 115–30.

———. "From Line to Story in Biblical Verse," *Poetics Today* 4 (1983), 615–37.

———. *The Art of Biblical Poetry*. New York: Basic Books, 1985.

———. "Samson Without Folklore," *Text and Tradition: The Hebrew Bible and Folklore*. Ed. S. Niditch. Atlanta: Scholars Press, 1990, 47–56.

Altman, C. B. See Loud, G.

Amit, Y. "'Manoah Promptly Followed His Wife' (Judges 13.11): On the Place of the Woman in Birth Narratives," *A Feminist Companion to Judges*. Ed. A. Brenner. The Feminist Companion to the Bible 4. Sheffield: Sheffield Academic Press, 1993, 146–56.

The Ancient Near East in Pictures Relating to the Old Testament. Ed. J. B. Pritchard. Princeton: Princeton University Press, 1954.

Ancient Near Eastern Texts Relating to the Old Testament. 3d ed. Ed. J. B. Pritchard. Princeton: Princeton University Press, 1969.

Anderson, G. A. *A Time to Mourn, A Time to Dance: The Expression of Grief and Joy in Israelite Religion*. University Park, PA: The Pennsylvania State University Press, 1991.

Andreasen, N.-E. A. "The Role of the Queen Mother in Israelite Society," *CBQ* 45 (1983), 179–94.

Arav, R. "Kedesh 2," *ABD* 4. Ed. D. N. Freedman. New York: Doubleday, 1992, 11a.

Arend, W. *Die typischen Scenen bei Homer*. Problemata 7. Berlin: Weidmann, 1933.

Aschkenasy, N. *Eve's Journey: Feminine Images in Hebraic Literary Tradition.* Philadelphia: University of Pennsylvania Press, 1986.

Attridge, H. W., and R. A. Oden, Jr. *Philo of Byblos: The Phoenician History. Introduction, Critical Text, Translation, Notes.* CBQMS 9. Washington, D.C.: The Catholic Biblical Association of America, 1981.

Bailey, R. C. *David in Love and War: The Pursuit of Power in 2 Samuel 10–12.* JSOTSup 75. Sheffield: JSOT Press, 1989.

Bal, M. *Lethal Love: Feminist Literary Readings of Biblical Love Stories.* Bloomington and Indianapolis: Indiana University Press, 1987.

———. *Murder and Difference: Gender, Genre, and Scholarship on Sisera's Death.* Bloomington and Indianapolis: Indiana University Press, 1988.

———. *Death and Dissymmetry: The Politics of Coherence in the Book of Judges.* Chicago: University of Chicago Press, 1988.

———. "A Body of Writing: Judges 19," *A Feminist Companion to Judges.* Ed. A. Brenner. The Feminist Companion to the Bible 4. Sheffield: Sheffield Academic Press, 1993, 208–30.

Baltzer, K. "Women and War in Qohelet 7:23–8:1a," *HTR* 80 (1987), 127–32.

Bargad, W., and S. F. Chyet. *Israeli Poetry: A Contemporary Anthology.* Bloomington: Indiana University Press, 1986.

Barnett, R. D. "The Nimrud Ivories and the Art of the Phoenicians," *Iraq* 2 (1935), 179–210.

———. *A Catalogue of the Nimrud Ivories, with other examples of Ancient Near Eastern Ivories in the British Museum.* 2d ed. London: Trustees of the British Museum, 1975.

———. "Syria and Phoenicia in the Iron Age," *Ancient Ivories in the Middle East and Adjacent Countries.* Qedem 14. Jerusalem: Hebrew University Institute of Archaeology, 1982, 43–55.

Barrois, A. See Thureau-Dangin, F.

Barthélemy, D. "La qualité du Texte Massorétique de Samuel," *The Hebrew and Greek Texts of Samuel.* 1980 Proceedings IOSCS, Vienna. Ed. E. Tov. Jerusalem: Academon, 1980, 1–44.

Bayer, B. "Dance in the Bible: The Possibilities and Limitations of the Evidence," *Papers of the International Seminar on the Bible in Dance*. Jerusalem, August 5–9, 1979. Jerusalem: The Seminar on the Bible in Dance, 1979, 1–10.

Beach, E. F. "The Samaria Ivories, *Marzeaḥ*, and Biblical Text," *BA* 56 (1993), 94–104.

Beck, P. "The Drawings from Ḥorvat Teiman (Kuntillet 'Ajrûd)," *Tel Aviv* 9 (1982), 3–86.

Ben-Barak, Z. "The Queen Consort and the Struggle for Succession to the Throne," *La femme dans le Proche-Orient antique*. Compte rendu de la XXXIIIᵉ Rencontre assyriologique internationale (Paris, 7–10 juillet 1986). Ed. J.-M. Durand. Paris: Recherche sur les Civilisations, 1987, 33–40.

———. "The Status and Right of the *Gĕbîrâ*," *JBL* 110 (1991), 23–34. Reprinted in *A Feminist Companion to Samuel and Kings*. Ed. A. Brenner. The Feminist Companion to the Bible 5. Sheffield: Sheffield Academic Press, 1994, 170–85.

Berlin, A. "Characterization in Biblical Narrative: David's Wives," *JSOT* 23 (1982), 69–85.

———. *Poetics and Interpretation of Biblical Narrative*. Sheffield: JSOT Press, 1983.

Bin-Nun, S. R. *The Tawananna in the Hittite Kingdom*. Heidelberg: Carl Winter; Freiburg: Universitätverlag, 1975.

Bird, P. "The Place of Women in the Israelite Cultus," *Ancient Israelite Religion: Essays in Honor of Frank Moore Cross*. Ed. P. D. Miller; P. D. Hanson; S. D. McBride. Philadelphia: Fortress, 1987, 397–419.

———. "Women's Religion in Ancient Israel," *Women's Earliest Records From Ancient Egypt and Western Asia*. BJS 166. Ed. B. S. Lesko. Atlanta: Scholars Press, 1989, 283–98.

———. "The Harlot as Heroine: Narrative Art and Social Presupposition in Three Old Testament Texts," *Narrative Research on the Hebrew Bible*. Semeia 46. Ed. M. Amihai; G. W. Coats; A. M. Solomon; 1989, 119–39.

———. "'To Play the Harlot': An Inquiry into an Old Testament Metaphor," *Gender and Difference in Ancient Israel*. Ed. P. L. Day. Minneapolis: Fortress, 1989, 75–94.

———. "Israelite Religion and the Faith of Israel's Daughters: Reflections on Gender and Religious Definition," *The Bible and the Politics of Exegesis: Essays in Honor of Norman K. Gottwald on His Sixty-Fifth Birthday.* Ed. D. Jobling; P. L. Day; G. T. Sheppard. Cleveland, OH: Pilgrim, 1991, 97–108.

———. "Women (OT)," *ABD* 6. Ed. D. N. Freedman. New York: Doubleday, 1992, 951a–57a.

Blau, Y. "Ḥătan Dāmîm," *Tarbiz* 26 (1956), 1–3 (Hebrew).

Bledstein, A. J. "Female Companionships: If the Book of Ruth Were Written by a Woman . . . ," *A Feminist Companion to Ruth.* Ed. A. Brenner. The Feminist Companion to the Bible 3. Sheffield: Sheffield Academic Press, 1993, 116–33.

———. "Is Judges a Women's Satire of Men Who Play God?" *A Feminist Companion to Judges.* Ed. A. Brenner. The Feminist Companion to the Bible 4. Sheffield: Sheffield Academic Press, 1993, 34–54.

Bleeker, C. J. *Hathor and Thoth: Two Key Figures of the Ancient Egyptian Religion.* Leiden: Brill, 1973.

Blenkinsopp, J. "Some Notes on the Saga of Samson and the Heroic Milieu," *Scripture* 11 (1959), 81–89.

———. "Ballad Style and Psalm Style in the Song of Deborah: A Discussion," *Bib* 42 (1961), 61–76.

———. "Structure and Style in Judges 13–16," *JBL* 82 (1963), 65–76.

Bloom, H. "The Author J," in H. Bloom and D. Rosenberg, *The Book of J.* New York: Vintage Books, 1990, 9–55.

Boardman, J. See Kurtz, D. C.

de Boer, P. A. H. "The Counsellor," *Wisdom in Israel and in the Ancient Near East.* VTSup 3. *Festschrift H. H. Rowley.* Ed. M. Noth and D. W. Thomas. Leiden: Brill, 1955, 42–71.

Boling, R. G. *Judges.* AB 6a. Garden City, NY: Doubleday, 1975.

———. "Judges, Book of," *ABD* 3. Ed. D. N. Freedman. New York: Doubleday, 1992, 1107a–17a.

———. "Introduction to and Annotations on Judges," *The HarperCollins Study Bible.* Ed. W. A. Meeks. New York: HarperCollins Publishers, 1993, 367–407.

Boogaart, T. A. "Stone for Stone: Retribution in the Story of Abimelech and Shechem," *JSOT* 32 (1985), 45–56.

Bos, J. W. H. "Out of the Shadows: Genesis 38; Judges 4:17–22; Ruth 3," *Reasoning with the Foxes: Female Wit in a World of Male Power. Semeia* 42 (1988). Ed. J. C. Exum and J. W. H. Bos, 37–67.

Boswell, J. *Same-Sex Unions in Premodern Europe.* New York: Villard Books, 1994.

Brekelmans, Chr. H. W. "Some Translation Problems," *OTS* 15 (1970), 170–76.

Brenner, A. *The Israelite Woman: Social Role and Literary Type in Biblical Narrative.* Sheffield: JSOT Press, 1985.

———. "Female social behaviour: two descriptive patterns within the 'birth of the hero' paradigm," *VT* 36 (1986), 257–73. Reprinted in *A Feminist Companion to Genesis.* Ed. A. Brenner. The Feminist Companion to the Bible 2. Sheffield: Sheffield Academic Press, 1993, 204–21.

———. "Introduction," *A Feminist Companion to Judges.* Ed. A. Brenner. The Feminist Companion to the Bible 4. Sheffield: Sheffield Academic Press, 1993, 9–22.

———. "A Triangle and a Rhombus in Narrative Structure: A Proposed Integrative Reading of Judges 4 and 5," *A Feminist Companion to Judges.* Ed. A. Brenner. The Feminist Companion to the Bible 4. Sheffield: Sheffield Academic Press, 1993, 98–109.

———, ed. *A Feminist Companion to Genesis.* The Feminist Companion to the Bible 2. Sheffield: Sheffield Academic Press, 1993.

———, ed. *A Feminist Companion to Ruth.* The Feminist Companion to the Bible 3. Sheffield: Sheffield Academic Press, 1993.

———, ed. *A Feminist Companion to Samuel and Kings.* The Feminist Companion to the Bible 5. Sheffield: Sheffield Academic Press, 1994.

———, and F. van Dijk-Hemmes. *On Gendering Texts: Female and Male Voices in the Hebrew Bible.* Leiden: Brill, 1993.

Briggs, C. A. See Brown, F.

Bronner, L. L. "Valorized or Vilified? The Women of Judges in Midrashic Sources," *A Feminist Companion to Judges.* Ed. A. Brenner. The Feminist Companion to the Bible 4. Sheffield: Sheffield Academic Press, 1993, 72–95.

Brown, F., S. R. Driver, and C. A. Briggs. *Hebrew and English Lexicon of the Old Testament, with an Appendix Containing the Biblical Aramaic.* Oxford: Clarendon, 1980.

Brown, R. E. "Luke's Method in the Annunciation Narrative of Chapter One," *No Famine in the Land: Studies in Honor of John L. McKenzie.* Ed. J. W. Flanagan and A. W. Robinson. Missoula, MT: Scholars Press (for the Institute for Antiquity and Christianity, Claremont), 1975, 179–94.

————. *The Birth of the Messiah: A Commentary on the Infancy Narratives in Matthew and Luke.* Garden City, NY: Doubleday, 1977.

Brown, S. "Perspectives on Phoenician Art," *BA* 55 (1992), 6–24.

Brueggemann, W. "'Impossibility' and Epistemology in the Faith Tradition of Abraham and Sarah (Gen 18 1–15)," *ZAW* 94 (1982), 615–34.

————. "I Samuel 1: A Sense of a Beginning," *ZAW* 102 (1990), 33–48.

Bunimovitz, S. "Area C: The Iron Age I Buildings and Other Remains," in "Excavations at Shiloh 1981–1984: Preliminary Report," *Tel Aviv* 12 (1985), 130–39.

Burney, C. F. *The Book of Judges.* London: Rivingtons, 1920.

Burns, R. J. *Has the Lord Indeed Spoken Only Through Moses? A Study of the Biblical Portrait of Miriam.* Atlanta: Scholars Press, 1987.

Burnshaw, S., T. Carmi, and E. Spicehandler. *The Modern Hebrew Poem Itself.* New York, Chicago, and San Francisco: Holt, Rinehart and Winston, 1965.

Calame, C. *Les choeurs de jeunes filles en Grèce archaïque* I: *Morphologie, fonction religieuse et sociale.* Filologia e critica 20. Roma: Edizioni dell'Ateneo & Bizzarri, 1977.

Camp, C. V. "The Wise Women of 2 Samuel: A Role Model for Women in Early Israel?" *CBQ* 43 (1981), 14–29.

————. "1 and 2 Kings," *The Women's Bible Commentary.* Ed. C. A. Newsom and S. H. Ringe. London: SPCK; Louisville, KY: Westminster/John Knox, 1992, 96–109.

Carmi, T. See Burnshaw, S.

Cartledge, T. W. *Vows in the Hebrew Bible and the Ancient Near East.* JSOTSup 147. Sheffield: JSOT Press, 1992.

Cazelles, H. "La Mere du Roi-Messie dans l'Ancien Testament," *Maria et ecclesia* 5: *Acta Congressus Mariologici-Mariani in civitate Lourdes anno 1958 celebrati.* Romae: Academie Mariana Internationalis, 1959, 39–56.

Childs, B. S. *The Book of Exodus: A Critical, Theological Commentary.* OTL. Philadelphia: Westminster, 1974.

Chyet, S. F. See Bargad, W.

Clines, D. J. A. "The Evidence for an Autumnal New Year in Pre-Exilic Israel Reconsidered," *JBL* 93 (1974), 22–40.

Clough, A. H. *The Poems of Arthur Hugh Clough.* Ed. H. F. Lowry; A. L. P. Norrington; F. L. Mulhauser. Oxford: Clarendon, 1951.

Coats, G. W. "Widow's Rights: A Crux in the Structure of Genesis 38," *CBQ* 34 (1972), 461–66.

Cogan, M. *Imperialism and Religion: Assyria, Judah and Israel in the Eighth and Seventh Centuries B.C.E.* SBLMS 19. Missoula, MT: Scholars Press, 1974.

Collins, J. J. *The Apocalyptic Vision of the Book of Daniel.* HSM 16. Missoula, MT: Scholars Press, 1977.

———. "Apocalyptic Genre and Mythic Allusions in Daniel," *JSOT* 21 (1981), 83–100.

———. *Daniel, with an Introduction to Apocalyptic Literature.* Forms of the Old Testament Literature 20. Grand Rapids, MI: Eerdmans, 1984.

———. *The Apocalyptic Imagination: An Introduction to the Jewish Matrix of Christianity.* New York: Crossroad, 1987.

———. *Daniel: A Commentary on the Book of Daniel.* Hermeneia. Ed. F. M. Cross. Minneapolis: Fortress, 1993.

Conzelmann, H. *The Theology of Saint Luke.* New York: Harper & Row, 1961.

Coogan, M. D. *Stories from Ancient Canaan.* Philadelphia: Westminster, 1978.

———. "A Structural and Literary Analysis of the Song of Deborah," *CBQ* 40 (1978), 143–66.

———. "Canaanite Origins and Lineage: Reflections on the Religion of Ancient

Israel," *Ancient Israelite Religion: Essays in Honor of Frank Moore Cross.* Ed. P. D. Miller; P. D. Hanson; S. D. McBride. Philadelphia: Fortress, 1987, 115–24.

Cooper, A., and B. R. Goldstein. "Biblical Literature in the Iron(ic) Age: Reflections on Literary-Historical Method," *HS* 32 (1991), 45–60.

Craigie, P. C. "A Note on Judges V 2," *VT* 18 (1968), 397–99.

———. "The Song of Deborah and the Epic of Tukulti-Ninurta," *JBL* 88 (1969), 253–65.

———. "Some Further Notes on the Song of Deborah," *VT* 22 (1972), 349–53.

———. "A Reconsideration of Shamgar ben Anath (Judg 3:31 and 5:6)," *JBL* 91 (1972), 239–40.

———. "Three Ugaritic Notes on the Song of Deborah," *JSOT* 2 (1977), 33–49.

———. "Deborah and Anat: A Study of Poetic Imagery," *ZAW* 90 (1978), 374–81.

———. *The Problem of War in the Old Testament.* Grand Rapids, MI: Eerdmans, 1978.

Craven, T. *Artistry and Faith in the Book of Judith.* SBLDS 70. Chico, CA: Scholars Press, 1983.

———. "Tradition and Convention in the Book of Judith," *Semeia* 28 (1983), 49–61.

Crenshaw, J. L. "The Samson Saga: Filial Devotion or Erotic Attachment?" *ZAW* 86 (1974), 470–504.

———. *Samson: A Secret Betrayed, a Vow Ignored.* Atlanta: John Knox, 1978.

Cross, F. M. "A New Qumran Biblical Fragment Related to the Original Hebrew Underlying the Septuagint," *BASOR* 132 (1953), 15–26.

———. "The Canaanite Cuneiform Tablet from Taanach," *BASOR* 190 (1968), 41–46.

———. *Canaanite Myth and Hebrew Epic: Essays in the History of the Religion of Israel.* Cambridge, MA: Harvard University Press, 1973.

———. "'ēl," *TDOT* 1. Ed. G. J. Botterweck and H. Ringgren. Grand Rapids, MI: Eerdmans, 1974, 242–61.

————. "A Response to Zakovitch's 'Successful Failure of Israelite Intelligence,'" *Text and Tradition: The Hebrew Bible and Folklore*. Ed. S. Niditch. Atlanta: Scholars Press, 1990, 99–104.

————, and D. N. Freedman. *Studies in Ancient Yahwistic Poetry*. SBLDS 21. Missoula, MT: Scholars Press, 1975.

Crowfoot, G. M. See Crowfoot, J. W.

Crowfoot, J. W., and G. M. Crowfoot. *Early Ivories from Samaria*. London: Palestine Exploration Fund, 1938.

Dahood, M. *Psalms* II. AB 17. Garden City, NY: Doubleday, 1968.

Daly, M. "The Women's Movement: An Exodus Community," *Religious Education* 67 (September/October 1972), 327–33. Reprinted in *Women and Religion: A Feminist Sourcebook of Christian Thought*. Ed. E. Clark and H. Richardson. New York, Hagerstown, San Francisco, London: Harper & Row, 1977, 265–71.

Darr, K. P. "Like Warrior, like Woman: Destruction and Deliverance in Isaiah 42:10–17," *CBQ* 49 (1987), 560–71.

————. *Far More Precious than Jewels: Perspectives on Biblical Women*. Louisville, KY: Westminster/John Knox, 1991.

Dawson, W. R., and T. E. Peet. "The So-Called Poem on the King's Chariot," *JEA* 19 (1933), 167–74.

Day, J. "Asherah in the Hebrew Bible and in Northwest Semitic Literature," *JBL* 105 (1986), 385–408.

Day, P. L. "From the Child Is Born the Woman: The Story of Jephthah's Daughter," *Gender and Difference in Ancient Israel*. Ed. P. L. Day. Minneapolis: Fortress, 1989, 58–74.

Dempster, S. G. "Mythology and History in the Song of Deborah," *WTJ* 41 (1978), 33–53.

Dever, W. G. "Iron Age Epigraphic Material from the Area of Khirbet el-Kôm," *HUCA* 40/41 (1969–70), 158–89.

————. "Recent Archaeological Confirmation of the Cult of Asherah in Ancient Israel," *Hebrew Studies* 23 (1982), 37–43.

————. "Material Remains and the Cult in Ancient Israel: An Essay in Archaeological Systematics," *The Word of the Lord Shall Go Forth: Essays in Honor of David Noel Freedman in Celebration of His Sixtieth Birthday.* Ed. C. L. Meyers and M. O'Connor. Winona Lake, IN: Eisenbrauns, 1983, 571–87.

————. "Asherah, Consort of Yahweh? New Evidence from Kuntillet 'Ajrûd," *BASOR* 255 (1985), 21–37.

————. "The Contribution of Archaeology to the Study of Canaanite and Early Israelite Religion," *Ancient Israelite Religion: Essays in Honor of Frank Moore Cross.* Ed. P. D. Miller; P. D. Hanson; S. D. McBride. Philadelphia: Fortress, 1987, 209–47.

————. *Recent Archaeological Discoveries and Biblical Research.* Seattle and London: The University of Washington Press, 1990.

————. "Archaeological Data on the Israelite Settlement: A Review of Two Recent Works," *BASOR* 284 (1991), 77–90.

————. "Unresolved Issues in the Early History of Israel: Toward a Synthesis of Archaeological and Textual Reconstructions," *The Bible and the Politics of Exegesis: Essays in Honor of Norman K. Gottwald on His Sixty-Fifth Birthday.* Ed. D. Jobling; P. L. Day; G. T. Sheppard. Cleveland, OH: Pilgrim, 1991, 195–208.

————. "Israel, History of (Archaeology and the 'Conquest')," *ABD* 3. Ed. D. N. Freedman. New York: Doubleday, 1992, 545b–58b.

————. "Cultural Continuity, Ethnicity in the Archaeological Record, and the Question of Israelite Origins," ErIsr 24 (1993). Abraham Malamat volume, 22*–33*.

————. "The Silence of the Text: An Archaeological Commentary on 2 Kings 23," *Scripture and Other Artifacts: Essays on the Bible and Archaeology in Honor of Philip J. King.* Ed. M. D. Coogan; J. C. Exum; L. E. Stager. Louisville, KY: Westminster/John Knox, 1994, 143–68.

Diakonoff, I. M. "Women in Old Babylonia Not Under Patriarchal Authority," *Journal of the Economic and Social History of the Orient* 29 (1986), 225–38.

Dietrich, M., O. Loretz, and J. Sanmartín. *Die keilalphabetischen Texte aus Ugarit: Einschliesslich der keilalphabetischen Texte ausserhalb Ugarits* I. *Transkription.* AOAT 24/1. Neukirchen-Vluyn: Neukirchener Verlag, 1976.

————, and O. Loretz. "*šb, šbm,* und *udn* im Kontext von KTU 1.3 III 35B–IV 4 und KTU 1.83:8," *UF* 14 (1982), 77–81.

Dijk-Hemmes, F. van, "Ruth: A Product of Women's Culture?" *A Feminist Companion to Ruth*. Ed. A. Brenner. The Feminist Companion to the Bible 3. Sheffield: Sheffield Academic Press, 1993, 134–44.

―――. "Mothers and a Mediator in the Song of Deborah," *A Feminist Companion to Judges*. Ed. A. Brenner. The Feminist Companion to the Bible 4. Sheffield: Sheffield Academic Press, 1993, 110–14.

―――. See further Brenner, A.

Donaldson, M. E. "Kinship Theory in the Patriarchal Narratives: The Case of the Barren Wife," *JAAR* 49 (1989), 77–87.

Donner, H. "Art und Herkunft des Amtes der Königinmutter im Alten Testament," *Festschrift Johannes Friedrich zum 65. Geburtstag am 27. August gewidmet*. Ed. R. von Kienle et al. Heidelberg: Carl Winter, 1959, 105–45.

―――, and W. Röllig. *Kanaanäische und aramäische Inschriften* 1–3. Wiesbaden: Otto Harrassowitz, 1962, 1964.

Dossin, G. See Thureau-Dangin, F.

Dressler, H. H. P. "The Metamorphosis of a Lacuna: Is *at.aḫ.wan* . . . a Proposal of Marriage?" *UF* 11 (1979), 211–17.

Driver, G. R. "Problems in Judges Newly Discussed," *ALUOS* 4 (1962–63), 6–25.

―――. *Canaanite Myths and Legends*. 2d ed. Revised by J. C. L. Gibson. Edinburgh: T. & T. Clark, 1978.

Driver, S. R. See Brown, F.

Drower, M. S. "Ugarit," *Cambridge Ancient History* 2, Part 2, ch. XXI (b). 3d ed. Ed. I. E. S. Edwards; C. J. Gadd; N. G. L. Hammond; E. Sollberger. Cambridge: Cambridge University Press, 1975, 130–60.

Dunard, M. See Thureau-Dangin, F.

Dyck, E. H. "Thebez," *ABD* 6. Ed. D. N. Freedman. New York: Doubleday, 1992, 443b.

Eaton, J. H. "Dancing in the Old Testament," *ExpTim* 86 (1975), 136–40.

Edgerton, W. F., and J. A. Wilson. *Historical Records of Ramses III*. Studies in Ancient Oriental Civilization 12. Chicago: The University of Chicago Press, 1936.

Edwards, M. W. *Homer: Poet of the Iliad*. Baltimore and London: Johns Hopkins University Press, 1987.

Emerton, J. A. "New Light on Israelite Religion: The Implications of the Inscriptions from Kuntillet 'Ajrud," *ZAW* 94 (1982), 2–20.

Exum, J. C. "Promise and Fulfillment: Narrative Art in Judges 13," *JBL* 99 (1980), 43–59.

———. "Aspects of Symmetry and Balance in the Samson Saga," *JSOT* 19 (1981), 3–29.

———. "The Theological Dimension of the Samson Saga," *VT* 33 (1983), 30–45.

———. "'You Shall Let Every Daughter Live': A Study of Exodus 1:8–2:10," *The Bible and Feminist Hermeneutics*. *Semeia* 28 (1983). Ed. M. A. Tolbert, 63–82.

———. "'Mother in Israel': A Familiar Figure Reconsidered," *Feminist Interpretation of the Bible*. Ed. L. M. Russell. Philadelphia: Westminster, 1985, 73–85.

———. "The Tragic Vision and Biblical Narrative: The Case of Jephthah," *Signs and Wonders: Biblical Texts in Literary Focus*. Ed. J. C. Exum. Decatur, GA: Scholars Press, 1989, 59–83.

———. "Murder They Wrote: Ideology and the Manipulation of Female Presence in Biblical Narrative," *USQR* 43 (1989), 19–39. Reprinted in *The Pleasure of Her Text: Feminist Readings of Biblical and Historical Texts*. Ed. A. Bach. Philadelphia: Trinity Press International, 1990, 45–67.

———. "The Centre Cannot Hold: Thematic and Textual Instabilities in Judges," *CBQ* 52 (1990), 410–31.

———. *Tragedy and Biblical Narrative: Arrows of the Almighty*. Cambridge: Cambridge University Press, 1992.

———. *Fragmented Women: Feminist (Sub)versions of Biblical Narratives*. Valley Forge, PA: Trinity Press International, 1993.

———. "Feminist Criticism: Whose Interests Are Being Served?" *Judges and Method: New Approaches in Biblical Studies*. Ed. G. A. Yee. Minneapolis: Fortress, 1995, 65–90.

Fauth, W. *Aphrodite Parakyptusa: Untersuchungen zum Erscheinungsbild der vorderasiatischen Dea Prospiciens*. Akademie der Wissenschaften und der Literatur, Abhandlungen der Geistes- und Sozialwissenschaftlichen Klasse, Jahrgang 1966, Nr. 6. Wiesbaden: Franz Steiner, 1967.

Feaver, V. *The Handless Maiden*. London: Jonathan Cape, 1994.

Fenik, B. *Typical Battle Scenes in the Iliad. Studies in the Narrative Techniques of Homeric Battle Description*. Hermes Einzelschriften 21. Wiesbaden: Franz Steiner, 1968.

Fensham, F. C. "The Shaving of Samson: A Note on Judges 16:19," *EvQ* 31 (1959), 97–98.

―――. "Widow, Orphan, and the Poor in Ancient Near Eastern Legal and Wisdom Literature," *JNES* 21 (1962), 129–39.

Ferguson, J. *Catullus*. Lawrence, KS: Coronado Press, 1985.

Fewell, D. N. "Judges," *The Women's Bible Commentary*. Ed. C. A. Newsom and S. H. Ringe. London: SPCK; Louisville, KY: Westminster/John Knox, 1992, 67–77.

―――. "Deconstructive Criticism: Achsah and the (E)razed City of Writing," *Judges and Method: New Approaches in Biblical Studies*. Ed. G. A. Yee. Minneapolis: Fortress, 1995, 119–45.

―――, and D. M. Gunn. "Controlling Perspectives: Women, Men, and the Authority of Violence in Judges 4 & 5," *JAAR* 58 (1990), 389–411.

―――, and D. M. Gunn. *Gender, Power, and Promise: The Subject of the Bible's First Story*. Nashville: Abingdon, 1993.

Finkelstein, I. "Organization, Method and History of the Excavations" in "Excavations at Shiloh 1981–1984," *Tel Aviv* 12 (1985), 123–30.

―――. "Shiloh Yields Some, But Not All, of Its Secrets: Location of Tabernacle Still Uncertain," *BARev* 12/1 (January/February 1986), 22–41.

―――. "Seilun, Khirbet," *ABD* 5. Ed. D. N. Freedman. New York: Doubleday, 1992, 1069a–72b.

―――. "Shiloh, Renewed Excavations," *The New Encyclopedia of Archaeological Excavations in the Holy Land* 4. Ed. E. Stern. Jerusalem: The Israel Exploration Society and Carta; New York: Simon and Schuster, 1993, 1366–70.

Fisch, H. "Ruth and the Structure of Covenant History," *VT* 32 (1982), 425–37.

Fisher, E. J. "Cultic Prostitution in the Ancient Near East? A Reassessment," *Biblical Theology Bulletin* 5 (1976), 225–36.

Folmer, M. L. "A Literary Analysis of the 'Song of the Vineyard' (Is. 5:1–7)," *JEOL* 29 (1985–86), 106–23.

Fox, M. V. *The Song of Songs and the Ancient Egyptian Love Songs.* Madison, WI: The University of Wisconsin Press, 1985.

Fraenkel, E. "Vesper adest," *JRS* 45 (1955), 1–8.

Frankfort, H. *The Art and Architecture of the Ancient Orient.* Harmondsworth: Penguin Books, 1954.

Freedman, D. N. "Divine Names and Titles in Early Hebrew Poetry," *Pottery, Poetry, and Prophecy: Studies in Early Hebrew Poetry.* Winona Lake, IN: Eisenbrauns, 1980, 77–129.

———. "Yahweh of Samaria and His Asherah," *BA* 50 (1987), 241–49.

———. See further Cross, F. M.

Friedman, R. E. *The Exile and Biblical Narrative: The Formation of the Deuteronomistic and Priestly Works.* Chico, CA: Scholars Press, 1981.

Frymer-Kensky, T. *In the Wake of the Goddesses: Women, Culture, and the Biblical Transformation of Pagan Myth.* New York: Fawcett Columbine, 1992.

Fuchs, E. "The Literary Characterization of Mothers and Sexual Politics in the Hebrew Bible," *Feminist Perspectives on Biblical Scholarship.* Ed. A. Y. Collins. Chico, CA: Scholars Press, 1985, 117–36.

———. "Who Is Hiding the Truth? Deceptive Women and Biblical Androcentrism," *Feminist Perspectives on Biblical Scholarship.* Ed. A. Y. Collins. Chico, CA: Scholars Press, 1985, 137–44.

———. "Marginalization, Ambiguity, Silencing: The Story of Jephthah's Daughter," *JFSR* 5 (1989), 35–45.

Furman, N. "His Story Versus Her Story: Male Genealogy and Female Strategy in the Jacob Cycle," *Feminist Perspectives on Biblical Scholarship.* Ed. A. Y. Collins. Chico, CA: Scholars Press, 1985, 107–16.

Garbini, G. "*Parzon* 'Iron' in the Song of Deborah?" *JSS* 23 (1978), 23–24.

Gaster, T. H. *Thespis: Ritual, Myth, and Drama in the Ancient Near East.* 2d ed. Garden City, NY: Doubleday, 1961.

———. *Myth, Legend, and Custom in the Old Testament: A Comparative Study with Chapters from Sir James G. Frazer's Folklore in the Old Testament.* New York and Evanston: Harper & Row, 1969.

Gerleman, G. "The Song of Deborah in the Light of Sylistics," *VT* 1 (1951), 168–80.

Gilula, M. "To Yahweh Shomron and to His Asherah," *Shnaton* 3 (1978/79), 129–37 (Hebrew).

Ginsberg, H. L. *The Legend of King Keret: A Canaanite Epic of the Bronze Age.* BASOR Supplementary Studies 2–3. New Haven, CT: American Schools of Oriental Research, 1946.

———. "The North-Canaanite Myth of Anath and Aqhat," *BASOR* 97 (1945), 3–10.

———. "The North-Canaanite Myth of Anath and Aqhat, II" *BASOR* 98 (1945), 15–23.

———. "The Tale of Aqhat," *ANET.* 3d ed. Ed. J. B. Pritchard. Princeton: Princeton University Press, 1969, 149–55.

Globe, A. "The Literary Structure and Unity of the Song of Deborah," *JBL* 93 (1974), 493–512.

———. "Judges V 27," *VT* 25 (1975), 362–67.

Goitein, S. D. "Women as Creators of Biblical Genres," *Prooftexts* 8 (1988), 1–33.

Goldstein, B. R. See Cooper, A.

Gordon, C. H. *Ugaritic Literature: A Comprehensive Translation of the Poetic and Prose Texts.* Rome: Pontificium Institutum Biblicum, 1949.

———. *Ugaritic Textbook.* Rome: Pontifical Biblical Institute, 1965.

———. "Ugaritic *RBT/RABĪTU*," *Ascribe to the Lord. Biblical and Other Studies in Memory of Peter C. Craigie.* JSOTSup 67. Ed. L. Eslinger and J. G. Taylor. Sheffield: JSOT Press, 1988, 127–32.

Gottlieb, F. "Three Mothers," *Judaism* 30 (1981), 194–203.

Gottwald, N. K. "Immanuel as the Prophet's Son," *VT* 8 (1958), 36–47.

————. *The Tribes of Yahweh: A Sociology of the Religion of Liberated Israel, 1250–1050 B.C.E.* Maryknoll, NY: Orbis, 1979.

Graffy, A. "The Literary Genre of Isaiah 5, 1–7," *Bib* 60 (1979), 400–9.

Gray, J. *I and II Kings: A Commentary.* OTL. London: SCM, 1964.

————. *The KRT Text in the Literature of Ras Shamra. A Social Myth of Ancient Canaan.* 2d ed. Leiden: Brill, 1964.

————. "Sacral Kingship in Ugarit," *Ugaritica* VI. Paris: Mission Archéologique de Ras Shamra. Librairie Orientaliste Paul Geuthner, 1969, 289–302.

————. *Joshua, Judges, Ruth.* Rev. ed. New Century Bible Commentary. Grand Rapids: Eerdmans; Basingstoke: Marshall Morgan & Scott, 1986.

Grdseloff, B. *Les débuts du culte Rechef en Egypte.* Cairo: L'Institut français d'archéologie orientale, 1942.

Greenberg, M. *Understanding Exodus.* New York: Behrman House for the Melton Research Center of the Jewish Theological Seminary of America, 1969.

Greenstein, E. L. "The Riddle of Samson," *Prooftexts* 1 (1981), 237–60.

Gressmann, H. *Die Anfänge Israels.* Göttingen: Vandenhoeck & Ruprecht, 1914.

————. *Alterorientalische Texte und Bilder* 1–2. Berlin und Leipzig: Walter de Gruyter, 1929.

Grieshaber, H. *Totentanz von Basel.* Dresden: VEB Verlag der Kunst, 1968.

Gruber, M. "Ten Dance-Derived Expressions in the Hebrew Bible," *Bib* 62 (1981), 328–46. Reprinted in *Dance as Religious Studies.* Ed. D. Adams and D. Apostolos-Cappadona. New York: Crossroad, 1990, 48–66.

Gunn, D. M. "Samson of Sorrows: An Isaianic Gloss on Judges 13–16," *Reading Between Texts: Intertextuality and the Hebrew Bible.* Ed. D. N. Fewell. Louisville, KY: Westminster/John Knox, 1992, 225–53.

————. See further Fewell, D. N.

Hackett, J. A. "In the Days of Jael: Reclaiming the History of Women in Ancient

Israel," *Immaculate and Powerful: The Female in Sacred Image and Social Reality.* Ed. C. W. Atkinson; C. H. Buchanan; M. R. Miles. Boston: Beacon, 1985, 15–38.

————. "Women's Studies and the Hebrew Bible," *The Future of Biblical Studies: The Hebrew Scriptures.* Ed. R. E. Friedman and H. G. M. Williamson. Atlanta: Scholars Press, 1987, 141–64.

————. "1 and 2 Samuel," *The Women's Bible Commentary.* Ed. C. A. Newsom and S. H. Ringe. London: SPCK; Louisville, KY: Westminster/John Knox, 1992, 85–95.

Hadley, J. M. "The Khirbet el-Qom Inscription," *VT* 37 (1987), 50–62.

————. "Some Drawings and Inscriptions on Two Pithoi from Kuntillet 'Ajrud," *VT* 37 (1987), 180–211.

Haines, C. R. *Sappho: The Poems and Fragments.* London: Routledge; New York: E. P. Dutton, 1926.

Halpern, B. "The Rise of Abimelek Ben-Jerubbaal," *HAR* 2 (1978), 79–100.

————. "The Resourceful Israelite Historian: The Song of Deborah and Israelite Historiography," *HTR* 76 (1983), 379–401.

————. *The First Historians: The Hebrew Bible and History.* San Francisco: Harper & Row, 1988.

————. "Kenites," *ABD* 4. Ed. D. N. Freedman. New York: Doubleday, 1992, 17b–22b.

Hanson, P. D. "War and Peace in the Hebrew Bible," *Int* 38 (1984), 341–62.

————. *The People Called: The Growth of Community in the Bible.* San Francisco: Harper & Row, 1986.

Haran, M. "Zebaḥ Hayyamîm," *VT* 19 (1969), 11–22.

Harris, R. "Women (Mesopotamia)," *ABD* 6. Ed. D. N. Freedman. New York: Doubleday, 1992, 947b–51a.

Hayes, J. H., and S. A. Irvine, *Isaiah. The Eighth-Century Prophet: His Times and His Preaching.* Nashville: Abingdon, 1987.

Heltzer, M. *The Internal Organization of the Kingdom of Ugarit.* Wiesbaden: Reichert, 1982.

Hendel, R. S. *The Epic of the Patriarch: The Jacob Cycle and the Narrative Traditions of Canaan and Israel.* HSM 42. Atlanta: Scholars Press, 1987.

Herbig, R. "Aphrodite Parakyptusa (Die Frau im Fenster)," *OLZ* 30 (1927), 917–22.

Hess, H. *Totentanz der Stadt Basel.* Basle: Alb. Sattler, n.d.

Hestrin, R. "The Lachish Ewer and the 'Asherah," *IEJ* 37 (1987), 215–20.

———. "The Cult Stand from Ta'anach and Its Religious Background," *Studia Phoenicia 5: Phoenicia and the East Mediterranean in the First Millennium B.C.* Orientalia Lovaniensia Analecta 23. Ed. E. Lipínski. Leuven: Uitgeverij Peeters, 1987, 68–71.

Hieratic Papyri in the British Museum. Third Series. Chester Beatty Gift 1. Ed. A. H. Gardiner. London: British Museum, 1935.

Hillers, D. R. "The Bow of Aqhat: The Meaning of a Mythological Theme," *Orient and Occident: Essays Presented to Cyrus H. Gordon on the Occasion of His Sixty-Fifth Birthday.* AOAT 22. Ed. H. A. Hoffner. Neukirchen-Vluyn: Neukirchener Verlag; Kevelaer: Butzon & Bercker, 1973, 71–80.

Holladay, J. S. "Religion in Israel and Judah Under the Monarchy: An Explicitly Archaeological Approach," *Ancient Israelite Religion: Essays in Honor of Frank Moore Cross.* Ed. P. D. Miller; P. D. Hanson; S. D. McBride. Philadelphia: Fortress, 1987, 249–99.

Houtman, C. "Exodus 4:24–26 and Its Interpretation," *JNSL* 11 (1983), 81–105.

Irvine, S. A. See Hayes, J. H.

Ishida, T. *The Royal Dynasties in Ancient Israel: A Study on the Formation and Development of Royal-Dynastic Ideology.* BZAW 142. Berlin: de Gruyter, 1976.

Jacobs, E. "Mourning," *IDB* 3. Ed. G. A. Butterick. Nashville: Abingdon, 1962, 452b–54b.

Jacobsen, T. *The Treasures of Darkness. A History of Mesopotamian Religion.* New Haven and London: Yale University Press, 1976.

———. *Toward the Image of Tammuz and Other Essays on Mesopotamian History and Culture.* Ed. W. L. Moran. Cambridge, MA: Harvard University Press, 1970.

Janzen, J. G. "A Certain Woman in the Rhetoric of Judges 9," *JSOT* 38 (1987), 33–37.

Jaroš, K. "Zur Inschrift Nr. 3 von Ḥirbet el-Qōm," *BN* 19 (1982), 31–40.

Jeansonne, S. P. *The Women of Genesis: From Sarah to Potiphar's Wife.* Minneapolis: Fortress, 1990.

Jenkins, I. "Is There Life After Marriage? A Study of the Abduction Motif in Vase Paintings of the Athenian Wedding Ceremony," *Bulletin of the Institute of Classical Studies* 30 (1983), 137–45.

Jepson, A. "'*emunah,*" *TDOT* 1. Ed. G. J. Botterweck and H. Ringgren. Grand Rapids, MI: Eerdmans, 1974, 316–20.

Johnson, A. R. "Hebrew Conceptions of Kingship," *Myth, Ritual, and Kingship: Essays on the Theory and Practice of Kingship in the Ancient Near East and in Israel.* Ed. S. H. Hooke. Oxford: Clarendon, 1958, 204–35.

———. "Living Issues in Biblical Scholarship. Divine Kingship and the Old Testament," *ExpTim* 62 (1950–51), 36–42.

Johnson, M. D. *The Purpose of the Biblical Genealogies with Special Reference to the Setting of the Genealogies of Jesus.* SNTSMS 8. 2d ed. Cambridge: Cambridge University Press, 1988.

Jones-Warsaw, K. "Toward a Womanist Hermeneutic: A Reading of Judges 19–21," *A Feminist Companion to Judges.* Ed. A. Brenner. The Feminist Companion to the Bible 4. Sheffield: Sheffield Academic Press, 1993, 172–86.

Kamuf, P. "Author of a Crime," *A Feminist Companion to Judges.* Ed. A. Brenner. The Feminist Companion to the Bible 4. Sheffield: Sheffield Academic Press, 1993, 187–207.

Kaplan, L. "'And the Lord Sought to Kill Him' (Exod 4:24): Yet Once Again," *HAR* 5 (1981), 65–74.

Katzenstein, H. J. "Who Were the Parents of Athaliah?" *IEJ* 5 (1955), 194–97.

Kidd, D. A. "Hesperus and Catullus LXII," *Latomus* 33 (1974), 22–33.

King, P. J. *Amos, Hosea, Micah—An Archaeological Commentary.* Philadelphia: Westminster, 1988.

Klein, L. R. *The Triumph of Irony in the Book of Judges.* Sheffield: Almond, 1988.

———. "A Spectrum of Female Characters in the Book of Judges," *A Feminist*

Companion to Judges. Ed. A. Brenner. The Feminist Companion to the Bible 4. Sheffield: Sheffield Academic Press, 1993, 24–33.

―――. "The Book of Judges: Paradigm and Deviation in Images of Women," *A Feminist Companion to Judges.* Ed. A. Brenner. The Feminist Companion to the Bible 4. Sheffield: Sheffield Academic Press, 1993, 55–71.

Klein, R. W. "The Song of Hannah," *CTM* 41 (1970), 674–84.

Korpel, M. C. A. "The Literary Genre of the Song of the Vineyard (Isa. 5:1–7)," *The Structural Analysis of Biblical and Canaanite Poetry.* JSOTSup 74. Ed. W. van der Meer and J. C. de Moor. Sheffield: JSOT Press, 1988, 119–55.

Kosmala, H. "The 'Bloody Husband,'" *VT* 12 (1962), 14–28.

Kramer, S. N. "The Weeping Goddess: Sumerian Prototypes of the *Mater Dolorosa,*" *BA* 46 (1983), 69–80.

Kugel, J. "On the Bible and Literary Criticism," *Prooftexts* 1 (1981), 217–36.

Kurtz, D. C., and J. Boardman, *Greek Burial Customs.* Ithaca, NY: Cornell University Press, 1971.

Laroche, E. See Nougayrol, J.

Lasine, S. "Guest and Host in Judges 19: Lot's Hospitality in an Inverted World," *JSOT* 29 (1984), 37–59.

Lattimore, R. *The Iliad of Homer.* Chicago and London: University of Chicago Press, 1951.

Lemaire, A. "Les inscriptions de Khirbet el-Qôm et l'Ashérah de Yhwh," *RB* 84 (1977), 597–608.

―――. "Date et origine des inscriptiones hebraiques et pheniciennes de Kuntillet 'Ajrud," *Studi epigraphici e linguistici* 1 (1984), 131–43.

―――. "Who or What Was Yahweh's Asherah?" *BARev* 10/6 (1984), 42–51.

Levine, B. A. *Numbers 1–20.* AB 4a. New York: Doubleday, 1993.

Levine, M. "The Polemic Against Rape in the Song of Deborah," *Beth Mikra* 25 (1979), 83–84 (Hebrew).

Lewis, T. J. "The Songs of Hannah and Deborah: ḤDL-II ('Growing Plump')," *JBL* 104 (1985), 105–8.

Lexora, I. *Ancient Egyptian Dances*. Praha, Czechoslovakia: Oriental Institute, 1935.

L'Heureux, C. *Rank Among the Canaanite Gods: El, Baʿal, and the Rephaʾim*. HSM 21. Missoula, MT: Scholars Press, 1979.

Lind, M. C. *Yahweh Is a Warrior: The Theology of Warfare in Ancient Israel*. Scottsdale, PA, and Kitchener, Ontario: Herald, 1980.

Lindars, B. "Deborah's Song: Women in the Old Testament," *BJRL* 65 (1983), 158–75.

Lipiński, E. "Juges 5, 4–5 et Psaume 68, 8–11," *Bib* 48 (1967), 185–206.

———. "The Goddess Aṯirat in Ancient Arabia, in Babylon, and in Ugarit," *OLP* 3 (1972), 101–19.

———. "Aḫat-milki, reine d'Ugarit, et la guerre du Mukiš," *OLP* 12 (1981), 79–115.

Liverani, M. "L'Histoire de Joas," *VT* 24 (1974), 438–53.

Long, B. O. See Stinespring, W. F.

Lonsdale, S. H. *Dance and Ritual Play in Greek Religion*. Baltimore and London: Johns Hopkins University Press, 1993.

Loretz, O. See Dietrich, M.

Loud, G., and C. B. Altman, *Khorsabad,* Part II: *The Citadel and the Town*. Oriental Institute Publications 40. Chicago: University of Chicago Press, 1938.

McCarter, P. K. *I Samuel*. AB 8. Garden City, NY: Doubleday, 1980.

———. *II Samuel*. AB 9. Garden City, NY: Doubleday, 1984.

———. "Aspects of the Religion of the Israelite Monarchy: Biblical and Epigraphic Data," *Ancient Israelite Religion: Essays in Honor of Frank Moore Cross*. Ed. P. D. Miller; P. D. Hanson; S. D. McBride. Philadelphia: Fortress, 1987, 137–55.

McKay, J. *Religion in Judah Under the Assyrians*. SBT (Second Series) 26. Naperville, IL: Alan R. Allenson, 1973.

Maier, W. A. *'Ašerah: Extrabiblical Evidence*. HSM 37. Atlanta: Scholars Press, 1986.

Malamat, A. "Mari and the Bible: Some Patterns of Tribal Organization and Institutions," *JAOS* 82 (1962), 143–50.

Mallowan, M. "The Excavations at Nimrud (Kalḫu), 1949–1950: Ivories from the N. W. Palace," *Iraq* 14 (1952), 1–23.

————, *The Nimrud Ivories*. London: British Museum Publications, 1978.

Marcus, D. *Jephthah and His Vow*. Lubbock, TX: Texas Tech Press, 1986.

Margalit, B. "Some Observations on the Inscription and Drawing from Khirbet el-Qôm," *VT* 39 (1989), 371–78.

Margalith, O. "More Samson Legends," *VT* 36 (1986), 397–405.

Mazar, A. *Archaeology of the Land of the Bible, 10,000–586 B.C.E.* Anchor Bible Reference Library. New York: Doubleday, 1990.

Mazar, B. "The Sanctuary of Arad and the Family of Hobab the Kenite," *JNES* 24 (1965), 297–303.

Mendenhall, G. E. "The Hebrew Conquest of Palestine," *BA* 25 (1962), 66–87.

Meshel, Z. "Kuntillet 'Ajrûd—An Israelite Site from the Monarchical Period on the Sinai Border," *Qadmoniot* 9 (1976), 118–24 (Hebrew).

————. "Kuntillet 'Ajrûd—An Israelite Religious Center in Northern Sinai," *Expedition* 20 (1978), 50–54.

————. *Kuntillet 'Ajrûd: A Religious Center from the Time of the Judean Monarchy*. Israel Museum Catalogue 175. Jerusalem: Israel Museum, 1978.

————. "Did Yahweh Have a Consort? The New Religious Inscriptions from Sinai," *BARev* 5/2 (1979), 24–35.

————, and C. Meyers. "The Name of God in the Wilderness of Zin," *BA* 39 (1976), 6–10.

Meyers, C. "Gender Imagery in the Song of Songs," *HAR* 10 (1987), 209–23.

————. *Discovering Eve: Ancient Israelite Women in Context*. New York and Oxford: Oxford University Press, 1988.

————. "Of Drums and Damsels: Women's Performance in Ancient Israel," *BA* 54 (1991), 16–27.

————. "'To Her Mother's House'—Considering a Counterpart to the Israelite *Bêt 'āb*," *The Bible and the Politics of Exegesis: Essays in Honor of Norman K. Gottwald on His Sixty-Fifth Birthday*. Ed. D. Jobling; P. L. Day; G. T. Sheppard. Cleveland, OH: Pilgrim, 1991, 39–51.

————. "Returning Home: Ruth 1:8 and the Gendering of the Book of Ruth," *A Feminist Companion to Ruth*. Ed. A. Brenner. The Feminist Companion to the Bible 3. Sheffield: Sheffield Academic Press, 1993, 85–114.

————. "The Hannah Narrative in Feminist Perspective," *"Go to the Land I Will Show You": Studies in Honor of Dwight W. Young*. Ed. J. Coleson and V. Matthews. Winona Lake, IN: Eisenbrauns, 1994, 117–26. Reprinted as "Hannah and her Sacrifice: Reclaiming Female Agency," *A Feminist Companion to Samuel and Kings*. Ed. A. Brenner. The Feminist Companion to the Bible 5. Sheffield: Sheffield Academic Press, 1994, 93–104.

————. See further Meshel, Z.

Miller, P. D. *The Divine Warrior in Early Israel*. Cambridge, MA: Harvard University Press, 1973.

————. "Psalms and Inscriptions," VTSup 32 (1981), 311–32.

————. "Israelite Religion," *The Hebrew Bible and its Modern Interpreters*. Ed. D. A. Knight and G. M. Tucker. Philadelphia: Fortress; Chico, CA: Scholars Press, 1985, 201–37.

————. "The Absence of the Goddess in Israelite Religion," *HAR* 10 (1986), 239–48.

Minear, P. S. "Luke's Use of the Birth Stories," *Studies in Luke-Acts*. Paul Schubert Festschrift. Ed. L. E. Keck and J. L. Martyn. Nashville: Abingdon, 1966, 111–30.

Mintz, R. F. *Modern Hebrew Poetry: A Bilingual Anthology*. Berkeley and Los Angeles: University of California Press, 1966.

Mittman, S. "Die Grabinschrift des Sangers Uriahu," *ZDPV* 97 (1981), 139–52.

Molin, G. "Die Stellung der Gᵉbira im Staate Juda," *TZ* 10 (1954), 161–75.

Moore, C. A. *Judith*. AB 40. Garden City, NY: Doubleday, 1985.

Moore, G. F. *A Critical and Exegetical Commentary on Judges*. ICC. Edinburgh: T. & T. Clark, 1903.

Morgenstern, J. "The Etymological History of the Three Hebrew Synonyms for 'to Dance,' HGG, ḤLL and KRR, and their Cultural Significance," *JAOS* 36 (1917), 321–32.

———. "The 'Bloody Husband' (?) (Exod 4:24–26) Once Again," *HUCA* 34 (1963), 35–70.

Morris, I. "The Use and Abuse of Homer," *Classical Antiquity* 5 (1986), 81–138.

Mosca, P. G. "Who Seduced Whom? A Note on Joshua 15:18/Judges 1:14," *CBQ* 46 (1984), 18–22.

Murray, D. F. "Narrative Structure and Technique in the Deborah-Barak Story (Judges IV 4–22)," *Studies in the Historical Books of the Old Testament*. VTSup 30. Ed. J. A. Emerton. Leiden: Brill, 1979, 155–89.

Myers, J. M. "Judges: Introduction and Exegesis," *IB* 2. Nashville: Abingdon, 1953, 677–826.

Naveh, J. "Graffiti and Dedications," *BASOR* 235 (1979), 27–30.

Neff, R. W. *The Announcement in Old Testament Birth Stories*. Unpublished Ph.D. dissertation; Yale University, 1969.

Nelson, R. D. *The Double Redaction of the Deuteronomistic History*. Sheffield: JSOT Press, 1981.

Niditch, S. "The Wronged Woman Righted: An Analysis of Genesis 38," *HTR* 72 (1979), 143–49.

———. "The 'Sodomite' Theme in Judges 19–20: Family, Community, and Social Disintegration," *CBQ* 44 (1982), 365–78.

———. "Eroticism and Death in the Tale of Jael," *Gender and Difference in Ancient Israel*. Ed. P. L. Day. Minneapolis: Fortress, 1989, 43–57.

———. "Samson as Culture Hero, Trickster, and Bandit: The Empowerment of the Weak," *CBQ* 52 (1990), 608–24.

———. *War in the Hebrew Bible: A Study in the Ethics of Violence*. New York and Oxford: Oxford University Press, 1993.

————. "Short Stories: The Book of Esther and the Theme of Woman as a Civilizing Force," *Old Testament Interpretation: Past, Present, and Future. Essays in Honor of Gene M. Tucker.* Ed. J. L. Mays; D. L. Petersen; K. H. Richards. Nashville: Abingdon, 1995, 195–209.

Niehr, H. "Zur Gattung von Jes 5, 1–7," *BZ* 30 (1986), 99–104.

Nofret—Die Schöne: Die Frau im Alten Ägypten, "Wahrheit" und Wirklichkeit. Mainz: Philipp von Zabern; Hildesheim: Roemer- und Pelizaeus-Museum, 1985.

North, R. "The Cain Music," *JBL* 83 (1964), 373–89.

Noth, M. *Die israelitischen Personennamen im Rahmen der gemeinsemitischen Namengebung.* Hildesheim: Georg Olms, 1980.

Nougayrol, J., and Ch. Virolleaud. *Le palais royal d'Ugarit* 1–6. Mission de Ras Shamra. Ed. C. F. A. Schaeffer. Paris: Imprimerie nationale, 1955–1970.

————, E. Laroche, Ch. Virolleaud, and C. F. A. Schaeffer, et al. *Ugaritica 5. Nouveaux textes accadiens, hourrites et ugaritiques des archives et bibliothèques privées d'Ugarit, Commentaires des textes historiques (première partie).* Mission de Ras Shamra 16. Paris: Imprimerie Nationale. Librairie orientaliste Paul Geuthner, 1968.

Obermann, J. *How Danil Was Blessed with a Son: An Incubation Scene in Ugaritic.* Supplement to *JAOS* 6. Baltimore: American Oriental Society, 1946.

O'Connor, M. *Hebrew Verse Structure.* Winona Lake, IN: Eisenbrauns, 1980.

————. "The Women in the Book of Judges," *HAR* 10 (1986), 277–93.

————. "Northwest Semitic Designations for Elective Social Affinities," *JANESCU* 18 (1986), 67–80.

————. "The Poetic Inscription from Khirbet el-Qôm," *VT* 37 (1987), 224–29.

Oden, Jr., R. A. "Method in the Study of Near Eastern Myths," *Religion* 9 (1973), 182–96.

————. "Theoretical Assumptions in the Study of Ugaritic Myths," *Maarav* 2 (1979–80), 43–63.

————. *The Bible Without Theology: The Theological Tradition and Alternatives to It.* New Voices in Biblical Studies. San Francisco: Harper & Row, 1987.

————. See further Attridge, H. W.

Oesterley, W. O. E. *The Sacred Dance: A Study in Comparative Folklore*. New York: Macmillan, 1923.

Oldenburg, U. *The Conflict Between El and Baʿal in Canaanite Religion*. Leiden: Brill, 1969.

Oliver, H. H. "The Lucan Birth Stories and the Purpose of Luke-Acts," *NTS* 10 (1963–64), 202–26.

Olyan, S. M. "*Hăšālôm*: Some Literary Considerations of 2 Kings 9," *CBQ* 46 (1984), 652–68.

————. "2 Kings 9:31—Jehu as Zimri," *HTR* 78 (1985), 203–7.

————. *Asherah and the Cult of Yahweh in Israel*. SBLMS 34. Atlanta: Scholars Press, 1988.

Pardee, D. "Will the Dragon Never Be Muzzled?" *UF* 16 (1984), 251–55.

Parker, S. B. "The Historical Composition of KRT and the Cult of El," *ZAW* 89 (1977), 161–75.

————. "Jezebel's Reception of Jehu," *Maarav* 1 (1978), 67–78.

————. *The Pre-Biblical Narrative Tradition*. SBLRBS 24. Atlanta: Scholars Press, 1989.

Pedersen, J. *Israel, Its Life and Culture* 1–4. Copenhagen: Branner og Korch; London: Oxford University, 1926, 1940.

Peet, T. E. See Dawson, W. R.

Penchansky, D. "Staying the Night: Intertextuality in Genesis and Judges," *Reading Between Texts: Intertextuality and the Hebrew Bible*. Ed. D. N. Fewell. Louisville, KY: Westminster/John Knox, 1992, 77–88.

Perrin, B. *Plutarch's Lives* I. LCL. Cambridge, MA: Harvard University Press, 1914.

Perrin, N. *The New Testament: An Introduction,* 2d ed. Revised by D. C. Duling. New York: Harcourt Brace Jovanovich, 1982.

Peterson, J. L. "Kedesh 3," *ABD* 4. Ed. D. N. Freedman. New York: Doubleday, 1992, 11b–12a.

Phipps, W. E. "A Woman Was the First to Declare Scripture Holy," *Bible Review* 6/2 (April 1990), 14–15, 44.

Pippin, T. "Jezebel Re-Vamped," *A Feminist Companion to Samuel and Kings*. Ed. A. Brenner. The Feminist Companion to the Bible 5. Sheffield: Sheffield Academic Press, 1994, 196–206.

Poethig, E. B. *The Victory Song Tradition of the Women of Israel*. Unpublished Ph.D. dissertation; Union Theological Seminary, 1985.

Polzin, R. *Moses and the Deuteronomist: A Literary Study of the Deuteronomistic History*, Part 1. New York: Seabury, 1980.

Pope, M. *'El in the Ugaritic Texts*. Leiden: Brill, 1955.

Poulsen, F. *Der Orient und die frühgriechische Kunst*. Leipzig: B. G. Teubner, 1912.

Rabin, C. "Judges V, 2 and the 'Ideology' of Deborah's War," *JJS* 6 (1953), 125–34.

Racine, J. *Théâtre complet* II. Ed. J.-P. Collinet. Paris: Gallimard, 1983.

von Rad, G. *Genesis: A Commentary*. OTL. Philadelphia: Westminster, 1961.

Rainey, A. F. "The Kingdom of Ugarit," *BAR* 3. Sheffield: Almond, 1970, 76–99.

Rasmussen, R. C. "Deborah the Woman Warrior," *Anti-Covenant: Counter-Reading Women's Lives in the Hebrew Bible*. Ed. M. Bal. JSOTSup 8. Bible and Literature Series 22. Sheffield: Almond, 1989, 79–93.

Redfield, J. "Notes on the Greek Wedding," *Arethusa* 15 (1982), 181–201.

Reed, W. L. *The Asherah in the Old Testament*. Fort Worth, TX: Texas Christian University Press, 1949.

Reinhartz, A. "Samson's Mother: An Unnamed Protagonist," *JSOT* 55 (1992), 25–37.

Roberts, J. J. M. "Isaiah and His Children," *Biblical and Related Studies Presented to Samuel Iwry*. Ed. A. Kort and S. Morschauser. Winona Lake, IN: Eisenbrauns, 1985, 193–203.

Robertson, N. "The Ritual Background of the Dying God in Cyprus and Syro-Palestine," *HTR* 75 (1982), 313–59.

Robinson, B. "Zipporah to the Rescue: A Contextual Study of Exodus IV 24–6," *VT* 36 (1986), 447–61.

Röllig, W. See Donner, H.

Sakenfeld, K. D. "Feminist Biblical Interpretation," *TToday* 46 (1989), 154–68.

Sanders, J. A. "Isaiah in Luke," *Interpreting the Prophets*. Ed. J. L. Mays and P. J. Achtemeier. Philadelphia: Fortress, 1987, 75–85.

Sanmartín-Ascaso, J. "*dôdh,*" *TDOT* 3. Ed. G. J. Botterweck and H. Ringgren. Grand Rapids, MI: Eerdmans, 1978, 143–56.

——. See further Dietrich, M.

Sasson, J. M. "The Worship of the Golden Calf," *Orient and Occident: Essays Presented to Cyrus H. Gordon on the Occasion of His Sixty-Fifth Birthday*. AOAT 22. Ed. H. A. Hoffner. Neukirchen-Vluyn: Neukirchener Verlag; Kevelaer: Butzon & Bercker, 1973, 151–59.

——. "Who Cut Samson's Hair? (And Other Trifling Issues Raised by Judges 16)," *Prooftexts* 8 (1988), 333–39.

Schaeffer, C. F. A. See Nougayrol, J.

Schuller, E. "Women of the Exodus in Biblical Retellings of the Second Temple Period," *Gender and Difference in Ancient Israel*. Ed. P. L. Day. Minneapolis: Fortress, 1989, 178–94.

Scott, R. B. Y. "Introduction and Exegesis: The Book of Isaiah, Chapters 1–39," *IB* 5. Nashville: Abingdon, 1956, 151–773.

Seaford, R. "The Tragic Wedding," *JHS* 107 (1987), 106–30.

Seibert, I. *Women in the Ancient Near East*. New York: Abner Schram, 1974.

Sendrey, A. *Music in the Social and Religious Life of Antiquity*. Rutherford, Madison, and Teaneck: Fairleigh Dickinson University Press, 1974.

Seow, C. L. *Myth, Drama, and the Politics of David's Dance*. HSM 44. Atlanta: Scholars Press, 1989.

Sheppard, G. T. "More on Isaiah 5:1–7 as a Juridical Parable," *CBQ* 44 (1982), 45–47.

Skehan, P. W. "The Hand of Judith," *CBQ* 25 (1963), 94–110.

Smith, J. Z. *Map Is Not Territory: Studies in the History of Religions.* Chicago and London: University of Chicago Press, 1993.

Smith, M. S. *The Early History of God: Yahweh and the Other Deities in Ancient Israel.* San Francisco: Harper & Row, 1990.

Soggin, J. A. *Joshua: A Commentary.* OTL. Philadelphia: Westminster, 1972.

———. "'Heber der Qenit.' Das Ende eines biblischen Personnennamens?" *VT* 31 (1981), 89–92.

———. *Judges: A Commentary.* OTL. Philadelphia: Westminster, 1981.

Sourvinou-Inwood, C. "A Series of Erotic Pursuits: Images and Meanings," *JHS* 107 (1987), 131–53.

Spanier, K. "The Queen Mother in the Judaean Royal Court: Maacah—A Case Study," *A Feminist Companion to Samuel and Kings.* Ed. A. Brenner. The Feminist Companion to the Bible 5. Sheffield: Sheffield Academic Press, 1994, 186–95.

Spencer, J. R. "Refuge, Cities of," *ABD* 5. Ed. D. N. Freedman. New York: Doubleday, 1992, 657b–58b.

Spicehandler, E. See Burnshaw, S.

Stager, L. E. "The Archaeology of the Family in Ancient Israel," *BASOR* 260 (1985), 1–35.

———. "Archaeology, Ecology, and Social History: Background Themes to the Song of Deborah," VTSup 40. Jerusalem Congress Volume, 1986. Ed. J. A. Emerton. Leiden: Brill, 1988, 221–34.

———. "The Song of Deborah—Why Some Tribes Answered the Call and Others Did Not," *BARev* 15/1 (January/February 1989), 50–64.

Stinespring, W. F., and B. O. Long. "Annotations on 2 Samuel," *The New Oxford Annotated Bible.* Ed. B. M. Metzger and R. E. Murphy. New York: Oxford University Press, 1991, 384–422.

Strommenger, E. "Ivory carving of a woman in a window," *Ebla to Damascus: Art and Archaeology of Ancient Syria.* Ed. H. Weiss. Washington, D.C.: Smithsonian Institution Traveling Exhibition Service, 1985, 355.

Tatum, W. B. "The Epoch of Israel: Luke I–II and the Theological Plan of Luke-Acts," *NTS* 13 (1966–67), 184–95.

Taylor, J. G. "The Song of Deborah and Two Canaanite Goddesses," *JSOT* 23 (1982), 99–108.

Thomsen, O. *Ritual and Desire: Catullus 61 and 62 and other Ancient Documents on Wedding and Marriage.* Aarhus, Denmark: Aarhus University Press, 1992.

Thureau-Dangin, F., A. Barrois, G. Dossin, and M. Dunard. *Arslan-Tash.* Bibliothèque archéologique et historique 16. Paris: Librairie Orientalist Paul Geuthner, 1931.

Tiede, D. *Prophecy and History in Luke-Acts.* Philadelphia: Fortress, 1980.

Tigay, J. "Israelite Religion: The Onomastic and Epigraphic Evidence," *Ancient Israelite Religion: Essays in Honor of Frank Moore Cross.* Ed. P. D. Miller; P. D. Hanson; S. D. McBride. Philadelphia: Fortress, 1987, 157–94.

————. *You Shall Have No Other Gods: Israelite Religion in the Light of Hebrew Inscriptions.* HSS 31. Atlanta: Scholars Press, 1986.

van der Toorn, K. "Judges XVI 21 in the Light of the Akkadian Sources," *VT* 36 (1986), 248–53.

————. "Torn Between Vice and Virtue: Stereotypes of the Widow in Israel and Mesopotamia," *Female Stereotypes in Religious Traditions.* Ed. R. Kloppenborg and W. J. Hanegraaff. Leiden: Brill, 1995, 1–13.

Trible, P. "Depatriarchalizing in Biblical Interpretation," *JAAR* 41 (1973), 30–48.

————. *God and the Rhetoric of Sexuality.* OBT 2. Philadelphia: Fortress, 1978.

————. "A Meditation in Mourning: The Sacrifice of the Daughter of Jephthah," *USQR* 36 (1981), 59–73.

————. *Texts of Terror: Literary-Feminist Readings of Biblical Narratives.* OBT 13. Philadelphia: Fortress, 1984.

————. "A Daughter's Death: Feminism, Literary Criticism, and the Bible," *Backgrounds for the Bible.* Ed. M. P. O'Connor and D. N. Freedman. Winona Lake, IN: Eisenbrauns, 1987, 1–14.

———. "Eve and Miriam: From the Margins to the Center," *Feminist Approaches to the Bible*. Ed. H. Shanks. Washington, D.C.: Biblical Archaeology Society, 1995, 5–24.

Urbrock, W. J. "Sisera's Mother in Judges 5 and Haim Gouri's '*Immô*," *HAR* 11 (1987), 423–34.

de Vaux, R. *Ancient Israel* 1: *Social Institutions* and 2: *Religious Institutions*. New York: McGraw Hill, 1965.

Vermule, E. *Aspects of Death in Early Greek Art and Poetry*. Berkeley, Los Angeles, and London: University of California Press, 1979.

Vickery, J. B. "In Strange Ways: The Story of Samson," *Images of God and Man: Old Testament Short Stories in Literary Focus*. Ed. B. O. Long. Sheffield: Almond, 1981, 58–73.

Virolleaud, Ch. See Nougayrol, J.

Wallace, H. N. *The Eden Narrative*. HSM 32. Atlanta: Scholars Press, 1985.

van de Walle, B. See Werbrouck, M.

Walls, N. H. *The Goddess Anat in Ugaritic Myth*. SBLDS 135. Atlanta: Scholars Press, 1992.

Webb, B. G. *The Book of the Judges: An Integrated Reading*. JSOTSup 46; Sheffield: JSOT Press, 1987.

Wegner, J. R. *Chattel or Person? The Status of Women in the Mishnah*. New York and Oxford: Oxford University Press, 1988

Weinfeld, M. "A Sacred Site of the Monarchic Period," *Shnaton* 4 (1980), 280–84 (Hebrew).

———. "Further Remarks on the 'Ajrûd Inscription," *Shnaton* 5–6 (1981–82), 237–39 (Hebrew).

———. "Kuntillet 'Ajrud Inscriptions and Their Significance," *Studi epigraphici e linguistici* 1 (1984), 121–30.

Wellhausen, J. *Der Text der Bücher Samuelis untersucht*. Göttingen: Vandenhoeck und Ruprecht, 1871.

Werbrouck, M., and B. van de Walle, *La Tombe de Nakht*. Bruxelles: Fondation Egyptologique, 1929.

Westenholz, J. "Tamar, *Qĕdēšā, Qadištu,* and Sacred Prostitution in Mesopotamia," *HTR* 82 (1989), 245–65.

Wharton, J. A. "The Secret of Yahweh: Story and Affirmation in Judges 13–16," *Int* 27 (1973), 48–65.

White, J. B. *A Study of the Language of Love in the Song of Songs and Ancient Egyptian Poetry.* SBLDS 38. Missoula, MT: Scholars Press, 1978.

White, S. A. "Esther: A Feminine Model for Jewish Diaspora," *Gender and Difference in Ancient Israel.* Ed. P. L. Day. Minneapolis: Fortress, 1989, 161–77.

———. "Esther," *The Women's Bible Commentary.* Ed. C. A. Newsom and S. H. Ringe. London: SPCK; Louisville, KY: Westminster/John Knox, 1992, 124–29.

Wiggins, S. A. *A Reassessment of 'Asherah': A Study According to Textual Sources of the First Two Millennia B.C.E.* AOAT 235. Kevelaer: Butzon & Bercker; Neukirchen-Vluyn: Neukirchener Verlag, 1993.

Williams, G. R. "Frustrated Expectations in Isaiah V 1–7: A Literary Interpretation," *VT* 35 (1985), 459–65.

Williams, J. G. "The Beautiful and the Barren: Conventions in Biblical Type-Scenes," *JSOT* 17 (1980), 107–19.

Willis, J. T. "The Song of Hannah and Psalm 113," *CBQ* 35 (1973), 139–54.

———. "The Genre of Isa 5:1–7," *JBL* 96 (1977), 337–62.

Wilson, A. *Such Darling Dodos and Other Stories.* London: Secker & Warburg, 1959.

Wilson, J. A. See Edgerton, W. F.

Winter, I. "Phoenician and North Syria Ivory Carving in Historical Context: Questions of Style and Distribution," *Iraq* 38 (1976), 1–22.

Winter, U. *Frau und Göttin: Exegetische und ikonographische Studien zum weiblichen Gottesbild im Alten Israel und in dessen Umwelt.* Freiburg: Universitätsverlag; Göttingen: Vandenhoeck & Ruprecht, 1983.

Wyckoff, E. *Sophocles I: Oedipus the King, Oedipus at Colonus, and Antigone.* Ed. D. Grene and R. Lattimore. New York: Washington Square Press, 1967.

Yadin, Y. "The 'House of Ba'al' of Ahab and Jezebel in Samaria, and that of Athaliah in Judah," *Archaeology in the Levant. Kathleen Kenyon Festschrift*. Warminster: Aris and Phillips, 1978, 127–35.

Yaron, R. "A Royal Divorce at Ugarit," *Or* 32 (1963), 21–31.

Yee, G. A. "The Form Critical Study of Isaiah 5:1–7 as a Song and a Juridical Parable," *CBQ* 43 (1981), 30–40.

———. "'Fraught with Background': Literary Ambiguity in II Samuel 11," *Int* 42 (1988), 240–53.

———. "Bathsheba," *ABD* 1. Ed. D. N. Freedman. New York: Doubleday, 1992, 627b–28a.

———. "By the Hand of a Woman: The Metaphor of the Woman Warrior in Judges 4," *Women, War, and Metaphor: Language and Society in the Study of the Hebrew Bible. Semeia* 61 (1993). Ed. C. V. Camp and C. R. Fontaine, 99–132.

———. "Introduction: Why Judges?" *Judges and Method: New Approaches in Biblical Studies*. Ed. G. A. Yee. Minneapolis: Fortress, 1995, 1–16.

———. "Ideological Criticism: Judges 17–21 and the Dismembered Body," *Judges and Method: New Approaches in Biblical Studies*. Ed. G. A. Yee. Minneapolis: Fortress, 1995, 146–70.

Yeivin, S. "Social, Religious, and Cultural Trends in Judaism Under the Davidic Dynasty," *VT* 3 (1953), 149–66.

Zakovitch, Y. "Sisseras Tod," *ZAW* 93 (1981), 364–74.

———. "Humor and Theology or the Successful Failure of Israelite Intelligence: A Literary-Folkloric Approach to Joshua 2," *Text and Tradition: The Hebrew Bible and Folklore*. Ed. S. Niditch. Atlanta: Scholars Press, 1990, 75–98.

Zevit, Z. "The Khirbet el-Qôm Inscription Mentioning a Goddess," *BASOR* 255 (1984), 39–47.

Zohary, M. *Plants of the Bible*. Cambridge: Cambridge University Press, 1982.

INDEX OF AUTHORS

INDEX OF SUBJECTS

INDEX OF SCRIPTURAL

AND OTHER ANCIENT SOURCES